The Golden Age of
Steam

The Golden Age of
Steam

A celebration of the locomotive
from 1830 to 1950

COLIN GARRATT

HERMES
HOUSE

ACKNOWLEDGEMENTS

The Publishers would like to thank the following for their kind permission to reproduce photographs in this book:

A. E. Durrant: pages 36 (bl), 38 (br).
Howard Ande: page 4.
British Waterways Archive: page 8 (t).
Colour Rail: page 64 (b).
Roger Crombleholme: pages 15 (t,b), 16, 17 (b), 18 (t,b), 19 (b).
Richard Gruber: pages 75 (t), 76 (b).
Alex Grunbach: pages 48, 49 (t,b), 116, 117.
John P. Hankey: pages 22 (t,m), 23 (t), 26 (t), 27 (m), 28 (top), 30 (b), 32 (t), 33 (b), 72 (b), 73 (t), 74 (t), 75 (m), 77 (m), 83 (t), 85 (t).
Michael Hinckley: page 15 (m).
Fred Hornby: pages 104 (t), 106 (br), 107 (t), 108, 109.

Locomotive Manufacturer's Association: page 67 (br).
Dennis Lovett: page 14 (b).
Arthur Mace: pages 10 (b), 13 (tr), 63 (t,b).
William D. Middleton Collection: pages 44 (b), 45 (t,b).
Mitchel Library: pages 29 (b), 33 (t,m), 39 (br), 44 (t), 45 (m), 47 (t), 49 (m), 50 (m), 52–3, 115 (t), 119 (m), 122 (b).
Alan Pike: pages 37 (b), 50 (t), 98, 99 (b), 100 (b), 101 (b), 102, 103.
Graham Pike: pages 105 (l).
Popperfoto: pages 23 (m), 29 (m), 32 (b), 35, 36 (br), 47 (b), 54 (t,b), 92 (m), 93 (m), 121 (tr).
William Sharman: pages 58 (b), 59 (t), 68 (b) 69 (t).
Brian Solomon: pages 23 (b), 24 (t,b), 28 (m,b), 30 (t), 31 (m,b), 70, 71 (m,b), 72 (t), 73 (m), 74 (b),

76 (t), 80 (t), 84 (b), 85 (m,b), 87 (b).
Richard J. Solomon: pages 71 (t), 73 (b), 77 (b), 80 (b), 82, 83 (b), 84 (t), 86 (t, br), 87 (t,m), 88, 89 (t,m), 90 (top), 91, 92 (t,b), 93 (t,b).
Gordon Stemp: pages 58 (t), 61 (b), 64 (b), 81 (t).
J. M. Tolson: page 104 (b).
Verkehrsmuseums Nürnberg: pages 36 (t), 37 (t).
Max Wade-Matthews: page 8 (b).
Neil Wheelwright: page 106 (bl).
Ron Ziel: pages 26 (t), 77 (t), 81 (b), 90 (b), 115 (br)

All other pictures courtesy of **Milepost 92^1/$_2$**.

t=top, b=bottom, l=left, r=right, m=middle.

This edition is published by Hermes House, an imprint of Anness Publishing Ltd, Hermes House, 88–89 Blackfriars Road, London SE1 8HA; tel. 020 7401 2077; fax 020 7633 9499

www.hermeshouse.com; www.annesspublishing.com

Anness Publishing has a new picture agency outlet for images for publishing, promotions or advertising. Please visit our website www.practicalpictures.com for more information.

Publisher Joanna Lorenz
Editorial Manager Helen Sudell
Assistant Editor Emma Gray
Designer Michael Morey

This book has been written and picture researched by the Milepost Publishing Production Team: Milepost also conserves and markets collections of railway transparencies and negatives. Milepost 92^1/$_2$, Newton Harcourt, Leicestershire LE8 9FH

ETHICAL TRADING POLICY
Because of our ongoing ecological investment programme, you, as our customer, can have the pleasure and reassurance of knowing that a tree is being cultivated on your behalf to naturally replace the materials used to make the book you are holding. For further information about this scheme, go to www.annesspublishing.com/trees

Previously published as part of a larger compendium, *The World Encyclopedia of Locomotives*.

For historical reasons, the measurements in this book are not always given with their metric or imperial equivalent. See page 128 for a conversion chart.

CONTENTS

The Birth of the Railway

The following section looks at the development of the railway, from
its very beginnings up to 1900, touching on both the technical changes
it underwent and the role it played in societies and industries around
the world. The text and photographs provide a comprehensive account
of the railway pioneers and the machines and lines they created, while
the technical boxes give an at-a-glance record of some of the most
influential and innovative locomotives.

FROM TRAMWAYS TO STEAM

● BELOW
Before railways, canals were the main means of moving heavy goods such as coal. With the coming of the railways, waterways fast fell into disuse. Today, they are basically used for pleasure.

In Britain, one of the first tramways was built about 1630 to serve collieries near Newcastle upon Tyne. The Tanfield Waggonway in County Durham was begun about 1725, and by 1727 included the Causey Arch, the world's first railway viaduct, built by Ralph Wood. At first, the rails were made of wood but these wore quickly, and in 1767 iron plates were affixed to them for durability. The first cast-iron plates were made by the Coalbrookdale Ironworks in Shropshire. Plate rails, that is iron-flanged rails, were introduced underground at Sheffield Park Colliery in 1787 and on the surface at Ketley Incline in 1788.

● STAGECOACH IMPROVES ROADS

Transportation in the 17th and 18th centuries was either by stagecoach or water. In 1658, the state of the roads was so bad that the stagecoach took two weeks to travel from London to Edinburgh. Even by the end of the 1700s, with responsibility for the maintenance of main roads handed from parishes to turnpike trusts, the state of the roads was not much better. In winter, they were blocked by snow or floods; in summer, hard-baked ruts made journeys uncomfortable. This was acceptable while most travel was on horseback. With the ever-increasing use of coaches for public transport, however, the roads improved. By the 1750s the stagecoach had come into its own.

● RAILWAYS REPLACE WATERWAYS

With industrialization, however, the need for transportation of heavy goods remained. By about the mid-18th century, artificial canals came into being as arteries for goods making their way to the larger rivers and to the sea for export to various parts of Britain. The waterways' half-century of posterity and public service ended, however, with the coming of the railways. Many became ruins or were bought by local railway companies. Turnpike roads ceased to be the chief arteries of the nation's lifeblood. Posting-inns were replaced by hotels springing up at railway termini. The Railway Era saw the demise of the public mailcoach and heavy family coach. In some instances, however, when such conservative-minded gentry as the Duke of Wellington travelled by rail, they sat in their coaches, which were placed on flat trucks. By 1840, with railways halving the cost of travel, canal and stagecoach were doomed.

● THE FIRST RAILWAYS

In 1804, the world's first public railway company, the Surrey Iron Railway Company, opened a horse-drawn line from Wandsworth Wharf, on the River Thames in south London, to Croydon in Surrey. The line was extended to Merstham, Surrey, but

never reached its intended destination, Portsmouth in Hampshire.

● RICHARD TREVITHICK

Another landmark in the history of railways also occurred in 1804 when British engineer Richard Trevithick (1771–1833) tested his newly invented steam locomotive. This drew five wagons and a coach with 70 passengers along the ten miles of track from the Pen-y-Darren Ironworks to the Glamorganshire Canal. This historic event saw the world's first steam locomotive to run on rails hauling a train carrying fare-paying passengers.

Trevithick continued his experiments and in 1808 erected a circular track in Euston Square, London, on which he ran his latest production "Catch Me Who Can". The public was invited to pay a shilling, almost a day's wages for the average working man, to ride on this novel method of transportation, but the venture failed financially and in a few weeks Trevithick had to close it.

● GEORGE STEPHENSON

Between 1814–21 Northumbrian engineer George Stephenson (1781–1848), born in Wylam, a village near Newcastle upon Tyne, built 17 experimental locomotives. Although he was not the first to produce a steam locomotive, he was the prime mover in introducing them on a wide scale. His turning-point came in 1821 when he was appointed engineer-in-charge of what became the 42 km (26 mile) long Stockton & Darlington Railway, between the County Durham towns of Stockton-on-Tees, a seaport, and Darlington, an industrial centre. It was opened in September 1825. Stephenson's Locomotion No. 1 drew the first train.

This historic event saw the world's first public railway regularly to use steam locomotives to haul wagons of goods (the main traffic was coal) and carriages of passengers. Passengers were carried in horse-drawn coaches until 1833.

In 1829, Lancashire's Liverpool & Manchester Railway, built mainly to carry cotton, offered a £500 prize to the winner of a competition for the best steam-locomotive design to work the line. The trials were held at Rainhill, near Liverpool. Of the three locomotives entered, George Stephenson's Rocket, gaily painted yellow, black and white, won at a speed of about 26 mph (42 kph).

ROCKET

Date	1829
Builder	George Stephenson
Client	Liverpool & Manchester Railway (L&MR)
Gauge	4 ft 8½ in
Type	0-2-2
Capacity	2 cylinders outside 8 x 17 in inclined
Pressure	50 lb
Weight	4 tons 5 cwt

BRITISH LOCOMOTIVES OF THE 1830S

By 1830 almost 100 locomotives had been built in Britain. These early experimental engines were of two main types: those with inclined cylinders and those with vertical cylinders. Then, in 1830 George Stephenson introduced the 2-2-0 Planet type. This was a radical step forward from the Rocket and its derivatives and established the general form that all future steam locomotives were to take. Planet combined the multi-tubular boiler with a fully water-jacketed firebox and a separate smokebox. The cylinders were now inside and horizontally mounted, while the engine's boiler and motion were carried on a sturdy outside frame of oak beams sandwiched by iron plates. The first Planet was a passenger-engine with 5 ft driving wheels and 3 ft carrying wheels, but Stephenson was quick to see that the frame arrangement would allow him to substitute two pairs of coupled 4 ft 6 in wheels to create a heavy-goods locomotive. The resulting engines, Samson and Goliath, were supplied to the Liverpool & Manchester Railway (L&MR) in 1831.

PATENTEE	
Date	1833
Builder	Robert Stephenson
Client	Liverpool & Manchester Railway (L&MR)
Gauge	4 ft 8$\frac{1}{2}$ in
Type	2-2-2
Driving wheels	5 ft
Capacity	2 cylinders 12 x 18 in
Pressure	50 lb

● **ABOVE**
Robert Stephenson (1803–59): at the age of 20 he was put in charge of his father's locomotive works in Newcastle upon Tyne. He became the leading locomotive engineer of his day. He built railway bridges and viaducts, notably the tubular bridge over the Menai Strait between Anglesey and mainland Wales.

● **BELOW**
Lion, built in the same year as Samson, shows how far heavy-goods engine design had really progressed. The first engine built by Todd, Kitson & Laird, this 0-4-2 had 5 ft driving wheels and is still in working order.

Hackworth, meanwhile, was still firmly wedded to the archaic vertical cylinder arrangement. In 1831 he built six engines of the Majestic class for heavy-coal haulage on the Stockton & Darlington Railway (S&DR). Their cylinders were carried on an overhanging platform at the back of the boiler and drove a crankshaft carried on a bracket below. The crankshaft in turn drove the nearest pair of the six coupled wheels, allowing all axles to be sprung. The boilers combined Hackworth's longitudinal flue with a return multi-tubular arrangement intended to provide the best features of both layouts. In the event, the small grate area possible in the single flue severely limited the engines' steaming power. Also, they were heavy on fuel as well as being cumbersome in appearance with a tender at each end of the locomotive. Their ponderous performance in traffic was such that the line's rigid speed limit of 6 mph (9.7 kph) did not trouble them.

Edward Bury had intended his first locomotive, Liverpool, to take part in the Rainhill Trials but it was not ready in time. Noting Rocket's superior features,

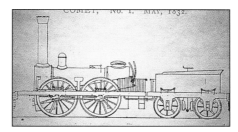

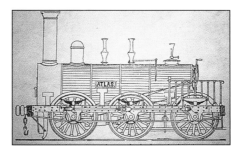

● **FAR LEFT**
George Stephenson (1781–1848): the world's most well-known locomotive engineer. He worked as an engineer for several railway companies and built the first railway line to carry passengers (1825).

● **ABOVE LEFT**
Comet was the first locomotive put into service on the Leicester & Swannington Railway (L&SR). On the inaugural run, in May 1832, the 13 ft high chimney was knocked down in the Glenfield Tunnel, near Leicester, covering the travelling dignitaries in soot. Swannington, in Leicestershire, is 19 km (12 miles) north-west of the county town.

● **BELOW LEFT**
Atlas was the first 0-6-0 goods engine built by Robert Stephenson. It was delivered to the L&SR in 1834. At the time, this was the largest, heaviest and most powerful locomotive running on any railway.

he was able to modify his design and deliver the engine to the L&MR in 1830. In its rebuilt form, it was bristling with innovations and became an international prototype. Most striking were the 6 ft coupled wheels, bigger than any previously made, but equally notable were the multi-tubular boiler, inside bar-frames and raised-dome firebox-casing. The cylinders, too, were inside, inclined slightly upwards to allow the piston rods to pass beneath the leading axle. On the line, Liverpool proved capable of hauling an 18-wagon train at an average of $12^{1}/_{2}$ mph (19 kph). In short, she was a stunning little creation, topped off by a small chimney with a procession of

cutout brass liver birds around its crown. (The liver is a fanciful bird on the arms of the city of Liverpool.)

With progress came the need for more powerful locomotives, and it had to be admitted that Planets were unsteady at any speed and their firebox capacity was limited. Robert Stephenson rectified this by extending the frames rearwards, adding a trailing axle behind a much-enlarged firebox. Thus was born the Patentee 2-2-2 Type, which became the standard British express-engine for the next four decades and was exported widely to inaugurate railway services across Europe. Stephenson's Patentees also incorporated great improvements in

boiler construction and valve gear. All had flangeless driving wheels.

The design could be varied to incorporate coupled driving wheels, as other manufacturers were quick to see. Perhaps the best known front-coupled Patentee is the 0-4-2 Lion, built for the L&MR in 1838 by Todd, Kitson & Laird of Leeds, Yorkshire.

● **BELOW**
Samson, built by Timothy Hackworth in 1838 for heavy-goods work on the Stockton & Darlington Railway (S&DR), already looked outdated by the standards of the time. Note the fireman feeding the single-flue boiler from the front end.

THE BATTLE OF THE GAUGES

Isambard Kingdom Brunel (1806–59) conceived railways on a grand scale. For his Great Western Railway (GWR), authorized in 1835, he dismissed the well-established 4 ft 8½ in gauge as inadequate to cope with the greater speeds, safety and smoother travel he planned for his relatively straight and level main line from London to Bristol. So he fixed his gauge at a spacious 7 ft. The main drawbacks were that this set the GWR apart from all other railways and meant that all goods and passengers had to change trains when travelling to or from areas not served by GWR trains.

The first GWR train steamed out of Paddington Station, west London, on 4 June 1838 behind the Stephenson 2-2-2 North Star, a large example of the Patentee type, which was originally built for the 5 ft 6 in gauge New Orleans Railway in the USA. A broken contract caused her to be altered to 7 ft gauge and to go to the GWR instead. A sister engine, Morning Star, entered service at the same time. North Star had 7 ft driving wheels and the inside-cylinders

● LEFT
A classic GWR broad-gauge single powers an express-train westwards through the Sonning Cutting, near Reading, Berkshire. It is late in the broad-gauge era for a third rail has been laid on each track to allow rolling stock of both gauges to operate.

were 16 x 16 in. Obsolescence was rapid in those days, but North Star was rebuilt with a large boiler and new cylinders in 1854, lasting in service for 33 years. When finally withdrawn, she was preserved at Swindon, Wiltshire, until, in an act of official vandalism, she was scrapped in 1906. In something of an atonement, GWR built a full-sized replica incorporating original parts in 1925. This is displayed at Swindon Railway Museum.

For the most part, the other original GWR broad-gauge locomotives were a collection of mechanical freaks, the best of a poor lot being six 2-2-2s with 8 ft driving wheels from Tayleur's Vulcan Foundry, which were Patentee copies but

IRON DUKE

Date	1847
Builder	Daniel Gooch, Swindon, Wiltshire, England
Client	Great Western Railway (GWR)
Gauge	7 ft
Type	4-2-2
Driving wheels	8 ft
Capacity	2 cylinders 18 x 24 in
Pressure	100 lb later 120 lb
Weight	35 tons

● **ABOVE LEFT**
The importance of the broad gauge and its hitherto unimagined speeds caught the imagination of the populace. People flocked to experience this revolutionary form of travel in which speeds of 90 mph (145 kph) had been reported.

● **ABOVE RIGHT**
Tiny: built by Sara & Co., of Plymouth, Devon, in 1868, this broad-gauge locomotive went into service on England's South Devon Railway (SDR).

● **OPPOSITE MIDDLE**
Isambard Kingdom Brunel (1806–59), the 19th-century English engineer who pioneered the broad gauge of the Great Western Railways, between London and Exeter in Devon. His father was a French engineer in England, Sir Marc Isambard Brunel (1769–1849).

● **OPPOSITE BOTTOM**
Iron Duke (replica): built by Gooch, this 4-2-2 of the Duke Class was named after Arthur Wellesley, the first Duke of Wellington (1769–1852), on whose birthday – 1 May – it first ran.

with small low-pressure boilers. They were delivered from Manchester, Lancashire, to London by sea and then on to West Drayton, Middlesex, by canal. Among their more bizarre stablemates were two 2-2-2s from Mather & Dixon with 10 ft driving wheels fabricated from riveted iron plates.

There was much opposition to the broad gauge, and in July 1845 the Gauge Commission sat to choose between the rival claims of both gauges. High-speed trial runs were organized, the honours going to Daniel Gooch's 7 ft GWR single "Ixion", which achieved 60 mph (96.6

kph) hauling an 80 ton (81,284 kg) train. The best standard-gauge performance was 53 mph (85.1 kph) behind a brand new Stephenson 4-2-0 with 6 ft 6 in driving wheels. Although the Commission considered the 7 ft gauge in every way superior, the standard gauge was selected on the basis of the greater mileage already in use. In 1848, Parliament decided there should in future be only one gauge, the narrow, and eventually the GWR had to bow to the inevitable, laying a third rail to give 4 ft 8½ in throughout its system and abolishing the broad gauge altogether in May 1892.

● **RIGHT**
Rain, Steam and Speed (National Gallery, London): Turner (1775–1851), the English landscape painter, welcomed the Industrial Revolution of the 18th and 19th centuries and painted this picture of one of Gooch's singles crossing the Maidenhead Viaduct, Berkshire, during a squally storm in the Thames valley.

BRITISH LOCOMOTIVES – 1840–60

Derwent: built by W.A. Kitching in 1845, this 0-6-0 went into service on the Stockton & Darlington Railway (S&DR) between Stockton-on-Tees port and Darlington, County Durham, the first passenger-carrying railway in the world (1825). This railway largely developed the industrial town.

In 1841, Robert Stephenson introduced the first of his "long-boilered" locomotives. In these, he sought to obtain greater boiler power by grouping all the axles in front of the firebox and having a much longer boiler barrel than usual. The necessarily short wheelbase was dictated by the small turntables of the period. "Long-boiler" engines also featured inside frames of iron-plate and the inside-cylinders shared a common steam-chest placed between them. The design could be built in almost any form: a 2-2-2 or 2-4-0 for passenger work and an 0-6-0 for goods-trains were the commonest configurations. But as line speeds rose, the passenger types were found to oscillate dangerously on their short wheelbase chassis and soon fell out of favour. For goods work, however, the design was an undoubted success and these were most numerous on Stephenson's home turf. The North Eastern Railway (NER), a successor to the Stockton & Darlington Railway (S&DR), had no fewer than 125 long-boiler 0-6-0s of the 1001 class built between 1852 and 1875. Fittingly, No. 1275 is preserved in the National Railway Museum at York.

Thomas Russell Crampton (1816–88) was an ambitious young engineer working at Swindon, Wiltshire, under Daniel Gooch. He began to develop his own ideas for an express-locomotive with a large boiler and driving wheels but low centre of gravity and took out his first patent in 1842. In his design, the driving axle was placed right at the base of the frame, behind the firebox. To keep the connecting-rods as short as possible, the cylinders were displaced rearwards outside the frames and fed from the smokebox by prominent outside steam-pipes. The motion and valve gear was all placed outside, allowing the boiler to

LARGE BLOOMER

Date	1852
Builder	W. Fairbairn/ E.B. Wilson
Client	London & North Western Railway (LNWR)
Gauge	4 ft 8 1/2 in
Type	2-2-2
Driving wheels	7 ft 6 in
Capacity	2 cylinders 18 x 24 in
Pressure	150 lb
Weight	31 tons 4 cwt

be sunk down in the frames but making the engine very wide. Crampton left the GWR to promote his design to a wider market. His first two engines were built by Tulk & Ley for the Liège & Namur Railway, Belgium, in 1846.

One of the Cramptons destined for Belgium was tested on the Grand Junction Railway (GJR), leading the London and North Western Railway (LNWR) to build one for themselves at Crewe, Cheshire, in 1847. This was the 4-2-0 Courier with 7 in driving wheels, inside-frames and a boiler of oval cross-section. At the same time, larger versions with 8 in driving wheels, the 4-2-0 London by Tulk & Ley and the 6-2-0 Liverpool by Bury, Curtis & Kennedy, were tried out by the LNWR, the latter with great destructive effect on the track. Cramptons could run at speeds approaching 90 mph (145 kph), but they never achieved great popularity in Britain because of their rough riding caused by the position of the driving axle. On the Continent, it was a different matter and the French Northern Railway in particular gained its reputation for lightweight fast expresses by the use of Crampton locomotives. "Prendre le Crampton" even entered the French

language as slang for "a quick getaway". These French Cramptons had very strong outside-frames, because the continental loading-gauge left room for the resulting enormous width over cylinders and cranks. A British example built the same

way by J.E. McConnell of LNWR earned the nickname "Mac's Mangle" following the trail of broken platforms and lineside structures left in its wake.

In 1847, from E.B. Wilson's Railway Foundry in Leeds, Yorkshire, emerged the first engine built to their most famous design, the Jenny Lind class. This 2-2-2 passenger-engine was the brainchild of the young chief draughtsman, David Joy. Built at a cost of about £2,500 each, the basic model had 6 in driving wheels powered by 15 x 20 in inside-cylinders, making it capable of a mile-a-minute in regular service. For the first time, railways could buy an off-the-peg express locomotive of peerless quality. This most elegant machine, with its polished mahogany boiler lagging and classically fluted bronze dome and safety-valve casings, rapidly became top-link motive power for many of Britain's main lines. The largest Jenny Lind was the Salopian built for Shrewsbury & Birmingham Railway (S&BR) in June 1849. It had a boiler with more than 1,270 sq ft of heating surface and a pressure of 120 lb with 15 1/2 x 22 in cylinders driving 6 ft 6 in wheels.

BRITISH LOCOMOTIVES – 1860–75

Patrick Stirling's early locomotives were cabless and had domed boilers. His first 2-2-2 was built for Scotland's Glasgow & South Western Railway (G&SWR) in 1857 and bore many of the design hallmarks that were refined into their finest flowering in his Great Northern 4-2-2 No. 1 of 1870. His crowning achievements were the 8 ft 4-2-2 singles, built at Doncaster, Yorkshire, from 1870 onwards, said to be one of the most handsome locomotives ever made. With modification these were used on all main-line trains for the next 25 years. In 1895, they took part in the railway Races to the North with average speeds of more than 80 mph (129 kph) between King's Cross Station, London, and York.

When William Stroudley became Locomotive Superintendent of the London, Brighton & South Coast Railway (LB&SCR) in 1870, he found a bizarre assortment of locomotives, which were

by no means a match for the work they had to do. Over the next two decades, he restocked with a fine series of soundly engineered machines for every purpose from express-passenger to branch-line

haulage. His smallest, yet most celebrated class, was the Terrier 0-6-0Ts of 1872. Fifty engines were built, originally for suburban work in south London but later widely dispersed to more rural

● **ABOVE**
William Stroudley's beautiful livery is captured to perfection on Terrier 0-6-0T No. 55 Stepney, built in 1875 and preserved in full working order on England's Bluebell Railway in Sussex.

● **LEFT**
Kirtley's double-framed 2-4-0 No. 158A breathes the spirit of the Midland Railway in the 19th century at the Midland Railway Centre, Butterley, Derbyshire. Butterley was a seat of ironworks and collieries.

● BELOW
A 4-2-2 Massey Bromley of 1879. Dübs & Co. built ten for the Great Eastern Railway (GER). Kitsons built ten more in 1881–2.

● BELOW
A 2-4-0 of Scotland's Highland Railway in about 1877. Note the louvred chimney, which produced a current of air with the object of lifting the exhaust above the cab.

surroundings. They had 4 ft driving wheels, a 150 lb boiler and 12 x 20 in cylinders. Most were rebuilt with slightly larger boilers without in any way spoiling their appearance. Always useful, they notched up a working life of more than 90 years. Today, nearly a dozen exist in preservation.

Joseph Beattie of the London & South Western Railway (L&SWR) was an ingenious Irishman who sought to increase the steaming power of the locomotive boiler by incorporating elaborate firebox arrangements. A typical Beattie firebox had two compartments, divided by a water-filled partition. Heavy firing took place in the rear portion, the forward fire being kept as far as possible in an incandescent state. Like Kirtley, he made great use of the 2-4-0 type, both in tender form as an express-engine and as a tank-engine for suburban work. He was determined to obtain the maximum steam output from every ounce of coal, and his express 2-4-0s also featured combustion chambers, thermic siphons and auxiliary chimneys. His 2-4-0 tank-engines carried their water supply in a well-tank between the frames. In 1874, 88 entered service.

● ABOVE
Joseph Beattie's L&SWR express 2-4-0 Medusa, fitted with double firebox and auxiliary chimney, as captured by artist Cuthbert Hamilton Ellis (born 1909).

STIRLING SINGLE

Date	1870
Builder	Doncaster, Yorkshire, England
Client	Great Northern Railway (GNR)
Gauge	4 ft 8½ in
Type	2-4-0
Driving wheels	8 ft 1 in
Capacity	2 cylinders 18 x 28 in outside
Pressure	140 lb
Weight	38 tons 9 cwt

BRITISH LOCOMOTIVES – 1875–1900

In 1882 Francis William Webb designed a three-cylinder compound express-engine with uncoupled driving wheels – the 2-2-2-0. The engine, LNWR No. 66 Experiment, had two outside high-pressure cylinders driving the rear axle and one huge low-pressure cylinder between the frames driving the leading axle. The absence of coupling-rods meant that one pair of wheels could slip without the other, and it was not unknown for the driving wheels to revolve in opposite directions when attempts were made to start the train. The best of this type were the Teutonics introduced in 1889, with their larger boilers and 7 ft 1 in driving wheels.

The first main-line 0-8-0 tender-engine to run in Britain was introduced on the newly opened Barry Railway in 1889. Built by Sharp, Stewart of Glasgow, they proved ideal for hauling heavy South Wales coal-trains, with their 18 x 26 in outside-cylinders and 4 ft-3 in driving wheels.

● **ABOVE**
The Jones Goods engines of 1894 were Britain's first 4-6-0s. No. 103 shows off its immaculate Highland Railway livery and Jones's louvred chimney.

● **ABOVE**
F.W. Webb's LNWR Precedent 2-4-0s were introduced in 1874. By 1882, the Crewe works had built 90 examples. They performed prodigious feats of haulage, culminating in No. 790 Hardwicke's performance in the 1895 Race to the North. Although Webb tried to displace them from top-link work with his compounds, the little 2-4-0s were the most reliable of all 19th-century LNWR passenger types.

● **LEFT**
A Neilson & Co. 4-2-2 with 7 ft driving wheels. Built in 1886, it is seen here in 1963, before heading the Blue Belle excursion.

● **OPPOSITE**
This Johnson Single of the former Midland Railway is one of a class known as Spinners, regarded by many as the most beautiful locomotives of all time. With variations, the class totalled 95 engines, all in service by 1900.

● **ABOVE LEFT**
Ivatt's Great Northern No. 990 was the first British Atlantic 4-4-2 and was built at Doncaster Works, Yorkshire, in 1898. Ten more were in service by 1900. In 1902, a larger boiler version appeared, No. 251, which was the first of one of Britain's most successful express-passenger types. Both the original engines are preserved and are shown here running together.

● **ABOVE RIGHT**
Nicknamed Cauliflowers because of the appearance of the LNWR coat of arms on their driving splashers resembling that vegetable, these were F.W. Webb's 18 in express goods-engines, 310 of which were built between 1880 and the turn of the century.

A serious problem on many railways was the blowing back of the exhaust into the crew's faces as they descended gradients. To remedy this, in 1877 David Jones of the Highland Railway introduced locomotives with a louvred chimney. This produced a current of air that lifted the exhaust above the cab. Jones also introduced a counter-pressure brake to assist in controlling trains descending the formidable Highland gradients. His most famous locomotives were his 4-6-0s of 1894, the first engines of this wheel arrangement to work in the

British Isles. Sharp, Stewart built 15, which were, at the time, the most powerful main-line engines in Britain.

Few inside-cylinder 4-4-0s surpassed Dugald Drummond's famed T9s of 1899 for the London & South Western Railway (L&SWR). By extending the coupled wheelbase of his earlier designs to 10 ft, he made room in his T9s for a large firebox. The new engines were a success. With their 6 ft 7 in driving wheels, they were fast and able to haul heavy expresses over the difficult South Western main line west of Salisbury, Wiltshire.

CAULIFLOWER

Date	1880
Builder	F.W. Webb, Crewe Works, Cheshire, England
Client	London & North Western Railway (LNWR)
Gauge	4 ft 8½ in
Type	0-6-0
Driving wheels	5 ft 2 in
Capacity	Cylinders 18 in x 24 in
Pressure	150 lb
Weight	36 tons

BRITISH BUILDERS OF THE 19TH CENTURY

Britain's railways were developed piece-meal by private companies with loco-motives coming from outside firms, but once the operating companies joined together to form larger organizations they established their own works for over-hauling and building. These company workshops caused places like Crewe (LNWR), Doncaster (GNR), Derby (MR) and Swindon (GWR) to become known as the Railway Towns. Tens of thousands of locomotives were built in these and other towns – over 7,000 in Crewe alone – all for home use rather than export.

The first centre of locomotive building in Britain was established in the mining town of Newcastle in 1821 when George Stephenson and his son Robert opened the world's first workshop dedicated solely to locomotive building. By 1855 the company had built more than 1,000 for Britain and the rest of the world. In 1899 the private company was shut down and a new limited company took its place.

One of the first builders of loco-motives in Leeds was Fenton, Murray & Wood. Founded in 1795, their first locomotive, "Prince Regent", was built for Middleton Colliery in 1812. Although the company only built five more

● **ABOVE LEFT**
Charles Beyer
(1813–76) of the
locomotive building
partnership Beyer
Peacock.

● **ABOVE RIGHT**
Richard Peacock of
the locomotive
building partnership
Beyer Peacock.

● **LEFT**
Beyer Peacock
letterhead.

● **ABOVE**
Works plate from Kitson & Co., Leeds, one of
the Leeds builders who made that city famous
across the world.

● **ABOVE**
Another great Glasgow builder, Sharp,
Stewart, who had moved to Springburn from
Great Bridgwater Street in Manchester.

● **ABOVE**
A plate of Falcon Engine and Car Works
Company of Loughborough – the forerunner
of the famous Brush Works, which continues
the tradition of building hi-tech locomotives
for today's railway.

● **RIGHT**
A 4-6-0 locomotive built by Robert Stephenson of Newcastle.

● **BELOW LEFT**
The Greek god of Fire used as the symbol for Charles Tayleur & Co., whose works became the famous Vulcan Foundry.

● **BELOW RIGHT**
James Naysmyth, legendary Victorian engineer and founder of Naysmyth Wilson Patricroft Locomotive Works.

locomotives, one of Murray's apprentices, Charles Todd, went on to found his own business, with James Kitson, in 1835. At first they built only parts, but by 1838 they had produced their first complete locomotive. It was so large that they had to pull down one of the workshop walls before it could be delivered.

One of the earliest manufacturers of locomotives in Manchester was William Fairbairn, who had founded an iron foundry in 1816 and who entered into locomotive building in 1839. In 1863, having built about 400 locomotives, the firm was taken over by Sharp, Stewart & Co., a firm which had been established in

● **ABOVE**
Dübs works plate from an early Spanish locomotive.

● **RIGHT**
Henry Dübs, one of the great Glasgow builders, whose works were in Polmadie.

1828 by Thomas Sharp and Richard Roberts. By the 1880s Sharp, Stewart had expanded so much that they left their Manchester foundries and relocated in Glasgow. In 1903 the three firms of Sharp, Stewart, Neilson Reid and Henry Dübs merged to become the North British Locomotive Company Ltd. Another of the great Manchester builders was Beyer, Peacock & Co., which, unlike the companies mentioned so far, had been founded, in 1854, purely as a locomotive building works.

One of the earliest building firms founded in Glasgow was that of Walter Neilson and James Mitchell. Although they had commenced the production of stationary engines in 1830, it was not

until 1843 that they produced their first locomotives. By 1860 the small works could not keep pace with orders, and a new foundry was built in Finniston. Even this factory soon became too small, and in 1861 work began on new premises in Springburn. The firm's locomotives were exported to many countries, including India, South Africa and Argentina. In 1864 Henry Dübs left the company to establish his own locomotive factory at Polmadie. Within three years the firm had achieved such a reputation that it was exporting to India, Cuba, Spain, Finland and Russia.

The great export trade that developed as Britain took railways to many parts of the world continued to be developed by private builders who in turn made cities like Manchester, Leeds, Newcastle and Glasgow famous throughout the world.

EARLY NORTH AMERICAN LOCOMOTIVES

Horse-drawn railways for hauling coal first appeared in the United States of America from about 1826. Then, having heard of events in England, in 1828 a commission of three American engineers visited the works of Robert Stephenson in Newcastle upon Tyne, the great engineering centre, and those of Foster, Rastrick & Co. in Stourbridge, a market-town and manufacturing centre in Worcestershire, west central England. The result of this visit was that, the next year, four locomotives were ordered, one from Stephenson and three from Foster, Rastrick. Stephenson's was delivered first in January 1829, but, for reasons which are unclear, it was not put into service. Foster, Rastrick's Stourbridge Lion arrived next and was the first steam-driven locomotive put into operation in the USA.

● MATTHIAS BALDWIN

The second Stephenson locomotive sent to America, a six-wheeler built in 1829, had, like the first, bar-frames. This type of design, soon to be abandoned in

● ABOVE
Ross Winans built vertical-boiler, vertical-cylinder locomotives called "grasshoppers" for the Baltimore & Ohio line, at its Mount Claire Shops, Baltimore, Maryland. In 1927, for its "Fair of the Iron Horse", B&O posed the Andrew Jackson of about 1835 as the Thomas Jefferson.

Britain, remained the standard in America for many years. Stephenson's third, a Planet-type 2-2-0, was delivered to the Mohawk & Hudson Railway (M&HR) in 1832. This was examined by Matthias Baldwin who went on to build Old Ironside, which on its first run reached 30 mph.

At about the same time, Stephenson sent another locomotive to the Camden & Amboy Railroad & Transportation Co. (C&AR&TC). Camden is a seaport in New Jersey, which became a terminus in 1834, Amboy is in Illinois. The locomotive had a circular boiler and domed "haystack" firebox. A year after its arrival, its front wheels were removed and a four-wheeled bogie with a cowcatcher substituted, to make it suitable for local conditions. It entered service in November 1831 at Bordentown, New Jersey. The oldest complete locomotive in the USA, it was brought out of retirement in 1893 to haul a train of two 1836-type C&A passenger-coaches. The train did the 1,481 km (920 miles) from New York City to Chicago in five days.

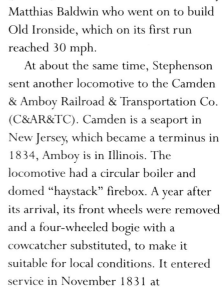

● LEFT
The De Witt Clinton was built for the Mohawk & Hudson line by the West Point Foundry, New York, in 1831.

● PETER COOPER

In 1830, the Baltimore & Ohio (B&O) line put into service Peter Cooper's Tom Thumb, on the 21 km (13 mile) stretch across Maryland between Baltimore and Ellicott's Mill. This was more of a scientific model than a proper locomotive, but it convinced American business that steam traction was a practical thing. The same year, the West Point Foundry of New York City constructed the first all-American-built locomotive, "The Best Friend of Charleston", for the South Carolina Railroad (SCR). In 1832, the same foundry completed Experiment, later named Brother Jonathan. This, the first locomotive in the USA to incorporate a leading bogie, was also the

first to operate on a regular scheduled run. The locomotive came to a premature end when its vertical bottle-like boiler burst.

In 1831, the De Witt Clinton, built by the West Point Foundry, made her first journey on the M&HR line. The locomotive, with cylinders mounted either side of the footplate's rear, reached 15 mph on the Albany-Schenectady line, which had been built across New York state to connect the two eponymous rivers. It could not have been a successful engine, for it was scrapped in 1835.

● **ABOVE AND INSET**
Camden & Amboy's first locomotive, John Bull, was built by Stephenson in England. It was assembled in the USA by Isaac Dripps. He added a pilot, making it the first locomotive in America to employ a cowcatcher pilot.

TOM THUMB

Date	1830
Builder	Peter Cooper, New York, USA
Client	Baltimore & Ohio (B&O)
Gauge	4 ft 8½ in
Driving wheels	2-2-0
Capacity	2 cylinders 3 x 14 in

● **RIGHT**
In 1830, New York businessman Peter Cooper demonstrated the first American-built locomotive on the Baltimore & Ohio railroad. This locomotive was later named Tom Thumb. A 1926 replica poses here.

EARLY BALDWIN LOCOMOTIVES

In 1834, Baldwin, having already built Old Ironside, produced his second engine, the E.L. Miller. This was for the Charleston and Hamburg Railroad (C&HR). Old Ironside's composite wood-and-iron wheels had proved fragile, so Baldwin fitted his six-wheeled machine with solid bell-metal driving wheels of 4 ft 6 in in diameter. A sister locomotive, Lancaster, appeared in June the same year and promptly set an American record by hauling 19 loaded cars over Pennsylvania's highest gradients between Philadelphia and Columbia. This persuaded the railway's directors to adopt steam power instead of horse traction and they placed an order with Baldwin for five more locomotives. The first Baldwin engine to

● **LEFT**
This Class 152 2-6-0 is typical of early wagontop boilered Moguls from Baldwin. The usual array of fluted and flanged domes, diamond chimney, short smokebox, cross-head-driven boiler-feed pump with back-up injector is completed by a decorated headlight.

have outside-cylinders, the Black Hawk, was delivered to the Philadelphia & Trenton Railroad (P&TR) in 1835.

● **POWER DEMANDED**
Railways were now demanding more powerful locomotives. Baldwin considered there was no advantage in the

OLD IRONSIDES

Date	1832
Builder	Baldwin, Philadelphia, Pennsylvania, USA
Client	Camden & Amboy Railroad (C&AR)
Gauge	4 ft 8½ in
Driving wheels	4 ft 6 in
Capacity	2 cylinders 9½ x 18 in

● **OPPOSITE TOP, INSET**
The builder's plate of the Baldwin-built 2-6-0 Mogul No. 20, Tahoe.

● **OPPOSITE TOP**
Matty Baldwin's first locomotive-building shop, in Lodge Alley, Philadelphia.

● **OPPOSITE BOTTOM**
The Tahoe, a Baldwin-built 2-6-0 Mogul-type, once operated by the Virginia & Truckee (V&T) line in Nevada, displayed at the Railroad Museum of Pennsylvania, Stroudsburg, Pennsylvania.

● **RIGHT**
From the early years, Baldwin built many saddle-tanks of distinctive generic appearance. This veteran, working at the E.G. Lavandero Sugar Mill, Cuba, is typical.

eight-wheeled engine, arguing it would not turn a corner without slipping one or more pairs of wheels sideways. None the less, in May 1837, he built his first eight-wheeler. Baldwin's outside-cylindered 0-8-0 Ironton of 1846 had the two leading coupled axles on a flexible beam truck, allowing lateral motion and the relatively long wheelbase to accommodate itself to curves.

● **CONCERNS ABOUT ADHESION**
As railroads spread, so 1:50 gradients or steeper were met, bringing concerns about adhesion. Baldwin's initial response was to incorporate a supplementary pair of smaller-diameter wheels on an independent axle, driven by cranks from the main driving wheels. The first such engine was sold to the Sugarloaf Coal Co. in August 1841. On a trial run,

it hauled 590 tons across Pennsylvania from Reading to Philadelphia, a distance of 87 km (54 miles) in 5 hours 22 minutes, yet another American speed-and-haulage record.

Baldwin's classic locomotive development for heavy freightwork was the 2-6-0- Mogul. In this design, he substituted an extra pair of coupled wheels and single carrying-axle for the leading bogie of the classic American 4-4-0 passenger-engine. The result was a machine that could also be turned to passenger work in mountainous country.

Baldwin's earliest locomotives were built at Matty, his modest assembly-shop in Lodge Alley, Philadelphia. The company he formed became the world's largest locomotive-builder. In the 117-year history of Baldwin Locomotives' work more than 7,000 engines were built.

AMERICAN LOCOMOTIVES – 1840–75

The years between 1840 and the American Civil War (1861–5) saw locomotive production treble. By the end of the 1850s, not only were there 11 main American builders but they had also progressed beyond the experimental stage to bulk production of well-defined standard types suited to local conditions.

With the development of the railroad over the Appalachian Mountains, separating the American East from the West, Richard Norris & Son of Philadelphia, Pennsylvania, extended the classic 4-4-0 by adding an extra coupled axle at the rear to become the 4-6-0 type ("Ten-Wheeler"). This allowed a much larger boiler and the extra pair of drivers gave 50 per cent extra adhesion to cope with steep gradients. The use of bar-frames by American locomotive builders allowed the simple enlargement of existing designs without needing to retool or create more workshop capacity.

● **RIGHT**
The Pioneer, a 2-2-2 single-driver "bicycle"-type built in 1851 by Seth Wilmarth for the Cumberland Valley Railroad. This was the first locomotive to operate in Chicago.

● **LEFT**
The railroad depot at Nashville, Tennessee, during the American Civil War.

● **BELOW**
This replica of the Central Pacific Railway's 4-4-0 Jupiter and Union Pacific Railroad's No. 119 stands at the Golden Spike National Monument, Promontory, Promontory Point, Utah.

• RIGHT
A typical American express train of the 1860s headed by a 4-4-0. This was the most important type of American locomotive providing the flexibility for running at speeds over lightly laid and often rough track beds.

● MOGULS AND CONSOLIDATIONS

Many American engineers became concerned that the increasing length of locomotive boilers interfered with the driver's view. In 1853 Samuel J. Hayes of the Baltimore & Ohio Railroad (B&OR) built a 4-6-0 with the cab perched on top of the boiler, surrounding the steam dome. It looked strange but the mechanical design was sound. The layout was copied by other builders.

In the 1860s, the New Jersey Railroad Co. (NJRC) was an early customer for the Baldwin 2-6-0 Mogul freight locomotives already described. As line speeds rose and trains became heavier still, an even larger freight engine was needed. In 1866, the Lehigh & Mahoning Railroad (L&MR), eponymous with rivers in Pennsylvania and Ohio, added a leading two-wheeled truck to the 0-8-0 design to create the Consolidation, the name by which heavy-freight 2-8-0s were henceforth known.

● ABOVE
The 1855 Brooks-built General, owned by the Western & Atlantic Railroad (W&AR), is famous for its role in the American Civil War. It was stolen from the Confederacy by Union spies and involved in a great chase. This is a typical 4-4-0 American-type of the period.

ATLAS

Date	1846
Builder	Baldwin, Philadelphia, Pennsylvania, USA
Client	Philadelphia & Reading
Wheels	0-8-0
Capacity	Cylinders 16½ x 18½ in
Weight	23.7 tons

Transcontinental links were planned in 1862 as part of President Lincoln's aim to unite the North and preserve the Union. As the 1860s ended, the last rails of the Union Pacific Railroad (UPR) and the Central Pacific Railway (CPR) were joined at Promontory, near Ogden, Utah. CPR President Leland Stanford, who had built eastwards from California, drove in the gold spike to fasten the track when the two lines met to form the first American transcontinental railway on 10 May 1869. The event, commemorated by the Golden Spike Monument, linked the Atlantic and Pacific Oceans by rail and left the way open to the large and powerful locomotives that were to come, serving settlement of the West, which now leapt ahead.

AMERICAN LOCOMOTIVES – 1875–1900

Industrialization and modernization meant free time and more spending money for the American workforce to buy things such as day trips and holidays. To meet this demand, in the late 1870s heavy traffic developed, especially weekend travel between Philadelphia and New Jersey. This called for longer passenger-trains and faster schedules.

● **AIR-BRAKES AND ANTHRACITE**

Until the 1870s, the 4-4-0 engine proved ideal for American railroads. Then, faster, heavier traffic began to demand something larger. Bigger locomotives led to heavier rails, stronger bridges, bigger turntables, better cars, longer passing-loops and, most important of all, air-brakes. George Westinghouse's

● **ABOVE**
The 4-4-0 American type was the universal locomotive from about 1850 to 1895. More than 24,000 were built. On this high-drivered Philadelphia & Reading camelback-design 4-4-0, the engineer rides above the boiler, the fireman behind.

● **LEFT**
The 2-8-0 type was popular with narrow-gauge railroads for high adhesion on mountain rails. This 1881 Baldwin, built for the D&RG, is displayed at the Colorado Railroad Museum, Golden, Colorado.

CHICAGO BURLINGTON & QUINCY 2-4-2

Date	1895
Builder	Baldwin, Philadelphia, Pennsylvania, USA
Client	Chicago Burlington & Quincy (CB&Q)
Gauge	4 ft 8½ in
Driving wheels	7 ft ¼ in
Capacity	Cylinders 19 x 26 in

● **LEFT**
This 1895 Baldwin-built 36 in gauge 2-8-0 Consolidation-type was typical of locomotives operating in Colorado before the turn of the century. It first operated on the Florence & Cripple Creek Railroad (F&CCR) and later on the Denver & Rio Grande (D&RG). It is displayed at Durango, Colorado.

● LEFT
When built in 1886, this Baldwin 2-10-0 "Decapod" was reported to be the world's largest locomotive. No. 500 and its sister No. 501 beat a temporary track across the mountains while a tunnel was being completed.

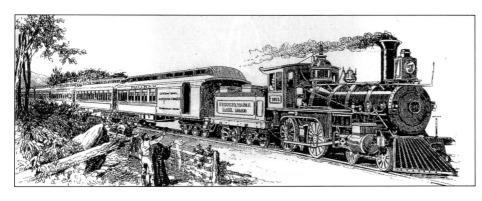

● ABOVE
A 4-4-0 on the Pennsylvania Railroad.

● BELOW
A 4-4-0 built in 1881 by Sharp, Stewart, of Glasgow, Scotland, for the St John & Maine Railroad (SJ&MR), linking St John and Maine.

compressed air-brake replaced hand-brakes almost immediately after he introduced it in 1868, allowing the high speed of modern trains.

Baldwin's 5,000th production was the 4-2-2 Lovett Eames. Built in 1880, the locomotive was fitted with a wide-grate Wootten firebox for burning anthracite coal, a fuel fast replacing coke and wood. The 6 ft 6 in driving wheels made the locomotive well suited for high-speed passenger service: Baldwin guaranteed it would maintain a 60 mph average speed pulling four cars. It was to have been No. 507 of the Philadelphia & Reading Railroad (P&RR) but only ran trials before the railroad went bankrupt and returned it to her builder.

● "DECAPOD" – WORLD'S LARGEST LOCOMOTIVE
Six years later, Baldwin produced what was reported to be the largest locomotive in the world – a 2-10-0 "Decapod". Its

ten 3 ft 9 in driving wheels were intended as much for spreading its great weight over as many axles as possible as they were for gaining adhesion on a temporary track over the mountains while a tunnel was being driven. To facilitate negotiating tight curves, the second and third pairs of drivers were flangeless. A rival claimant for the title of largest engine in the world was the 4-8-0 Mastodon heavyfreight engine of the 1890s.

The American type 4-4-0 was eclipsed on all major railroads by the end of the century. Its final flowering, in 1893, was the L Class of New York Central Railroad (NYCR). That year, No. 999 topped 100 mph at the head of the Empire State Limited between New York City and Buffalo.

AMERICAN LOCOMOTIVE BUILDERS

The first British locomotive was imported into the USA in 1829. Within a year the first American-built machine, "The Best Friend of Charleston", from the West Point Foundry of New York City, was on the rails. By the end of the 1830s, about a dozen workshops had tried their hands at locomotive-building. By 1840, as railways were being built or projected in all parts of the USA, the three main American builders – Baldwin, Norris and Rogers – had made 246 locomotives between them, the first two in Philadelphia, the third in New Jersey.

● **LEFT**
The builder's plate for Florence & Cripple Creek Railroad's No. 20, a Schenectady-built 4-6-0. Schenectady was one of several builders consolidated into the American Locomotive Company (Alco) in 1901.

● STANDARDIZATION OF COMPONENTS

In the USA, as in Britain, there were operating-company workshops as well as private builders. Generally, company shops concentrated on repair and maintenance, leaving building of complete locomotives to private companies. An exception was the Pennsylvania Railroad's Altoona Works, which began locomotive production in 1866 and quickly standardized components within classes. This was a great improvement because, at this time, locomotives were still mainly handbuilt, meaning it was rarely possible to interchange parts, even on locomotives of the same type from the same builder.

● **ABOVE**
Baldwin's erecting shop (*The American Railway*, 1892).

● **BELOW**
The William Crooks was the first locomotive to operate in Minnesota. It was built by the New Jersey Machine Works in Paterson, New Jersey, in 1861 for the St Paul & Pacific Railroad (SP&PR), a predecessor of American railway pioneering entrepreneur James J. Hill's Great Northern Railway (GNR). Hill was nicknamed "the Empire Builder".

● SPECIALISTS TAILOR-MADE FOR INDUSTRY

Apart from main-line railroads, rail transport was spreading widely across industry, and specialist locomotive-manufacturers sprang up to tailor-make machines for industry's needs. Doyen of these was Ephraim Shay, a sawmill-owner from Haring, Michigan. He brought timber down from forests on temporary, corkscrew tracks. As these could not stand the weight of a conventional locomotive, he designed his own. In 1880, he mounted a boiler in the centre of a flat bogie-car. This was offset to one side, to allow a pair of vertical cylinders to drive a horizontal shaft turning along the locomotive's right-hand side at wheel-centre level. This engine was nothing like a conventional locomotive, but it was perfect for its job.

● VOLUME OUTPUT FROM FACTORIES

Before 1880, most American locomotives were fairly small machines of weights rarely exceeding 30 tons. This meant they could be built in small workshops without the need for big overhead cranes and their bar-frame components could be made by hand in an ordinary blacksmith's forge. However, by 1890, locomotives had grown so much in size that traditional shops had become useless. The largest builders, such as Baldwin and Cook, set up multi-storied factories with heavy-duty power cranes to build locomotives on a volume-production scale. Smaller firms could no longer compete and collapsed financially.

CANADIAN LOCOMOTIVES

Canada's first railway was a wooden tramway in Quebec extending just more than 27 km (17 miles) between Laprairie and St Johns. The line, opened for traffic in 1832, was for combining rail and water transport via the Hudson and Richelieu rivers. In the first winter of operation, the wooden rails were torn up by adverse weather. The next spring, metal rails replaced them.

● AMERICAN ENGINES

In July 1836, the Champlain & St Lawrence Railroad (C&SLR) was opened. Its first train was pulled by horses because the Canadian engineer could not get the English-built locomotive, Stephenson's 0-4-0 Dorchester, nicknamed "Kitten", to work. An engineer from the USA found that all it needed was "plenty of wood and water", and eventually it built up steam and managed an "extraordinary" 20 mph.

Canadian steam locomotives displayed British and American characteristics and the classic American-outline 4-4-0 was popular. Canadian winter conditions could play havoc with the track, and the American design proved more satisfactory than the British-style 2-4-0 with its relatively rigid wheelbase. American 4-4-0s were supplied in quantities to Canada in the 1870s and were regarded as a general-service type.

● ABOVE
The Samson was built in 1838 by Hackworth, of Wylam, Northumberland, in England for use in Canada. It was the first locomotive to operate in Nova Scotia and one of the earliest used in Canada.

● BELOW
The Countess of Dufferin, a typically Canadian 4-4-0, was the first locomotive put into service on the Canadian Pacific Railway (CPR).

● **LEFT**
A 4-4-0 built in 1870
by Dübs, of
Glasgow, Scotland,
for the Canadian
ICR. Note the ornate
headlamp and wheel
bosses.

● **RIGHT**
In 1868, a 4-4-0 was
built by Neilson of
Glasgow, Scotland,
for the 5 ft 6½ in-
gauge Canadian
Grand Trunk
Railway (CGTR).
The massive spark-
arrester chimney top
was 6 ft wide.

● **COUNTESS OF DUFFERIN**

The Countess of Dufferin was built by
Baldwin in 1872 and used on
governmental contracts in Manitoba,
Canada's easternmost Prairie Province,
before going to the Canadian Pacific
Railway (CPR) in 1883 – the same year
the CPR built its first locomotive.
Designed by the Scottish engineer F.R.F.
Brown, it was a typical "American" type
4-4-0 with 5 ft-2 in coupled wheels.
Canada followed American locomotive

practice very closely, but there were
subtle differences. The Countess featured
a British-style parallel boiler, not the steeply
coned American wagon-top pattern; the
spark-arresting stack's shape bespoke
Canadian rather than American design.

However, the wagon-top boiler did
feature in the early Canadian 4-6-0 and
2-8-0 designs. Its provision for additional
steam space over the firebox crown, the
hottest part of the boiler, helped avoid
priming, particularly when locomotives

were tackling the 1:25 gradients of the
CPR's Rocky Mountain section. On this
section, passenger- and freight-trains were
handled by small-wheeled 2-8-0s, loads
often limited to no more than two bogie-
cars per locomotive. When a long train
had to be worked over the mountains,
engines were interspersed through the
train at two-car intervals. By the end of
the 19th century, coal replaced wood as
fuel, and the need for hitherto prominent
spark-arrester chimneys ceased.

A 4-4-0

Date	1868
Builder	Neilson, Glasgow, Scotland
Client	Canadian Grand Trunk Railway (CGTR)
Gauge	5 ft 6½ in
Driving wheels	4-4-0
Capacity	Cylinders

● **LEFT**
The Albion, often
cited as the third
locomotive to
operate in Canada,
was made by Rayne
& Burn at Newcastle
upon Tyne, England.
This locomotive is
often misrepre-
sented as a
Hackworth
product.

EARLY EUROPEAN LOCOMOTIVES

The first locomotive built on mainland Europe was the unsuccessful Berliner Dampfwagen 1, a 0-4-0, constructed in Germany in 1816 for the horse-drawn Köningsgrube Tramway. The first successful steam trials in Europe were on the Saint-Etienne & Lyons Railway in 1828, using a pair of early Stephenson engines. In November 1829, French engineer Marc Séguin put his own engine into service on the line. It had a multi-tubular boiler with huge rotary fans, mounted on the tender and blowing fire through leather pipes. It could pull up to 18 tons but could not exceed 2 mph.

AJAX

Date	1841
Client	Austrian North Railway
Gauge	1,435 mm
Driving wheels	0-6-0

● **BELOW**
Der Adler, the first steam locomotive used on the Nuremberg-Fürth Railway, Bavaria, on 7 December 1835.

● **ALTERNATING SAWS**
Séguin produced two more locomotives. They went into service but had problems with belt-driven bellows mounted in the tender. These continually broke down from lack of steam. To allow for this, a wagon with four horses always accompanied the locomotive to provide traction should it be needed. These faults were ironed out, and by 1835 Séguin had completed 12 more locomotives of the same type that, because of the action of the levers, were referred to as *scieurs de long*, "alternating saws".

• FIRST IN GERMANY AND THE NETHERLANDS

The inaugural locomotive used in 1835 on Germany's first steam railway, in Bavaria, between Nuremberg and Fürth, was Der Adler. This 2-2-2 Patentee-type, built by Stephenson, had outside-frames and an enormously tall chimney of small diameter. It became popular in Europe and was the first locomotive introduced into several countries, including the Netherlands in 1839 when one opened the country's first line, in North Holland province, between Amsterdam, the commercial capital, and Haarlem 19 km (12 miles) west.

• AUSTRIAN EMPIRE'S FIRST

The first steam railway in the Austrian Empire was the Kaiser Ferdinand Nordbahn, which opened in 1837 using two Stephenson Planet-type locomotives, the Austria and the Moravia. Robert Stephenson's assistant John Haswell (1812–97) accompanied the engines to Vienna and stayed on to take charge of the rail workshops there. He was responsible for much early Austrian locomotive development.

• BRITISH INFLUENCE IN RUSSIA

Russia's first public railway was opened in 1837 between the royal centres of St Petersburg, the capital (1712–1914), and Tsarskoye Selo – "The Tsar's Village" summer residence 24 km (15 miles) south. Its first three locomotives were all Patentee 2-2-2s, one each from Timothy Hackworth, Robert Stephenson & Co. and Tayleur & Co. However, the first Russian-built engine was already at work on an industrial line in the Urals. This was a 2-2-0, built in 1833 by M. Cherepanov, a man who had seen early Stephenson locomotives in action in England.

• **ABOVE**
A Buddicom 2-2-2 locomotive built for the Paris-Rouen Railway in 1843. It could average 38 mph and is pictured arriving for display at the Festival of Britain in London in 1951.

• **BELOW**
Ajax, built by Isambard Kingdom Brunel in 1841 for the Austrian North Railway, entered service on the Floridsdorf-Stockerau stretch of the line, north out of Vienna.

EUROPE – MID-19TH CENTURY

The Alps are a mountain barrier in south Central Europe extending more than 1,000 km (650 miles) from the Mediterranean coast of France and north-west Italy through Switzerland, northern Italy and Austria to Slovenia. Their highest peak is 4,807 m (15,771 ft) Mont Blanc.

From 1844, the Austrian Government built the main line southwards from Vienna over the Alps via the Semmering Pass, 980 m (3,215 ft) above sea level. Engineer Karl Ghega used heavy gradients and severe curvature to conquer this barrier. The 29 km (18 mile) ascent from Gloggnitz to the summit is graded almost continually at 1:40. No existing locomotive was powerful enough to work trains over the pass, and it was at first thought that trains would have to be cable-hauled or worked by atmospheric power. Finally, a German technical magazine suggested a locomotive competition, on the lines of the Rainhill Trials, to find the best design of engine for mountain haulage. The Government Locomotive

● **ABOVE**
Wesel, built in 1851 by Borsig of Berlin, ran on the Cologne-Minden line across what since 1946 has been the Federal German state of North-Rhine Westphalia.

● **BELOW LEFT**
RENFE locomotive No. 030-2016, built by Kitson, Thomson & Hewitson, of Leeds in 1857, is seen here working as a station-pilot at Valencia, eastern Spain, in 1962.

● **BELOW RIGHT**
Gmunden was built in 1854 by Gunther, of the Lower Austrian town of Wiener Neustadt, for the narrow-gauge (1.106 metre) Linz-Gmunden line crossing Upper Austria.

Superintendent, Baron Engerth, agreed. The Semmering Trials were held in July 1851.

● **SEMMERING TRIALS**
Of the four entrants, three became milestone-makers in articulated-locomotive development. All four competitors more than fulfilled the test conditions, climbing the pass with the test-load faster than the required minimum speed. The winner of the first prize of 20,000 gold florins was the German entry Bavaria

LIMMAT

Date	1846
Builder	Emil Kessler, Karlsruhe, Baden, Germany
Client	Swiss Northern
Gauge	1,435 mm
Driving wheels	4-2-0
Capacity	Cylinders 14.25 x 22 mm

● **BELOW**
Pfalz, a Crampton-type locomotive, was built in 1853 by Maffei of Munich for the Bavarian Palatine Railway. This replica is pictured in front of locomotive sheds at Nuremberg, Bavaria.

locally by Wilhelm Günther.

The railway bought all the engines, and Bavaria was rebuilt in 1852 by Engerth as an 0-6-0 with its tender-frames extended forward to support the firebox's weight. Thus was created the Engerth-type of semi-articulated locomotive, which became popular in Austria, France, Switzerland and Spain. Seraing was progenitor of the double-boiler Fairlie-type articulated. Wiener Neustadt's design led to the Meyer articulated-locomotive layout. Both types achieved worldwide acceptance.

built by Maffei of Munich, a 0-4-4-4 tender-locomotive with rod-coupled groups of driving wheels linked by roller chains. The other entries were Vindobona, a rigid-framed 0-8-0 by John Haswell of Vienna; Seraing, a double-boilered articulated machine by John Cockerill of Belgium; and Wiener Neustadt, a double-bogie articulated with a single boiler, built

● **ANATOLE MALLET**

The first compound engine was built by Swiss-born, French-educated engineer Anatole Mallet (1837–1919) in 1876 for the Bayonne and Biarritz Railway in south-western France. Steam was admitted to a single high-pressure cylinder from where it was exhausted into a larger-diameter low-pressure

cylinder, working twice over. The claimed advantage was fuel efficiency. Right to the end of steam operation, French Railways were strongly committed to compounds. Two-cylinder compounding was developed in Germany by von Borries of Hanover State Railways, who introduced his compound 2-4-0s for express work in 1880.

● **RIGHT**
Limmat, a long-boilered engine built by Emil Kessler of Karlsruhe, Baden, in the German state of Württemberg, was the first locomotive to run from Zurich, Switzerland, to Baden, south-western Germany, on 19 August 1847. The line became known as the "Spanische Brötli Bahn" – a popular type of confectionery.

EUROPE TO 1900

● BELOW
This de Glehn compound running on France's Nord railway is typical of the closing years of the 19th century. Similar engines played a prolific part in express service across France and were also exported to many countries by French and other continental builders.

By 1879, the total track length on Russian railroads was 20,125 km (12,500 miles). Between 1860–90 the ever-growing demand for locomotives could not be met by Russian building alone, and many engines were imported from Britain, France, Germany and Austria. Two features of Russian locomotives of this period were the fully enclosed cabs, giving protection from harsh winters, and the promenade-deck effect, produced by handrails extending round the footplating on either side of the boiler to stop the crew slipping off in icy weather. In 1895, the first of 29 0-6-6-0 Mallet articulated-compound tender-engines was put into service, on the 3 ft 6 in gauge Vologda-Archangel railway in north Russia.

● ALFRED DE GLEHN

Alfred de Glehn (1848–1936), an inspired British engineer working in France as technical chief of Société Alsacienne, evolved a system of compounding using two high- and two low-pressure cylinders. His first locomotive was an advanced 4-2-2-0 in which the outside high-pressure cylinders were set well back in Crampton fashion and drove the rear-pair of uncoupled wheels. The low-pressure cylinders, set forward between the frames, drove the leading driving-axle. In partnership with Gaston du Bousquet (1839–1910), chief engineer of the Northern Railway of France, bigger, better and faster derivatives with coupled driving wheels were introduced in the 1890s, placing the Nord at the fore of high-speed locomotive performance. The first four-cylinder de Glehn compound was made in 1886 – the last in 1929.

● KARL GÖLSDORF

Compound locomotives were also developed in Austria by Karl Gölsdorf (1861–1916), engineer to Austrian State Railways – Österreichische Bundesbahnen (ÖBB). His earliest two-cylinder engines were freight 0-6-0s introduced

● LEFT
One of Europe's early, huge, heavy-hauling 0-8-0 tender-engines from the German builder Hartmann, exported to Spain in 1879.

● ABOVE
This Czech 0-8-0 was originally built in 1893 for the Austrian State Railways as their locomotive No. 73175, by STEG, of Vienna.

EMMETT 2-6-0T

Date	1886
Builder	Emil Kessler, Karlsruhe, Baden, Germany
Client	Portuguese CN Railway
Gauge	Metre
Driving wheels	3 ft 3½ in
Capacity	Cylinders 13 x 19 mm

in 1893. Gölsdorf's main concern was to provide both passenger- and freight-engines capable of hauling trains over Alpine passes. His heavyfreight 2-8-0s, designed for the Arlberg Tunnel, and of which more than 900 were built, were so successful they lasted in service until the 1950s.

● **CAESAR FRESCOT**

In 1884, Caesar Frescot, chief mechanical engineer (CME) of the Upper Italian Railway, gave Europe its first standard-gauge 4-6-0 tender-locomotive, Vittorio Emanuele II. These locomotives, built at Turin's works, were

● **BELOW LEFT**
An early Portuguese Railways 5 ft 6 in gauge saddle-tank built by Beyer Peacock, of Manchester, England.

● **BELOW RIGHT**
This type 0-8-0 of the Volga Dam Railway was imported from Britain's Sharp, Stewart in 1871.

intended for heavy passenger and freightwork over the 8 km (5 mile) long Giovi Pass railway tunnel at an altitude of 329 m (1,080 ft), across the Apennine mountain range of central Italy, linking Genoa, Turin and Milan in northern Italy.

They had outside-cylinders and were decorated with much ornamental brasswork, though their appearance was spoilt by the short wheelbase bogie. They were built into the 1890s and lasted well into the 20th century.

EUROPEAN BUILDERS OF THE 19TH CENTURY

One of Europe's first locomotive builders was Matthias von Schönner, the architect of the horse-drawn Budweis & Linz Railway linking the then German-named brewing city of České Budějovice, in southern Bohemia (now Czech Republic) and the Upper Austrian commercial city. Von Schönner visited America in the 1830s and was greatly influenced by the Philadelphian builder William Norris. He returned home to build the Vienna & Raub line which opened in 1842.

The Vienna & Gloggnitz Railway, immediately after opening in 1841,

● **ABOVE**
European builders, such as Kuntze & Jürdens of Germany, exported their locomotives as far afield as Cuba.

● **ABOVE**
One of Germany's most prolific locomotive builders was Henschel & Sohn whose works were in Kassel. The company built its first locomotive in 1848. Henschel produced for domestic railways and world export.

● **ABOVE**
Another prolific world-export market builder was Richard Hartmann, of Chemnitz, a town known as the "Saxon Manchester", standing at the base of the Erzgebirge, the "Ore Mountains" chain.

● **ABOVE**
The former German builder BMAG of Berlin was initially known as Schwartzkopff, as shown by this ornate maker's plate.

● **ABOVE**
A lesser-known German builder was Rheinische Metalfrabrik of Düsseldorf, capital of North-Rhine Westphalia and commercial hub of the Rhine-Ruhr industrial area. Its name is pictured on a Class 20 2-6-0, built in 1922, of Yugoslav Railway – Jugoslovenske Železnice (JŽ).

● **ABOVE**
Borsig of Berlin was a prolific builder for home and export markets.

● **ABOVE LEFT TO RIGHT**
Orenstein & Koppel builder's plates.

erected its own works to maintain its existing engines and to build new ones. The Scottish engineer John Haswell was in charge and his first locomotive, Wien, was built the same year. In 1842 Wenzel Günther, who worked with Haswell, left to take over as manager of the Wiener Neustadt locomotive works. In 1844, Haswell produced the first 4-4-0 for the Vienna & Gloggnitz. This was followed by his two famous locomotives Grosse Gloggnitzer and Kleine Gloggnitzer. Such was the former's success that it hauled 160 ton passenger-trains and 380 ton freight-trains between Mürzzuschlag, south-west Wiener Neustadt, and Leibach.

● AUGUST BORSIG

August Borsig's first locomotive, built in Berline-Moabit, was completed in July 1841 for use on the Berlin & Anhalt Railway, linking the then Prussian capital with the then duchy Prussia surrounded by Saxony. In this production he sought to improve on the American Norris 4-2-0 design by adding a pair of trailing-wheels behind the firebox. This helped weight distribution but robbed the engine of vital adhesive weight on the driving-axle. In his 2-2-2 locomotive Beuth of 1843, also for the Berlin & Anhalt, Borsig embodied the best of English locomotive practice of the time, owing much to Edward Bury but with Stephenson's inclined outside-cylinders.

Borsig went on to become one of Germany's most prolific locomotive factories, supplying a worldwide market.

The firm of Henschel & Sohn, founded in 1817 and based in Kassel, then the capital of Westphalia before becoming part of the Prussian province of Hesse-Nassau, built its first locomotive, Drache (Dragon), in 1848. It was a 4-4-0 of hybrid appearance, combining the Stephenson long-boiler and haystack-firebox with the short-wheelbase Norris leading-bogie. Henschel's output was quite modest – no more than eight engines a year up to 1860 when its 50th locomotive emerged. After the works was extended in 1865, production soared.

INDIAN LOCOMOTIVES

India's first stretch of railway was part of the Great Indian Peninsular Railway (GIPR) between Bombay City and Thana, Maharashtra, 34 km (21 miles) away. It opened in April 1853. For the opening, Tayleur's Vulcan factory at Newton-le-Willows supplied eight inside-cylindered 2-4-0s with domeless boilers, haystack-fireboxes and 5 ft driving wheels.

Just as the GIPR originated in Bombay, so the East Indian Railway (EIR) began in Calcutta. In 1862, ten 2-2-2 express-locomotives with outside-cylinders were built for EIR priority train services. Large canopies over the cabs protected crews from the sun's heat and glare. Their 6 ft 6 in driving wheels equipped them for high-speed running, and they had surprisingly large tenders. The firebox was also relatively large for the period, having an 18 sq ft grate area.

● LEFT
The Indian metre-gauge Class E was an 0-4-2 mixed-traffic version of the D Class. Between 1874–91, 147 examples of a standard design entered service.

● **WESTERN GHATS OBSTACLE**

From its start, the GIPR had problems operating trains over the 900-1,500 m (3,000-5,000 ft) high Western Ghat range. Banking over the mountains' zigzag inclines with heavy tank-engines was common practice. In 1862, Sharp, Stewart & Co., of Glasgow, Scotland, built a tough-looking outside-framed 4-6-0 saddle-tank to the requirements of GIPR engineer J. Kershaw. The first engine of this wheel arrangement to be built in a British works, it was fitted with

sledge-brakes. These were applied to the rails during descent of the western escarpments of the hills where gradients reached 1:37. It was superseded in 1891 by a massive 59 ton 0-8-0ST from the Vulcan Foundry and Neilson of Glasgow.

Webb's three-cylinder compounds were much admired in some quarters, despite precocious behaviour on Britain's LNWR. It may have been that, seen from India, distance lent enchantment to their engineering peculiarities. So it was that the Oudh & Rohilkhand Railway (ORR),

● LEFT
The metre-gauge F Class 0-6-0 dominated Indian railways and is one of the most celebrated locomotive types in world history. The engines worked on many railways. More than 1,000 examples were constructed with little more than detailed variations, between 1884–1922 by 12 different builders.

● RIGHT
The Indian metre-gauge Class D 0-4-0 was a
standard design comprising ten engines built
at Sharp, Stewart's Great Bridgewater Street
Foundry, Manchester, England, in 1873.

● RIGHT
The Indian metre-gauge Class D 0-4-0 was a
standard design comprising ten engines built
at Sharp, Stewart's Great Bridgewater Street
Foundry, Manchester, England, in 1873.

in what today is the state of Uttar
Pradesh, ordered a 5 ft 6 in gauge
version from Dübs of Glasgow in 1883.
Despite different cab and valve
arrangements, it closely resembled the
Crewe original, right down to the
uncoupled driving wheels.

● BENGAL-NAGPUR LEADS
DEVELOPMENT

In the late 19th century, Indian broad-
gauge locomotive practice often mirrored
that on British main lines with 4-4-0s for
passenger work and 0-6-0s for goods.
Increasing train weights, however, pressed
for the development of the small-wheeled
six-coupled engine into something rather
bigger for Indian conditions. Hence, the
Bengal-Nagpur Railway, which linked
Calcutta and the capital of the Central
Provinces (later Madhya Pradesh) and was
always at the fore of technical
development, commissioned a class of
mixed-traffic 4-6-0s, delivered between
1888–91. Aside from their headlamps and
cowcatchers, they were of typical British
appearance with straight running-plates,
outside-cylinders and inside valve-gear.

● LEFT
The coat
of arms of
India's
Bengal-
Nagpur
Railway
(BNR).

● LEFT
The most celebrated of all Indian 2 ft gauge
designs are the 0-4-0 saddle-tanks built for the
Darjeeling Railway from 1889. The line took
Bengal government officials to their hot-
weather headquarters.

● BELOW
The metre-gauge O Class 4-4-0 was an outside-
cylinder version of the early M Class. It was
the standard passenger-engine on most lines.
Some were superheated. The class totalled 297
examples, from six different builders between
1883–1912.

F CLASS 0-6-0

Date	1874
Builder	Various: Britain, Germany, India
Client	Various: Indian State Railways
Gauge	Metre
Driving wheels	3 ft 6 in
Capacity	Cylinders 13 x 20 in
Weight in full working order	20 tons

CHINESE LOCOMOTIVES

China's first railway was opened in 1876 in the eastern province of Kiangsu. It was an 8 km (5 mile) long stretch of 2 ft 6 in gauge between Shanghai and Wusung, Shanghai's outport, that is a subsidiary port built in deeper water than the original port. The first locomotive on the line was the Pioneer, built by Ransomes & Rapier of Ipswich, Suffolk, England. Used by the railway's builders, this 1½ ton engine with 1 ft 6 in driving wheels had a service-truck attached on which the driver sat. The line had a short history. After it had operated for only a month, a local man was fatally injured. Riots ensued and the line was closed. A few months later, it was reopened with two 9 ton 0-4-2STs, Celestial Empire and Flowery Land, both with outside-cylinders and 2 ft 3 in wheels. On these locomotives the water-tanks, a combination of side and saddle, completely enveloped the boiler but left the smokebox clear. However, by the end

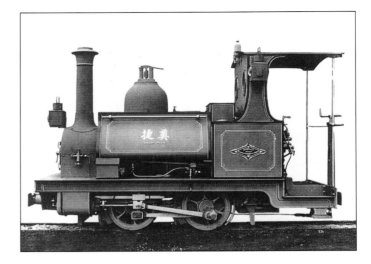

ROCKET OF CHINA

Date	1881
Builder	C.W. Kinder
Client	Kaiping Tramway
Gauge	Narrow gauge
Driving wheels	0-6-0
Capacity	Cylinders 14.25 x 22 mm

of 1877, the Chinese authorities ordered line and engines dismantled.

● **KAIPING TRAMWAY**

The next attempt to provide a railway in China was in 1881 in the northern province of Hopeh. A mining company built the narrow-gauge Kaiping Tramway as an 8 km (5 mile) link between the Kaiping coalfield near Tangshan, north of Tientsin, and the canal that connected with the Pehtang River. At first, because of Chinese prejudices against steam locomotion, mule traction was used. C.W. Kinder, the company's resident engineer, decided nonetheless to build a steam locomotive. Using odds and ends recovered from various scrap-heaps, he secretly built a small 2-4-0 locomotive, which he named Rocket of China. When the Chinese authorities heard about the locomotive, they sent a commission to investigate. Forewarned of their imminent arrival, Kinder dug a pit and buried his engine.

● **THE CHINESE IMPERIAL RAILWAY**

In 1886 Dübs & Co. of Glasgow, Scotland, built two 0-4-0STs for a 2 ft gauge section of the Imperial Chinese Railway (ICR). Named Speedy Peace and Flying Victory, they were instantly opposed by the Chinese, who were convinced that the

● **ABOVE**
The Kaiping Tramway in Hopeh Province was China's first permanent railway. The 2-4-0 Rocket of China pictured here was built in China by British engineer C.W. Kinder and was the tramway's first locomotive.

● **RIGHT**
Sung Wu Railway
2-4-2T No. 2 was
built by Brooks
Locomotive Works,
Dunkirk, New York,
USA. This celebrated
American builder
produced more than
4,000 locomotives
until it combined
with seven others in
1901 to form the
American
Locomotive
Company (Alco).

● **RIGHT**
A 2-6-2 saddle-tank built by Dübs in 1887
entered service on the Tientsin Railway in
Hopeh Province.

"devil's machines" would desecrate
ancestral graves. To prevent this, many
trains were halted by Chinese being
thrown in front of the locomotives. Many
were run over and killed. After about 20
of these deaths, the line was eventually
closed and the locomotives scrapped.

● **BELOW**
This engine is an example of how American
locomotives exported to China exerted
permanent influence on developments. It was
built by Baldwin in 1899 and was No. 230 on
the Chinese Eastern Railway (CER). Although
the CER was operated by Russians, most of its
motive power was of American origin. No. 230
was one of 121 Vauclain compound 2-8-0s
built for the line by Baldwin in 1899. Samuel
Vauclain (1856–1940) worked for Baldwin for
51 years, becoming chairman in 1929. He
invented his compounding system in 1899.

EAST ASIAN RAILWAYS

● RIGHT
Indonesian State Railways (ISR) C12 Class 2-6-0 Tank No. C1206 was a two-cylinder compound built for the Staats Spoorwegen by Hartmann of Chemnitz, Germany, in 1895.

In Malaya, the first train service started in 1885 in Perak State, between Taiping and Port Weld. Then, in 1886, the first section of the metre-gauge Perak Government Railway (PGR), the 11 km (7 mile) stretch between Kelung and Kuala Lumpur, Perak's capital, was opened. The railway came when the country was covered in dense jungle and transport was entirely by river. The first locomotive was a little 0-6-0 tank by Ransomes & Rapier, of Ipswich, Suffolk, England, similar to the Pioneer and one of the few built by the firm. Small tank-engines were the most suitable for the infant railway system, with the Class A 4-4-0Ts favoured. The larger B Class engines of 1890 were later developed into a tender-engine version. Malayan locomotives were distinguished by their huge headlight – a necessary item on line in dark jungle. Nonetheless, one of these locomotives was charged and derailed by a bull elephant, which lifted the tender clear off the track.

● SINGAPORE-PENANG
By 1909 passengers could travel by train between Singapore and Penang. Completion of the Johore Causeway in

1923 brought the line into Singapore. Singapore had had a railway from Tank Road to Bukit Timah since 1903. In eastern Malaya, goods and passengers could go by train from Gemas to Kota Bharu from 1931.

● BRITISH INFLUENCE IN JAPAN
Japan's first line was built by British engineers in 1872. The first locomotive, a 14¾ ton 2-4-0T with 4 ft 3 in driving wheels, to run on the 3 ft 6 in gauge line was built in 1871 by the Vulcan Foundry of Newton-le-Willows, England. The early equipment on Japanese railways was almost entirely British and included some outside-cylinder 4-4-0s supplied by Dübs & Co. of Glasgow. Other British locomotives to run in Japan were made

● LEFT
One of Java's Staats Spoorwegen B50 Class 2-4-0s, No. B5012, built by Sharp, Stewart of Great Bridgewater Street, Manchester, England, in 1884. When built, these were main-line passenger-engines for Java's 3 ft 6 in gauge lines.

● **RIGHT**
A 3 ft 6 in-gauge 4-4-0 engine with inside-cylinders, built in 1899 for the Imperial Government Railways of Japan, by Neilson, of Glasgow, Scotland.

● **OPPOSITE CENTRE**
Another Indonesian State railwy B5014, also from Sharp, Stewart's foundry in 1884, wheezes along the Madian Slahung line. Burning both coal and wood the engine issues shrouds of fire from its chimney.

by Sharp, Stewart of Manchester and by Kitson of Leeds.

One of Kitson's creations was a 0-6-0 goods-engine built in 1873, which three years later was rebuilt in the shops at Kobe, Honshu, as a 4-4-0, a type which became the standard Japanese passenger-locomotive. In 1876 Kitson built another 4-4-0, of typical British appearance, its only oriental feature being the small louvred shutter in the cab side. Class 1800s were introduced in 1881. These engines were fitted with smart copper-capped chimneys bearing the number in brass.

● **AMERICAN INFLUENCE IN JAPAN**
In 1897, Baldwin exported to Japan the Mikado-type. These were the first locomotives built with a 2-8-2 wheel arrangement with a tender. Named in honour of the Japanese head of state, these locomotives were designed to burn an inferior quality of coal,

requiring a large grate area and a deep, large firebox.

One of Japan's steepest railways, up to 1:40 gradient, was the Hakone line serving the eponymous mountain resort near Mount Fuji, on Honshu. For this, Moguls were bought from Rogers in 1897. Japanese railways were Americanized even more in 1900 by the introduction of Schenectady-built 4-4-0s.

● **JAVA**
Perhaps East Asia's most remarkable railway system was on Java whose network serving the islands was developed during the Dutch East Indies

period. The main lines were developed in the last 20 years of the 19th century. Innumerable feeder lines, known as steam tramways, joined them. A gauges battle occurred between the 3 ft 6 in gauge and the standard. For a while, a third rail was laid over the 4 ft 8½ in gauge to enable through 3 ft 6 in gauge trains to operate. The gauge was finally standardized at 3 ft 6 in.

The multiplicity of state and private enterprises that built Java's railways produced a wide diversity of motive power primarily of Dutch, German and British origin.

● **LEFT**
A rare example of Java's standard-gauge network of the NISM, that is Nederlandse Indische Spoorwegen Maatschappij. These 0-6-0 goods-engines, from Beyer Peacock, of England, resemble that company's Ilfracombe goods class. This rare veteran was pictured at Indonesia's southern Javan city of Yogyakarta.

● **BELOW**
The standard O Class outside-cylinder 4-4-0 of the metre-gauge lines of the Indian subcontinent heading the Royal Train on the Burma State Railway.

INDONESIAN STATE RAILWAYS (ISR) B50 CLASS 2-4-0

Date	1880
Builder	Sharp, Stewart, Manchester, England
Client	Staats Spoorwegen
Gauge	3 ft 6 in
Driving wheels	1,413 mm
Capacity	Cylinders 381 x 457 mm

AUSTRALASIAN RAILWAYS

In the 19th century, Australia consisted of a series of separate colonies, all with administrations operating independently of each other. This, added to personalities and poor communications, led to the mess of gauge problems from which the country has suffered ever since.

The first steam locomotive to run in Australia was locally built by Robertson, Martin, Smith & Co. It entered service on the Colony of Victoria's Melbourne and Hobsons Bay Railway on 12 September 1854. New South Wales (NSW) followed by opening a 21 km (13½ mile) line from Sydney to Parramatta on 26 September 1855.

● DIFFICULT TERRAIN

Australian locomotive design was much governed by the difficult country to be traversed with mountainous country close to coast. The standard gauge in NSW had many 1:30 gradients with curves as tight as 8-chains radius on the main lines. Branch and narrow-gauge states' lines were even worse.

Early locomotives that became standards were generally of the 4-4-0 or 0-6-0 wheel arrangements and of British design or styling. Australia's most significant development was probably the

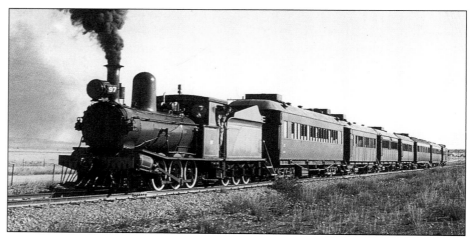

● **BELOW**
Baldwin supplied ten K(294) Class goods engines in 1885. They were put on lesser duties, including working water-trains between Lake Menindee and Broken Hill mining-town in NSW's dry west. The large wagon behind the locomotive is a 32,000 litre (7,000 gallon) water "gin" to augment the tender's supply.

● **ABOVE**
One of South Australia's Y Class "Colonial Moguls" introduced in 1886. This class originally totalled 134 examples, 58 of which were converted to YX Class with higher-pressure boilers from 1907.

CLASS K TANK

Date	1892
Builder	Neilson Reid
Client	Western Australian Government Railways (WAGR)
Gauge	3 ft 6 in
Driving wheels	2-8-4
Capacity	Cylinders 19 x 24 in

● LEFT
One of six D(55) Class 4-4-0s with 6 ft ½ in driving wheels supplied to NSW Railways by Beyer, Peacock in 1882. Able to achieve 70 mph, they were soon dubbed the "Peacock High-fliers". Ten similar locomotives were supplied to Victorian Railways as their old A Class.

● OPPOSITE TOP
"Number 10" was the first locomotive built in NSW. She was a 2-4-0 designed on the Stephenson long-boiler principle. Completed in 1870, she was used as an express passenger-locomotive. She is pictured at Picton Station, south-west of Sydney, soon after entering service.

● ABOVE
A New Zealand Government Railways (NZGR) 1873-built A Class 0-4-0 tank by Dübs. These little engines, nicknamed "Dodos", worked well and lasted into the 1920s.

● RIGHT
One of 77 members of the New South Wales (NSW) A(93) Class 0-6-0s, shunting at Sydney's Darling Harbour goods yard.

4-6-0 type, well before Jones introduced it to the Highland Railway in Britain. The 30 R Class was introduced from 1886 in South Australia. The P6 Class introduced in NSW in 1892 eventually numbered 191 units.

On the narrow gauge, Beyer, Peacock's development of the "Colonial Mogul" had the most impact, with 134 Y Class in South Australia, 47 G Class in Western Australia and 28 C Class in Tasmania.

● NEW ZEALAND'S GAUGES
New Zealand also started with a mess of gauges. South Island had a 3 ft gauge horse-drawn railway from Nelson, in 1862; a 5 ft 3in gauge steam railway from Christchurch in 1863; a wooden-railed line, worked unsuccessfully on the Davies

or Prosser principle, from Invercargill in 1864; and a 4 ft 8½ in gauge steam-line from Invercargill in 1866. Finally, the 3 ft 6 in gauge was selected as standard and introduced, with double Fairlie loco-motives, at Dunedin in September 1872.

New Zealand had, as well as regular designs, a great variety of types: vertical-boilered locomotives, single- and double-Fairlies, flangeless Prosser-types, Fell locomotives and locally made curiosities. Mainly, short lines radiated from coastal ports, so the most significant design would have been the 88-strong F Class 0-6-0T saddle-tanks.

American locomotives were more successful in New Zealand, starting with eight K Class supplied by Rogers Locomotive works in 1878.

SOUTHERN AFRICAN RAILWAYS

South Africa's first public railway was a 3 km (2 mile) stretch in Natal between Durban and The Point, opened in June 1860. The locomotive was the "Natal". It was built by Carrett Marshall & Co., of Leeds, England, stripped down, crated and sent to Durban, where it was rebuilt by Henry Jacobs. The engine had a large dome cover and its chimney, of typical American design, incorporated a wire-mesh spark-arrester. This locomotive,

CLASS 6

Date	1893
Builder	Dübs, of Glasgow, Scotland
Client	Cape Government Railway (CGR)
Gauge	3 ft 6 in
Driving wheels	4 ft 6 in
Capacity	Cylinders 17 x 26 in
Weight in full working order	80 tons

● **LEFT**
South Africa's first steam locomotive, which operated in Cape Province, was a contractor's engine for building the Cape Town – Wellington Railway in 1859. She was built by Hawthorn & Co.'s works in Leith, Scotland, as a 4 ft 8 in gauge 0-4-2. Here is the preserved veteran, proclaimed a national monument in 1936.

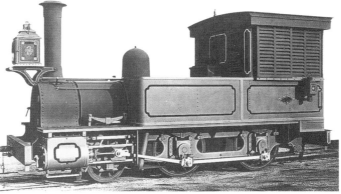

● **LEFT**
The first locomotive to serve the Ugandan Railway was this Dübs 2-4-0T, one of two locomotives bought secondhand from Indian State Railway (ISR). Dübs of Glasgow built 25 of these engines in 1871–2.

however, was not the first to run in South Africa, for in September 1859, E. & J. Pickering had imported a 0-4-2 built by Hawthorn & Co. of Leith, Scotland.

● **KITSON VERSUS FAIRLIE**
In 1875, the Cape Government Railway (CGR) introduced a back-to-back from Kitson & Co. of Leeds, Yorkshire, and a

0-6-0+0-6-0 Fairlie-type from Avonside Engine Co. of Bristol. In 1864, Robert Fairlie introduced his double-ender. This could be driven in either direction and was adopted in hilly countries where curves and gradients challenged ordinary locomotives. When the two machines were tested against each other, the Fairlie worked around curves with facility, up

● **RIGHT**
The Class 6s were one of the most important types in South African locomotive history. Between 1893–1904, almost all the 268 engines being built to a basic design came from Glasgow. They operated express passenger-trains across the entire republic, with the exception of Natal.

and down gradients, and the Kitson lurched badly descending a decline and was much heavier on fuel.

In 1887, Black Hawthorn, of Gateshead, County Durham, England, built a woodburning 0-4-2ST for the Cape of Good Hope & Port Elizabeth 3 ft 6 in gauge line. It had spark-arrester rails above the tank for wood storage, single slide-bars and Ramsbottom safety-valves with single exhaust.

● EAST AFRICAN LINES

The two pioneer public railways in East Africa were Kenya's Mombasa & Nairobi laid in 1896 and the Usambara Railway through the eponymous highlands of

Tanga Province of German East Africa (later Tanganyika) on which work began in 1893 but was not completed until 1911. A private railway was built from Tanga to Sigi, to serve the logging interests of the Deutsche Holtzegesellschaft für Ostafrika. The first engine used on this line, naturally a woodburner, was a 0-4-2 tank built in 1893 by Vulcan of Stettin, then capital of Pomerania, a province of Prussia.

In May 1896 the first locomotives were delivered to the Ugandan Railway. They were secondhand 2-4-0Ts, bought from Indian State Railways (ISR), built in 1871 by Dübs of Glasgow, Scotland.

● **ABOVE**
The Cape Government Railway (CGR) Class 7 was a small-wheeled freight version of the Class 6 passenger-locomotive. It was introduced in 1892. More than 100 were built, all by the three Glasgow builders Dübs, Neilson and Sharp, Stewart.

● **BELOW**
These locomotives began as main-line 4-10-2Ts on the Natal Government Railway (NGR). They were among more than 100 engines built by Dübs in Polemadie, Glasgow. Replaced by tender-engines, they were converted to 4-8-2Ts for further use as shunting- and trip-engines.

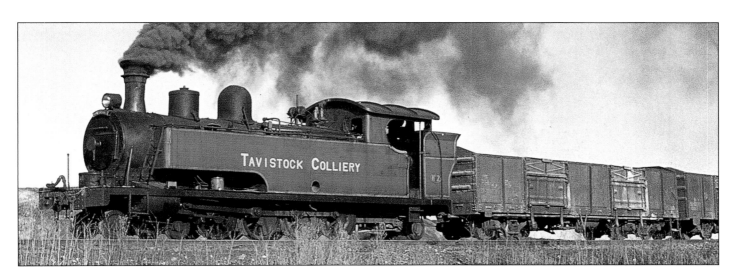

NORTHERN AFRICAN RAILWAYS

Although the first steam tramway in North Africa was built at Egypt's El Dikheila quarries near Alexandria as early as 1838, the first public railway in the region was the British-built Cairo-Alexandria line opened in 1854. By 1870, Egyptian State Railway (ESR) took delivery of a mixed collection of 241 locomotives of over 50 classes supplied by 16 builders from five countries. Besides the usual types, there were a few exotic 2-2-4T saloon locomotives to carry visiting royalty.

MOGUL	2 - 6 - 0
Date	1891
Builder	Baldwin, Philadelphia, Pennsylvania, USA
Client	Bône-Guelma Railway, Algeria
Gauge	3 ft 6 in
Driving wheels	4 ft
Capacity	Cylinders 18 x 22 in

● F.H. TREVITHICK'S IN THE NILE VALLEY

British occupation of the Nile Valley in 1882 put railways under the direction of F. H. Trevithick, grandson of the Cornish pioneer. The first new locomotives he introduced were Great Western in concept, with inside-cylinders and strong double-frames. These frames were essential to negotiate Egypt's rough tracks. For the lightest and fastest duties, he ordered 25 2-2-2s from Kitson and the Franco-Belge Company of La Coyère. These sturdy locomotives were the last singles to work in Africa. Some were still in use in World War II.

● **ABOVE**
A type 0-6-0 tender built by North British, of Glasgow, Scotland, for ESR. The driving wheels are 5 ft ¼ in diameter, the cylinders of 18 x 24 in capacity.

Built by Neilson, of Glasgow, Scotland, this design was on display at the Great Exhibition of 1862, where it was seen by Said Pasha, Viceroy of Egypt, who later ordered one for Egyptian State Railways (ESR).

● FRENCH DESIGN FOR ALGERIA

Algeria's railway development was put in the hands of the French Paris, Lyons & Mediterranean Company in 1863. Secondhand PLM 0-6-0s of characteristic French design were shipped to get services started. Some of these redoubtable 0-6-0 designs, as SNCFA classes 3B, 3E and 3F, were destined to last almost until the end of steam on the Algerian standard gauge. The Algiers-Oran main line opened in 1871 when more 0-6-0s were supplied, with the first of the successful 0-8-0 goods-engines of classes 4A and 4C for the 1:80 gradients up from Philippeville. Operations between Algeria and Tunisia were begun with 0-6-0s built by Batignolles. By 1883, 39 of these, assisted by 18 0-6-0Ts built by the same firm for shunting and banking, were in operation. On the 300 km (184 mile) of the Algerian Western, the sparse service was operated by 26 0-6-0s that were built by Fives Lille and SACM. These ultimately became SNCFA classes 3L and 3M. In 1899 the Bône-Guelma Railway in eastern Algeria turned to Baldwin for ten of its ready-made American-style Moguls. These performed well but were rebuilt as tank-engines in the early 20th century.

● BRITISH PRESENCE IN TUNISIA

Tunisia's first railway was built with British capital and equipment, as part of a move to extend British influence in the region. The standard-gauge line was opened from Tunis to La Marsa in 1874 using four little Sharp, Stewart 2-4-0 tanks. The Italians took over the line in 1876 and ran it until it was acquired by Algeria's Bône-Guelma Co. in 1898. In 1895, under Bône-Guelma's auspices, an extensive metre-gauge network was inaugurated along the coastal region south of Tunis. As motive power, a fleet of no fewer than 135 Mallet articulated engines was built – the largest concentration of these tank-engines in Africa. The first batch of eight 0-4-4-0s came from Batignolles to start services, and larger machines were delivered early in the new century.

SOUTH AMERICAN RAILWAYS

In 1836, three Baldwin locomotives were exported to Cuba, then a Spanish territory. These would have been for the line between the capital, Havana and the small town of Bejueal in La Habana Province. It opened in July 1837.

● **LEFT**
The 4-4-0 was the classic locomotive type in the first few decades of rail-roading in America, because it provided a good turn of speed and stability over inevitably roughly laid tracks. This example, from the 1840s-50s, was exported to Chile and is pictured in Santiago.

● ARGENTINE CAUTION

Railways came to Argentina in 1857 when a line opened between the towns of Parque and Floresta. The line manager had so little faith in his own product that he rode on horseback to the opening rather than trust himself to his own railway. The four-wheeled engine used on this occasion was La Portena, a locomotive which had been used in the Crimea, Ukraine.

● AMERICAN INFLUENCE IN BRAZIL

The first railway in Brazil, a short 5 ft 3 in gauge line in the neighbourhood of Rio de Janeiro, the then capital, opened in 1854. The inaugural train was hauled by the 2-2-2 Baroneza. The bulk of Brazil's railway track was laid to metre gauge, though in 1889 the Huain railway was built to the peculiar gauge of 3 ft 1¾ in. Most Brazilian woodburning locomotives of the 19th century were supplied by American builders. Typical was a series of relatively small 2-8-0s from Baldwin with driving wheels of only 3 ft 1 in diameter.

● **BELOW**
This classic 4-6-0 two-cylinder compound was built by Beyer, Peacock for the British-owned 5 ft 6 in gauge Buenos Aires and Great Southern Railway (BAGS). These locomotives were a principal express-passenger type for many years.

B CLASS

Date	1906
Builder	Beyer, Peacock, Manchester, England
Client	Buenos Aires and Great Southern (BAGS)
Gauge	5 ft 6 in
Driving wheels	6 ft
Capacity	Cylinders 19 x 26 in (high pressure) 27½ x 26 in (low pressure)
Weight in full working order	115 tons

● **LEFT**
Another early 4-4-0, almost certainly of European origin and sporting a cowl, is pictured heading a tourist-train in the desert border region between Tacna in Peru and Arica in Chile, disputed territory until 1930.

● LEFT
 Superficially American in style, this British engine has no running-plate but plate-frames, splashers and a brass dome. It was built by Sharp, Stewart at Springburn Works, Glasgow, Scotland, in 1892 for Brazil's metre-gauge Mogiana Railway. It hauled trains of varnished teak coaches through the Atlantic seaboard's lush tropical scenery.

MEXICAN CHOICES

In Mexico, a 424 km (265 mile) line opened in 1873 between the capital Mexico City and the seaport Veracruz. The railway was an early user of double-boilered Fairlie 0-6-6-0 tanks. These were successful, unlike the totally impractical American-built Johnstone articulateds of 1888. These were so large they had to be partly dismantled to pass through the 2,608 m (8,560 ft) high Raton Tunnel, Colorado, during delivery. The Mexicans, ever willing to try another form of flexible wheelbase engine, in 1890 bought two Baldwin Mason-Fairlie articulated 2-6-6 tanks. This engine was essentially an American interpretation of the single Fairlie principle, with a power-bogie and a trailing-truck supporting a large boiler with deep firebox.

● ABOVE
Numberplate and worksplate of the Leopoldina Railway.

● RIGHT
This metre-gauge 2-6-0 was one of a class of 15 engines built by Beyer, Peacock of Manchester, England, at the end of the 19th century for Brazil's Leopoldina Railway. The Leopoldina system, all on the metre gauge, has approximately 3,200 km (2,000 miles) of track and was owned by the British-controlled Leopoldina Railway Co.

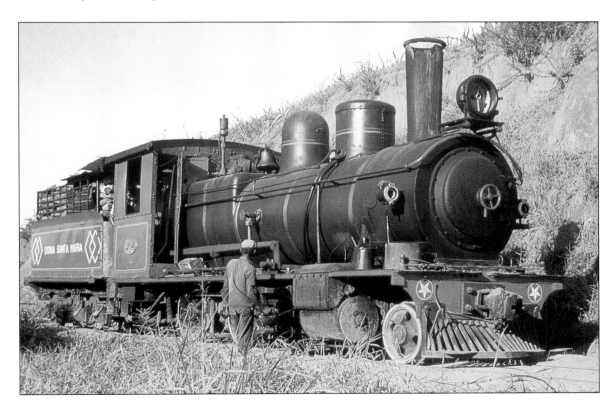

The Golden Age
1900–50

The first half of the 20th century may truly be called the Golden Age of railways. The railway was the primary form of transport for moving people and freight. The railway was perceived as being the heartbeat of society. Furthermore, throughout the period the vast majority of the world's railways were powered by steam. The period began with a legacy of modest 19th century locomotive designs, which rapidly gave way to 20th century concepts – larger, heavier and more powerful engines, which by the advent of World War II had evolved almost to the ultimate potential within the existing loading gauges. One of the many precepts that accelerated the world change from steam to modern forms of traction was that the necessary power and speeds demanded by railway administrations were outstripping the capacity of steam within the physical restrictions imposed on it.

● **OPPOSITE**
One of Germany's magnificent unrebuilt Reichbahn Standard 01-class Pacifics seen in the soft countryside north of Dresden, Saxony, with an express from Berlin. The Pacific is pictured in charge of a 450-ton train. Coal-fired, these engines operated on timings faster than a mile a minute and were Europe's last high-speed steam expresses.

● **ABOVE**
In the late 19th century the principle of compounding was adopted by many railways throughout the world. Shortly after the turn of the century, Britain's Midland Railway produced a set of 4-4-0s in which two high-pressure cylinders exhausted into a larger low-pressure one. Building continued after the grouping under the London, Midland & Scottish (LMS) Railway and the Midland. Compounds have gone down in locomotive history as one of the most successful classes and remained in Britain until their demise in the 1950s.

BRITISH MAIN-LINE LOCOMOTIVES – PASSENGER

The turn of the century saw the elegance of the Atlantic-type locomotive established on the main lines of Britain. The type soon led to the Pacific, which in essence was an Atlantic with an extra pair of driving wheels. When Gresley introduced his A1 Pacifics to the Great Northern Railways (GNR) in 1922, they represented in terms of size and power as large an increase over the GN's biggest Atlantic as the first Atlantics of 1898 exerted over the earlier 4-4-2 singles. The Pacific represented the end of the evolutionary line. Nothing bigger ever appeared in Britain, apart from Gresley's incursions into huge 2-8-2 Mikados and his solitary 4-6-4.

The Pacific captured the popular imagination, especially during the competition for Scottish traffic over

Britain's East and West Coast routes in the early 1930s. Worldwide, the streamlined Pacifics of this decade generated much publicity. Gresley's A4s proved to be the "Concordes" of their day and have become the most celebrated British locomotive type. No. 4468

Mallard achieved the world speed record for steam traction of 126 mph in 1938.

The Pacific as an express passenger locomotive was backed up by the 4-6-0, which began to become profuse after the turn of the century. By 1923, the 4-6-0 in both two- and four-cylinder form was

● **RIGHT**
In the 1920s, need arose for an extra passenger locomotive on Britain's Southern Railway, one able to work a 500-ton train at an average speed of almost one mile a minute. So, four-cylinder Lord Nelsons were introduced. They totalled a class of 16 engines named after famous British Sea Lords. These engines worked the Continental Expresses between Victoria Station, London, and the English channel port of Dover, and served the south-western sections of Britain's Southern network.

widespread, largely replacing the Atlantic. Not until 1933 did the first Stanier Pacific take the title of the most powerful express-passenger-locomotive type away from the 4-6-0. In 1930, the 4-4-0 made its last flourish with Britain's Southern Railway's three-cylinder Schools engine, the most powerful of this wheel arrangement ever to run in the country.

From the mid-1930s, the 4-6-0 became increasingly used as the basis for powerful mixed-traffic types. In this guise, it continued to play an important role in main-line passenger duties. With Britain's policy of frequent and relatively light trains, the 4-6-0, despite its restrictive firebox capacity, was sufficient, with the quality of coal available, to provide the necessary power and adhesion for most express duties until the end of steam. The next logical step, to the 4-8-0, although proposed, was never taken.

● **BELOW**
Britain's Great Western Railway experimented with compounding in 1903 when Churchward introduced several engines on the De Glehn system. The first engine was built at Belfort, France, and named Le France. These compound Atlantics did not convince the Great Western to adopt the principle and they progressed to ultimate success with conventional 4-6-0s of two- and four-cylinder varieties.

PRINCESS CORONATION CLASS

Date	1937
Builder	Crewe Works, Cheshire, England
Client	London, Midland & Scottish Railway
Gauge	Standard
Driving wheels	6 ft 9 in
Capacity	4 cylinders 16 x 28 in
Total weight in full working order	165 tons

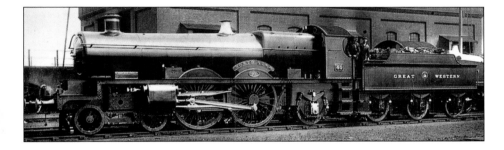

● **OPPOSITE**
William Stanier followed up his Princess Royal Pacifics with the Princess Coronations introduced in 1937. They hauled many of the heaviest trains on Britain's West Coast route until the end of steam.

● **ABOVE**
One of W.P. Read's Atlantics. These were the largest engines built for the North British Railway. They were introduced in 1906 and given Scottish names such as Aberdonian, Waverley and Highland Chief. They worked on the North British main lines, especially on the heavily graded Waverley route between Edinburgh and Carlisle in Cumbria.

BRITISH MAIN-LINE LOCOMOTIVES – FREIGHT

● BELOW
Stanier's class 8F 2-8-0s were freight engines and provided Britain's LMS with a robust heavyfreight locomotive. They were a huge advance on the 0-6-0 and 0-8-0 types.

The freight locomotive's evolution was less dramatic than that of its express passenger-hauling counterpart. The inside-cylinder 0-6-0s and 0-8-0s so prolific in the late-19th century continued to be built into the 20th century, although a major advance occurred in 1903 when Churchward introduced his 2800 class 2-8-0s. The 2-8-0 was pre-eminent until the end of steam. Churchward's engines were followed by Robinson's 04s for the Great Central Railway in 1911. Two years later, the 2-8-0 was taken up by Gresley on the Great Northern Railway. The London, Midland and Scottish (LMS) built most 2-8-0s: Stanier's 8Fs for LMS totalled 772 locomotives.

The modest size of British freight engines was given a massive boost in 1927 when the LMS introduced its 2-6-6-2T Garratts. These were built by Beyer Peacock of Manchester, northern England, to alleviate the double-heading of inside-cylinder 0-6-0s on Britain's Midland main line. Of these four-cylinder giants, 33 went into operation and demonstrated a potency hitherto

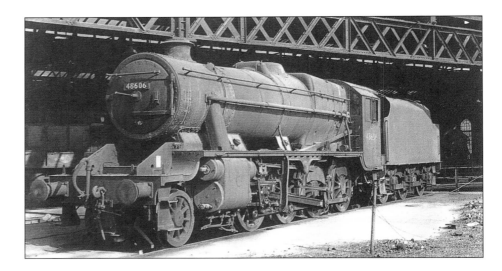

● BELOW
Stanier's class 8F 2-8-0s were freight engines and provided Britain's LMS with a robust heavyfreight locomotive. They were a huge advance on the 0-6-0 and 0-8-0 types.

unknown on Britain's railways. Gresley turned to the 2-8-2 with his P1s of 1925. Two of these giants were built and hauled coal-trains weighing upwards of 2,000 tons.

The 2-8-2 was the next logical phase of development; as compared with the 2-10-1, it readily provided for a deep firebox with adequate space for the ashpan. Sadly, however, no further heavyfreight hauling 2-8-2s were ever built for use on the home railway, and the ultimate in British freight locomotives

● BELOW LEFT
Britain's first 2-10-0s were built for the Ministry of Supply in World War II by the North British works in Glasgow. With their more numerous 2-8-0 counterparts, they served in many countries during the war. The example shown here was taken into the stock of Greek State Railways.

● BELOW RIGHT
Gresley's V2 2-6-2 Green Arrow was one of the most successful classes in British locomotive history. They were true mixed-traffic engines capable of enormous haulage. They did monumental service in World War II and were popularly known in Britain as "the engines which won the war". Here, one is seen on the rollers of the British locomotive-testing plant at Swindon, Wiltshire.

was the 2-10-0. This was not truly established until the 1950s, under the British Railways (BR) standard locomotive scheme. The 2-10-0s had first appeared as an Austerity version of the World War II 2-8-0s used for military operations, but these were primarily for light-axle loadings rather than sustained heavy haulage. The BR 9Fs were mineral haulers in their own right and building continued until 1960. An engine of this design became the last main-line locomotive built for Britain. It was named Evening Star. The 9Fs had a very short life for by 1968 steam operation in Britain ceased. They went to the scrapyard with all earlier forms of British freight locomotives – inside-cylinder 0-6-0s and 0-8-0s and the main 2-8-0 types.

LMS GARRATT

Date	1927
Builder	Beyer Peacock, Manchester, England
Client	London, Midland & Scottish Railway
Gauge	Standard
Driving wheels	5 ft 3 in
Capacity	4 cylinders 18 x 26 in
Steam pressure	190 lb sq in
Total weight in full working order	156 tons
Tractive effort	45,620 lbs

● **ABOVE LEFT**
The inside-cylinder 4-6-0 appeared on Scotland's Caledonian Railway in 1902. Over the next 12 years, the company's chief mechanical engineer (CME) J. F. McIntosh produced six different designs totalling 42 locomotives.

● **ABOVE RIGHT**
One of Churchward's 2800-class 2-8-0s introduced in 1903. The design caused his successor, Collett, to produce more between 1938-42 with only slight variations. Very few classes in British locomotive history have been built over a period as long as 40 years.

● **BELOW**
The LMS Garratt was a most exciting development in British freight-locomotive history. The engines were built for the LMS by Beyer Peacock. The class totalled 33 engines and hauled coal-trains over the Midland main line between Toton (Nottingham) and Cricklewood (north London). They took the place of two inside-cylinder 0-6-0s.

BRITISH SHUNTERS AND INDUSTRIAL LOCOMOTIVES

The traditional main-line shunting tank has been either an 0-4-0 or, more commonly, an 0-6-0. Numerous designs were created, especially Britain's LMS Jinty 0-6-0, of which more than 500 were built, and the Great Western 5700-class 0-6-0 pannier tanks, totalling 863 examples. Many more classes of 0-6-0 and even 0-8-0 tanks would have been built for shunting had not these forms of locomotives been heavily supplemented by downgraded inside-cylinder 0-6-0s and 0-8-0s. These engines, important main-line freight haulers in the closing years of the 19th century, became ideal heavy shunters and tripping engines in their later years. Wagons had grown bigger, loads much heavier and the abundance of these downgraded freight engines meant the traditional 0-6-0 tank-engine did not evolve to any great size, remaining largely unchanged for almost a century.

Some larger marshalling yards – especially those with humps – needed something bigger than the 0-6-0, so special designs evolved to fill this niche. The first of these giants appeared in 1907 when John George Robinson introduced a three-cylinder 0-8-4T for humping at the Great Central Railway's Wath Yards, in the North Riding of Yorkshire. Two years later, the ever-prolific Wilson Worsdell, CME of the North Eastern Railway, put into traffic some three-cylinder 4-8-0Ts. The LNWR introduced the first 30 0-8-2Ts in 1911, followed by 30 0-8-4Ts. These two classes were, in effect, a heavy tank-engine version of their standard 0-8-0 freight engines.

The definitive industrial locomotive evolved as either a side or saddle tank, four- or six-coupled. Larger industrial locomotives invariably came in the form of former main-line engines, which had been sold out of service. This practice led to tender-engines appearing on industrial lines. These environments often gave a massive extension of life to engines that

GWR 5700 CLASS

Date	1929
Builder	Swindon Works, Wiltshire, England
Client	Great Western Railway
Gauge	Standard
Driving wheels	4 ft 7 in
Capacity	2 cylinders 17 x 24 in
Steam pressure	200 lb sq in
Total weight in full working order	51 tons
Tractive effort	2,255 lbs

● **LEFT**
Britain's Great Western Railway adopted the pannier tank for shunting operations. GWR's ultimate design was Collett's 5700-class with 4 ft 7 in wheels. Between 1929-49, 863 engines were built. When building ended, they were the largest class in Britain.

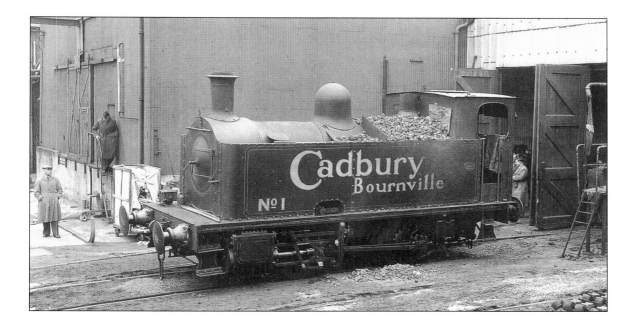

had outlived their normal life span on
main lines.

The basic industrial engine changed
little in its century of pre-eminence. One
fascinating variation, however, occurred
in the form of the Fireless, of which
some 200 worked in Britain. These
engines were a low-cost shunting unit for
industries with a ready supply of high-
pressure steam. They took their steam
secondhand from the works' boilers.

Up until World War II, several
thousand industrial engines were active
the length and breadth of Britain. Many
survived in their industrial habitats after
main-line steam working ended in 1968.
This was historically appropriate.
The world's first steam locomotive,
created in a South Wales ironworks in
1804, was an industrial.

● BELOW LEFT
Andrew Barclay &
Son, locomotive
builders of
Kilmarnock,
Strathclyde, south-
west Scotland, were
famous for a long
range of 0-4-0 and
0-6-0 saddle-tanks,
which formed a
distinctive family of
engines built almost
unchanged over a
70-year period.
Here, one of their
0-4-0s works on the
Storefield Ironstone
system in
Northamptonshire,
in the English
Midlands, taking
iron ore to the
connection with
British Railways'
main line.

● BELOW LEFT
Britain's LMS Jinty 0-6-0s represented the
ultimate manifestation of a long line of
Midland Railway 0-6-0 shunting-tanks. They
were found all over the English part of the
LMS system in the years before most freight
carriage was transferred from rail to road.

● BELOW RIGHT
Andrew Barclay pioneered the Fireless type in
Britain and built many examples, both 0-4-0
and 0-6-0, for industrial establishments. The
Fireless was arguably the most efficient and
economical shunting unit ever devised.

BRITISH MAIN-LINE TANK ENGINES

The engines that worked suburban trains around Britain's great cities and conurbations were almost exclusively tank designs. The absence of a tender facilitated ease of running in either direction and cut out cumbersome and time-consuming turning. Also, the water's weight above the coupled wheels provided adhesion useful for rapid starts from stations. For similar reasons, tank-engines were favoured on branch lines across Britain.

In the 19th century, the urban and branch-line tank-engine evolved in many forms: 2-4-0, 4-4-0, 4-4-2, 0-4-2, 0-4-4 and 0-6-0.

The 0-4-4 was particularly favoured. It had flexibility to run in either direction. Its boiler and cylinder blocks were often interchangeable with sister inside-cylinder 0-6-0s and inside-cylinder 4-4-0 express-passenger engines.

● **LEFT**
Britain's London and North Western Railway used many tank engines on suburban and branch lines, particularly 0-6-2 and 2-4-2 types. For faster intermediate work, Bowen Cooke introduced this class of 4-6-2 superheated tank engine.

As the population of Britain's cities grew, so did the suburban tank's proportions. It graduated to the 4-4-2 and by the turn of the century, with the harmonious 4-4-4, in sheer aesthetic terms, reached its pièce de résistance, the ultimate in balanced proportions.

The most remarkable suburban engine was Holden's Decapod 0-10-0T for the Great Eastern Railway (GER). Advocates of electrification claimed that a 315-ton train could be accelerated to 30 mph in 30 seconds. Holden, in producing his Decapod, proved that this achievement could be bettered with steam. As a result, the proposed electrification of GER's suburban services from London's Liverpool Street Station was shelved.

● **BELOW**
An 0-6-0 shunting-tank of Britain's North Eastern Railway, from a class of 120 engines built between 1886–95. The type's suitability is shown by the introduction of a second and similar batch in 1898 of which 85 were built by 1925. Then, 28 more were built between 1949–51, under British Railways. This created the unique situation of a design being built over a 54-year period. Possibly no other class in world locomotive history has achieved this distinction.

The 0-4-4 T's flexibility was shown by this example from England's North Staffordshire Railway. Classified as "M", five examples of the type were built in 1907–8.

● BELOW
Britain's Great Western Railway (GWR) achieved excellent standardization in all categories of motive power. For suburban and branch-line work, Churchward introduced a range of 2-6-2s.

Alas, the Decapod was so heavy on the track that it never entered service.

Six-coupled engines in the form of 0-6-2s and 0-6-4s progressed to 2-6-2s and 2-6-4s, the preferred power from the 1930s onwards. Many of these engines were mixed-traffic types, equally suited for cross-country and branch-line work as well.

Electrification – especially of metropolitan and suburban services – progressively eroded the need for tank engines, particularly on Britain's Southern Railway. A partial erosion of need also occurred on branch lines, where demoted express-passenger designs of earlier years were used, 2-4-0s and 4-4-0s being especially common.

The tank-engine is popularly thought of as something of a plodding machine. In truth, many were extremely fast runners, and speeds of 70 mph were quite normal on many suburban and outer-suburban workings, some of which were very tightly timed and had to be fitted in between the paths of more important, longer-distance trains.

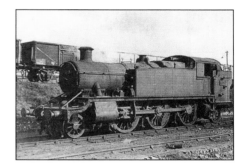

● BELOW
This engine belonged to a class of Ivatt 0-6-2Ts with 5 ft 8 in wheels, built for the Great Northern Railway (GNR) between 1906–12. The class totalled 56 engines. These appeared prolifically on suburban workings out of London's Kings Cross Station. Many had condensing apparatus for working through metropolitan tunnels. In their later years, many were found on suburban workings around Leeds and Bradford, in west Yorkshire.

LNER CLASS J72
0-6-0T

Date	1898
Builder	Darlington Locomotive Works, Co. Durham, England
Client	North Eastern Railway; London & North Eastern Railway; British Railways
Gauge	4 ft 8 in
Driving wheels	4 ft 1 in
Capacity	2 cylinders 17 x 24 in
Steam pressure	140 lb sq in
Weight	43 tons
Tractive effort	16,760 lbs

BRITISH EXPORTS

The steam-locomotive was arguably Britain's greatest technological contribution to mankind. Her lead in railways ensured wide opportunities, and she became railway builder to her empire and the world. A vast locomotive industry developed quite separately from that of the famous railway towns, which served Britain's domestic needs. Legendary foundries in Glasgow, Scotland, and in the English provinces at Leeds in Yorkshire, Newcastle upon Tyne in Northumberland (now Tyne and Wear), Darlington in Durham, Manchester and other parts of Lancashire, and in Stafford, west central England, sent

● LEFT
Manning Wardle of Leeds, west Yorkshire, built this Crane Tank locomotive in 1903. It lifted tree trunks at an Indian sawmill, replacing elephants.

locomotives worldwide, often exporting the industrial revolution with them. Lands beyond the British Empire were served, including those having no political affinity with Britain. Exported locomotives reflected the designs of engines running in the mother country, and the types of engines seen rolling through the soft English countryside

were soon found crossing barren, rugged and jungle-clad landscapes in many countries of Africa, Australia, South-east Asia and South America.

Britain's role as locomotive-builder to the world remained largely unchallenged throughout the 19th century, but the early 20th saw serious competition for the first time, especially from America and, to a lesser extent, from builders in continental Europe. America's engines were a commercial threat and also challenged conventional British design. These, though produced by skilled craftsmen, nonetheless had deficiencies. These, not apparent in Britain, caused problems in the rough-and-tumble of world railways.

● LEFT
The lineage of these British build Pacifics is fully shown in this scene of a South African Railways 3 ft 6 in gauge 16CR heading over flood waters of the tidal Swartkops River in Port Elizabeth, Cape Province, South Africa.

● RIGHT
One of a group of Moguls built in 189 by Beyer Peacock of Manchester, Lancashire, for Brazil's Leopoldina Railway. This Mogu is an example of exported types being used abroad before coming into service in the country of manufacture.

● **RIGHT**
In East Africa, the scrublands of Tanzania resounded to the wail of British locomotives in the 1920s after the territory was mandated to Britain at the end of World War I, when it was known as Tanganyika. This light-axle 2-8-2 was ideal for riding the lightly laid and rough track beds common in Africa.

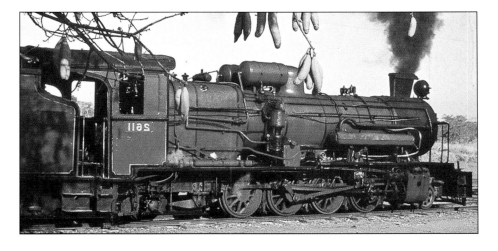

BAGNALL 2-8-2

Date	1947
Builder	Bagnall's of Stafford, Staffordshire, England
Client	Tanganyika Railway, East Africa
Gauge	Metre
Driving wheels	3 ft 7 in
Capacity	Cylinders 17 x 23 in
Steam pressure	180 lb sq in
Total weight full working order	100 tons
Tractive effort	25,050 lb

Most British locomotives had small fireboxes set between the frames, a restriction that caused steaming difficulties when inferior coal was used.

Traditional British plate frames gave problems when engines ran on the developing world's poor quality tracks. American engines had wide fireboxes suitable for inferior fuel. Their bar-frames enjoyed greater tolerance in adverse conditions. Some British loco-motives' limited bearing surfaces also gave trouble in rough conditions.

American engines' bearing proportions were more generous.

An immediate effect of America's aggressive export drive in the early 20th century was the amalgamation in 1903 of Glasgow's three big builders – Sharp Stewart, Neilson and Dübs – to form the North British Locomotive Company. Although there was a shift towards a more international design of locomotive, created in the light of world experience, British builders retained a significant role right to the end of the steam age.

● **RIGHT**
Britain's private loco-motive builders often built for companies in Britain whose works were unable to supply engines quickly enough. Here, at the North British Works in Glasgow, Scotland, an LNER class B1 4-6-0 is in the background, by a light-axle loaded 2-8-2 for East African Railways.

BRITISH RECORD-BREAKERS AND STREAMLINERS

The commonly held view that the steam-locomotive was replaced because it was slow is incorrect. Many of today's diesel and even electrically operated services are not appreciably faster than steam was 50 or more years ago.

The magical three-figure speed was reached in 1903 by the Great Western Railway's 4-4-0 City of Truro. This achieved 102.3 mph down Wellington Bank in Somerset, south-west England, with an Ocean Mails train, the first time any form of transport reached 100 mph.

GWR featured in another speed dash, with a Churchward Saint Class 4-6-0, which allegedly reached 120 mph while running light engine on a test trip after an overhaul at Swindon works in Wiltshire. This alleged achievement is not authenticated, but over the years authorities have claimed it to be true.

The 1930s, the "streamlined era", were a time of epic record-breaking runs all over the world. Streamlining was in vogue. It inspired and fascinated the public, but its usefulness in reaching high speeds was soon questioned.

The legendary speed records of the

LNER A4 PACIFIC

Date	1935
Builder	Doncaster Works, south Yorkshire
Client	London & North Eastern Railway
Gauge	Standard
Driving wheels	6 ft 8 in
Capacity	3 cylinders 18 x 26 in
Total weight in full working order	167 tons
Steam pressure	250 lb sq in
Tractive effort	33,455 lb

● **BELOW**
Great Western Railway's Castles were distinguished among British express-passenger designs. They first appeared in 1923. Their exploits on the Cheltenham Flyer were legendary, and for some years the Flyer was the world's fastest train. In 1924 the engine shown, No. 4079 Pendennis Castle, running from Paddington, London, to Plymouth, Devon, averaged 60 mph between Paddington and Westbury, Wiltshire, with a 530-tonne train.

● **LEFT**
The LNER's plaque affixed to the boiler of Mallard to commemorate its world record-breaking run in 1938.

● **BELOW**
The LNER class-A4 No.4468 Mallard, dubbed the world's fastest steam locomotive. Mallard's record may remain unbeaten.

The Princess Royals were followed by the Princess Coronations. One of these engines, streamlined, briefly held the world record for steam traction of 114 mph. Over the years after World War II, all streamlined examples lost their casing.

● ABOVE
Stanier's record-breaking Princess Royal Pacific No. 6201 Princess Elizabeth, which in 1936 covered the 401 miles between Glasgow, Scotland, and London Euston in 5 hours 44 minutes – an average speed of 70 mph. Almost 60 years later, in November 1996, the *Daily Telegraph* reported that many electrically operated services on the West Coast route were slower than Princess Elizabeth's epic run.

1930s were again the result of competition between the East and West Coast routes linking London and Scotland. Both the LMS and the LNER had brand new designs of Pacific locomotives in service – streamlined Coronations on the former and Gresley A4s on the latter.

In terms of maximum speed, the LMS bid for the world speed record on 29 June 1937 when a special run of the Coronation Scot was made for the press six days before the service's official start. The locomotive, No. 6220 Coronation, reached 114 mph down Madeley Bank on the approaches to Crewe, Cheshire, in northern England. Alas, the bank was not long enough and the train was still doing 60-70 mph when the platform signal came into sight and rapid braking for a standstill in Crewe Station smashed all the crockery in the dining car.

The LNER would not countenance the LMS taking the honour in this way. Almost a year later, on 3 July 1938, the A4 class Pacific Mallard, ostensibly on a special run to test braking, achieved 126 mph on the descent of Stoke Bank, between Grantham in Lincolnshire and Peterborough in Cambridgeshire, eastern England, thus beating the LMS and setting a never-beaten world speed record for the steam locomotive.

Non-streamlined activity in the 1930s was also exciting, not least with the Cheltenham Flyer express, which was booked to run the 77.3 miles from Paddington, London, to Swindon, Wiltshire, in 65 minutes. On one occasion the distance was covered in 56 minutes. This involved a start-to-stop average of 82 mph.

World War II ended any such performances and in the postwar period the railway network's recovery was slow. Not until the 1950s did three-figure speeds with steam reappear.

AMERICAN MIKADOS

The 2-8-2 Mikado-type locomotive was developed in 1897 for Japanese Railways by the Baldwin Locomotive Works, the largest and most prolific locomotive-builder in the United States of America.

● **AN AMERICAN ENGINE FOR JAPAN**

The Mikado-type locomotive derives its name from this first owner, though during World War II, when America was fighting Japan, American nationalists tried to change the name to "MacArthur-type". Many Americans call these locomotives "Mikes".

In 1905, the Northern Pacific Railway was the first railroad to embrace the Mikado in large numbers. The locomotive quickly caught on, and many were produced for many railroads until about 1930. Some 10,000 were built for domestic use, and more than 4,000 were built for export.

● **A SOLID DESIGN**

The 2-8-2 wheel arrangement was a natural progression from the popular 2-8-0 Consolidation-type and 2-6-2 Prairie-type. The Mikado's overall design was outstanding. It was well balanced, providing excellent tractive effort and a good ride. The trailing truck allowed for a larger firebox, therefore more steam capacity and larger cylinders, giving the engine greater power than earlier designs which it rendered obsolete. When technological advances such as superheating were developed, they were used on the Mikado to great success. The

locomotive's primary application was heavy freight service, though many railroads used lighter Mikes on branch lines.

● **NARROW-GAUGE APPLICATION**

The Mikado type was particularly well adapted to narrow-gauge freight service because of its balanced design and four sets of drivers. These provided the traction needed on heavy mountain grades, while producing only minimum wear and tear on lightweight track and right-of-way. In the West, Denver & Rio Grande Western (D&RGW) operated four classes of Mikado on its rugged mountain grades. Its

● LEFT
Pennsylvania Railroad (PRR) No. 1596, a Class-L1s Mikado-type, features a boxy Belpaire-type firebox, standard on most late-era PRR steam locomotives. It is pictured near the end of its active life, at Enola, Pennsylvania.

line over the 3,048 m (10,003 ft) high Cumbres Pass, in the San Juan Mountains of south Colorado, featured gruelling 4 per cent grades, which gave the 3 ft narrow-gauge Mikado a real proving ground. In the East, narrow-gauge coal hauler East Broad Top also preferred the Mikados, owning several from Baldwin. Many of these narrow-gauge locomotives are preserved in working order.

● RIGHT
The Duluth & Northern Minnesota's Mikado No. 14 clips along north of Duluth, Minnesota. This light Mikado was built by Baldwin in 1913.

MISSOURI PACIFIC MIKADO TYPE

Date	1923
Builder	American Locomotive Co. (Alco)
Client	Missouri Pacific
Gauge	4 ft 8½ in
Driving wheels	65 in
Capacity	2 cylinders 27 x 32 in
Steam pressure	200 lb
Weight	305,115 lb
Tractive effort	62,950 lb

● RIGHT
This 2-8-2 Mikado-type was built by the American Locomotive Company (Alco) at its Brooks Works in 1920. It worked for the Aberdeen & Rockfish Railroad, and serves the Valley Railroad at Essex, Connecticut, New Maryland.

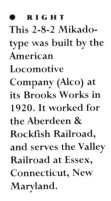

AMERICAN ARTICULATED LOCOMOTIVES

The Mallet-type compound articulated steam locomotive, named after Swiss inventor Anatole Mallet, had been popular in Europe for decades before its eventual introduction in the United States of America.

● B&O EMPLOYS THE MALLET

After the turn of the century, a need for greater tractive effort led American railroads to employ articulated steam locomotives with two sets of driving wheels. The compound articulated

BALTIMORE & OHIO MALLET-TYPE NO. 2400 "OLD MAUD"

Date	1904
Builder	American Locomotive Co. (Alco)
Client	Baltimore & Ohio Railroad
Gauge	4 ft 8½ in
Driving wheels	56 in
Capacity	4 cylinders: 2 (20 x 32 in) and 2 (32 x 32 in)
Steam pressure	235 lb
Weight	334,500 lb
Tractive effort	71,500 lb

● **OPPOSITE TOP**
The Baltimore & Ohio's articulated 2-8-8-2 Class KK1 was an experimental locomotive that featured a water-tube boiler (most American locomotives had fire-tube boilers). It delivered a 90,000 lb tractive effort.

● **LEFT**
Union Pacific (UP) 4-6-6-4 Challenger-type simple articulated No. 3985 at Portola, California. UP owned more than 100 locomotives of this type for heavy-freight service in western USA.

engine reused steam from high-pressure cylinders, in low-pressure cylinders, to achieve maximum efficiency. On most Mallets, very large low-pressure cylinders were used at the first set of drivers, while high-pressure cylinders were used at the second.

In 1904, the American Locomotive Company (Alco) built the first American Mallet-type, a 0-6-6-0 compound articulated nicknamed "Old Maud", for the Baltimore & Ohio Railroad (B&O), a

coalhauler facing many steep grades. While Mallet-types were effective for slow-speed service, few railroads used them for general service on the main line.

● THE SIMPLE ARTICULATED GAINS POPULARITY

The articulated concept achieved greater popularity in a more traditional format. This was the simple articulated engine, which has two sets of cylinders but does not reuse steam. Most articulated engines

● **LEFT**
The Baltimore & Ohio's No. 2400 was the first American locomotive to use the Mallet design. It was built in 1904 by Alco and widely known as "Old Maud". It weighed 334,500 lb and had a 71,500 lb tractive effort.

built after about 1910 were not compounds and thus not true Mallets. While many railroads preferred simple articulated engines, the Norfolk & Western (N&WR) continued to perfect the Mallet. The N&WR class-Y6b built by the railroad's Roanoke shops in North

Carolina for main-line service represented the zenith of the type. N&WR was one of the last American railroads to use Mallets in regular main-line service.

The development of articulated steam locomotives, combined with other improvements such as mechanical stokers and superheaters, eventually led to the building of the world's largest locomotives. Among the largest articulateds were the 2-8-8-4 Yellowstone type used by Northern Pacific and ore-hauler Duluth, Missabi & Iron Range (DM&IR); the 2-6-6-6 Allegheny type built by the Lima Locomotive works for the Chesapeake & Ohio and Virginian Railway, in 1941 and 1945 respectively; and the 4-8-8-4 Big Boy type built for Union Pacific lines between 1941–44.

● SOUTHERN PACIFIC CAB FORWARD

The Southern Pacific (SP) developed a unique variation of the articulated engine. The traditional steam locomotive configuration featuring the cab behind the boiler proved unsatisfactory on the big articulateds when operating in the long tunnels and snowsheds found on the 2,174 metre (7,135 ft) Donner Pass in California's Sierra Nevada. Crews suffered from smoke inhalation. So SP turned the engine around, placing the cab in front of the boiler. The first of SP's 256 cab-forward articulated was a Mallet-type built in 1910. The last were Baldwin-built articulated 2-8-8-4 types, the SP class-AC-12, built in 1944.

● **ABOVE**
Among the heaviest articulated steam locomotives ever built were 2-8-8-4 Yellow-stone types made for Northern Pacific (NP) and Duluth, Missabi & Iron Range (DM&IR).

● **RIGHT**
Norfolk & Western continued to perfect the Mallet compound-articulated-locomotive design long after other railroads adopted the simple articulated. An N&WR Y6 Mallet 2-8-8-2 pictured near Blue Ridge Summit, West Virginia, in 1958.

AMERICAN PACIFICS

The 4-6-2 Pacific-type steam locomotive came into favour shortly after the turn of the century and was produced widely for many American railroads until the 1930s.

● PREMIER PASSENGER POWER

This locomotive followed the logical developmental progression from the 4-4-0 American-type, 4-4-2 Atlantic-type and, to a lesser extent, the 2-6-2 Prairie-type. Most Pacifics, designed for high-speed passenger service, had relatively large fireboxes and high drivers. By 1915, this type had supplanted 4-6-0 Ten Wheelers and 4-4-2 Atlantics on crack passenger-trains. All around America, flashy high-drivered Pacifics were hauling name trains. These included Northern Pacific's luxurious North Coast Limited, Southern Pacific's Sunset Limited and the Pennsylvania Railroad's Broadway Limited.

● BELOW
The Baltimore & Ohio's Pacific type, No. 5305.

● OPPOSITE TOP
The Louisville & Nashville's Pacific-type No. 152 was built by Alco's Rogers Works in January 1905. This locomotive served the railroad for nearly 50 years.

● THE PACIFIC ADAPTS WELL TO NEW TECHNOLOGY AND STYLES
The Pacific-type was well suited to technological improvements. Superheating, mechanical stokers and roller bearings were developed. Superheating recirculated hot steam through the engine's firetubes, allowing for more power and greater efficiency. These developments were applied to both new and existing Pacifics, dramatically improving the performance of the engines. In the 1930s, when streamlined trains became the latest thing in railroad style, some railroads dressed up their Pacifics in snazzy shrouds.

● PENNSYLVANIA RAILROAD K4
The best-known, most loved and perhaps the best-performing Pacific was the Pennsylvania Railroad's Class K4. PPR received its first Pacific-type from Alco in 1907, an experimental locomotive Class K28. This locomotive led to several other

classes of Pacific, with the culmination of design exhibited in the 1914 Class K4. A masterpiece of engineering, the K4 was an outstanding performer. Eventually, Pennsylvania rostered some 425 K4s, an exceptional number for a single class of locomotive. They were the railroad's preferred passenger locomotive for nearly 30 years. Some K4s were built by Baldwin but many were constructed at the railroad's Juniata Shops. Like many PRR steam locomotives, the K4 featured the boxy Belpaire-type firebox. The last K4 was retired from regular service in 1957.

● **LEFT**
The Southern Pacific's No. 2472 was one of 15 Class-P8 Pacific types in the railroad's passenger fleet. These 1912 Baldwin-built locomotives had a 43,660-lb tractive effort.

● **ABOVE**
A highly polished Pennsylvania Railroad K4 Pacific, No. 5475.

PENNSYLVANIA RAILROAD K4 PACIFIC

Date	1914 –28
Builder	Juniata Shops, Baldwin, Pennsylvania, USA
Client	Pennsylvania Railroad
Gauge	4 ft 8½ in
Driving wheels	80 in
Capacity	2 cylinders 27 x 28 in
Steam pressure	205 lb
Weight	468,000 lb
Tractive effort	44,460 lb

SHAYS AND SWITCHERS

American logging railroads had special locomotive requirements because their track, often crudely built, used very sharp curves and negotiated grades as steep as 10 per cent. Also, these railroads required locomotives that could haul relatively heavy loads at very slow speeds.

● SHAYS AND OTHER GEARED LOCOMOTIVES

To meet these requirements, three builders specialized in constructing flexible, high-adhesion steam locomotives that operated with a geared drive, rather than the direct drive used on conventional locomotives. These builders were Lima, at Ohio, with the Shay-type; Heisler Locomotive Works, at Eire, Pennsylvania, and Climax Locomotive and Machine Works at Corry, Pennsylvania. Each builder used the same basic principle – a cylinder-driven shaft that connected to the driving wheels using bevelled gears – but each approached the concept slightly differently.

● **ABOVE**
This is a stock Shay, built by Lima in 1928. It was sold to the Mayo Lumber Company and operated in British Columbia, Canada. It is preserved, with other Shays, at the Cass Scenic Railroad, West Virginia, USA.

Lima's Shay was the most popular type. It used a row of vertical cylinders on the fireman's side, that is the right-hand side of the engine, to power a shaft that connected two or three sets of driving wheels. Two-cylinder Shays had two sets of driving wheels; three-cylinder Shays had three sets of driving wheels. The Shay-type was first constructed in the 1880s.

Heisler used two cylinders facing one another crosswise, one on each side of the locomotive, forming a V-pattern. These cylinders turned a shaft to power two sets of driving wheels. Climax used two parallel, sharply inclined cylinders, one on each side of the locomotive, to power a shaft connecting two sets of driving wheels.

● SWITCHERS

Most railroads used specialized locomotives of a conventional design for switching service at yards, terminals and industrial sites. Because most switchers were relatively small locomotives, operated at slow speeds, and needed high adhesion to move long cuts of cars, they normally did not have pilot or trailing trucks – commonly used on road locomotives.

The smallest switchers were 0-4-0 types. This sort of locomotive, however, had low adhesion and a notoriously bad-ride quality, so locomotives with more driving wheels were generally preferred. The 0-6-0 switcher was the most popular for general switching and about 10,000 were built. Some railroads used 0-8-0 switchers for heavier switching duties and, after the turn of the century, 0-10-0 switchers saw only limited service in hump yards.

Specialty tenderless switchers, with water-tanks built over the boilers, and "fireless" steam engines saw limited use in areas where conventional locomotives were inappropriate.

TYPICAL 0-6-0 SWITCHER

Date	About 1905
Builder	American Locomotive Co. (Alco)
Gauge	4 ft 8½ in
Driving wheels	51 in
Capacity	2 cylinders 19 x 24 in
Steam pressure	180 lb
Weight	163,365 lb
Tractive effort	26,510 lb

● **OPPOSITE**
Heisler's geared locomotives use two cylinders in a V position. This Heisler was built in 1912 for the Louise Lumber Company of Hawkes, Mississippi. It operates on the Silver Creek & Stephenson Railroad in Freeport, Illinois, USA.

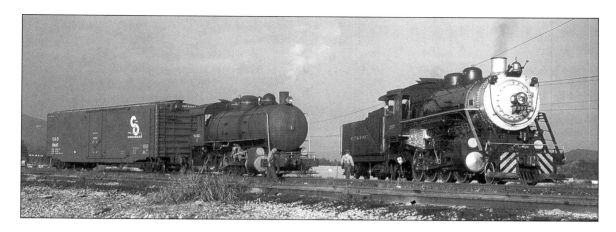

● **RIGHT**
The last of the Lima-built Shay-types were heavy, three-cylinder locomotives built in 1945. The Western Maryland railroad in the USA owned several of these big Shays. They weighed 324,000 lb and generated a 59,740 lb tractive effort.

● **ABOVE**
Locomotive 2-8-0, No. 207 (formerly Southern 630), and North American Rayon Company's fireless 0-6-0T, No. 1, on the East Tennessee and Western North Carolina Railroad, USA.

● **BELOW**
Surrounded by lumber, this Ely Thomas Lumber Company's Lima-built Shay-type No. 2 waits for its next run in 1958 near Gauley, West Virginia, USA.

AMERICAN EXPORTS

Nations around the world relied on the locomotive prowess of the United States of America to supply their motive-power needs. Of some 175,000 steam locomotives built in the USA in the 120 years between 1830 and 1950, about 37,000, more than 20 per cent, were built specifically for export. Many varieties of locomotives were sold, depending on customers' needs, but five types were particularly popular in the export market and represented the lion's share of those sold.

● **CONSOLIDATIONS**

The most popular export model was the 2-8-0 Consolidation. More than 10,000 were sold outside the USA. This model was the second most-popular domestic locomotive, too. More than 22,000 were built for use in the USA where only the 19th-century 4-4-0 American-type was more popular.

A distant second to the Consolidation was the 2-8-2 Mikado-type. More than 4,000 were exported. This type was specifically designed by Baldwin Locomotive Works for Japanese Railways in 1897. Later, it was adapted for domestic use. Many were used for freight service in the USA.

● **DECAPODS FOR RUSSIA**

The 2-10-0 Decapod was the third most-popular model. Many of the heavy locomotives went to Russia and to the Soviet Union during World Wars I and II. The Decapod was also popular in Germany, Greece, Poland and Turkey. Oddly, it was not very popular in the

MACARTHUR 2-8-2 USATC

Builder	Baldwin Locomotive Company, Eddystone, Pennsylvania, USA
Client	United States Army Transport Corps (USATC)
Gauge	Metre
Driving wheels	4 ft
Capacity	Cylinders 16 x 24 in
Weight in full working order	112 tons

● **LEFT**
One of the last surviving MacArthur 2-8-2s. These metre-gauge engines were built for the United States Army Transport Corps (USATC) for operations during World War II. They saw wide service in India, Burma, Thailand and the Philippines. After the war, survivors remained active. In India, they were classified MAWD (McArthur War Department) and found in the country's Northeast Frontier region.

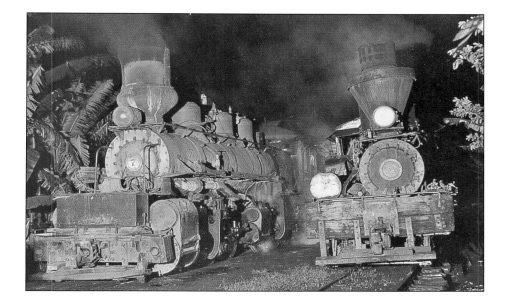

● **ABOVE**
Cuba's Manuel Isla sugar mill is host to this vintage Baldwin 0-4-2 tank believed to have been built in 1882. A retired employee at the mill, 88-year-old Jose Alfonso Melgoragio, remembers knowing the engine all his life. He worked on it for 25 years.

● **ABOVE LEFT**
A night scene in the mountains of the Philippines island of Negros. Two last survivors of their respective types are seen at the Insula Lumber Company. On the left, a Baldwin-built, four-cylinder compound Mallet; on the right, a vertical-cylinder Shay. These are classic American locomotives of the American Pacific Northwest.

● **LEFT**
This classic American ten-wheeler, built by Rogers of New Jersey in 1896, pictured at the San Barnado Locomotive Works near Santiago, Chile, where the veteran was ending its days as work's pilot.

● **LEFT**
A rare Baldwin 2-6-2 saddle-tank, known as the "Lavras Rose", which as Baldwin export order No. 372 of 1927 operated as a work's shunter at Lavras in Mina Gerais State, Brazil.

● **BELOW LEFT**
This classic American switcher once worked for the 5 ft 3 in gauge Paulista Railway serving the city and Pernambuco state in eastern Brazil. It was built by Baldwin of Philadelphia, Pennsylvania, USA, in 1896. The veteran is pictured here pensioned off to industrial service at the Cosim Steelworks at São Paulo, Brazil.

domestic market. Only the Santa Fe and Pennsylvania Railroad owned large numbers. The Frisco picked up Decapods intended for Russia and used them successfully for many years. Of the 4,100 American-built Decapods, 3,400 were exported around the world.

● **EXPORTS OF MOGULS AND TEN-WHEELERS**

Nearly 3,000 2-6-0 Mogul-types were built for export. This locomotive was popular for heavy freight in the mid-19th century. Some 1,600 4-6-0 ten-wheeler types were also exported, nearly 10 per cent of American production. Of 3,800 geared locomotives built in the USA for use on steep grades and for specialty railroads, such as logging, 600 were exported.

STREAMLINED STEAM

In 1934, at the height of the Great Depression, the Burlington railroad's Budd-built stainless-steel streamlined Pioneer Zephyr streaked across America.

● STREAMLINING TAKES OFF

Everywhere Pioneer Zephyr went, it inspired railroad managers and the riding public. In a similar vein, Union Pacific's streamlined City of Salina toured the West. These Winton engine-powered diesel articulated "trains of the future" soon resulted in the streamlining of a great many steam locomotives for passenger service. New locomotives, steam, diesel-electric and electric, were ordered as well, along with whole streamlined trains of luxurious passenger cars.

● DRESSING UP THE OLD GUARD

The railroads were quick to send crack passenger locomotives to shop for a fancy new dress. In 1936, Pennsylvania Railroad hired noted industrial designer

● BELOW
The Chesapeake & Ohio railroad operated four Class L1 streamlined 4-6-4 Hudson types in passenger service. These odd-looking, yellow and stainless-steel adorned locomotives were nicknamed "Yellowbellies".

Raymond Loewy to improve K4 No. 3768 aesthetically. The result was a flashy-looking locomotive. Many railroads dressed up their older locomotives with elaborate shrouding, though in some cases with less than superlative results. In many cases, shrouding hampered maintenance and was later removed.

● NEW STREAMLINERS

The Milwaukee Road was one of the first railroads to order new streamlined steam locomotives. In 1935, it ordered high-speed 4-4-2s with 84 in driving wheels and shrouds designed by Otto Kuhler. Assigned to its Hiawathas, these fast engines would regularly zip at more than 100 mph between Chicago, Illinois, and Milwaukee, Wisconsin.

Beginning in the late 1930s, Southern Pacific's fleet of semi-streamlined 4-8-4 Northern types, painted in its flashy orange, red and silver "Daylight" scheme, marched about California. The epitome of this famous class were the 30 GS-4s and GS-5s built by the Lima works in 1941–42. These powerful engines exhibited some of the finest styling found on any North American locomotive.

Among the last types of streamlined locomotive built were the Norfolk & Western's J Class 4-8-4s, for service with its passenger-trains.

● RIGHT
The Norfolk & Western Railroad's Class-J Northerns, Nos. 600 to 612, were its most famous streamliners. These powerful locomotives could operate to a top speed of 110 mph but rarely needed to. N&WR operated other streamline steam as well, including its 800 Series Class K-2, 4-8-2 Mountains. Two N&WR Js pause for servicing in 1958.

● **ABOVE**
Canadian National Railway 4-8-4 No. 6402 passing through Toronto.

● **BELOW**
Southern Pacific owned a fleet of semi-streamlined, "Daylight"-painted 4-8-4 Northern types for fast passenger service. Of these, the best performing and most aesthetically pleasing were 30 Class GS-4s and GS-5s built in 1941–42.

SOUTHERN PACIFIC GS-4

Date	1941
Builder	Lima, Ohio, USA
Client	Southern Pacific
Gauge	4 ft 8½ in
Driving wheels	80 in
Capacity	2 cylinders 26 x 32 in
Steam pressure	300 lb
Weight	475,000 lb
Tractive effort	78,650 lb

THE NETWORK EXPANDS – DECAPODS, MOUNTAINS, SANTA FES AND OVERLANDS

The railroads of the United States of America had an insatiable appetite for ever-larger, more powerful and more efficient locomotives. It stemmed from their belief that more powerful locomotives would produce lower operating costs through the ability to haul more goods, faster, with fewer crews and locomotives.

In the 19th century, locomotive output was limited to the size of the firebox and the fireman's ability to shovel coal. Early attempts at producing big locomotives usually resulted in curious behemoths that did not steam well and languished for lack of power. The development of superheating (recirculation of steam through a locomotive's firetubes, significantly increasing power) and of the trailing truck (enabling an increase in firebox capacity) allowed for significant increases in practical locomotive size and for the development of several large new locomotive types. The further

development of devices such as the mechanical stoker (moving coal from tender to firebox without a shovel) allowed for maximum performance from new larger locomotives.

CHESAPEAKE & OHIO CLASS J1 MOUNTAIN TYPE

Date	1911–12
Builder	American Locomotive Co. (Alco)
Client	Chesapeake & Ohio Railroad
Gauge	4 ft 8½ in
Driving wheels	62 in
Capacity	2 cylinders 29 x 28 in
Steam pressure	180 lb
Weight	499,500 lb
Tractive effort	58,000 lb

● DECAPOD AND MOUNTAIN-TYPES

The 2-10-0 Decapod-type, first introduced in 1870 by the Lehigh Valley Railroad, Pennsylvania, proved too big for its time. After 1900, it was built with limited success for several American railroads. It was most successful in the export market.

The 4-8-2 was introduced in about 1910 for use on the Chesapeake & Ohio railroad and soon proved a very popular design. This versatile type of locomotive was well suited for fast passenger-trains.

● SANTA FE AND OVERLAND-TYPES

Western railroads, which operated over great distances across the open plains, mountains and deserts, had a special need for large, powerful locomotives and

● **ABOVE**
The 2-10-0 Decapod type was not popular among American railroads, but Pennsylvania Railroad owned more than 500. The Decapod was used for heavy, slow-speed freight service.

● **RIGHT**
The Norfolk & Western Railroad operated streamlined 4-8-2 Mountain types in passenger service. These locomotives, Class K2, looked very similar to the J Class Northern types.

were better able to handle those with a long wheelbase. Shortly after the turn of the century, the Santa Fe Railway took delivery of 2-10-2 locomotives called Santa Fe types. This type did not attain popularity with other railroads until World War I, when changes in technology made it more appealing and the type was mass produced. In the 1920s, the Union Pacific railroad took delivery of a three-cylinder 4-10-2 locomotive named after that railroad's primary corridor, the Overland Route. Southern Pacific also ordered this type and referred to it as the Southern Pacific type. The 4-10-2 was not very popular. Fewer than 100 were built.

● **ABOVE**
This Baltimore & Ohio railroad's 4-8-2 brand new Mountain type poses for its builder's photograph. This locomotive had 74 in driving wheels, 30 x 30 in cylinders, operated at 210 lb per sq in and produced a 65,000 lb tractive effort.

AMERICAN SUPERPOWER

American locomotive builders were constantly looking to improve the steam locomotives' output and fuel economy, and in doing so developed many important innovations.

● FOUR-AXLE TRAILING TRUCK KEY TO POWER

The development of the four-axle trailing-truck or -tender allowed for a larger firebox, and thus increased the heating surface and power. "Superpower" also took advantage of other improvements, such as automatic stokers, superheating and, later, roller bearings.

The first locomotive exhibiting the radial, outside-bearing, four-axle truck and enlarged firebox was a Lima 2-8-4 built in 1925 for the New York Central railroad. It was designed for heavyfreight service. NYC used its 2-8-4s on the Boston & Albany (B&A) line in western Massachusetts. This line featured the

steepest grades on NYC's system. As a result, this new type was named the "Berkshire", after the mountain range in which it operated. The Berkshire type was the logical progression from the Mikado type, long popular for freight service. NYC was pleased with the Berkshires' performance and ordered a fleet of them for service on the B&A line. There they served for more than 20 years, until the introduction of diesel-electric.

● SUPER PASSENGER POWER

The four-axle trailing-truck and larger firebox principle worked so well on the freight-hauling Berkshire that the same principle was tried on fast passenger locomotives. In 1927, NYC took delivery of its first 4-6-4 locomotive from Alco. This type was named after the Hudson River, NYC's famed Water Level Route, which runs parallel to the line between New York City and Albany, the state capital.

● LEFT
One of the most impressive types of steam locomotive ever built was Atchison, Topeka & Santa Fe's 2900 Series, 4-8-4 Northerns. They weighed 510,000 lb, operated at 300 lb per sq in and had 80 in driving wheels. They regularly ran at more than 100 miles an hour.

In 1945, Reading Railroad built eight 4-8-4 Northerns, Class T1, at its shops in Reading, Pennsylvania. Designed for freight service, the T1 weighed 809,000 lb, had 70 in driving wheels and operated at 240 lb per sq in.

● **RIGHT**
The Baltimore & Ohio Railroad's 4-6-4 Hudson type. Many American railroads used Hudsons in passenger service. The superpowered Hudson was the natural progression from the Pacific type.

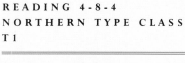

READING 4-8-4 NORTHERN TYPE CLASS T1

Date	1945
Builder	Reading Shops, Reading, Pennsylvania, USA
Client	Reading Railroad
Gauge	4 ft 8½ in
Driving wheels	70 in
Capacity	2 cylinders 27 x 32 in
Steam pressure	240 lb
Weight	809,000 lb
Tractive effort	68,000 lb

Continued development of the Hudson type produced some of the finest passenger locomotives ever built. About 500 Hudson types were built for service in America.

● **NORTHERNS**

The 4-8-4 Northern type was first developed in 1927 for the Northern Pacific. The Northern was an excellent locomotive for high-speed passenger service and fast freight service and remained in production throughout World War II. Some of the finest examples of the Northern type were

● **RIGHT**
Union Pacific has maintained No. 844. While used mainly for excursion services, it occasionally hauls freight. In September 1989, it led a westbound freight across Nebraska from Omaha to North Platte.

● **ABOVE**
Milwaukee Road took delivery of Class S-3 Northerns from Alco in 1944. These powerful locomotives were used for freight and passenger service but were too heavy to operate on some routes.

Union Pacific railroad's 800-class, built by Alco in 1937; Milwaukee Road's S-Class, built by Alco in 1944; Santa Fe's 2900 Series, built by Baldwin that same year; and NYC's 6000 Series locomotives, built in 1946 and usually referred to by the railroad as Niagaras rather than as Northerns.

Some Northerns were delivered in streamlined shrouds, notably Norfolk & Western Railroad's J Class and Southern Pacific's GS-2 to GS-6 Class. (SP's Class GS-1, GS-7 and GS-8 did not feature streamlining.)

More than 1,000 Northern types were built for North American railroads. Union Pacific has the distinction of maintaining a Northern well past the end of steam in the 1950s. In 1996 its famous Northern No. 844 emerged from a multi-million dollar overhaul and paraded around the system in excursion service.

AMERICAN ELECTRIC AND EARLY DIESELS

The first use of electric locomotives in the United States of America was in the Baltimore Railway Tunnel, by the Baltimore & Ohio Railroad (B&O) in 1895.

● ELECTRICS

Electrification gained popularity after the turn of the century and through the 1930s many American railroads electrified portions of their main lines. Most notable were the Pennsylvania Railroad (PPR) extensive 11,000-volt alternating current (a.c.) electrification in New York, New Jersey, Maryland and Pennsylvania; the New York Central (NYC) 660-volt direct current (d.c.) third-rail electrification; New Haven's 11,000-volt a.c. suburban main-line electrification in Connecticut; and Milwaukee Road's famous 3,000-volt d.c. overhead electrification through the mountains of Montana, Idaho and Washington State. PRR owned many classes of electric locomotives, from the

small 0-C-0 switchers, Class B1, to the famous Raymond Loewy-styled 4-C+C-4, Class GG1. The GG1 served PRR and its successors for nearly 50 years.

NYC operated several classes of motors in the New York City area. Its first electric, Class S1, No. 6000, was in service from 1904 until the 1970s.

PENNSYLVANIA RAILROAD CLASS GG1 ELECTRIC LOCOMOTIVE

Date	1934–43
Builder	Baldwin, General Electric, Juniata Shops
Client	Pennsylvania Railroad
Gauge	4 ft 8½ in
Voltage	11,000 volts a.c.
Power	4,680 hp
Weight	460,000 lb
Tractive effort	75,000 lb

The PRR operated 139 GG1 electrics in freight and passenger service on its electrified lines. These Raymond Loewy-styled locomotives operated for nearly 50 years.

New Haven's electrics could operate from both 660-volt d.c. third rail and 11,000-volt a.c. overhead wire. New Haven used EF-class motors in freight service and EP-class motors in passenger service. Its last passenger electrics were 10 EP-5s, delivered by General Electric in 1955.

● ABOVE
A PRR GG1 leads a high-speed passenger-train through Frankford Junction, near Philadelphia, Pennsylvania, in 1959.

● LEFT
The Rio Grande Zephyr on the Denver & Rio Grande Western Railroad, seen at Thistle, Colorado, in 1982.

Milwaukee Road's most famous electrics were its 6-D+D-6, Class EP-2, Bipolars, built by GE in 1918 for use on its Washington State lines; and its 1949 GE-built Little Joes for its Montana and Idaho lines. These double-ended, baby-faced locomotives were intended for operation in Russia but not delivered because of the start of the Cold War. Hence their nickname, after Joseph Stalin. Milwaukee discontinued the last of its electric operations in 1974, and six years later abandoned its tracks to the Pacific Coast.

● DIESEL-ELECTRIC INTRIGUE

America's first successful commercial diesel-electric was a 60 ton, 300 hp boxcab built by Alco-GE-Ingersol Rand for the Central Railroad of New Jersey in 1925. At first, the diesel-electric was primarily used for switching, but its passenger application became evident with the introduction of the Budd-built Pioneer Zephyr on the Burlington railroad in 1934. This articulated, streamlined, stainless-steel wonder changed the way railroads viewed the diesel-electric.

In 1939, General Motors Electro-Motive Corporation introduced the FT, a 1,350-hp, streamlined locomotive designed to be operated in sets of four in heavyfreight service. This amazing locomotive outperformed contemporary steam locomotives in nearly every service in which it was tested. The diesel had proved it could handle all kinds of service and, in most respects, in a more cost-efficient way than steam. Only World War II prolonged the inevitable. Following the war, the diesel-electric quickly took over from the steam locomotive. By the mid-1950s, many railroads had completely replaced

locomotive fleets with new diesels. By 1960, the steam locomotive was relegated to the status of a historical curiosity.

The diesel-electric enabled American railroads to "electrify" their lines without stringing wires. In some cases, the diesel-electric replaced true electric operations as well.

● **LEFT**
One of the New Haven railroad's EP-5 passenger electrics leads a train through Sunnyside Yard, in Queens, New York, in 1960. New Haven's 10 EP-5s, built by General Electric in 1955, were the railroad's last new passenger electrics.

● **BELOW TOP**
The Electro-Motive E7 was one of the most popular passenger locomotives. More than 500 were built. Here, a pair of the Louisville & Nashville railroad's E7s rest at Louisville, Kentucky, in 1958.

● **BELOW BOTTOM**
Electro-Motive Corporation's EAs built in 1937 for the Baltimore & Ohio railroad were the first streamlined passenger diesel-electrics not part of an articulated-train set.

AMERICAN INTERURBANS

Between the 1890s and World War I, lightweight interurban electric railways were built throughout the United States of America. Their greatest concentration was in the Northeast and Midwest.

● INTERURBANS' PERFORMANCE ACROSS AMERICA

Interurbans were mainly passenger carriers, but many developed freight business as well. Interurbans were badly affected when automobile travel became popular, and very few interurban companies survived the Great Depression of the 1930s. A handful of interurban lines operated passenger services into the 1950s and early 1960s. Others survived as freight carriers. Only a few segments of the once-great interurban system exist today, mostly as freight carriers. Three are still electrified, and one line, the Chicago, South Shore & South Bend, still carries passengers.

● INTERURBAN CARS

Early interurban car design emulated that of steam railroad passenger cars. Ornate, heavyweight, wooden cars prevailed until about 1915 when steel cars became standard. Interurban cars were built by several companies including the American Car Company, Brill, Cincinnati Car Company, Holman Car Company and the Jewett Car Company, most of which also built street cars and elevated rapid-transit cars.

● ABOVE

The North Shore operated two articulated, streamlined electric train sets called Electroliners on its high-speed line between Chicago, Illinois, and Milwaukee, Wisconsin. An Electroliner is seen here on the streets of Milwaukee – on 19 July 1958.

● BELOW

The Chicago, South Shore & South Bend Railroad operated a fleet of Standard Steel Car interurban cars. Here, a typical South Shore interurban is seen at Gary, Indiana, in 1958.

● **RIGHT**
The North Shore painted some of its
heavyweight interurban cars to make it appear
as if they were modern, stainless-steel,
streamlined cars.

CHICAGO, SOUTH SHORE & SOUTH BEND INTERURBAN COACH

Date	1929
Builder	Standard Steel Car
Client	South Shore & South Bend Interurban
Gauge	4 ft 8½ in
Voltage	1,500 d.c.
Axles	Four
Weight	133,600 lb
Propulsion	Westinghouse
Seating	48 seats

A few interurbans ordered high-speed, lightweight cars in the 1930s, notably the Fonda, Johnstown & Gloversville railroad in New York State, which acquired five streamlined Bullet cars from Brill in 1932; the Cincinnati & Lake Erie railroad, which acquired 20 high-speed cars from the Cincinnati Car Company in 1932; and the Northern Indiana Railway, which acquired ten lightweight cars from Cummings in 1930.

● **ARTICULATED STREAMLINERS**
The Chicago, North Shore & Milwaukee (the North Shore) received two streamlined, articulated interurban train sets from the St Louis Car Company in 1941. Named Electroliners, these flashy trains were painted in a unique emerald-and-salmon multistriped scheme. The North Shore was one of few interurbans integrated with a city rapid-transit system. For more than 20 years, the Electroliners zipped between Milwaukee, Wisconsin, and Chicago's "L" Loop. After the North Shore's demise in 1963, the Electroliners were sold to Philadelphia, where they operated for another ten years as Liberty Liners on the Norristown Highspeed Line (the former Philadelphia & Western). The Illinois Terminal also operated St Louis Car streamlined articulated interurbans.

● **RIGHT**
The Chicago, Aurora & Elgin (CA&E) railroad's No. 20 was built by the Niles Car & Manufacturing Company in 1902. It weighs 85,000 lb and seats 52 passengers. The CA&E powered its cars by third-rail and overhead wire.

CANADIAN PASSENGER

In 1948, about 4,100 steam locomotives were serving Canada's two main railroads, Canadian National (CN) and Canadian Pacific (CP).

● LOCOMOTIVE BUILDERS

Two commercial Canadian builders provided most of these locomotives. The Montreal Locomotive Works (MLW), a subsidiary of the American Locomotive Company (Alco), built more than 3,600 steam locomotives between the turn of the century and the early-1950s when it switched to producing diesel-electric locomotives. The Canadian Locomotive Company (CLC), founded in the 1850s, built more than 2,500 steam locomotives, including about 500 export models. In 1950, CLC was given the licence to build Fairbanks-Morse diesel-electric locomotives.

● CANADIAN NATIONAL

The CN railroad introduced the 4-8-4 to Canada in 1927, only a few months after Northern Pacific first tried it in the United States of America. CN called the 4-8-4 the Confederation type and during 20 years ordered more than 200 for freight and passenger service. Of CN's 4-8-4s, 11 were streamlined. One of the most impressive types of 4-8-4 was CN's Class U-2-h, intended for dual service. They operated at 250 lb per sq in,

● ABOVE

Canadian Pacific's most famous locomotives were its Royal Hudsons, built by the Montreal Locomotive Works from 1938. Like many CP steam-locomotives, they were semi-streamlined and had recessed headlights.

● BELOW

Canadian Pacific Railway G-5 4-6-2s, Nos. 1246 and 1293, pictured at Brockways Mills, Vermont, USA.

weighed 400,300 lb, featured 73 in driving wheels, and produced a 56,000 lb tractive effort. CN also maintained a fleet of 4-8-2 Mountain types, many working exclusively in passenger service.

● CANADIAN PACIFIC

The late-era steam locomotives of CP feature several distinctive hallmarks. Most were semi-streamlined and featured

CANADIAN PACIFIC CLASS H1D, 4-6-4 ROYAL HUDSON

Date	1938
Builder	Montreal Locomotive Works
Client	Canadian Pacific
Gauge	4 ft 8½ in
Driving wheels	75 in
Capacity	2 cylinders 22 x 30 in
Steam pressure	275 lb
Weight	628,500 lb
Tractive effort	45,300 lb

centred, recessed headlights. As with CN locomotives, CP used vestibule cabs to give crews greater comfort when operating in extremely cold temperatures.

CP preferred 4-6-2 Pacific types and 4-6-4 Hudson types for its passenger service. It began buying Pacifics in 1906 and continued acquiring them until 1948. Its Hudsons were notable locomotives, with outstanding performance records and excellent aesthetic qualities. Some CP Hudsons regularly operated on 800-mile-long runs. Its best-known 4-6-4s were its H1 Royal Hudsons, so named because two of their class hauled the special trains that brought King George VI and Queen Elizabeth across Canada in 1939. The Royal Hudsons were decorated with an embossed crown.

● ABOVE
A Canadian National 4-8-4, No. 6218, races with a passenger excursion. CN owned more 4-8-4s than any other railroad.

● ABOVE
A Canadian National 4-8-4, No. 6218, rolls a passenger-train off a bridge in 1964.

● LEFT
Canadian National railroad preferred four-coupled steam locomotives and owned many Mikados, Mountains and Confederations (known elsewhere as Northerns). Here, a 4-8-2 Mountain Class N-7b, No. 6017, rests at Turcot Yard, Montreal.

CANADIAN FREIGHT

Canadian National was a publicly owned company formed in 1922 from a number of failing railroad lines. It was the larger line of the two Canadian systems and spanned Canada from coast to coast.

● CANADIAN NATIONAL

In the 1920s, the unified CN acquired many 4-8-2 Mountain types and smaller 2-8-2 Mikados. In 1927 it was one of the first railroads to adopt the 4-8-4 Northern type, which it called the Confederation type. CN and its American subsidiary, Grand Trunk Western (GTW), eventually owned more than 200 4-8-4s, far more than any other North American railroad. These high horsepower 4-8-4s were ideal suited for heavy freight service and passenger service.

In 1929, CN experimented with an alternative form of motive power. It ordered two diesel-electrics from Westinghouse and was the first North American railroad to use the diesel in main-line service. However, these experimental locomotives were unsuccessful and not duplicated.

● LEFT
A 40-ton Shay "Old One Spot", standard gauge, built in 1910: the last of the woodburners.

Ultimately, CN converted from steam to diesel operations, but at a more gradual rate than railroads in the USA.

● CANADIAN PACIFIC

Privately owned CP took a different approach to its freight locomotives from CN. Where CN used many four-coupled locomotives, 4-8-2s, 4-8-4s, etc., CP preferred three-coupled locomotives for many applications. It owned many 4-6-2 Pacific types and 4-6-4 Hudson types. It used light Pacifics in branch-line freight service as

● RIGHT
A Canadian National 4-8-4, No. 6168, leads a mixed train near Brantford, Ontario, in 1959. CN used many 4-8-4s in freight and passenger service.

CANADIAN PACIFIC CLASS T1b, 2-10-4 SELKIRK TYPE

Date	1929–49
Builder	Montreal Locomotive Works
Client	Canadian Pacific
Gauge	4 ft 8½ in
Driving wheels	63 in
Capacity	2 cylinders 25 x 32 in
Steam pressure	285 lb
Weight	447,000 lb (engine only)
Tractive effort	76,905 lb

well as in passenger service. CP was also one of the few railroads to employ its Hudsons in freight service. Most railroads used this type exclusively for passenger trains.

CP did own some big locomotives. In 1928 it built two 4-8-4s but acquired no more. However, for heavy freight service in the Canadian Rockies, it owned 36 semi-streamlined 2-10-4 Texas-types that it called Selkirks. These locomotives were well suited for steep grades and heavy tonnage and performed well. In 1931, CP built an experimental three-cylinder 2-10-4. This locomotive was not particularly successful, CP did not bother to duplicate it and it was eventually scrapped.

● **ABOVE**
A Canadian National 2-8-0 Consolidation sits at Turcot Yard, Montreal. Most CN steam locomotives were built by Montreal Locomotive Works.

● **ABOVE**
A 45-ton, two-truck Climax logging locomotive, No. 9, built in 1912.

● **LEFT**
In the 1920s, the newly formed Canadian National began buying many 2-8-2 Mikados.

THE PRUSSIAN INFLUENCE

Prussian influence is seen by many to be confined to the large class of 4-6-0 locomotives known as the P8. After Germany's unification in 1871 as an imperial power, Prussia continued to go its own way in railway matters. Other states in the German Empire followed suit under Prussia's sway.

● THE EARLY DAYS

At the end of the 19th century, most railway locomotive authorities were trying to cope with the pace of advance in design, Prussia included. Because of the fairly level nature of Prussian territory, lightweight locomotives with a fair turn of speed lasted for many years and in various guises. Compounding was in fashion and classes were turned out seemingly almost at random, some being compound locomotives and others simple locomotives.

● ABOVE
The Prussian P8 also lasted to the end of the days of steam in West Germany. Here, in the late 1960s, No. 038 509-6 trundles under a bridge.

PRUSSIAN P8

Date	1906
Builder	Schwarzkopff, Berlin
Client	Prussian State Railways
Gauge	1,435 mm
Class	Prussian P8; Deutsche Reichsbahn (DR) 38
Type	4-6-0
Driving wheels	1,750 mm
Capacity	2 cylinders 575 x 630 mm
Weight in working order	78.2 tonnes
Maximum service speed	100 kph

● THE SCHMIDT SUPERHEATER

Then came a most important event for Prussia and railway administrations worldwide. This was the development of a successful superheater. Steam was dried in a further set of tubes in the boiler to remove water drops in suspension. This superheated steam worked far more efficiently than those preceding it.

In the early 1890s, a Prussian physicist working in this field, Dr Wilhelm Schmidt, was encouraged to try out his results on the Prussian State Railways (PSR) system, by Mr Geheimiath Garbe of PSR. The first Schmidt superheater was fitted in 1897, but, as with many innovations, there were problems of lubrication and leaks. Further, locomotives fitted with superheaters cost more to build. In 1900, a simple 4-4-0 was fitted with the Schmidt superheater and achieved much interest and some success. Compared with nonsuperheated compound 4-4-0s of the same class, the nonsuperheated machines used 12 per cent more coal and 30 per cent more water.

● THE PRUSSIAN P8

The cost-savings of a simple machine against a compound being most

● RIGHT
AND OPPOSITE
BOTTOM
Turkish State Railways (TCCD) operates a system separated from the main network to take coal from collieries in the Armutçuk Mountains to the docks at Eregli on the Black Sea. On shed at the port, these Prussian G8-2, two-cylinder 2-8-0s, dating from 1919, are ready for the night's work.

attractive, superheaters began to be fitted more widely and to more types of locomotive, including a class of sturdy 2-6-0 mixed-traffic locomotive. Compounding was not abandoned, however, for high-speed work. PSR had gained experience of the De Glehn compounds and developed their own compound 4-6-0 version. When a simple two-cylinder version for mixed traffic came out in 1906, the scene was set for the expansion of the Prussian Class P8. The first was built by Schwarzkopff of Berlin. Between 1906–21, the PSR bought 3,370 machines. Many others were constructed, including for export. More than 6,000 were built in total. After World War I, reparations demanded from Germany led to the arrival of the P8 in many other countries including Belgium and France.

● THE WIDER IMPLICATIONS
Several other classes of Prussian-designed locomotive were also distributed widely, including to Germany's allies, especially Turkey. This distribution and the reparations possibly extended Prussian influence far wider, and interest in these relatively

simple and robust designs grew. The German locomotive-building industry's need to gear up to replace stocks distributed elsewhere increased its design and production capacity. From this, German builders outside Prussia also benefited while, in Germany, the foundations were laid for German State Railways – the Deutsche Reichsbahn (DR) and, after 1945, the Deutsche Bundesbahn (DB).

● BELOW LEFT
The Deutsche Bundesbahn (DB) Class 078 4-6-4T lasted right to the end of the days of steam, in the early-1970s in then-West Germany. One of the class is pictured in a familiar role on a light passenger-train. This class, as Prussian Class T18, was built in batches between 1912-27.

● BELOW
Also on shed at Eregli in Turkey, in the 1970s, a driver is oiling round on a Prussian Type-G8 44071, an 0-8-0 dating from 1902, before moving off to pick up his train.

THE REICHSBAHN STANDARDS

After World War I, Germany's need to reorganize its railways led in 1920 to formation of a national system, the Reichsbahn. It is not surprising that Prussian management and methods were prominent.

● THE FOUNDATIONS

An engineering-management centre was set up in Berlin. One of its decisions was to produce a series of locomotive classes that would operate across the network. A man called Wagner was placed in charge. In the years to 1939, at least, Wagner's stature as an engineer and manager grew.

● FIRST STEPS

One of his first decisions was to categorize all the locomotives from

● **RIGHT**
This unmodified 01-798 had a trailing load of 450 tonnes as it neared Grossenhain, in the then-East Germany, on the 06.37 hours express from Berlin to Dresden in 1977.

various sources under his control. This was so successful that its basic tenets were widely followed elsewhere in the operation. It pointed to strengths and weaknesses in the stock. Once more, Prussian influence emerged.

This is not to say that the other German States' railways had little to offer. Saxony and Württemberg were well advanced. Further, private locomotive builders contributed high technical input to many designs.

KRIEGSLOK – DEUTSCHE REICHSBAHN (DR) CLASS 52

Date	1942
Builder	Borsig of Berlin
Client	Deutsche Reichsbahn
Gauge	1,435 mm
Class	52
Type	2-10-0
Driving wheels	1,400 mm
Capacity	2 cylinders 500 x 600 mm (stroke)
Weight in working order	85.3 tonnes
Maximum service speed	80 kph

● **RIGHT**
A Class 050 2-10-0, No. 050 383-9, pulling away from Freudenstadt Station in the Black Forest, in the then West Germany of the late 1960s.

● **DESIGN CRITERIA**
Compounding was on the way out. Two-cylinder, simple expansion locomotives were to be adopted, although, in the 1930s, three small specialist classes had three cylinders. Robust engineering was assisted by raising the axleload on main lines to 20.4 tonnes. Ease of maintenance was improved by mounting ancillaries on the boiler and adopting bar-frames as favoured by the locomotive-builders, J.A. Maffei of Munich. Commodious cabs eased the lot of footplate crews. Many other decisions affected components and fittings, some of which carried on Prussian practice. Despite radical changes to external appearance, the Prussian style continued to dominate.

● **OPPOSITE**
A Kriegslok of Turkish State Railways (TCDD), No. 56533, pictured about to move off to pick up a freight train in the nearby yard.

● **RIGHT**
Class 01 Pacific 4-6-2s were still working between Berlin and Dresden, Saxony, in the then East Germany, in 1977, when this rural scene was briefly disturbed near Weinböhla.

● **STANDARDS AT HOME AND ABROAD**
No fewer than 29 classes were brought into service between 1925–45. They ranged from small classes of 0-6-0T and 2-4-2T, to the 6,292 Class 52 Kriegslok introduced in 1942. These ranged far and wide across Europe, surviving well beyond designers' expectations.

Standard designs proved attractive to other countries. Some bought almost identical designs from German builders, or built them under licence in their own works. For example, Poland had modified Prussian P8s in 1922; Turkey had a range of types in regular use in the 1970s and, in small numbers, even later than this.

Many examples remained in regular use in the former East Germany until the late 1980s. A substantial number, especially of Kriegsloks, have been recovered for restoration and use on special trains in European countries.

GÖLSDORF AND THE AUSTRIAN EMPIRE

The Austro-Hungarian Empire, before its eventual collapse in 1918 as a result of World War I, was one of the most powerful political and economic entities in continental Europe.

● BACKGROUND

Its railways' main axis ran generally east-west with few topographical problems in the easterly direction from Vienna, in Austria, to Budapest, in Hungary. To the south, the only real geographical challenge between Vienna and Graz, in Austria, was surmounted by the opening in 1853 of the Trieste Railway line over the Austrian Alps and through the 980 m (3,215 ft) high Semmering Pass. A similar problem faced railway builders for the line going southward to Italy from Innsbruck in Austria. This crossed the mountains through the 1,369 m (4,494 ft) high Brenner Pass whose railroad was

completed 1867. Apart from the relatively level lines to the German border to the west, other lines westward tended to be regarded as secondary. Moreover, they faced the main European Alpine barrier. The best route was a single line through Austria's Tirol and Vorarlberg. This reached Buchs, Kanton St Gallen on the Swiss border, with hard climbing on both sides of the 1,798 m (5,900 ft) high Arlberg Tunnel, 6 km (3¾ miles) long and opened in 1884.

● DR KARL GÖLSDORF

Karl Gölsdorf was born into a railway family in 1861. By the age of 30 he was chief mechanical engineer (CME) of the Austrian State Railway. In the early 1900s, he was made responsible for all mechanical engineering under the purview of the Austrian Railway Ministry, which also influenced the notionally

independent Hungarian railways. His achievements include the rack-and-pinion Erzberg line. The 1,533 m (5,032 ft) high Erzberg Mountain, rich in iron ore, stands above the mining commune of Eisenerz in Austria's Styria province.

● DESIGN PROBLEMS AND SOLUTIONS

The empire's level routes required locomotives capable of sustained high speed, while the curving, mountainous lines called for machines capable of a long, hard slog. Both criteria needed free steaming. However, Gölsdorf faced the severe limitation of lightweight track and, consequently, a maximum axleload of no more than 14.5 tons.

He achieved high power:weight ratios by relatively high boiler pressures and by applying his own dictum that it is easier to save weight on each of a thousand

● **LEFT**
This scene in Strasshof locomotive depot north of Vienna in 1987 includes BBO, Bundesbahnen Österreich, class 30.33. This engine dates from 1895 and is sporting two steam domes and joining-pipe.

● **ABOVE LEFT AND RIGHT**
These locomotives are Gölsdorf designs or derivatives active as late as the 1970s in what was then Yugoslavia.

● **BELOW RIGHT**
The elegance of Gölsdorf's express passenger locomotives is well known. Less well known is this class of three rack-and-pinion locomotives. Its life was spent mostly on trains loaded with iron ore from the Erzberg, the Iron Mountain at Eisenerz, in Austria's Styria province, to the point where trains were handed over to pure adhesion traction at Vordernberg.

GÖLSDORF'S DESIGN FOR THE RACK AND PINION ERZBERG LINE

Date	1912
Builder	Dr Karl Gölsdorf
Gauge	1,435 mm
Class	BBO 269; OBB 197
Type	BBO category F: Whyte notation 0-12-0T
Capacity adhesion: pinion:	2 cylinders 570 x 520 mm 2 cylinders 520 x 450 mm
Coupled wheel diameter	1,030 mm
Weight in working order	88 tonnes
Maximum service speed	Adhesion, 30 kph; rack, 15 kph

small parts than on a few large ones. Wide firegrates helped to ensure a plentiful supply of steam. Very large driving wheels on express locomotives, up to 7 ft in diameter, gave the opportunity for high speed. Up to 12 small coupled wheels offered the adhesion and formed part of the tractive-effort calculations for heavy hauling in the mountains.

● COMPOUNDING

Gölsdorf's designs are often regarded as unusual. One obvious feature was visible early on. Two domes were mounted on the boiler barrel, both to collect steam. They were linked by a large pipe through which steam from one passed to the regulator in the other. More important

was a hidden device. Gölsdorf was a great proponent of compounding, often using just two cylinders, one high- and the other low-pressure. Difficulty was often experienced in starting compounds from rest. Instead of the usual starting-valve requiring skilled operation, high-pressure steam was automatically admitted to the low-pressure cylinder when the valve gear was fully in fore or back gear.

His designs were generally adopted by the Hungarian railways, although in some cases they used simple machines based on Gölsdorf's compounds. After the empire's break-up, many of his numerous types of locomotive could be found in Czecho-slovakia, Hungary and Yugoslavia where, as in Austria, some can be seen today.

THE FRENCH INFLUENCE – STEAM

1900 to 1950 truly was the "Golden Age" for steam in France. Designers were pushing at the frontiers of knowledge of locomotive design and performance. The age also bred a class of driver who not only had to learn about the new technology but also had to adapt driving techniques to take best advantage of it. The French *mécanicien* was an outstanding footplate technician.

● COMPOUNDING

To a railway historian, compounding is immediately identified with France and two names: Alfred De Glehn and André Chapelon. De Glehn was born in Britain.

Compounding works like this. A basic steam locomotive creates steam under pressure in its boiler. The steam expands in cylinders to drive the pistons and is then exhausted to the atmosphere. But a lot of power is still left in the exhausting steam. If this steam is channelled to a larger, low-pressure cylinder, this power, otherwise wasted, can be used to save fuel and water.

As with much engineering, there are disadvantages. The machines are more complicated. They demand top-quality maintenance and skilled driving.

● DESIGNERS AND THEIR WORK

Other French engineers who made great contributions to worldwide development included Gaston Du Bousquet, a contemporary of De Glehn, and, towards the end of the steam era, Mark de Caso. Chapelon always acknowledged Du Bousquet's groundwork, which led to some of his successes.

As always, locomotive designers had to work under constraints. In France, where railways have been strictly controlled since 1857, there was a requirement before World War II for the shortest possible journey-times to be achieved without exceeding 75 mph. This meant that uphill speeds with heavy loads had to be high. The De Glehn compounds built up to 1914, economical and free running, were more than adequate in their day. As loads increased and they had to be worked harder, however, efficiency fell away, and little real work was obtained from a four-cylinder compound's low-pressure cylinders.

● **ABOVE LEFT**
This former Paris-Orleans railway's 231E Pacific heads the Flêche d'Or Calais-Paris express in the later days of steam, as shown by the standard rolling stock. In its heyday, it was a luxury train, but the locomotive, a Du Bousquet/Chapelon design for the Paris-Orleans railway, is truly from the golden age.

● **ABOVE RIGHT**
These 2-8-2 tanks simmering on shed recall scenes once familiar in a typical French roundhouse.

SNCF (ETAT) 241A

Date	1927
Builder	Compagnie de Fives-Lille, Fives, France
Client	Société Nationale des Chemins de Fer (SNCF)
Gauge	1,435 mm
Type	241 (Whyte notation, 4-8-2)
Driving wheels	1,790 mm
Capacity	2 cylinders 510 x 650 mm 2 cylinders 720 x 700 mm
Weight in working order	114.6 tonnes
Maximum service speed	120 kph

● **REDOUBLING POWER AND EFFICIENCY**
In the late 1920s, Chapelon began to stand out as a great railway engineer. He had entered railway service in 1919 but in 1924 joined a telephone company. His research abilities, recognized while he was a student, then led to him accepting an appointment in the Paris-Orleans railway's research department. There, Monsieur Paul Billet charged him to improve specific machines' exhaust systems. This was the platform on which his career really began.

Studies had confirmed that power was being wasted in getting steam from boiler to cylinder. The reasons included inadequate and indirect steam passages. Redesign under Chapelon's expert guidance led almost to redoubling the power and efficiency of rebuilt compound locomotives.

However, these improvements applied equally to simple expansion locomotives, and the techniques were eagerly adopted across the world. They strengthened the argument of those who considered that simple locomotives with high superheat were, overall, more economical. To Chapelon's credit, he was not a slavish devotee of compounding, and he caused similar significant improvements to classes of simple expansion locomotives.

● **LEFT**
231 G 558 drifts into the port of Le Havre, northern France, with a train of 1930s stock. Were it not for the overhead-line equipment, the scene might have been soon after 1935 when the SNCF rebuilt this 1922-constructed Batignolles Pacific. In fact, the picture was taken in 1992.

THE SWISS INFLUENCE – MOUNTAIN RAILWAYS

● BELOW
Switzerland's Vitznau-Rigi Bahn (VRB) owns two steam locomotives that regularly operate on vintage trains. H2/3 No. 17 built by SLM in 1925, is pictured at Rigi Kaltbad in 1986. The sturdy nature of Riggenbach's ladder rack is shown.

Mountain railways are usually powered either on the funicular principle (the weight of a descending car pulls another up) or on the "rack-and-pinion" principle of toothed rails.

● THE RIGGENBACH SYSTEM

The first successful rack-and-pinion system was developed not in Switzerland but in the USA. Development was proceeding in both countries, but neither of their two respective engineers knew of the other's work.

In Switzerland, Niklaus Riggenbach took out a patent on 12 August 1863 but did not develop it then. In 1869, he heard about the railway up 800 m (2,624 ft) high Mount Washington, in Berkshire County, USA, with its rack system designed by Sylvester Marsh. He visited that railway and on his return successfully developed his "ladder rack". Its first application was to a short quarry line at Ostermundigen, near Bern, in 1870. The locomotive that worked the

RIGI BAHN NO. 7

Date	1873
Builder	Swiss Locomotive and Machine Works (SLM), Winterthur
Client	Rigi Bahn
Gauge	1,435 mm
Rack system	Riggenbach
Capacity	2 cylinders 270 x 400 mm
Weight in working order	15.1 tonnes (as built)
Maximum speed	7.5 kph

● BELOW
The first SLM-built steam railway locomotive, Rigi Bahn No. 7, was taken from Luzern Transport Museum in 1995 and restored by SLM for the 125th anniversary of Switzerland's Vitznau-Rigi Bahn (VRB) in 1996, when it was pictured pushing a fully loaded vintage coach from Rigi Staffel to Rigi Kulm summit station.

line, "Gnom", has been preserved.

The success was soon followed by another when his system was applied to the Vitznau-Rigi Bahn (VRB), a standard-gauge line linking Vitznau, on Lake Lucerne, with the isolated 1,800 m (5,906 ft) high Rigi Mountain. This line

There is no difficulty in fitting pinion gear to electric vehicles. The 800 mm-gauge Wengernalp Bahn (WAB), which provides the intermediate stage of the journey from Interlaken to the 4,758 m (13,642 ft)-high Jungfrau Mountain in central Switzerland's Bernese Alps, uses the Riggenbach-Pauli rack to reach Kleine Scheidegg. These trains are pictured at Grindelwald Grund in 1989 before tackling their climb. Some stock dates from 1947.

● BELOW
The Locher rack's unique construction is shown in this picture, taken in 1991 from the traverser well at the Pilatus railway depot, Alpnachstad, at the foot of Mount Pilatus, near Luzern.

● LEFT
The opening of the Filisur-Bever section of Switzerland's Rhaetische Bahn in 1903 signalled the conquest of river, valley and mountain to reach a plateau at 1,800 m (6,000 ft). Steam was the original power but in 1921 the 61-tonne electric locomotives pictured here came on the scene.

or system celebrated its centenary in 1996 by operating one of the original vertical-boilered locomotives, No. 7, the first locomotive to be built by the Swiss Locomotive and Machine Works (SLM), of Winterthur, near Zürich.

● **THE RIGGENBACH-LOCHER SYSTEM**

It was Riggenbach who came up with the germ of an idea from the fitting of hooks that ran under the rails on the funicular from Territet to Glion near Montreux at the eastern end of Lake Geneva. The actual design is credited to Colonel Eduard Locher who became engineer to the Pilatus line in Unterwalden Canton, central Switzerland, with its 1:2 gradients. The design amounted to a pair of horizontally mounted guide pinion wheels with deep, plain flanges which run underneath the specially designed rack-rail. In effect, traction and guidance

were performed by the rack-rail and pinion wheels. The rails on which the carriage wheels run are merely for balance.

● **ADHESION LINES**

Numerous, mostly metre-gauge, lines wind their way into the mountains, in some cases tackling gradients of about 1:13 (7.7 per cent) without rack assistance. Two examples are popular with tourists. One is the Montreux-Oberland-Bernoise, which runs from Montreux through valley and alp to Zweisimmen. The other is the extensive spread of metre-gauge routes on the Rhaetische Bahn, which covers the Rhaetian Alps and Switzerland's largest canton, Graubünden (Grisons).

The Rhaetische Bahn offers spectacular scenery and benefits from remarkable engineering feats, which enable the line to reach the fertile flatlands of the Engadine, that is the 97 km (60 mile)

long valley of the River Inn, some 1,800 m (6,000 ft) above sea level. Much of the area is devoted to sports in winter when there is only one reliable means of access and egress – the railway. Spirals and tunnelling had to be used similar to that adopted by Swiss Federal Railways on two earlier lines. The section of the SFR over the St Gotthard Pass, with an inter-cantonal 15 km (9½ mile) long tunnel at 1,154 m (3,788 ft), completed in 1872–81, links Göschenen and Airolo and the Bern-Loetschberg-Simplon line between Frütigen and Brig with the Loetschberg Tunnel.

The 20 km (12½ mile) long Simplon Tunnel built in 1898–1905, between Brig and Domodossola, lies partly in Switzerland and partly in Italy. In its day it was the world's longest railway tunnel, famous for carrying the Simplon–Orient Express, with connections, from Calais, over the Alps at 705 m (2,313 ft), to Istanbul, Athens and Asia Minor.

SOUTHERN EUROPE – IBERIAN, ITALIAN AND GREEK PENINSULAS

The railways of Peninsular Europe – Iberia (Spain and Portugal), Italy and Greece – have long been concerned not only with national and international services but with intercontinental links between Europe and Africa, across the Western and Eastern Mediterranean Sea. Since 1869, proposals to build a rail-and-road fixed link between Spain and Morocco, across the Strait of Gibraltar, making Tangier the gateway to Africa, have been discussed. (Similarly, proposals to link Eurasia and North America by a rail tunnel across the Bering Strait, between Russia's Siberia and Alaska, have been discussed since 1905.)

● SPAIN

In Spain, locomotive design and construction was well developed and most steam locomotives not only entered the 20th century but continued to operate beyond the 1950s – apart from those most heavily used or taxed by mountainous terrain. Nevertheless, from the 1920s, many large and well-proportioned loco-motives were obtained for the standard gauge from various domestic and foreign builders, the 4-8-2 wheel arrangement

● LEFT
In Greece, the sun glints on a chunky USA-built 2-8-0 of a general type familiar across Europe immediately after World War II.

● BELOW
Locomotives 2-8-2 No. 7108 and doubled-domed Es Class No. 7721 head a special train at Diakofto, Greece in 1980.

being preferred. There were even Garratts, built in 1930 for passenger work.

Electrification began in 1911 on 21 km (13 miles) of steeply graded line on the Spanish Southern Railway between Gérgal and Santa Fé de Montdújar, in the Sierra Nevada of Almeria province, and was slowly extended to Almeria town, on the coast, 44 km (27 miles) in all. Overhead-line a.c. 5.5kv 3 phase was used. Some massive locomotives were supplied for these lines, including 12 2CC2s in 1928 from Babcock & Wilcox-Brown Boveri.

Steady progress came to a grinding halt with the Civil War (1936–9), but new steam and electrics began operating fairly quickly thereafter. Further, the process of building new lines to make a more effective network continued, forming a firm base for the sound rail system Spain has today.

● **FAR RIGHT**
Visible on FS Italia
2-8-0 No. 741 046
are the Crosti
preheater drum,
beneath the
smokebox door, and
the exhaust
replacing the
conventional
chimney.

F S   I T A L I A   C L A S S   7 4 1

Date	1911 (rebuilt 1955)
Builder	Breda
Client	F.S. Italia (rebuild)
Gauge	1,435 mm
Class	741 (rebuilt from 740)
Driving wheels	140 (Whyte notation 2-8-0)
Capacity	2 cylinders 540 x 700 mm
Driving wheel diameter	1,370 mm
Weight in working order	68.3 tonnes
Maximum service speed	65 kph

● **BELOW**
This Alco 1,500 hp
diesel-electric,
delivered in 1948, is
one of 12 in the van
of Portugal's diesel
revolution. It is
pictured at Tunes,
Algarve, in 1996.

● **PORTUGAL**

At the turn of the century, Portugal's steam-locomotive stock was varied and of good lineage. It included De Glehn compounds built in 1898-1903 and typical Henschel outline 4-6-0s, built at Kossel, Germany. Indeed, most European builders of note were represented. It was 1924 before Pacifics arrived from Henschel. Several series of 2-8-0s for freight came into service between 1912-24, built by Schwarzkopf of Berlin and North British of the United Kingdom. The first 4-8-0 arrived from Henschel in 1930. Tank locomotives ranging from 0-4-0T to 2-8-4T helped to cover remaining duties, including suburban passenger-train services.

The metre gauge had some fine machines, many of them big Mallet 2-4-6-0T tanks. The suburban services around Oporto, the country's second-largest city, were shared by 0-4-4-0Ts and 2-8-2Ts dating from 1931.

● **ITALY**

Italy's steam development was reasonably conventional for the period, subject to disruption in World Wars I and II. The unusual took the form of a novel and effective preheating system for feed water. Dr Ing Piero Crosti designed boilers in which combustion gases pass in the normal way through the main, simple boiler and then in reverse direction through a drum or drums. The feed water introduced into the drum(s) thereby captured more heat from flue gases and reduced scale on the firebox wall. This cut fuel costs but the locomotives' conventional appearance suffered. They had no obvious chimney and exhaust gases were disposed of by a series of pipes near the boiler's rear.

Italy is probably best known in the diesel world for its export of railcars. The names Fiat and Breda are on worksplates across the world. These companies began to develop in this field in the mid-1930s, as did Ganz of Hungary. The Fiat railcar started a vogue in 1935 for wheel spats over the bogie wheels, as in aircraft of the day. FS Italia Class Aln 56 was just one example.

● **GREECE**

In Greece, locomotives were haphazardly obtained from various builders and by purchase of secondhand engines from Germany, Austria and Italy. USA-built locomotives were brought to Greece in 1914 and, again, after damage done to the railways in World War II.

SCANDINAVIAN RAILWAYS

From 1900 the railways of the Scandinavian countries – Norway and Sweden forming the Scandinavian Peninsula and Denmark and Finland respectively to its south and east – were gradually extended, in some cases upgrading from metre to standard gauge, especially in Norway, and moved from steam to electrification, except for Finland whose 805-unit fleet included 766 steam locomotives (95 per cent) as late as 1958.

Apart from Denmark, whose insular component presented other physical difficulties, problems facing the railways were the same as in all cold countries. Frost heave disturbed the permanent way in the level wet areas. Heavy snow, with the ever-present risk of avalanche, was a burden in the mountains of Norway and northern Sweden.

● **DENMARK**

Denmark remains different from the other Scandinavian countries because of its islands, its population density and its closely sited communities. Here, speed and frequency of services became paramount together with the desire,

● **RIGHT AND OPPOSITE BOTTOM LEFT AND RIGHT** These pictures of steam in Finland capture the sense of an age long past and illustrate Russian design influence. The balloon stack and high stacking-rails on the tender of the wood-burner, No. 1163, can be seen.

● **BELOW RIGHT** The simple outlines of this 1-C-1 diesel, No. HP 15, of the Danish Hjörringer Privatbanen, the railway operating in north-east Jutland's Hjörring county, are appropriate for this workhorse. It was built in about 1935 by Frichs and is pictured at Randers, the east Jutland seaport.

gradually being achieved, to link the mainland Jutland Peninsula to all the islands and to the Scandinavian Peninsula at Malmo by bridge and tunnel rather than conveying trains on albeit very efficient train ferries.

In the 1930s, route length was 5,233 km (3,250 miles), of which only 2,512 km (1,560 miles), that is 48 per cent, was state-owned. The level terrain put no great demands on steam locomotives and it was the light diesel-

● **LEFT** This 2-6-0T No. 7 sports typical features of Danish steam locomotives, including the smokebox saddle and the national colours in the band around the chimney. Vintage coaches with clerestorey roofs and torpedo vents enhance the nostalgic scene at Helsingor, near Copenhagen, on the Danish island of Zeeland, in 1980.

railcar that became attractive for passenger work as an alternative to steam.

Electrification came late to Denmark, starting with the suburban system in the capital, Copenhagen, in 1934 employing a line voltage of 1,500 dc. The state system owned a good stock of steam power, mostly built in Germany, but, to develop high-speed services, three-car diesel-electric units called Lyntog ("Lightning") were introduced, which cut journey times dramatically.

● FINLAND

From 1809 to 1917, Finland was part of what was then the Russian Empire and so adopted the Russian 5 ft gauge for main lines and 2 ft 5½ in gauge for minor lines. The terrain was relatively level and, in the earlier part of the 20th century, schedules were not demanding, so that comparatively light, often woodburning, locomotives were sufficient. In the latter days of steam, a small class of coalfired Pacifics with good lines and particularly commodious cabs worked the heaviest passenger services. Local and semifast services around Helsinki, the capital, were served by the neat, most attractive Class N1, built by Hanomag in Germany.

● SWEDEN

The "Golden Age" of Sweden's railways may be said to be firmly linked to the enormous supplies of iron ore in the inhospitable mountains on the northern borders of Sweden and Norway. Near the town of Kiruna, at 509 m (1,670 ft) above sea level Sweden's highest, established mines work night and day. Some 16 million tons were produced in 1960, the bulk being moved by rail for export.

Electrification of the lines at 16,000 volt single phase ac 16⅔ Hz began in 1910

● LEFT
One of the later versions of the Lyntog ("Lightning") train pictured at Struen, western Jutland, Denmark, in 1980. The four-car unit is powered by a Maybach diesel engine with Voith (Heidenheim, Germany) hydraulic transmission. The power-car is Class MA, No. 467.

with the Frontier Railway between Lulea and Rikseransen. By 1914, the first of the massive electric locomotives 1+CC+1 for freight and B-B+B-B were being delivered by the builders ASEA/Siemens. Electrification continued apace until, by 1923, some 450 km (280 miles) had been completed. Even more powerful locomotives were provided, ten -D- for freight, producing 1,200 hp and capable of working in multiple, as well as two 2,400 hp B-B+B-B passenger machines.

For general electrification, SJ, the Swedish State Railway, decided on a single class of locomotive to work passenger and freight trains. 1-C-1,

whose gearing can easily be changed to operate either 500-ton passenger-trains at 65 mph or 900-ton freight trains at 45 mph. Electrification did not supplant steam rapidly. Main routes were electrified in the 1930s with considerable success, including the Stockholm–Gothenburg line.

In the early days, locomotives were bought from Britain. Later, designers adapted and developed them to suit local needs. This may be why inside-cylinders continued to be used long after most mainland countries had adopted the more convenient outside form. The practice continued until in 1930 the

● LEFT
This private Traffic-Ab Grangesberg-Oxelosunds Jarnvagar (TGOJ) operated noncondensing turbine locomotives. Class MT3 71 joins a parade at Stockholm in 1981.

Swedish Motala works built a massive inside-cylinder 4-6-0 for the private Kalmar Railways operating in the south-eastern province of Kalmar.

The private Traffic-Ab Grangesberg–Oxelosunds Jarnvagar (TGO), basically an iron-ore mining company, had three noncondensing turbine locomotives in its stock, which achieved a degree of successful operation.

The three-cylinder locomotive was rare in Sweden. In 1927, Nydkvist and Holm of Trollhättan, Sweden, built a class for the Bergslagernas Railway. This class's golden days on the expresses between Gothen-burg and Mellerud, on Lake Vanern, ended with electrification in 1939.

As late as 1955, 10 per cent of train miles were operated by steam and 63

SWEDISH STATE RAILWAY (SJ) 4-6-0

Date	1918
Builder	Nyakvist and Holm, Trollhättan, Sweden
Client	Swedish State Railway (SJ)
Gauge	1,435 mm
Class	B
Driving wheels	1,750 mm
Capacity	2 cylinders 590 x 620 mm
Weight in working order	69.2 tonnes (excluding tender)
Maximum service speed	90 kph

per cent by electricity. The remaining 27 per cent was diesel, but during the period under consideration, up to 1950, diesel traction had yet to become significant.

● NORWAY

Norway, politically linked with Sweden under the Swedish Crown between 1814–1905, is the most mountainous of Scandinavian countries. Its railway lines spread out from the capital, Oslo, like fingers, seeking natural routes to a scattered population.

Norway's railways developed late and in a scattered fashion. In the more benign terrain north of Oslo, steam traction was successful. British designs were the basis for further development.

Locomotives had been bought from the USA since 1879. When purchase of new locomotives became necessary during World War I, Baldwin Works of Philadelphia, USA, were asked to supply 2-8-0s, ostensibly to Norwegian design. Certainly, the boiler fittings and enclosed cab were Norwegian, but the rest was

● LEFT
The beauty of polished wood adorning bodywork is a striking feature of SJ Class Du 1-C-1 E109 as it waits with its train of period coaches at Malmø Central Station, in the southern Swedish seaport, in 1981.

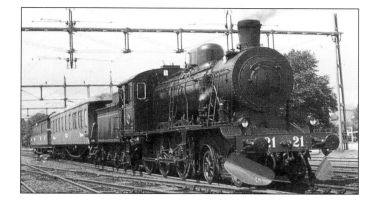

pure Baldwin. Two 0-10-0 yard-shunters came from the same source in 1916, as well as three 2-8-2 for freight. In 1919, a 2-6-2T arrived, which now had the stamp of real Norwegian design.

Later classes show German influence. An unusual design of 1935 was a 2-8-4, a wheel arrangement previously seen only in Austria for an express-locomotive. The class were four-cylinder compounds for the Dovre line, across the Dovrefjell, the 2,285 m (7,565 ft) high central Norwegian plateau, between Dombås and Trondheim (formerly Trondhjem), the seaport and the country's third largest city. The first engine was called The Dovre Giant. However, much smaller and ageing 2-6-0s and 4-6-0s worked main-line and branch services into the mid-1960s.

Electrification, especially in the far north, followed the Swedish pattern. Because there was plenty of water for hydroelectric power, electrification began in 1922 between Oslo and Drammen, the seaport on a branch of Oslo Fjord.

At the same time, work was in hand to link the main centres to Oslo. Trondheim was first in 1921, followed by Christiansand, the seaport on the Skagerrak in 1938 and Stavanger seaport in 1944.

Almost all the route mileage of about 4,300 km (2,700 miles) is state-owned, about a third of which is electrified at 15 kv single phase $16\frac{2}{3}$ Hz. Few narrow-gauge systems operated by state and private companies have survived.

Narvik, which exports iron ore, is the terminus for the railway that cuts across the peninsula from the Swedish port of Lulea on the Gulf of Bothnia. It is one of the world's two most northerly railway stations.

INDIAN RAILWAYS

Of all world railways influenced by Britain, those of India best reflected the British presence. Railway development proceeded further in India than in any other part of Asia and by the 1950s 64,400 km (40,000 miles) were operating, comprising broad-gauge trunk lines, connecting large centres of population, and a network of narrow-gauge lines.

In the 19th century, four gauges emerged on the Indian subcontinent: 5 ft 6 in; metre; 2 ft 6 in; and 2 ft. The variety of companies operating these gauges had ordered a diversity of designs, which, with the exception of some metre-gauge standards , were largely unco-ordinated. The Central Provinces (from 1950 Madhya Pradesh), for example, had three railway systems.

● ENGINEERING STANDARDS COMMITTEES

This led the British Engineering Standards Committee (BESA) to appoint

a subcommittee, composed of several leading British locomotive mechanical engineers, to prepare a set of standard designs for the subcontinent. In 1905, eight locomotive types were suggested to cover all broad-gauge requirements across India. The designs were classic British products: inside-cylinder 0-6-0s and 4-4-0s with common boilers, Atlantics, 4-6-0s and 2-8-0 heavy goods.

In 1924, the newly appointed Locomotive Standards Committee (LSC) was asked to make a new set of designs, in accordance with the need for more powerful locomotives. The committee presented eight basic types. The main ones were three Pacifics, XA, XB and XC, for branch-, medium- and heavy-passenger work; two Mikados, XD and XE, for medium and heavy goods respectively; and XT 0-4-2Ts for branch-line work.

Standard designs for metre and narrow gauge were also produced. Following the prefix X for the broad gauge came Y for metre gauge, Z for 2 ft 6 in gauge and Q for 2 ft gauge.

● AMERICAN INFLUENCE

A dramatic change occurred during World War II, Britain could not supply sufficient locomotives for India's increased traffic requirements and many new designs were ordered from North

● LEFT
A typically British 2-8-0 classified HSM from India's South Eastern Railway. These were once main-line heavy-freight haulers on the Bengal & Nagpur Railway. This last survivor is pictured on tripping duties in the Calcutta area.

America. These designs contrasted
dramatically with the British engines and
set a precedent for the remainder of
steam development in India, because of
suitability and popularity.

Three notable designs appeared on
the 5 ft 6 in gauge: the AWC, which was
an Indian version of Major Marsh's
famous S160 of World War II; the class
AWE, which was an Americanized
version of the XE 2-8-2; and a lighter
mixed-traffic Mikado 2-8-2 classified
AWD/CWD. These three classes totalled
909 locomotives, 809 (89 per cent) of
them being the light Mikado from
mixed-traffic work. All entered service
between 1943–9.

INDIAN XE CLASS 2-8-2

Date	1930
Builder	William Beardmore Dalmuir, Vulcan Foundry, Lancashire, England
Client	East Indian Railway
Gauge	5 ft 6 in
Driving wheels	5 ft 1½ in
Capacity	Cylinders 23 x 30 in
Total weight	200 tons

CHINESE LOCOMOTIVE TRADITIONS

Railway development came late in China, and an incredible locomotive-building programme and standardization of types occurred in the years following World War II.

● EARLY DEVELOPMENT WITH FOREIGN LOANS

As recently as 1930, China had fewer than 16,000 km (10,000 miles) of railway. During the early years of the 20th century, China's railways were developed by a number of organizations, but

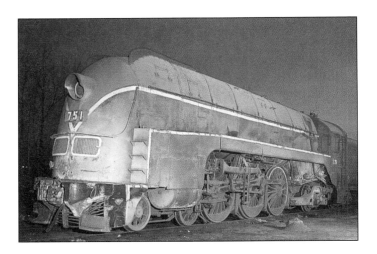

● **LEFT**
This streamlined Pacific classified SL7 is of a type built in Japan by Kawasaki and at the works of the South Manchurian Railway. These engines worked the high-speed Asia day-train between Dairen (the Japanese name for Dalian) and Mukden (modern Shenyang). The class was introduced in 1934.

invariably they turned to American imported locomotives of modest proportions. America's vigorous drive to promote the export of locomoties proved effective in China. The similarity in size between America and China, along with the varied terrain which the two countries

● **LEFT**
In the years following World War II, a number of Major Marsh's classic S160 2-8-0s were transferred to China in a programme to rebuild the country's railways.

USATC S160 2-8-0

Date	1943
Builders	American Locomotive Company (Alco); Baldwin Locomotive Company; Lima Locomotive Company
Client	United States Army Transportation Corps of Engineers (USATE)
Gauge	4 ft 8½ in
Driving wheels	4 ft 9 in
Capacity	2 cylinders 19 x 26 in
Total weight	125 tons

● RIGHT
A China Railway's JF Class 2-8-2 Mikado on heavy shunt duties at Sankong Bridge, Haerbain (Harbin), the capital of Heilongjiang Province, north-eastern China.

had in common, rendered the American locomotive relatively easy to sell and well suited to the task in hand.

● THE SOUTH MANCHURIAN RAILWAY

The most developed part of China was Manchuria, and the South Manchurian Railway, although Japanese owned, was almost entirely American in its equipment and operation as a result of America having provided most of Japan's railway. In 1931, Japan took over Manchuria and with it the North Manchurian Railway. Locomotives operated in Manchuria were locally made as well as imported from Japan.

The advancement of railway and industrial operation in Manchuria led to the South Manchurain Railway's introducing the streamlined "Asia" train in 1934, which operated a fast air-conditioned service between Dalian and Shenyang, or Makden as it was then known. Streamlined Pacific locomotives were built for this service both in Japan and South Manchuria.

● RAILWAYS UNDER CHAING KAI-SHEK

Under the nationalist government of Chiang Kai-shek, development of railways was proceeding in other parts of the country in the 1930s. In 1937, the outbreak of the Sino-Japanese War ended new building. As this war went on, 80 per cent of China's railways were either destroyed or fell into Japanese hands.

However, China's central government continued to build lines in the west, in areas not occupied by the Japanese.

● KMT: RAILWAYS UNDER COMMUNISTS

Japan's surrender in 1945 found China's railways in an appalling state. Aid came through the United Nations Relief and Rehabilitation Adminstration (UNRRA) scheme, which again brought huge numbers of American locomotives to Chinese soil. The ongoing Chinese Civil War caused further damage.

By the time of Mao's victory in 1949, the railways were in terrible disarray. Only half of the system was active. The following decades provided some stability under a powerful national identity and a centrally planned economy. The railways flowered under this regime. Herein lay the seeds of China's "Golden Age" of railways, expanding from the 1950s to the present day.

● RIGHT
A former Soviet Union FD Class 2-10-2 engine, introduced in 1931. About 1,250 of these engines were transferred to China in the 1950s. The Chinese railway's standard QJ Class was derived from them. The FDs were themselves derived from an American design.

● RIGHT
Little British design influence permeated China's railways. American, Russian and indigenous factors were all the more prevalent. An exception is this Mogul, believed to be designed in Glasgow, Scotland, but built in China.

SOUTH-EAST ASIAN RAILWAYS

This section covers the railways of Peninsular Malaysia, from 1957 the successor-state to the British-controlled Federation of Malaya; of Thailand proper and Peninsular Thailand, which joins Peninsular Malaysia at the Kra Isthmus; of Indonesia, the Philippines and Taiwan.

● PENINSULAR MALAYSIA

In 1909 the last link of the line between two island cities of the then-British colony called the Straits Settlements, Penang and Singapore, respectively at the north and south ends of Peninsular Malaysia, was opened. Termini were on the mainland, at ferry ports serving the islands. The engines used on this line were the Pacifics, which, although small by British and continental standards, were robust machines weighing about 76 tons. With a 4-6-4 wheel arrangement, the locomotives had large headlights and cowcatchers.

In 1938, three-cylinder Pacific express-passenger locomotives were introduced on the Malayan metre-gauge line between Singapore, Kuala Lumpur,

capital of Perak State, and Prai, the railway terminus and seaport on the mainland, opposite George Town on Penang Island. Part of this line ascended the 1,000 m (3,300 ft) high Taiping Pass near Ipoh, the commercial centre of the Kinta Valley tin-mining region of Perak. These heavy gradients called for a special type of locomotive. The three-cylinder 4-6-2 Pacifics had a relatively small boiler but at high pressure provided the latent energy needed for developing a high tractive power.

The Pacifics were used on long runs but there were branch lines on which a tender-engine was unsuitable. For these, a 4-6-4 two-cylinder tank-engine was

● ABOVE
The Insular Lumber Company on the Philippine island of Negros operated the world's last four-cylinder compound 0-6-6-0 Mallet. It was built by Baldwin in the 1920s.

● ABOVE
One of South-east Asia's most remarkable systems is the stone railway at Gunung Kataren in northern Sumatra, Indonesia. The line conveys stones from a riverbed to a crushing plant for use as track ballast. Built to 60 cm gauge, this veteran came from Orenstein & Koppel in 1920.

● LEFT
Three standard Japanese 3 ft 6 in gauge designs working in Taiwan. Left, a Taiwan Government Railway Class DT595 2-8-0 (Japanese National Railway 9600 Class); centre, a Class CT192 Mogul (JNR Class 8620); right, a Class DT673 Mikado (JNR Class D51) – 1,100 of these mixed-traffic 2-8-2s were built between 1936–45.

● RIGHT
A 4-6-0 built for metre-gauge Royal Siamese
State Railways in 1919 by North British of
Glasgow, Scotland.

4 - 6 - 0

Date	1919
Builder	North British Glasgow, Scotland
Client	Royal Siamese State Railways
Gauge	Metre
Driving wheels	4 ft
Capacity	Cylinders 14½ x 22 in

used. It was fitted with cowcatchers at
both ends so that it was suitable for
running in both directions. Like the
Pacifics, these 4-6-4Ts were fitted with
Caprotti valve gear.

● THAILAND
In Siam (Muang-Thai to Thais and
since 1949 Thailand), in the rice-
growing and jungle country, the metre-
gauge railway was laid with relatively

light rails on a soft road bed. Powerful
locomotives were needed, and in
1925 26 Pacific 2-8-2s were bought from
the USA. They were woodfired,
and routes were arranged so that the
engines would travel out and back to
their home station on one tenderful
of fuel. The round trips were
193–225 km (120–140 miles) long.
This arrangement meant frequent
engine changes *en route*.

● ABOVE
A battered, hybridized, American-built
Mikado, believed to have been constructed
by Alco in 1921, at work on the metals of
the Ma Ao Sugar Central railway on the
Philippine island of Negros. These
locomotives draw freshly cut sugar cane
from the fields to the mills.

● RIGHT
A Thai railways metre-gauge Pacific 4-6-2, No.
823, which, with the MacArthur 2-8-2s, was
one of Thailand's last steam locomotives.

AUSTRALASIAN RAILWAYS

New South Wales (NSW) entered the 20th century with a scheme to have main-line traffic handled by standard classes for passenger services, the P6 (later C32) Class 4-6-0; for goods traffic, the 1524 (later D50 Class) 2-8-0, of which 280 were built; and for suburban working the S636 (later C30) Class, numbering 145 units.

● NEW SOUTH WALES

In the mid-1920s, as traffic grew, 75 C36 Class units took over major passenger services. From 1929, 25 4-8-2 D57 Class units were introduced for heavyfreight. With extreme traffic during World War II, 30 new C38 Class Pacifics were built, becoming the foremost express-locomotive. With the need for new goods locomotives after the war, 42 4-8-4+4-8-4 Garratts were obtained to carry the brunt of the load prior to the arrival of diesels.

● TASMANIA

Tasmania also used Garratts – the 2 ft gauge K Class of 1910 being the first Garratt in the world. The 3 ft 6 in lines followed, with the L Class 2-6-2+2-6-2 for goods traffic and the M Class 4-4-2+2-4-4s for passenger traffic.

K167, an example of Australia's Victorian Railways K Class Consolidations introduced in 1922, pictured with a tour-train at Bandiana, near the New South Wales (NSW) border, in 1965.

● LEFT
After 1924, the P96 Class was reclassified as the C32 class. With regular floods in the Hunter Valley, in eastern NSW, this class was able to maintain traffic in conditions no diesel-electric could handle. The cover over the crosshead keeps out dust in the almost desert country in the far west of NSW.

● SOUTH AUSTRALIA

In South Australia, ten 4-6-2 passenger, ten 2-8-2 goods and ten 4-8-2 mixed-traffic locomotives entered service in 1926. These were of American design but built in England. On the narrow gauge, the T Class were the mainstay of the traffic, almost to the end of steam.

● WESTERN AUSTRALIA

Western Australia introduced 57 F Class 4-8-0s in 1902. These were accompanied by 65 E Class 4-6-2s for passenger services. Larger Pacifics entered service from 1924 onwards. Following World War II, the fleet was augmented by 60 light-line Beyer Peacock 4-8-2 W Class and 25 heavy 2-8-2 V Class from Robert Stephenson & Hawthorn.

● AUSTRALIAN NETWORK AND THE TCR

The development of Australia's railway network was complicated but striking. The gauge was not uniform (New South Wales was mostly the standard 4 ft 8½ in, South Australia mostly broad 5 ft 3 in gauge and all Queensland was narrow 3 ft

● LEFT
Imported from the North British Works, Glasgow, Scotland, in 1950, this Pmr726 Pacific is pictured outside the Midland workshops in 1968. Unsuccessful at speed, these locomotives did excellent goods-traffic work.

● **RIGHT**
The pride of Australia's NSW Railways, No. 3801, introduced in 1943, waiting to depart with an air-conditioned passenger-train in 1963.

● **RIGHT**
In 1899, South Australian Railways (SAR) started converting 30 R Class 4-6-0 locomotives to Rx Class by providing higher-pressure boilers. An additional 54 were newly built in 1909. This example, RX93, is pictured at the Mile End depot in 1965.

SAR RX 4-6-0	
Date	1909
Builder	SAR Islington/NBLC Walker (SA)
Client	NSWGR
Gauge	4 ft 8½ in
Wheels	5 ft 9 in
Capacity	Cylinders 18 x 24 in
Weight	201 tons

6 in gauge). Of the continent's some 45,000 km (28,000 miles) of railway, all but about 3 per cent, 1,290 km (800 miles), was state-owned by the 1950s. Of that length, 1,694 km (1,052 miles) were occupied by the Transcontinental (East-West) Railway completed in 1917. The TCR crosses South Australia and Western Australia, linking Port Augusta, at the head of the Spencer Gulf, and Perth with its port of Fremantle on the Indian Ocean. It crosses the Great Victoria Desert and the Nullarbar Plain, serves the goldfields of Kalgoorlie and the agricultural industry, and runs link lines to Port Pirie and to Alice Springs in the Northern Territory.

● **NEW ZEALAND**
New Zealand's main claim to fame is the development of the world's first true Pacific locomotive, 13 of which were supplied by Baldwin in 1901. These engines had a long life, the last being

● **BELOW**
Designed for traffic on light lines, this example of a J Class was one of 40 delivered to New Zealand at the start of World War II. A modified Ja Class supplied in 1946 is in front. The two locomotives are pictured at Fielding-Marton in 1972.

written off in 1957. The Pacific was further developed, eventually to the Ab class of 1915, of which 141 were built, and to a tank-engine, the Wab class. The Ab Class is claimed to be the first locomotive in the world to have been capable of 1 hp for each 100 lb of weight.

Tank engines played a major part on the lines of this small nation, the 4-6-4T W Class of 50 units being one of the more prolific. Garratts were also tried in 1928 but failed, due less to design faults than to the light drawgear on New Zealand rolling stock and the short crossing loops, making economical running almost impossible. Heavier conventional locomotives followed.

AFRICAN RAILWAYS

The years before the start of World War I were exciting and dynamic on South Africa's railways, many designs being produced. The 20th century brought a foretaste of the giants to come, powerful 2-8-2s, 4-8-0s and 4-8-2s being put into traffic with some racy Pacific designs.

● **UNION OF SOUTH AFRICA**

The immense distances and sparsely populated country called for strong locomotives, many of which had four-wheeled leading bogies to cope with cheaply laid track beds.

South African Railways (SAR) were formed in 1910 by the amalgamation of Africa's main railway companies. These were the Cape Government Railway (CGR), the Natal Government Railway (NGR) and the Central South African Railway (CSAR).

The country's first articulated locomotives were 2-6-6-0 compounds built by the American Locomotive Company (Alco). The type was introduced on to Natal's heavily graded, sharply curved routes.

Just as the giant Mallet conquered

● **BELOW**
Garratts on the Greytown Line in Natal, South Africa. One of SAR's pugnacious GMA Class 4-8-2+2-8-4 Garratts prepares to leave New Hanover, Natal, with full freight for Greytown. These powerful secondary Garratts, descended from the GM Class of 1938, climbed 1:40 gradients with only 60 lb weight.

● **ABOVE**
In contrast with the typical four- and six-coupled tanks of British industry, South Africa's engines were fully fledged mainliners to haul trains over undulating tracks to SAR connections often many miles from collieries. This North British-built 4-8-2T is one of a standard class exported from Glasgow, Scotland, to South Africa for industrial use.

● **LEFT**
SAR 3 ft 6 in-gauge 4-8-2s of the 1930s.

America, so the Garratt articulated conquered Africa. South Africa's railways were one of the largest users of Garratts from their introduction to the country in 1920. They quickly proved themselves superior to the Mallet on a network that ran through difficult terrain abounding in heavy gradients and curves with relatively lightly laid track.

The Garratt's boiler and firebox are free of axles and so can be built to whatever size is needed. A deep firebox allowed for ample generation of steam and full combustion of gases. By placing the engine's wheels and cylinders under a front water unit and with the rear coal units situated either side of the boiler, the engine's weight is spread over a wide area. With the front and rear units articulated from the boiler, a large, powerful locomotive can be built capable of moving heavy loads over curved gradients and

SAR "BIG BILL" 4-8-2

Date	1925
Builder	Baldwin, American Locomotive Company (USA), Breda (Milan, Italy), North British (Glasgow, Scotland)
Client	South African Railways (SAR)
Gauge	3 ft 6 in
Wheels	5 ft
Capacity	Cylinders 24 x 28 in
Weight	173 tons

● **FAR LEFT**
The SAR Class 15CA, 4-8-2 "Big Bills" were the first large American engines imported to South Africa. They had a profound influence on locomotive development. This Italian-built example is seen leaving Panpoort, Transvaal.

● **NAMIBIA (FORMERLY SOUTH WEST AFRICA)**
In the years following World War II, 100 2-8-4 Berkshires were put into operation for branch-line work, particularly over the 45 lb rail lines in South West Africa (Namibia since independence in 1990). They had cylindrical bogie tenders for long-range operation in waterless areas. The type displaced the ageing Class 7 and Class 8 4-8-0s of half a century earlier.

lightly laid lines. SAR used more than 400 Garratts, mostly British-built.

The 1920s also saw the introduction of large 4-8-2s and Pacifics of pure American construction. These set the precepts for the giants that followed, such as the 15F Class and 23 Class 4-8-2s. These formed the mainstay of steam motive power from the 1930s until the end of steam operations.

● **ABOVE RIGHT**
The Mallett was little used in South Africa but this 2-6-6-2, four-cylinder compound Class MH was one of five built by North British in 1915. At their introduction, they were the largest locomotives in the world on 3 ft 6 in gauge track.

● **RIGHT**
A South African Railways (SAR) Class 23 4-8-2 heads northwards from Bloemfontein, capital of Orange Free State. These American-inspired engines of 3 ft 6 in gauge were constructed in the late 1930s by both British and German builders and totalled 136 examples.

● **LEFT**
A former
Tanganyika Railway
ML Class 2-8-2,
complete with Geisl
ejector and air
brakes – and one of
Tanganyika
Railway's last
designs.

● **OPPOSITE
TOP LEFT**
The plate from a
locomotive built for
Rhodesian Railways
by Beyer Peacock of
Manchester,
England.

● **ZIMBABWE**

Railways were essential to the rich
development potential of landlocked
Zimbabwe (Southern Rhodesia until
1964, Rhodesia 1964–78). Routes
extended to the Indian Ocean ports, eastwards to Beira in Mozambique, southwards through South Africa to Durban in
Natal. A third route was opened up northwards, across the Victoria Falls at Hwange
(until 1982 Wankie) and on through the
copper belt. This route reached the
Atlantic Ocean ports via the Bengeula
Railway in Angola. By 1920, when
Rhodesia Railways (RR) was formed, a
unified 3 ft 6 in gauge was in operation.

Motive power was not dissimilar from
that of South Africa, with 4-8-0s and 4-
8-2 Mountains. As the national wealth of
this vast region was developed, however,
the demand for heavier trains became

huge and articulated locomotives vital.
After a Kitson-Mayer phase, the Garratt
phase was introduced to standardize the
system. Almost half the locomotives built
for Rhodesian Railways were British-built
Garratts, embracing all duties from
branch-line work, through heavy freights
to expresses with the racy 15th Class
4-6-4+4-6-4s. These handled mixed-
traffic duties and reached speeds of
70 mph with passenger-trains.

● **EAST AFRICA**

In East Africa, the British-built Kenyan
and Ugandan lines and the German-built

● **LEFT**
Following the lead
by the USA the wide
firebox appeared
early on Britain's
locomotive exports,
especially those
bound for African
countries. A typical
example was the
Rhodesian Railways
12A Class 4-8-2. The
example shown is
No. 190, built in
1926 by North
British, Glasgow,
Scotland.

● **RIGHT**
A former Rhodesian
Railways 16th Class
Garratt 2-8-2+2-8-2,
built by Beyer
Peacock of
Manchester,
England, in 1929,
working at the
Transvaal
Navigation Colliery,
South Africa.

A typical African plantation-train during the early 20th century at Lugazi, Uganda. The unidentified engine, with ornate spark-arresting chimney, is of European origin.

railways of neighbouring Tanzania (formerly Tanganyika) were metre gauge. The Ugandan railway in its early years used early Indian metre-gauge types, notably E Class 0-4-2s and the celebrated F Class 0-6-0s. Invariably, motive power

CLASS 54 2-8-2+2-8-2 GARRATT

Date	1944
Builder	Beyer Peacock, Manchester, England
Client	Kenya & Ugandan Railway (via UK Ministry of Supply)
Gauge	Metre
Wheels	3 ft 9½ in
Capacity	4 cylinders 19 x 24 in
Weight	185 tons

blossomed and embraced a Mallet stage and some Garratts, although the 4-8-0 was adopted as a general standard, many examples being to Indian BESA designs.

By the time the Kenya & Ugandan Railway (KUR) was formed in 1926, extremely powerful 2-8-2s worked the line linking the Kenyan Indian Ocean port of Mombasa and the Kenyan capital at Nairobi. The network also had a wide variety of Garratts, although these remained in a minority compared with the conventional locomotives, many of which were used on lighter sections of this vast area of Africa.

● ANGOLA

The 1,347 km (837 mile) long Angola Railway (Benguela Railway) was built by the Portuguese to link their then west and east coast possessions in southern Africa, respectively Angola and Mozambique. From the west, it runs from the Atlantic Ocean ports of Lobito and Benguela, to the Democratic Republic of Congo (formerly Zaire),

linking to Port Francqui (Ilebo), the Copper Belt of Zambia (formerly Northern Rhodesia) and Zimbabwe, and on to the Indian Ocean ports of Sofala (formerly Beira) and Maputo (Lourenço Marques until 1975) in Mozambique, and Durban, then on to the Cape.

It achieved world renown for the eucalyptus-burning Garratts, which worked over one of the sections climbing the steep coastal escarpment inland from the Atlantic. These red-liveried mammoths shot columns of fire into the sky at night and were regarded by some as one of the railway sights of the world.

NORTHERN AFRICAN RAILWAYS

Railway development in Africa was essential to open up the industrial potential of the continent's interior and provide vital lifelines for the movement of materials. Africa has benefited vastly from her railways but their piecemeal, often parochial, building defied the obvious ideal of a Pan-African system. Had the railways been built with this vision, Africa would be an infinitely more prosperous continent than she is today.

● ALGERIA

Algeria's railways were built and engineered by the French from the mid-19th century. A large network of lines of various types emerged, including through links with neighbouring Tunisia and Morocco. The standard gauge, fed by metre-gauge lines, saw many 0-6-0s. Moguls and standard De Glehn compounds of types commonly seen in Europe.

In the 1920s, 2-10-0s appeared for hauling heavy mineral trains. Famous types working in Algeria included some Prussian G8s and three-cylinder G12s. Most celebrated, however, were the Algerian Garratts. These, built in France in 1932, were the most powerful express-passenger-locomotives ever to

● LEFT
Nameplates from former Gold Coast Railway's steam locomotives commemorating British governors, tribes and slaving forts.

EGYPTIAN STATE RAILWAYS (ESR) ATLANTIC 4-4-2

Date	1906
Builder	North British, Glasgow, Scotland
Client	Egyptian State Railways (ESR)
Gauge	4 ft 8½ in
Driving wheels	6 ft 3 in
Capacity	Cylinders 17 x 26 in

● BELOW
These British-styled Atlantics were delivered to ESR in 1906 from the North British Works in Glasgow, Scotland, for operation on Egypt's standard-gauge network.

operate outside the USA.

By the 1950s, a rail network of more than 4,800 km (3,000 miles) penetrated all parts of Algeria. Two lines stretched into the Sahara to link with motor routes stretching to then French West Africa.

● TUNISIA

Tunisia had both standard- and metre-gauge lines, although no standard-gauge locomotives were delivered into the country after 1928. During World War II, American S160 2-8-0-s, British Hunslet Austerity 0-6-0STs and some British Great Western Dean goods were all introduced for military operations.

● MOROCCO

Morocco's railways were also French-dominated, the country having become a French protectorate in 1912. Through-services were run between Marrakech in

● LEFT
Two 0-6-0 well-tanks made by Orenstein & Koppel at the Nsuta Manganese System in Ghana, West Africa. The engines' Works Nos. 10609/10 respectively were exported to Ghana (until 1957 the British colony called Gold Coast) in 1923.

established. Sudan has a great will to operate a good, viable railway system. Additions to the network were being made as late as 1960.

Pacifics and Mikados, many with light axle loadings, were a mainstay of Sudan's motive power. Sudan also operated 4-6-4+4-6-4 Garratts pulling 1,600 ton trains between Atbara, Khartoum and Wad Medani. In contrast, English-looking 0-6-0Ts handled shunting and local tripping work. The last of these was not built until 1951, notwithstanding Sudan received diesel-shunters as early as 1936.

The pièce de résistance of conventional Sudanese motive power came with the 42 500 Class 4-8-2s delivered by North British, of Glasgow, Scotland, in 1954.

the west and Tunisia in the east, a distance of 2,400 km (1,491 miles).

● EGYPT

The Egyptian State Railway (ESR) is the oldest in Africa and blossomed following British occupation of the Nile Valley in 1882. The railway was built and run by the British. Though the ESR operated a vast diversity of types, British operating methods and many British designs were in evidence. Much of Egypt's express-passenger work was handled by the Atlantic 4-4-2s, backed by either 0-6-0s or Moguls for mixed-traffic work.

World War II's North African Campaign demanded movement of really heavy freight trains. Many British Stanier 8F 2-8-0s were sent, of which 60 were adopted by the ESR after the war.

Egypt's rich locomotive tradition ended with a class of oil-burning, French-built Pacifics delivered as late as 1955.

● SUDAN

Egypt's standard-gauge lines contrast with the 3 ft 6 in gauge network of neighbouring Sudan where railway building proper began around the turn of the century. One of the earliest systems ran from the Nile Valley to the Red Sea then southwards through the capital, Khartoum. Although much of this early railway building had a military purpose, the beginnings of a national railway were

● ABOVE
The spinning driving wheels of a Class 500 4-8-2 of Sudan Railway.

● BELOW
A mixed train on Sudan State Railways headed by a standard oilburning Mikado 2-8-2 built by North British, of Glasgow, Scotland.

● WEST AFRICA

In West Africa, Britain, France and Germany all introduced railways to their colonial possessions.

SOUTH AMERICAN RAILWAYS

South America's railways are of great diversity, reflecting the vast geographical contrasts of a continent that ranges from the tropical rain forests of the Amazon, to the passes of the Andes standing at 4,266 m (14,000 ft), through to the verdant beef-rearing flatlands of the Argentine pampas.

● ARGENTINA

Argentina had by far the greatest density of railways, with over 100 different types of locomotive operating over five different gauges. The British-owned railways of Argentina constituted the largest commercial enterprise ever to operate outside an investing nation. With many of the country's railway systems operated by Britain, Argentina was a huge recipient of British products. British-built steam locomotives fired on Welsh coal gave Argentina one of the world's most successful economies, exporting vast tonnages of meat, grain and fruit.

● URUGUAY

The railways of neighbouring Uruguay were also British-owned. Beyer Peacock of Manchester, England, was a principal

builder over many years. Manchester was connected with the vast Fray Bentos meat corporation based on Fray Bentos town in Uruguay.

● BRAZIL

The vastness of Brazil, with its network of 5 ft 3 in and metre-gauge lines and a huge diversity of secondary routes, plantation and industrial railways, also ensured an incredibly rich locomotive heritage. American-built locomotives predominated with British classics on the metre-gauge Leopoldina system.

● PARAGUAY

Neighbouring Paraguay's standard-gauge main-line railway linked the capital and chief port, Asunción, with Encarnación

● LEFT
Mixed freight to Fray Bentos, in Uruguay. The Uruguayan Railway's last-surviving T Class 2-8-0 named Ing Pedro Magnou is heading a train bound for the meat-canning port on the Uruguay River. This 2-8-0 has a distinctive Scottish Highland Railway aura about it.

● OPPOSITE
A 5 ft 6 in gauge survivor of the Chilean Railway's 38 Class on pilot duties at San Bernardo works, outside Santiago in Chile. It is probably the last survivor from Roger's of New Jersey, USA, having come from those works in 1896.

386 km (240 miles) away on the Argentine border. This railway was also British-owned and operated. The main motive power for much of the present century has been provided by woodburning Edwardian Moguls, exported from the North British Works in Glasgow, Scotland.

● BOLIVIA AND CHILE

The railways of Bolivia, South America's other landlocked nation, connected Chile, over the Andes to the west, with Brazil and Argentina, over the humid lowlands to the east. The country's locomotive heritage was diverse, with a rich mixture of European, American and British schools of design.

● TRANS-ANDEAN
RAILWAY (TAR)

The Trans-Andean Railway (TAR) completed in 1910 links Valparaiso, Chile's greatest seaport, with Buenos Aires, the Argentine capital, crossing the Andes and desolate Patagonia at the Uspallata Pass between Mendoza in Argentina and Santiago in Chile. The near 3 km (2 mile) long Trans-Andean RR tunnel crosses at the pass's highest point, at 3,986 m (13,082 ft), near the Western Hemisphere's highest peak, 6,958 m (22,835 ft) high Mount Aconcagua. The link cut the 11-day

● OPPOSITE MIDDLE
A woodburning Edwardian Mogul from North British, of Glasgow, Scotland, heads along the standard-gauge main line from the Paraguayan capital Asunción to Encarnación on the Argentine border. This railway is the last all-steam worked international main line in the world.

● RIGHT
A 2-8-2, No. 183, of Guatemalan Railways, at Gualán in 1971.

BUENOS AIRES & GREAT SOUTHERN 11B CLASS 2-8-0

Date	1914
Builder	Beyer Peacock, North British and Vulcan Foundry
Client	Buenos Aires & Great Southern Railway (BAGS)
Gauge	5 ft 6 in
Driving wheels	4 ft 7½ in
Capacity	Cylinders 19 x 26 in
Total weight	105 tons

journey by boat via the Magellan Strait to 40 hours overland. The line climbs hills so steep that part of it uses cog-wheel apparatus.

● COLOMBIA, ECUADOR
AND PERU

Colombia, Ecuador and Chile drew their locomotive traditions mainly from American builders. Peru had a mixture of American and British designs.

There were no locomotive-building traditions in South America or Africa. Both these continents were entirely dependent on the building traditions developed in Britain, Europe and America.

● LEFT
The last surviving Kitson-Meyer 0-6-6-0 – known as "The Dodo of the Atacama" – at work in Chile's Atacama Desert. These locomotives once brought gold and nitrates to Pacific coast ports.

INDEX

CONVERSION CHART

To convert:	Multiply by:
Inches to centimetres	2.54
Centimetres to inches	0.3937
Millimetres to inches	0.03937
Feet to metres	0.3048
Metres to feet	3.281
Miles to kilometres	1.609
Kilometres to miles	0.6214
Tons to tonnes	1.016
Tonnes to tons	0.9842

Complete
English as a
Second Language
for **Cambridge IGCSE®**
Teacher Resource Pack

Chris Akhurst
Lucy Bowley
Dean Roberts

d excelle

XFOR

Great Clarendon Street, Oxford, OX2 6DP, United Kingdom

Oxford University Press is a department of the University of Oxford. It furthers the University's objective of excellence in research, scholarship, and education by publishing worldwide. Oxford is a registered trade mark of Oxford University Press in the UK and in certain other countries

British Library Cataloguing in Publication Data
Data available

978-0-19-839289-7

16

Paper used in the production of this book is a natural, recyclable product made from wood grown in sustainable forests. The manufacturing process conforms to the environmental regulations of the country of origin.

Printed in Great Britain by CPI Group (UK) Ltd., Croydon CR0 4YY

Acknowledgements

®IGCSE is the registered trademark of Cambridge International Examinations. The questions, example answers, marks awarded and/or comments that appear in this book and CD were written by the authors. In examination, the way marks would be awarded to questions like these may be different.

The publishers would like to thank the following for permissions to use their photographs:

Cover image: City art paint/Shuttertock

p8: Jacopin/BSIP/Science Photo Library; **p15:** Pressmaster/Shutterstock; **p23:** iStock; **p27:** Jackin/Fotolia; **p32:** Ayzek/Shutterstock; **p48:** iStock; **p96:** Rainer Lesniewski/Shutterstock

Artwork by Six Red Marbles and OUP

The author and publisher are grateful for permission to reprint extracts from the following copyright material:

Anna De Filippo: adapted from 'Old games in Italy' by Anna De Filippo, from http://www.lifeinitaly.com, editor Francesca Bezzone, reprinted by permission.

FilmMakers.com: excerpts adapted from 'The Film Director Part I' from FilmMakers.com, copyright © FilmMakers.com, reprinted by permission, all rights reserved.

Any third party use of this material, outside of this publication, is prohibited. Interested parties should apply to the copyright holders indicated in each case.

Although we have made every effort to trace and contact all copyright holders before publication this has not been possible in all cases. If notified, the publisher will rectify any errors or omissions at the earliest opportunity.

Links to third party websites are provided by Oxford in good faith and for information only. Oxford disclaims any responsibility for the materials contained in any third party website referenced in this work.

Contents

Notes for the teacher

The Student Book is based on teaching 'segments' and each of these segments is based on a theme which is drawn from the broader chapter topic. For example, in Chapter 1, there is a segment on inventors and inventions. We have left it to you to decide how long to spend on each of the segments, and indeed, when and where to use them in terms of a wider teaching scheme or unit of work. There is no need to use the segments in a particular order as each one is interchangeable in the context of the whole chapter.

You might even like to use a series of segments from different chapters to form a teaching scheme, perhaps focusing on skills you wish to introduce or particular examination questions you wish to practice. We have tried to offer a highly flexible book therefore, to be used in the English as a Second Language classroom by the teacher irrespective of any particular curricular programme. Indeed, the Student Book is not set out as a planned programme of study, but rather, a resource to be used in the classroom to generate interesting and lively activities, which allow students to practise the key skills, cover appropriate content, and prepare in a focused manner for achieving success in their final examinations.

The Student Book comprises several key sections:

- Thinking out loud. These are to be used before teaching begins and to 'set the scene' for the learning to follow. We recommend that you encourage time for thought and we strongly advise that these sections are not formally assessed.

- Building your vocabulary. In each chapter, there are several of these. Our aim is to help students build up an IGCSE-relevant vocabulary. We use a variety of ways to check vocabulary - e.g. sentence completion, filling in crossword puzzles, word matching; and each of these is intended to be informal and operate as formative assessment. There is a glossary of all of the words in these sections on the support CD.

- Check your understanding. These are also intended as formative and informal means of assessment; for example, we encourage students to work through these in pairs. In our view, it would be counter-productive to use these sections as summative assessment. It is permissible therefore for students to approach these collaboratively and to make mistakes. In these sections, we are building up confidence and improving the key receptive skill of understanding what has been read or heard.

- Literary connections. Where relevant, some chapters have a segment which utilises literary texts. While we appreciate that this is not used or assessed in the examination, we feel that it provides some light relief from reading exam-style articles, and literature is very useful in generating discussion and of course, in encouraging further reading.

- The Big Issue. Each chapter has a segment where we focus on an issue, relating to the topic. In some cases, these are intended to be controversial. It is important that students engage with contemporary issues, and that they are able to speak about them, listen to others presenting their views on them and read further to explore some issues. Students who possess global awareness are likely to perform better in the series of examinations.

- Key skills and language focus. These sections highlight language-learning skills which we feel are essential for success in the examinations. The range of language learning we have included is not intended to be complete or exhaustive, but areas which we find that students of IGCSE need further practice in.

- Reflection. At the end of each chapter, there is a collaborative activity which invites students to work in groups and generate a 'product' which can be displayed or presented to others. This is intended as a fun activity, with the emphasis on peer-based, and therefore student-centred, learning.

- Study tips. There are four of these in each chapter - i.e. an opportunity for teachers to focus on summative assessment for each of the four key skills of reading, writing, speaking and listening. In these sections the focus is the final examination, and once we have described and commented upon the nature of the key skill, we provide some sample student responses to exemplify this. We provide opportunities for students to discuss these examination skills, practise them, and extend them. These sections function therefore as semi-formal assessment.

- My progress. At the very end of the chapters, we invite students to do some self-evaluation and to select a key study skill that they feel they need to improve on. There is a an Action Plan template for students to work from. All of the skills featured in the 'My progress' charts are key examination skills (so we have provided 48 of these in the whole book); improvement here should improve a student's success in the examinations.

Reading, writing, speaking and listening

- Reading activities. We have tried to provide a range of international and interesting articles. Our main purpose when selecting reading material was to mirror the style of articles that appear in the Reading and Writing examination. We feel that providing reading material of a very different nature would distract from students' success. However, there are shorter and longer pieces, and there are pieces which function as information texts, pieces which lend themselves to note making, and pieces which can easily be summarised.

- Writing activities. We have tried to cover a wide range of authentic situations, and we have incorporated modern electronic formats. You will see students asked to write emails, to complete blogs, to add comments to webpages, etc. However, we have also ensured that traditional modes of writing are covered, particularly those which feature in the Reading and Writing examination paper.

- Speaking activities. We feel that there is sufficient practice for students preparing for the Speaking Test in the Study tips sections and elsewhere in this Teacher Pack. The focus in the Student Book is therefore on a wider range of platforms where speaking is prevalent. We have incorporated speaking skills into collaborative activities (e.g. role-playing, acting out scenes from a play, themed discussions among peers) but we have also included opportunities for students to speak at length; giving talks, making oral presentations, etc. We hope that this approach will build up confidence and will enable students to feel more comfortable when the formal assessment of speaking occurs in the Speaking Test. It is the authors' belief that speaking should be an integral and natural part of any language-learning programme.

- Listening activities. Each chapter has a number of scenarios, some of which mirror the scenarios used in the Listening examination, others are more playful and entertaining. All of the audio recordings have a 'Check your understanding' section and we encourage you to use these as informal and formative assessment. There is additional listening material accompanying the Teacher Pack which can be used solely for examination practice and summative assessment. When using the audio material, you can manage the playback as you prefer and to suit your students' needs. You might like to pause the recording several times for instance, so that each Check your understanding question can be attempted carefully. Or you may choose to play the whole recording (perhaps for more able students).

The Teacher Pack is designed to clarify the content and rationale for each of the teaching segments in every chapter.

The first part of the book tabulates each segment. We have included the following:

syllabus objectives - the main assessment objectives drawn from the syllabus

introducing the session - in many cases, Thinking out Loud will function as an ice-breaker, but we have also provided alternative ideas here

ensuring a skills balance - where one or more of the main skills has not been covered in depth, we have provided some ideas for activities here for the less prominent skill(s)

differentiated activities - the segment will have covered a range of activities which can be modified to suit the learning stage or skills level of students. However, here we offer additional activities for stronger students.

learner outcomes - a clear statement of the expected learning at the end of the segment.

workbook content - the page references in the workbook where additional and related activities can be located.

links to web sites - while we appreciate that these are somewhat temporal in nature, we have provided a current list of appropriate web pages that teachers and students might find useful.

The second part of the book focuses on examination practice and we re-visit each of the Study tips sections in the Student Book Our purpose here is to:

- describe how each part of each examination works
- differentiate between the Core and the Extended examination papers
- offer expert guidance on how best to prepare for and practice each examination question and exercise
- provide answers to the Study tips questions, and full commentaries on the sample student responses
- (for two of the Study tips in the chapters) supply model answers and a commentary which describes in detail strong and competent performance, focusing on how to improve performance and secure high achievement
- provide additional exam-style material that the students will have not had access to in the Student Book
- create a resource for the teacher which can be used to generate formal exam questions (or a full paper) which can serve as a mock or practice examination
- position the key study skills and associated tasks precisely on the examination papers. Please refer to the exam question mapping table on page vii.

Scope and sequence

The scope and sequence chart which follows summarises the teaching segments in each chapter, and maps these with the additional Workbook activities, and planning for assessment.

Please note:

1. In the Workbook: follow up activities column:
   R = reading comprehension W = writing, followed by the register/purpose L = listening
   S = speaking, followed by context
   LF = language focus, followed by specific area
   BV = building vocabulary

2. In the Exam Practice: unseen exam-style material, we list questions, exercises, speaking tasks and audio recordings which are not in the Student Book - i.e. new material for the teacher, unseen by the students, and intended to be used for objective and probably summative assessment purposes. By utilising this material, a full mock exam can be generated, for example.

The Workbook, and additional worksheets in the Teacher Pack provide further resources for students and teachers.

In the Workbook, students can engage with further related content, practice key language skills, complete hands-on activities and build up more vocabulary. The Workbook stays with the students so can be used as a self-access resource, or can be used in conjunction with the Student Book as teacher-led activities. There are some sections where it might be sensible to direct the learning, but others where individual and solo work is preferable. It should be possible to set extension and homework using the workbook, but it should also function as an aide-memoire to students. We recommend that teachers plan ahead and decide early which parts of the Workbook will be teacher-led and which parts self-access.

On the Teacher Pack CD, we have supplied additional worksheets. These are intended as enhancement and extension activities, and of course, will not have been seen by the students. This is a resource therefore which is ideal for homework, or for work in the classroom Some of the worksheets encourage working in pairs or groups, while other worksheets suit individual work Each worksheet relates directly to an activity in the Student Book, and the scope and sequence chart indicates this connection.

 What's on the CD?

English as a Second Language for Cambridge IGCSE® Teacher Resource Pack includes a CD with additional material:

- Audio recordings and transcripts from the Student Book CD
- Audio recordings and transcripts from the Workbook CD
- Additional exam practice audio and transcripts
- Interactive activities from the Student Book CD to revise and practise vocabulary and language skills
- Links to online resources
- Worksheets to use in class
- A grammar reference from the Student Book CD
- A glossary of key vocabulary from the Student Book CD

Exam question mapping

	Reading	Writing	Listening	Speaking
1. Science and Technology	**Exercise 4**	Exercise 6	**Question 7**	Developing vocabulary
2. Food and Fitness	**Exercise 2**	Summaries	Recognising attitudes	**Prompt 3**
3. Communities	**Exercise 3 Core**	Exercise 6	Covering question types	The warm up phase
4. Animals and us	Note taking	Extended writing	**Question 8**	**Prompt 4**
5. Working life	**Exercise 3 Extended**	Exercise 6	1, 2 word Gap filling	**Development and Fluency**
6. Travel and Transport	**Exercise 1**	Completing a form	Question 5 scenario	**Prompt 2**
7. Leisure and Entertainment	Recognising numbers	**Exercise 5 Extended**	Question 8b	Prompts 1 and 2
8. Hobbies and interests	**Exercise 5 Core**	Topic sentences	**Question 6**	Paraphrasing and examples
9. Customs and cultures	Recognising balance	Proper sentences	**Accurate inference**	**Influencing discussion**
10. The past and the future	redundant material	Own words in summary	**Question 5**	**Prompt 5**
11. Communication	Getting the gist	**Exercise 7**	**Q1 to Q4**	Structures
12. Global issues	Diagrams and charts	Note taking	Recogising attitudes	Using open questions
	NOTE - items in bold are sections which have full Model Answers and Examiner commentaries			

Coverage by Exam question / exercise

Reading		Listening
Ex 1 ✓		Q1-4 ✓
Ex2 ✓		Q5 ✓
Ex 3 ✓		Q6 ✓
Ex 3 ✓		Q7 ✓
Ex 4 ✓		Q8 ✓
Ex 5 ✓		
Ex 5 ✓		
Ex 6 ✓		
Ex 7 ✓		
Speaking ✓		
Note that there are several full Speaking Exam		
Topic Cards included for exam practice:		
Ch 2		
Ch 4		
Ch 5		
Ch 9		

EXAM PRACTICE	STUDENT WORKBOOK	STUDENT BOOK ACTIVITIES
Unseen exam material	Follow-up activities	Tasks and activities
Exercise 4 - the science of sleep	Comparatives and superlatives - LF	Debating the importance of technology
Question 7 - balloons into space	Edwin Hubble - R, BV	Writing a letter to request something
	A great scientist - W blog	Delivering a persuasive speech
	James Bond - R	Discussing opposing points of view
	Ali and the patent office - L	Carrying out a survey
	Thomas Edison - R	Collaborating on a group presentation
	Carnivals and festivals - W advert	Writing an advertisement
Topic card - Keeping fit	Let's cook - W blog	Writing a recipe
	Restaurant review - R, BV	Writing a blog entry
Exercise 2 - Old games in Italy	Being a top chef - W diary	Writing a persuasive letter
	Signature dish - W recipe	Making a one minute speech
	Food standards officer - L	Researching a biography
	Life of a farmer - S interview	
	Personal trainer - L	
	Joseph Pilates - R, BV	
	Rafa Nadal tennis foundation - R, BV	
	Angus Macfadyen - L	
	Zumba - R, BV, S group presentation	
	Honey bees - R	Making a PowerPoint presentation
	Bee keeper - LF	Researching books about communities
Exercise 3 - student exchange visit	Life in Maasai Kraal - R, BV, W notes	Writing a story based on a community
Exercise 6 - living in a different community	A Maasai villager - L	Debating the usefulness of jobs
	The Eco Truly Park, Peru - R, BV, W email	Designing your own community
	A good community? - S discussion	
	Advice for pet owners - R, BV	Collating the results of a survey
	Animal metaphors - LF	Role playing being given a pet
	Puppy training - R, BV,	Planning for writing
Question 8b - how rats can help humans	A guide dog owner - L	Establishing point of view
Topic card - animals and us	Giant pandas- R, BV	Conveying an anecdote
	World Wildlife Fund - W email	Writing a fable
	Aesops' fables - W fable	
	Sponsor an animal - S discussion	
	Summer jobs - R, BV, W diary	Writing a resignation letter
Exercise 3 - application for a job in Finance	Rose, a social worker - L	Considering case studies
	Aid worker - R, BV, LF reported speech	Re-creating a counselling session
Topic card - university and work	Site of an earthquake - W formal report	Writing a job application
	Puppetry - R, BV	Creating a scene for a play
	Choosing a career - S pair discussion	Preparing a display stand about careers
	A cyclist promoting a new route - L	Sending an email to a friend
Exercise 1 - route 66 by motorbike	Scott of the Antarctic - R, BV	Writing a travel guide
Prompts 1 and 2 - technology and transport	A modern-day Arctic explorer - L	Role playing the first ever long-haul flight
	A deep sea diver - L	Sending a post card home
Unseen exam material	Shipwrecks - W application letter	Writing a diary entry
	Amelia Earhart - R, BV, W blog	Making a promotional pitch
	A holiday complex - S group presentation	

	TEACHING SEGMENTS	WORKSHEETS IN TEACHER PACK CD	PLANNING FOR ASSESSMENT
	Content and context	Extension and enhancemant work	Study Tips. Full model answers*
7 Leisure and entertainment	Music	7.1 Writing a song lyric	
	Crime fiction and drama	7.2 Using persuasive vocabulary	Speaking - the early part of the discussion
	Going out	7.3 Short-answer questions	*Writing - using linking words in a summary
	Organising large scale events	7.4 More practice with adverbs	Reading - numbers and figures
	Apps	7.5 Short-answer questions	*Listening - making sound inferences
	Gaming	7.6 Writing a summary	
8 Hobbies and interests	Hobbies	8.1 Hobbies and pastimes vocabulary	
	Collecting	8.2 A talk on autograph collecting	Speaking - paraphrasing, and examples
	Listening to music	8.3 Your desert island discs	*Listening - recognising opinions, attitudes
	Learn to play an instrument	8.4 Building your vocabulary	Writing - paragraphing techniques
	Literary connections	8.5 Questionnaire for a reading survey	*Writing - using notes for a summary
	Getting away from it all	8.6 To fish or not to fish	
9 Customs and cultures	Greetings all!	9.1 Building your vocabulary	
	Birth customs	9.2 Giving a presentation	Writing - accurate sentences
	Coming of age	9.3 Language focus - trick or treat?	*Speaking - influencing the discussion
	Marriage customs in Europe	9.4 Composing a speech	Reading - a balanced argument
	Chinese wedding traditions	9.5 Building your vocabulary	*Listening - understanding implication
	Death customs	9.6 Understanding what is implied	
10 The past and the future	Progress	10.1 Your top 10 life-hanging things	
	Life in England 100 years ago	10.2 Note making	*Speaking - prompt 5
	Family life in ancient Egypt	10.3 Using synonyms	Reading - redundant material
	The Terracotta Army	10.4 Building your vocabulary	Writing - using own words in a summary
	The future	10.5 Writing about life in 2050	*Listening - grammatical accuracy
	A Golden Age	10.6 Building your vocabulary	
	Literary connections	10.7 Reflection - speaking activity	
11 Communication	Why do we need to communicate?	11.1 Building your synonym vocabulary	
	How do we communicate?	11.2 A guessing game	*Writing - a formal essay
	Communication in the past	11.3 Using persuasive language	Speaking - accurate structures
	Communication in children	11.4 Writing a communication passport	*Listening - follow on information
	Communication without speaking	11.5 Writing a letter	Reading - getting the gist of the theme
	Alternative ways to communicate	11.6 E-mailing about the Deaflympics	
	Literary connections	11.7 Communiacting with your idol	
12 Global issues	Global trade and advertising	12.1 Writing an email	
	Early traders	12.2 Language focus on conjuncts	Speaking - open questions
	Global population	12.3 Speaking about global population	Listening - recognising opinions, attitudes
	Carbon neutral	12.4 Writing a newspaper report	Reading - diagrams and charts
	Global hunger	12.5 Using vocabulary in a recipe	Writing - improving notes
	Global energy and recycling	12.6 Delivering a news report	
	Cyber bullying	12.7 Using global issues vocabulary	
	Each of these segments is based on a theme which is drawn from the broader chapter topic. The teacher should decide how long to spend on each of the segments, and when and where to use them in terms of a wider teaching scheme or unit of work.	These are intended as enhancement and extension activities and will not have been seen by the students. This is a resource therefore which is ideal for homework, or for work in the classroom. Some of the worksheets encourage working in pairs or groups, while other worksheets suit individual work.	*Model answers and a commentary which describes in detail strong and competent performance, focusing on how to improve performance and secure high achievement

EXAM PRACTICE	STUDENT WORKBOOK	STUDENT BOOK ACTIVITIES
Unseen exam material	Follow-up activities	Tasks and activities
	Lego - R, BV	Interviewing an actor
	A.R. Rathman - L	Compiling a job description
Exercise 5 - film directors	Sea of Tears - R, LF adverbs	Writing an outline for a detective novel
	Richard Whitehead - R, W persuasive	Sharing first impression writing
Question 8b	Plays within plays - R, W review	Creating a story board for a film
	The History Boys - L	Adapting a book for the stage
	Producing a film - S discussion	
	Collecting postcards - R, BV, W describing	Miming a hobby
	Renate's collection - L	Role playing meeting a famous person
Question 6 - people talking about hobbies	The effect of music - R, BV	Selecting only the required information
Exercise 2 - Old games in Italy	What music means to me - S pair discussion	Carrying out a survey about reading habits
Exercise 4 - the science of sleep	Playing the drums - R, BV, W advert	Responding to a poem
	Leisure week - S individual presentation	Constructing a short teaching scheme
	Childcare in different cultures - L	Writing for a web page
	Putting a baby to bed! - R	Delivering a short speech
Topic card - traditions	Greek marriage customs - R, BV	Being interviewed on the radio
	A greek wedding - W email	Writing an article for a wedding magazine
Question 6 - various views about marriage	Caring for the dead - R, BV	Designing a multi-media project
	What is culture today? - S individual talk	Organising a campaign
	Life in the past - R, BV, W - letter	Chatting to a guest from the past
"The future is the past, re-appearing"	Daily life in Egypt - R, BV	Writing a letter to a friend from the past
	Life in the future - L	Researching a historical event
	Antiques in 2115 - L	Debating the best period ever to have lived
Question 5 - a futuristic home	My future - S individual talk	Interviewing someone from the future
		Re-create and act out a scene from the past
	Every picture tells a story - W blog	Designing an application form
Exercise 7 - a one way trip to Mars	A chimpanzee handler - L	Sending a message in the past
	Formal and informal language - LF	Giving a talk about graffitti
Questions 1 to 4	A company director - L	Contrasting two accounts with the same theme
	Esperanto - R, BV	Asking open questions
	Two friends chatting - L	Compiling a secret code
	Creating a new word - S individual talk	
Note - there is no model answers section or unseen exam exam material in the final chapter	Ethical brands - R, BV	Writing a review of a product
	Jennifer and free-cycle - L	Writing a travelogue
	Centre for 21st century energy - R	Attending a public meeting
	Providing concise responses - LF	Writing a protest song
	Recycled clothing - R	Role playing a modern job
	Earth hour - S individual talk	Delivering a talk about water preservation
		Planning a major festival

Questions, exercises, speaking tasks and audio recordings which are not in the Student Book - i.e. new material for the teacher, unseen by the students, and intended to be used for objective and probably summative assessment purposes. By utilising this material, a full mock exam can be generated, for example.	R = reading comprehension W = writing, followed by the register/purpose L = listening S = speaking, followed by context LF = language focus, followed by specific area BV = building vocabulary

1 Science and technology

Student book content coverage

Segment 1	Pages 1–3 Teenage brains
Syllabus objectives	**R1** Identify and retrieve facts **S1** Communicate clearly and effectively
Broader skills development	• Discuss as a class. • Talk about modern technology. • Select appropriate notes.
Introducing the session	"Thinking out loud" (page 2): Allow five minutes to let students compare how people's brains might be different. This could be a whole-class activity.
Ensuring a skills balance	Suggested writing activity: Ask students to tweet what they think the advantages of a teenage brain are (giving up to three).
Differentiated activities	Stronger students can, in pairs, talk about the last "brainy" thing they did. Ask them to explain to each other what prompted them to do it.
Teaching and learning methodologies	**1** Discuss in groups and feed back to class. **2** Learn to select and use appropriate notes.
Building your vocabulary	Ask students, in pairs, to think of words to do with the brain and thought. They can use the reading on page 2 of the student book to help them.
Check your understanding	Page 3: The teenage brain – ask students to complete this in pairs in no more than five minutes.
Learner outcomes	By the end of this segment, learners should be able to: • participate in a discussion • understand how to make notes about an article.
Workbook	Page 1: Science facts Pages 1–2: Check your understanding
Worksheet	1.1: Teenage brains vocabulary

Segment 2	Pages 4–6 Science museums
Syllabus objectives	**W2** Convey information and express opinions effectively **L1** Identify and retrieve facts and details
Broader skills development	• Write a letter to make a request. • Give a persuasive talk. • Think about and use linking words.

Introducing the session	"Thinking out loud" (page 4): Ask students, in pairs, to tell each other when and where they learn about science. Spend up to five minutes on this.
Ensuring a skills balance	Suggested reading activity: Ask students to look at the Deutsches Museum website and imagine they could spend a morning there. Which three exhibits would they go and see?
Differentiated activities	Stronger students can imagine that they have been to the Deutsches Museum. Ask them to write a letter to a friend telling them why they were there and who they were with, and to describe one exhibit they particularly enjoyed seeing.
Teaching and learning methodologies	1 Write a formal letter to request something. 2 Use a variety of linking words.
Building your vocabulary	Page 4: The Deutsches Museum. Ask students to work alone when answering the questions. Give them up to five minutes to complete the questions.
Check your understanding	Page 4: José – listen and give the answers in pairs. Page 5: The Deutsches Museum – ask students to complete this individually.
Learner outcomes	By the end of this session, learners should be able to: • use persuasive language • discuss answers with a partner.
Workbook	Page 2: Language focus – comparatives and superlatives Page 2: Discussion point – "Who is the greatest scientist?" Ask students to discuss this in small groups for up to five minutes. They can then report back to the whole class. Who does the class believe is the greatest scientist?
Worksheet	1.2: Science museum speaking activity

Segment 3	**Pages 7–9 Inventors and inventions**
Syllabus objectives	**R2** Understand and select relevant information **L2** Understand and select relevant information
Broader skills development	• Learn about an inventor. • Practise how to answer multiple-choice questions. • Talk about inventions.
Introducing the session	Ask students to read and complete the sentences in the "Building your vocabulary" box. They can work alone and take up to five minutes to complete it.
Ensuring a skills balance	Suggested writing activity: Tell students that they think Q sounds really interesting and is someone they would like to work with. Ask them to write Q a letter of application explaining why they would be an asset to his team of inventors.
Differentiated activities	Stronger students can imagine that the listening with Ruth Amos was an interview for a newspaper. They can now write up the newspaper report. Give them a time limit by telling them that the newspaper has to go to press in 20 minutes' time.
Teaching and learning methodologies	1 Work in pairs to make a decision. 2 Learn to answer multiple-choice questions.

Building your vocabulary	Page 7: James Dyson – ask students to complete this in small groups.
Check your understanding	Page 8: James Dyson – give students up to five minutes to complete this individually. Page 8: Ruth Amos – ask students to complete this in pairs.
Learner outcomes	By the end of this session, learners should be able to: • find solutions using discussion • know how to answer multiple-choice questions.
Workbook	Page 3: Building your vocabulary crossword Page 4: Edwin Hubble reading Page 4: Check your vocabulary on Edwin Hubble. Page 5: Write a blog imagining that you are a famous scientist.
Worksheet	1.3: Reading and answering short-answer questions

Segment 4	Pages 10–15 Literary connections
Syllabus objectives	**R3** Recognize and understand opinions, ideas, and attitudes **L3** Recognize and understand opinions, ideas, and attitudes and the connections between related ideas
Broader skills development	• Develop the range of vocabulary students use. • Have a discussion. • Practise comparatives.
Introducing the session	In pairs, students can look at the "Developing a discussion" box and tell each other what they think of when they hear the words "science fiction". Spend about five minutes talking about this.
Ensuring a skills balance	Suggested speaking activity: In small groups, ask students to tell each other about a science fiction novel they have read and would recommend to the group. If they have not read one, ask them to give their opinion of *The Coming of the Terraphiles* extract.
Differentiated activities	Stronger students can pick one of the science fiction passages in the student book and continue it, adding another paragraph. Ask them to use relevant vocabulary where they can.
Teaching and learning methodologies	**1** Use comparatives. **2** Develop a discussion.
Building your vocabulary	Page 11: Doctor Who – ask students to complete this in small groups.
Check your understanding	Page 12: Doctor Who – ask students to spend no more than five minutes completing this in pairs.
Learner outcomes	By the end of this session, learners should be able to: • use and include comparatives in their language • discuss science fiction using task-specific vocabulary.
Workbook	Page 6: Speaking – what would you put in your perfect car? Ask students to share their ideas in small groups. Page 6: Reading – James Bond Page 6: Check your understanding – James Bond Page 7: Check your understanding – a patent
Worksheet	1.4: More on comparatives

Segment 5	Pages 16–19 Medical science and sight
Syllabus objectives	**W4** Demonstrate knowledge and understanding of a range of appropriate vocabulary **L4** Understand what is implied but not actually stated
Broader skills development	• Complete a class survey. • React to a blind teenager. • Write an article.
Introducing the session	Ensure that students understand what is meant by echolocation. Ask them for examples of echolocation in real life – who or what uses it, and why. Spend up to five minutes on this activity, which may be done as a whole class.
Ensuring a skills balance	Suggested speaking activity: Once they have watched the video on Ben Underwood, ask students, in pairs, to talk for one minute about him – how did they feel when watching him?
Ensuring a skills balance	Stronger students can, individually, think of up to six jobs which use science and technology in them. Ask them to choose which job they would like to do for a day and blog their ideas; remind them to use task-specific vocabulary during this activity.
Differentiated activities	1 Use language to attract the reader's attention. 2 Make inferences.
Teaching and learning methodologies	Ask students, in small groups, to think of ten words they could use when talking about science and technology. Look back at the reading on page 16 if they need ideas.
Building your vocabulary	Page 18: Ben Underwood. Ask students 'how would life be different if you were unable to see, or had very limited vision? Think of about ten adjectives you could use to describe your life.' Ask students to complete this in pairs. Pages 18–19: Louise. Ask students 'why do you think it's important to get your eyes checked regularly? Think of five reasons why it is a good thing to do.' Ask students to complete this individually.
Check your understanding	Page 18: Watch Ben before answering the questions on page 18. Pages 18-19: Listen to the interview with Louise before answering the questions on page 19.
Learner outcomes	By the end of this session, learners should be able to: • develop three prompts in a writing task • make inferences from information they have been given.
Worksheet	1.5: Reading and answering short-answer questions

Segment 6	Pages 20–22 Advances in modern technology
Syllabus objectives	**W1** Communicate clearly, accurately, and effectively **S4** Demonstrate knowledge of a range of appropriate vocabulary
Broader skills development	• Broaden active vocabulary. • Talk about the positive and negative aspects of flying. • Discuss scientific advances in groups.
Introducing the session	In pairs, allow students up to five minutes to complete the "Building your vocabulary" box on page 20.

Ensuring a skills balance	Suggested listening activity:
	Ask students, in small groups, to make a list of the benefits and drawbacks of flying in the past (different groups can take different decades). They can then report back to the whole class. Each listening group must ask the reporting group one question about what they have said.
Differentiated activities	Stronger students can imagine that they are sitting in a cockpit watching the pilot. Ask them to say how they feel and what they can see. Do they feel differently as the plane comes in to land?
Teaching and learning methodologies	**1** Think about positives and negatives in language.
	2 Work in a group discussion.
Building your vocabulary	Page 20: Pilot vocabulary – ask students to complete this exercise individually.
Check your understanding	Page 20: Pilot. Listen to Ajay talking about his life as a pilot before answering the questions on page 20.
Learner outcomes	By the end of this session, learners should be able to:
	● talk about flying, using task-specific vocabulary
	● use language to express advantages and disadvantages.
Workbook	Page 7: Reading – Thomas Edison
	Page 8: Check your understanding – Thomas Edison
	Page 8: Discussion point. Divide the class up and give them a role. Allow students up to five minutes to prepare their ideas before the discussion, which should take no longer than ten minutes.
Worksheet	1.6: Writing a formal letter
Further practice	**On completion of the chapter, ask students to complete questions 1–20 of the science and technology interactive activities.**

Links

If you choose only one link to use with your students, try this:

- www.bbc.co.uk/podcasts/series/discovery

  Listen and find out more about the latest discoveries.

You might also try:

- www.newscientist.co.uk – science stories from around the world.
- www.scientificamerican.com – more science stories from around the world.
- www.t3.com – every new gadget you can think all, all explained and reviewed.
- www.howitworksdaily.com – explanations of how things work.
- www.flipside.theiet.og – all the latest technology news.

If your students enjoyed reading about the Deutsches Museum, they may want to try researching another science museum. Many capital cities have one. Another interesting piece of research could result from looking up the Evoluon in the Netherlands, which used to be a science museum. The students could find out what it is now and where the science museum once based there has moved to.

Study tips: reading

Selecting appropriate notes (see page 3 of the student book)

This section focuses on developing note-making skills, and while there is a slight difference here between the number of notes generated in the core and extended paper, the skills are the same. Students need to develop the confidence to skim, scan, and select relevant parts of the text, while also having the confidence to ignore redundant areas.

Evaluating the sample student responses

- **Student 1** has better note-taking skill: the notes are succinct, accurate, and convey only what is needed.

- **Student 2** has worse note-taking skill: note 1 uses too many words, note 2 is inaccurate, and note 3 provides irrelevant information.

Exam focus: reading and writing

A student taking both of the Reading and Writing papers, at core and extended level, will need to complete a note-taking exercise (Exercise 4) based on a text of approximately 500 words. The difference between the two papers is:

- for the core paper, students are required to use their notes to write a summary

- at extended level, additional notes are required and students write a summary based on a new passage.

> ## Assessment objectives
>
> **R1** Identify and retrieve facts and details
>
> **R2** Understand and select relevant information
>
> **R3** Recognize and understand ideas, opinions, and attitudes and the connections between related ideas

Notes are always asked for, using subheadings; usually two to three areas are provided. The following example shows how it works in a typical examination paper. Quite often, students will be prompted to make appropriate notes for a talk they will be giving later.

Read the article below and complete the notes that follow it.

The Biology of Sleep

Every living creature restores their bodies naturally, often every 24 hours, during the time we call sleep. For most creatures, this period of rest will take place at night.

There are several reasons why our bodies need sleep each night. Our brains allow our bodies to detoxify every 24 hours, removing the waste which has built up during that time. Researchers believe this removal of toxins is one of the main reasons why we need sleep.

Sleep also allows us to go over what has gone on during our waking hours, and to allow the memory to process what has happened, storing events and conversations which we will later recall, and generally sort out what has happened to us. Increased levels of sleep thus help not only the memory, but the learning process in general.

It seems the capacity of the brain may be finite and so it needs to process past events and filter out the ones which do not need to be recalled at a later date. It is when we are asleep that this filtering out of past events and memories takes place and so we wake fresher than when we fell asleep.

Sleep also allows our bodies to repair properly, mending body tissues and allowing the body to develop and grow during this period of rest. Hormones which promote growth are released during sleep, which is perhaps a reason why children sleep more than adults.

Sleep also allows us to conserve energy, resting before an early rise on the lookout for food in the morning.

However, the removal of toxins is the main reason for sleep. As the brain rests during sleep mode, the cells in the brain retract and fluid takes up the space and fills in the mini gaps so there is no air gap. As the brain wakes and the cells expand, the fluid is expelled and takes with it the toxins which have built up in it. The whole system of using fluid for the removal of toxins in the brain is called the glymphatic system, similar to the lymphatic system in the rest of the body. The glymphatic system flows through pipes to wash away toxins in the brain, a bit like the pipes which carry away waste water in your house or flat.

The molecules which are telling our brains we are tired have been cleared after we have had enough sleep; we feel more tired during the day as these molecules build up again. The system of waste removal using fluid around the cells in the brain works primarily when we are asleep; the removal of toxins when we are awake, and when the brain cells are fully expanded, is minimal. It is possible that this waste removal is up to ten times more efficient during sleeping, rather than waking hours.

Much is already known about the brain and the restorative effect periods of sleep can have, not only on the brain but also on the whole body. However, there is still much to learn and much research is being done to teach us more about the benefits of sleep. We need to learn more about the relationship between physical sleep and the chemical processes which occur in the brain during sleep. Getting enough sleep may allow the brain cells to repair, and perhaps restore some brain-cell function.

Lack of sleep and the resulting failure to eliminate the toxic molecules in the brain may be a contributory factor in diseases like Parkinson's and dementia. The pathway of the glymphatic system may slow or stop working as we get older. We need to learn more about the relationship between sleep, the molecules in the brain, and how they function before and after sleep. Once we understand this relationship, we may also understand the causes of these diseases and will therefore be one step closer to finding their cures as well.

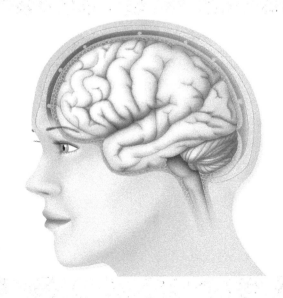

Make notes on the following:

1 Some of the roles that sleep plays:

- ....
- ....
- ....

2 Specific details about the removal of toxins from the brain:

- ....
- ....
- ....

3 Implications of the research:

- ....
- ....
- ....

[9 marks available at extended level; at core level two more challenging notes would be omitted = 7 marks available]

Answers

1 Roles that sleep plays:
- The removal of toxins which have built up
- allows memory to work better
- allows the brain to filter out past events
- Repairs the body
- Conserve energy

2 Specific details about the removal of toxins:
- as brain cells retract, fluid takes up the space
- toxins build up during the day and are taken away at night
- toxins are removed in the glymphatic system
- is up to ten times more efficient during sleep

3 Implications of research
- we need to learn more about physical sleep and the chemical processes which occur in the brain during sleep
- sleep may help to repair brain cells and restore brain-cell function
- lack of sleep and therefore the non-removal of toxins may cause some disorders (allow specific disorders)
- we may even find a cure for some of these disorders

Model answers and how to improve performance

The key skill here is to be succinct in conveying the notes needed. Students can either simply lift or copy the appropriate segment from the original text, or use their own words to shorten or clarify it. A highly competent note-taker would bear in mind that notes are created as an aide memoire and are usually used for another purpose – e.g. writing an article after making notes from a speech; or creating a speech based on notes from researching articles.

Here are some model answers for the notes above, one for each subheading, followed by some examples that are not accurate and are therefore problematic.

1   Roles that sleep plays:
    to remove waste... to remove toxins...

> **Our expert says:** Students need to ensure that they do not offer notes that are too short and lack key details. The response "to remove waste" is too general and would therefore not be accepted. Some sense of the removal of toxins is needed – at the very least some idea that a waste-removal system is operating. Since notes cannot usually be reduced to a single word, encourage your students to use short phrases.

2   Specific details about the removal of toxins:
    toxins are waste removed from the body; waste removal is up to ten times more efficient

> **Our expert says:** Since specific details are asked for, a general response such as "toxins are waste removed from the body" would not be credited. The specific nature of the system is that it is the fluid which carries out the toxins in it. You may encounter spelling issues here, but examiners expect accurate spelling of the word glymphatic since it is in the text for students to see. Slight slips would be tolerated but not inaccurate or phonetic spelling.

3   Implications of the research:
    we can understand disorders like Parkinson's... we can understand how the brain works...

> **Our expert says:** A potential trap here is that students put things into their notes that aren't in the text. The examiners will be scrutinizing any such additional information. For example, a response declaring that "some brain diseases can be cured... brain disease can be treated..." etc. would not be credited as this is not what the text says and is an incorrect inference from the details given. Notes need to be accurate versions of the original if alternative wording is used.

Study tips: listening

Answering multiple-choice questions (see page 9 of the student book)

The Listening examination papers at core and extended level feature questions that assess listening skill by offering three potential answers for each question, known as multiple-choice questions or MCQs. Students need to understand the nature of this type of question and the methodology used by setters of such questions.

The student book introduces students to MCQs and offers some informal practice. The exam focus section below offers further guidance in this important skill of processing multiple-choice answers.

Track 1.2 (student book)

Q1: The correct answer here is c) Cambridge when he was a little older at 19. This is a direct question and all the potential answers are simple factual statements, two of which are wrong.

Q2: The correct answer here is a) he has an active mind. Students need to do a little inferring here as b) seems initially to be reasonable. However, "the job keeps him active" suggests physical activity and there is no evidence of this. Answer c) offers a different meaning, i.e. that Q is a key part of the team. Again, we have no evidence to support this: quite the opposite.

Q3: The correct answer here is c) English. It is a straightforward question but students might be expecting answer a) engineering, as Q is clearly a scientific person. He has also conducted research so answer b) research is not unreasonable. These distractors are common elements of MCQs, so give students plenty of practice in recognizing them.

Q4: This is included to test the student's ability to infer something, a useful skill that features in several places in both examination papers (core and extended levels). The only way to answer this question is to work out Q's attitude from what he says and how he says it. The correct answer is b) that he is just another agent and wastes Q's time. It is a relatively easy inference to make, but students need to be able to explain why answers a) and c) are wrong and present evidence to support their explanation.

Exam focus: listening

Question 7 of the Listening paper is the point in the examination where multiple-choice questions are introduced. The exercise is the same for core- and extended-level candidates, with eight MCQs being asked, each with three possible options: A, B, or C, so Question 7 carries eight marks at both levels.

A common format used is the interview, which relates to an aspect of a person's career, job, or hobby. The information provided is therefore about the person and the work that he or she does. Question 7 is testing higher-level skills, and MCQs can be used effectively for this purpose. Candidates are not going to be asked to locate simple information in this exercise.

Assessment objectives

L3 Recognize and understand ideas, opinions, and attitudes and the connections between related ideas

L4 Understand what is implied but not actually stated, e.g. gist, relationships between speakers, speaker's purpose/intention, speaker's feelings, situation, or place

Here's a full examination exercise to illustrate how Question 7 works.

🎧 **Track 1.1 Space balloons**

First, play the interview about space balloons to the students. The transcript is on the CD.

For each question below, students must choose the correct answer (i.e. the answer that fits the best) from the three offered.

1 How long did it take the designers to solve the initial problems with the balloon?

   A Two years

   B Three years

   C Two to three years

2 What was used during the initial work of taking photographs?

   A A foam bed

   B A GPS tracker

   C A weather balloon

3 How did they make the idea known to other people?

   A They contacted people in Canada

   B They sent emails to interested people

   C They showed it working on the Internet

4 How was the kit made?

   A With expensive but simple parts

   B With simple but reliable parts

   C With simple but difficult-to-find parts

5 What did special events feature?

   A A university where 20 balloons were used

   B A 10-metre balloon

   C Help for a team of sociologists

6 What is the most important part for making everything work as it should?

   A The parachute

   B The black box

   C The tracking device

7 What does a typical flight do?

   A Takes 38 days to enter near space

   B Covers 38 kilometres before ending

   C Travels 38 kilometres in 20 hours

8 What is the most important part for returning any items to Earth?

   A The parachute

   B The GPS tracker

   C The software

Answers

1.A; 2.C; 3.C; 4.B; 5.B; 6.B; 7.B; 8.A

Model answers and how to improve performance

The main skill being tested is the ability to select the most appropriate answer from the three offered. A feature of MCQs is that for each question (the stem) the three answers look very similar to elements of the content. Students should be made aware, however, of the subtle differences between the source text and the answers.

It is not possible to provide model answers for MCQs, so instead you could explore with students why each of the incorrect answers is wrong. For example:

3 How did they make the idea known to other people?

   A They contacted people in Canada

       – *wrong, because it was the other way round*

   B They sent emails to interested people

       – *wrong, because there is no evidence for this*

   C They showed it working on the Internet

       – *correct*

8 What is the most important part for returning any items to Earth?

   A parachute

       – *correct; "Without this there's no point to the whole journey."*

   B GPS tracker

       – *wrong, because it is not the most important part, just a part*

   C software

       – *wrong, because this is used to locate the items after they have landed.*

Note how candidates need to use inference and gist understanding to answer Q8. This is assessment criterion L4, which will often be used in question 7.

> **Our expert says:** Another approach to answering MCQs might be to go through a process of elimination. This means running through all three options and striking out the ones that are definitely not correct. The one that remains must be the right answer. This process of deduction probably works better than a process of induction.

Study tips: speaking

Developing vocabulary (see page 10 of the student book)

One of the three criteria used to assess speaking skills is vocabulary – or, rather, the range and accuracy of the words used in a focused discussion. In the student book agricultural words are used to illustrate and practise this, but you could also use other science-based subjects such as earth science, and prepare a list of the typical vocabulary used in that context. Since speaking is a different skill from writing in terms of vocabulary use, you will need to work with your students to develop their oral skills from a wide range of perspectives.

It's important to remember that it is not the number of words known that will be assessed but the student's skill in using words appropriately. When candidates stretch their vocabulary to the limit, it's obvious to examiners whether a word is really understood or whether it's a thesaurus talking. However, an important skill for success across all three examination papers is to possess a wide and varied vocabulary. Learning new and specialist words is therefore encouraged.

Evaluating the sample student responses

Track 1.4 (student book)

Obviously Ashram has much stronger skills. Not only is he able to use specialized vocabulary but he is also able to use non-specialized vocabulary at a more sophisticated level than the other two agricultural students. It is clear that Ashram would perform best in an IGCSE speaking test.

However, it is not as easy to distinguish between the other two students because they both present ideas about changes in farming that show insight. However, if we concentrate on vocabulary alone we can see that James has the edge because he uses a wider range of appropriate vocabulary. A feature of the Speaking test is that it may show whether a candidate has stronger skills in vocabulary or in sentence structure. It is important, therefore, if you are acting as an assessor, that you are able to make judgments about each criterion rather than the speaking skills of a candidate as a whole. If you are acting as a teacher/examiner **you must** apply the three criteria as directed by the Oral Assessment Criteria Grid.

It is therefore a useful exercise to ask your students to extract the vocabulary words that each of the three agricultural students uses. They should put them in two columns – specialized and non-specialized – and then contrast the three students' usage.

Ashram: 10 marks; James: 6 marks; Sabina 5 marks

> **Our expert says:** Cambridge offers training and accreditation for teachers to act as examiners and conduct the speaking tests. Indeed, a centre must have at least one accredited examiner to be able to conduct the speaking test.

Study tips: writing

Developing the three prompts (see page 18 of the student book)

This section invites students to engage with three prompts used as a stimulus, or guide, for a piece of extended writing.

In Exercise 6 of the examination papers, at both core and extended level, students will be asked to produce a piece of guided or directed writing. Three prompts will be supplied to help structure the piece of writing. As stated in the student book, it is possible to rearrange the prompts and it is not necessary therefore to structure the essay in a linear manner. Students are invited to play around with paragraphs so that they can see how this works but, at the same time, they must ensure that they respond to all three prompts.

It is sensible to generate a response of equal length to each of the three prompts; using three paragraphs per prompt is an acceptable approach. Writing one sentence for one prompt and 15 sentences for another are not likely to lead to a balanced piece of writing.

There is a pattern to how these prompts relate to each other. Here's an example of an Exercise 6 with a science theme:

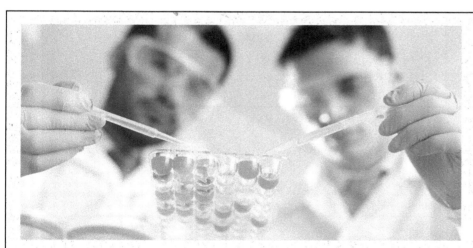

You have just attended your school's science fair. Write a letter to a friend describing your day.

In your letter, you should:

- tell your friend about the day as a whole
- describe a particular science display or experiment you liked
- mention a person at the fair whom you found interesting.

The pattern is to interweave descriptive writing to make the three prompts blend together... and to do this in a lively and readable way. This is quite a challenge, and stronger candidates tend to achieve this by balancing the writing so that one of the prompts leads naturally into the other two. It doesn't matter which prompt is utilized first but it matters very much that there is a natural flow to the development of the experience.

Encourage students to experiment with re-ordering the prompts above to generate extended writing. An A grade could be achieved by using the three prompts in any order you like.

☑ My progress

The four study skills – reading, writing, speaking, and listening – are key skills for success in each of the examinations. In the "My progress" section at the end of the chapter in the student book, we invite students to select one skill that they can focus on and develop. However, you may like to ask your students to prepare action plans to develop all four of the skills.

The table shows where the skills feature in the examination papers and how they are applied. Unless otherwise indicated, the skills and tasks are common to both levels.

Skill	Task	Positioning in examination papers
Selecting appropriate notes from an information text	Locate 7 notes (core) Locate 9 notes (extended)	Reading and writing ● Exercise 4
Answering multiple-choice questions	Answer eight three-option MCQs	Listening ● Exercise 7
Using a wide and accurate range of vocabulary in a conversation	Respond to all five prompts of the speaking test	Speaking test ● The whole of Part D; the assessed phase (the discussion)
Using prompts to bind together a piece of extended writing	Directed writing: 100–150 words (core) Directed writing: 150–200 words (extended)	Reading and writing ● Exercise 6

2 Food and fitness

Student book content coverage

Segment 1	Pages 23–27 Traditional food celebrations
Syllabus objectives	**R1** Identify and retrieve facts and details **S1** Communicate clearly, accurately, and appropriately
Broader skills development	• Think about how food is celebrated. • Identify food used in celebrations around the world. • Read about Chinese New Year celebrations.
Introducing the session	"Thinking out loud" (page 24): Allow five minutes to let students decide what they think about their favourite festivals and celebrations.
Ensuring a skills balance	Suggested writing activity: Ask students to write a short article on a celebration they go to at the beginning of the year. They should include information about why the celebration takes place, where it takes place, and why they enjoy it.
Differentiated activities	Stronger students can read the articles on celebrations (above) and then tell each other which one they like the most, and why.
Teaching and learning methodologies	**1** Think about celebrations around the world. **2** Read about Chinese New Year.
Building your vocabulary	Ask students to make a list of five unfamiliar words on pages 25–26. They should check the meaning of the word and, if appropriate, the context it is in, to confirm the definition.
Check your understanding	Page 25: Chinese New Year celebrations. Ask students to complete this individually. Page 25: Harbin International Ice and Snow Festival. Ask students to complete this in pairs.
Learner outcomes	By the end of this segment, learners should be able to: • talk about celebrations • talk about the food used in celebrations around the world.
Workbook	Page 9: Writing an advertising leaflet Page 9: Speaking – information about a carnival
Worksheet	2.1: Writing about food

Segment 2	Pages 28–9 Carnival
Syllabus objectives	**R2** Understand and select relevant information **W1** Communicate clearly, accurately, and appropriately
Broader skills development	• Learn how to use context clues. • Find and use specific information. • Make a brief oral presentation.
Introducing the session	Allow five minutes for students to plan on their own how they will participate next time there is a carnival in their local area.
Ensuring a skills balance	Suggested speaking activity: Ask students to tell each other why they like taking part in carnival, listening to what their partner is saying before asking their partner a question about what they have just said.
Differentiated activities	Stronger students can review the destination chosen after the oral presentation on page 29, and then update their blog, having been to the destination.
Teaching and learning methodologies	**1** Pick out specific information to help understand a text (written and spoken). **2** Discuss carnival with peers.
Building your vocabulary	Ask students to make a list of five unfamiliar words on page 28. Working in pairs, they can compare these and decide on the five most useful words to add to their vocabulary.
Check your understanding	Ask each student to pick out three interesting facts they have learned about carnival and in small groups compare what they have chosen.
Learner outcomes	By the end of this segment, learners should be able to: • use context clues to help understanding • communicate clearly about carnivals.
Workbook	Page 10: Writing an update of your blog
Worksheet	2.2: Building your food vocabulary – crossword

Segment 3	Pages 30–3 Taking food from field to plate
Syllabus objectives	**W2** Convey information **L1** Identify and retrieve facts and details
Broader skills development	• Learn how to describe ingredients precisely. • Learn how to use collocations in your language. • Read a blog and then write your own.
Introducing the session	"Thinking out loud" (page 30): Allow students five minutes to think about unusual or rare foods.
Ensuring a skills balance	Suggested reading activity: Ask students to read the recipes their peers have written as a result of the activity on page 32 and then decide which one they might make this week. Tell them to give reasons for their choice.
Differentiated activities	Stronger students can continue the work they have done on collocations in the writing activity on page 32, ensuring that the ingredients they have used have been appropriately collocated.

Teaching and learning methodologies	1 Think about appropriate language to use in a recipe.
	2 Learn about what to put in a blog.
Building your vocabulary	Ask students to pick out five collocations from a recipe they feel they can use in the future.
Check your understanding	Page 30: Truffles in France – students can complete this in pairs.
	Page 31: An interview with a chef – students can complete this individually.
Learner outcomes	By the end of this segment, learners should be able to:
	● use words which collocate
	● write a short personal blog.
Workbook	Page 11: Building your vocabulary – a restaurant review
	Pages 11–12: Reading about a restaurant and answering the questions
	Page 12: Thinking about the restaurant review
	Page 12: Writing a diary entry
	Page 13: Writing about your signature dish
Worksheet	2.3: Food – speaking in a restaurant

Segment 4	Pages 34–38 Fitness
Syllabus objectives	R2 Understand and select relevant information
	S2 Convey information and express opinions effectively
Broader skills development	● Learn how to write an effective summary.
	● Use persuasive language in different contexts.
	● Understand how to give short and precise answers when needed.
Introducing the session	"Thinking out loud" (page 34): Allow students five minutes to think about staying fit and healthy.
Ensuring a skills balance	Suggested listening activity:
	Ask students to listen to the speeches resulting from the activity on page 38. Which speech is the most persuasive? Ask them to try to explain what was in the speech that was so persuasive.
Differentiated activities	Stronger candidates could respond in the appropriate way to the email they produced on page 35, as the friend receiving it.
Teaching and learning methodologies	1 Learn about writing a good summary.
	2 Develop and extend the range of persuasive language.
Building your vocabulary	Page 36: Allow students, in pairs, up to five minutes to match the words to their correct definitions.
Check your understanding	Ask students to pick out three words after the suggested listening exercise that has made the speech persuasive.
Learner outcomes	By the end of this segment, learners should be able to:
	● use persuasive language in a variety of contexts
	● give short and precise answers when needed.
Workbook	Page 14: Listening – a foods standards officer
	Page 14: Check your understanding – a food standards officer
	Page 14: Writing – interview answers
Worksheet	2.4: Fitness – reading an extract and answering questions

Segment 5	Pages 39–43 Food and literature
Syllabus objectives	**W2** Convey information and express opinions effectively
	S2 Convey information and express opinions effectively
Broader skills development	• Talk about a favourite novel.
	• Practise using adjectives in an effective way.
	• Use language to describe something.
Introducing the session	"Thinking out loud" (page 39): Allow students five minutes to think about their favourite novel – what is it about and when did they first read it?
Ensuring a skills balance	Suggested listening activity:
	Ask students to listen to their classmates describing their favourite novel. Once they have heard them all, they choose one that they will try to read, explaining why they made that decision.
Differentiated activities	Stronger students could compare a favourite novel to the film version of it and decide which is better at describing the action and characters the writer created.
Teaching and learning methodologies	**1** Learn to use adjectives in an appropriate and creative way.
	2 Create and maintain interest by using descriptive detail.
Building your vocabulary	Ask students to choose five adjectives to describe their favourite novel. Can their partner guess the novel from these five words?
Check your understanding	Ask students to pick out three adjectives they have used and find a synonym for each which they could add to their vocabulary.
Learner outcomes	By the end of this segment, learners should be able to:
	• use a wider range of adjectives in their descriptive writing
	• use language to describe something.
Workbook	Page 16: Building your vocabulary – Fitness
	Pages 16–17: Reading – A fitness guru
	Page 17: Check your understanding – A fitness guru
	Page18: Building your vocabulary – A sporting hero
	Pages 18–19: Reading – A sporting hero
	Page 19: Check your understanding – A sporting hero
Worksheet	2.5: Fitness – vocabulary in a dialogue

Segment 6	Pages 44–49 Outstanding achievement
Syllabus objectives	**L2** Understand and select relevant information
	L3 Recognize and understand ideas, opinions, and attitudes
Broader skills development	• Listen to ideas, opinions, and attitudes, and how we respond to this information.
	• Think about people who have overcome the odds.
	• Write biographical information about a person who has overcome the odds.
Introducing the session	Page 44: Ask the students to watch the clip about Alex Zanardi and explain what "achieving against the odds" means. Ask the students, in no more than five minutes, to give their initial response to Zanardi.

Ensuring a skills balance	Suggested reading activity: Ask the students to research a famous sportsperson and note down five interesting facts about their lives, then, in small groups, to give a brief one-minute report about their chosen person and explain their choice.
Differentiated activities	Stronger candidates can finish the discussion on page 47 and then write a short biography of their partner, using the list of things that they have already noted make a good biography.
Teaching and learning methodologies	**1** Recognize people's opinions and attitudes when they are expressing their ideas. **2** Understand and explain how someone has overcome difficulties to succeed.
Building your vocabulary	Page 44: Alex Zanardi listening. Ask students, in pairs, to match the words to their definitions.
Check your understanding	Page 46: Marathon on crutches listening. Students can complete the multiple-choice questions individually.
Learner outcomes	By the end of this segment, learners should be able to: • reflect on the language they have seen in the chapter to write a biography of someone they admire • complete the "My progress" chart and pick one skill for their action plan.
Workbook	Page 20: Listening – Channel swim Page 20: Check your understanding – Channel swim Page 21: Building your vocabulary – fitness trends Page 21: Reading – fitness trends Page 22: Check your understanding – fitness trends Page 22: Discussion topic
Worksheet	2.6: Fitness – writing a diary
Further practice	**On completion of the chapter, ask students to complete questions 1–20 of the food and fitness interactive activities.**

Links

If you choose only one link to use with your students, try this:

- www.freerice.com

  This is an excellent way to practise vocabulary – and the more questions you answer correctly the more rice you will earn, which the organization will give to feed people in the poorest parts of the world.

You might also try:

- www. jamieoliver.com – read more recipes and ideas for eating healthily.
- www. nhs.uk/change4life – advice on healthy living and activities and games to keep you active – now, and as an adult.
- www. food.gov.uk – learn more about food standards and hygiene.
- www. food.com – top recipes from chefs, covering many favourite cuisines.
- www. kids.usa.gov – exercise, fitness and nutrition for teenagers.

If your students enjoyed reading *The Hunger Games*, suggest that they try the second book in the trilogy, *Catching Fire* – or watch the film.

Study tips: speaking

Responding to Prompt 3 of the oral test (see page 29 of the student book)

Level of achievement	Sample response
Student A: high achievement	<ul><li>Clearly understands the topic</li><li>Able to add shades of meaning and come up with additional ideas to develop the topic</li><li>Can change the direction of the discussion and be proactive</li><li>Vocabulary is sophisticated</li><li>Sentence structures are natural and highly competent</li></ul>
Student B: average achievement	<ul><li>Understands the topic but is only able to develop it partially</li><li>Occasionally drifts away from the main thrust of the prompt</li><li>Is passive rather than proactive</li><li>Vocabulary is sufficient but not impressive</li><li>Sentence structures are simple without too much error</li></ul>
Student C: lower achievement	<ul><li>Has only a basic understanding of the theme</li><li>Misinterprets some questions</li><li>Settles on a related and simpler idea – can't develop the discussion as intended</li><li>Vocabulary is limited</li><li>Sentence structures contain basic errors</li></ul>

Exam focus: the Speaking test

There is no distinction between the levels for the oral (Speaking) test: all students take the same test. There is only one set of assessment criteria (printed in the syllabus) and these cover all marks and grades. The oral test is marked out of 30, with the following mark scheme:

- structure – 10 marks
- vocabulary – 10 marks
- fluency and development – 10 marks.

The assessed phase of the oral test is based on a topic card, chosen for the student by the nominated examiner. The card will list five prompts, which must all be utilized, and in the sequence in which they appear on the card.

Assessment objectives

S1 Communicate clearly, accurately, and appropriately

S2 Convey information and express opinions effectively

S3 Employ and control a variety of grammatical structures

S4 Demonstrate knowledge of a range of appropriate vocabulary

S5 Engage in and influence the direction of conversation

S6 Employ suitable pronunciation and stress patterns

An oral test topic card will look like this:

Keeping fit

Oral test topic card

Many people like to keep fit but how this is achieved often varies.

Discuss this theme with the examiner.

The following ideas *must* be used in sequence to develop the conversation:

1 How you keep fit on a regular basis

2 How some people you know keep fit and healthy

3 The pros and cons of exercising, and why some people struggle to exercise

4 The suggestion that there are more important things in life than fitness

5 The idea that the fitness industry is more interested in making money than anything else.

You are free to consider any other *related* ideas of your own.

Remember, you are not allowed to make any written notes.

Model answers and how to improve performance

For a highly competent performance in the Speaking test, a student will need to speak fluently about the topic and have some additional ideas to contribute to the development of the discussion. A wide range of vocabulary will need to be demonstrated and spoken structures will need to be sound and varied.

The student should aim to speak on equal terms with the examiner and at times involve the examiner in developing the discussion. The aim is to have a two-way conversation – so the greater the role the student plays the more likely it is that a high mark/grade will be issued.

The student should use the 2–3 minutes of preparation time carefully to plan the structure of the 6–9-minute discussion based around the five prompts. Ideally, the student should respond to each prompt with one or two minutes of dialogue. At no point should a monologue occur; the examiner is trained to intercede should this happen.

Level of achievement	Level descriptor
A grade	Speaks clearly and confidently in response to other speakers; occasionally takes the initiative
C grade	Speaks clearly with some confidence, mostly in response to the directions of other speakers; shows a readiness to listen to others and respond appropriately
E grade	Speaks with some confidence, but usually in response to the directions of other speakers; shows readiness to listen to others and to respond

In a model response at A grade level to the topic about keeping fit:

> A student would stay on task throughout, respond in depth to most of the Examiner's questions and prompts, and show an enthusiasm to talk. A student at this level would pause for thought on occasions, and make corrections naturally. He or she would think carefully about which words to use so that a varied vocabulary is present. It's always good to hear a student closing the topic with a concluding comment. An Examiner is likely to award this approach a clear Band 1, and in all likelihood, a mark of 28–29 out of 30. Students should not be too concerned about slight slips therefore - it is the fluency and pertinence of the discussion which generates higher marks.

Study tips: writing

Writing a summary (see page 35 of the student book)

Level of achievement	Sample response
Summary 3: strong performance	• Has a sense of confidence • Uses accurate language • Covers the appropriate content • Flows naturally
Summary 1: average performance	• Covers the key points, but repeats them in a mechanical, systematic way • Competent, but not highly competent.
Summary 2: weak performance	• Has understood the article and selected the main points but conveyed them in limited language with some errors • Uses generally simple, short sentences • Is quite short • Contains some lifted/copied segments and is like a snapshot of the original

> **Our expert says:** Summary writing on the extended paper tests reading *and* writing skills but the core-level paper tests only writing.

(Further in-depth work on summaries appears on pages 112–16 and 131–2 of this teacher guide.)

Study tips: reading

Questions requiring short and precise answers (see page 38 of the student book)

When reading for comprehension in the exam, students will be asked to show their understanding by answering questions on the text, and their answers should be as brief and precise as possible.

Question 1 answers

Answer a) is the best response because it communicates the required information succinctly. Answer b) would be acceptable, but it adds unnecessary information. Answer c) is not correct because it lifts details from the text that do not respond to the question.

Question 2

Answer a) is correct here. However, less detail could have been provided and the mark would still have been awarded, 'no need to carry backpacks' would have sufficed. This demonstrates that lifting the correct phrase is acceptable but reducing that phrase to a shorter version is even better. Answer b) does not relate to the carrying of items, and is this not specific enough. Answer c) suggests that the organisers carry the backpacks and there is no evidence of this.

Question 3

Answers a) and b) are both correct and would both receive a mark. However, note how the first answer provides all that is required, and the second answer provides more than is required. A student who writes too much is penalising himself/herself as it takes longer to do this. Where a short answer can be supplied, it should always be preferred. Answer c) does not relate to the tour and is provided as an additional feature. This would therefore be marked wrong.

Exam focus: the reading and writing paper

In Exercise 2 of the Reading and Writing examination, students are asked to read a text and answer a series of questions to test their comprehension. The article will usually be a report or a newspaper article, and it will always incorporate a graphical element such as a bar chart, a pie chart, or a line chart.

> ## Assessment objectives
>
> **R1** Identify and retrieve facts and details
>
> **R2** Understand and select relevant information
>
> **R4** Understand what is implied but not actually written, e.g. gist, relationships, writer's purpose/intention, writer's feelings, situation, or place

The following article is based on how people in Italy used to keep themselves active and entertained by playing traditional games.

The questions that follow are for both core and extended levels, with an additional question at extended level that invites students to scan the whole text to extract a theme.

Old games in Italy

Once upon a time, people in Italy used to play games that no longer exist; these games were often played in the streets, safer then as there was not very much traffic. Friends' houses, bars or *circoli*, and special clubs, were the places where people met and gathered to entertain themselves and spend their free time. The most common meeting places, however, were the *circoli* and people's houses.

These games had been played for centuries, generation after generation, before technology became such a huge part of people's lives. Today, computer games, social networks, and the Internet have replaced what are now considered old-fashioned games; games that used to be part of Italian tradition and social history. One of the key differences in the two different approaches to game playing is that traditional games involved people socializing in one place and interacting, while games that use technology often mean that a person is playing on his or her own.

These are among the most famous:

- **The *trottola*, the spinning top.** The *trottola* dates back 6,000 years and was found in the excavation works in Pompeii. This game was also very famous in Rome, where politicians and plebes alike used to play with it. Mostly made from wood, it rotated through a rope. From the north to the south of the country, you will still find *nonni*, grandparents, who remember playing it.

- **The *campana*, hopscotch.** This is one of the oldest and best-known street games, also well known in many other countries. It is said to have been invented by the Romans, who taught it to children when they conquered new places. There are several ways to play it, which change from place to place, and also sometimes within the same region. The campana was usually played by girls, at home or at school, using a chalk to draw numbers on the ground. One of the most ancient drawings of a *campana* was found on the paving of the *Foro Romano*, the Forum of Rome, and it showed lots of children gathered around a *campana* grid.

- **The *album di figurine*, the stickers' album.** Another popular game among children and teenagers was the game of *figurine*. It was usually played at school, during breaks. This passion boomed, above all, thanks to the *Panini* album and stickers collections. The game consisted of throwing a sticker with a single finger, and if the sticker fell on top of another sticker, same side up, the person who managed this feat won that sticker: this was not only entertaining but it also allowed people to win more stickers and increase their collection. This is a game that is pointless to play on your own.

- ***Calcio balilla* or *biliardino*, table football.** Until recently, one would have found a *calcio balilla* or *biliardino* in almost every coffee shop and on almost every beach in Italy. Children used to love it and adults adored it too. Two teams, with two or three players each, were formed and tried to simulate a football match by manoeuvring the little wooden players on a board, scoring as many goals as possible.

- **The *scubidù*, scoubidou.** The *scubidù* mania boomed in the 1970s and lasted up to the end of the 1990s. It was about crafting shapes with plastic thread, formed by intertwining two strings of different colours. They were so pretty and colourful that they were often used as key chains or decorations for school bags. Some teenagers also used to sell them. It was popular for friends to swap halfway through and complete each other's designs, adding a further creative element and encouraging collaboration.

Playing games has been a traditional activity since Roman times. Children are said to have a natural aptitude for playing games from a very young age. Games are also a good occasion to socialize and develop creativity: and some of those described above certainly fulfilled both points. Some of them are still played in rural Italian villages, where traditions have been kept alive, and where modern technology has not quite had the impact that it has had in the towns and cities.

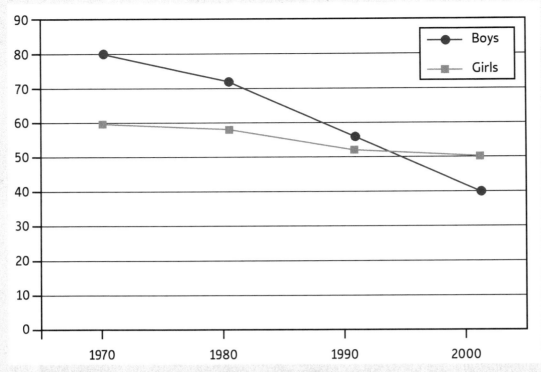

The percentage of boys and girls who played traditional games over a period of 30 years

Article adapted from www.lifeinitaly.com, Anna De Filippo, author; Francesca Bezzone, editor

Questions common to both papers

a) Why used it to be safer for people to play traditional games in the streets? [1]

b) Where did people most often meet to play their games? Give two places. [2]

c) What was the main factor that caused traditional game-playing to decline? [1]

d) How do we know that the spinning top was played around 6,000 years ago in Italy? [1]

e) Which main material was used to manufacture the *trottola*? [1]

f) When did the Romans particularly enjoy their *campana* and how do we know the Romans played it? [1]

g) In the game of *figurine*, how were the stickers thrown? [1]

h) In which two places was table football played in Italy? [1]

i) Give two reasons why some teenagers found the *scubidù* attractive. [1]

j) According to the graph, what significant change occurred in the year 2000? [1]

The question on the extended paper only

k) Give four examples of games being used for socialization, quoting some evidence in each case. [4]

[Total marks: 15]

Answers

a) Less traffic (on the streets)

b) People's houses and bars/*circoli*

c) Technology

d) It was found in (the excavation works in) Pompeii

e) Wood

f) After they had conquered somewhere *and* drawings were found in the Forum

g) With a (single) finger

h) Beaches and coffee shops

i) It made colourful decorations and could be sold for money

j) More girls were playing traditional games than boys / fewer boys were playing traditional games than girls

k) Four examples of games being used for socialization purposes:

- *campana* – drawing of lots of children playing it
- *figurine* – no point playing on your own
- table football – involved teams playing each other
- *scubidù* – friends collaborate on the designs

Model answers and how to improve performance

The main skill being tested in Exercise 2 is scanning for specific information. It is sensible therefore to skim-read the article initially to get the gist of what is it about, and then answer the questions in order. This is because the answers to the questions are found in the same order as the questions – i.e. they are linear and follow a logical sequence.

We recommend that students use as few words as possible when responding to Exercise 2 questions. Full sentences are certainly not required and it is acceptable to "lift" text from the article if it contains the information needed.

Only content (reading comprehension) is being assessed and not the accuracy of language. The examiners will therefore tolerate some awkward language, slight slips in spelling, inappropriate grammar, etc. However, poor language competence will affect the marks awarded because a lack of clarity can reflect a lack of understanding.

Level of achievement	Level descriptor
A grade	Selects material from texts and develops it in relationship to the question, sufficient to show some independence of thought
C grade	Selects material from texts in answer to questions and provides straightforward explanations and developments to show relevance
E grade	Selects material from texts in answer to questions and provides basic explanations.

Here are some model answers to some of the questions above. The first response is the ideal response, but the other responses are acceptable and would be credited by an examiner.

a) Why used it to be safer for people to play traditional games in the streets? [1]

There was less traffic... there were fewer cars on the roads.... the traffic wasn't as busy...

> **Our expert says:** With a "why" question, there needs to be a secure understanding and an explanation. A student responding with "traffic" would not therefore be allowed the mark. However, "less traffic" would be allowed.

c) What was the main factor that caused traditional game-playing to decline? [1]

Technology... it was technology... the growth of technology

> **Our expert says:** All that is needed here is "technology", illustrating that a single-word response is fine for Exercise 2. If a student chooses to add to this, care needs to be taken to ensure that the meaning does not change. For example, "there were only technology games available" would not be credited.

g) In the game of *figurine*, how were the stickers thrown? [1]

By using a single finger... with a finger... a finger was used... the finger on one hand

> **Our expert says:** For "how" questions, an explanation is required. This is unlikely to be possible by using a single word. "Finger" on its own would not be credited because it shows no clear understanding of the action of throwing the stickers. Also, students should be careful not to lose specificity: "with their hands", for example, would not be given credit because it is not specific enough.

h) In which two places was table football played in Italy? [1]

Beaches and coffee shops... coffee shops and beaches... places that sell coffee and the beach... on the beach and in a café...

> **Our expert says:** Only two places need to be listed. Students should provide the information as succinctly as possible. Synonyms are accepted, so café could be used for coffee shop, but "tea shop" would not be credited, and neither would "on the sand" for beach. Students should remember that, where two pieces of information are required, they need to show this clearly. Using "and" is the best way to do this, but responses separated by commas would be allowed and responses where there is a clear space between the two responses are fine also.

j) According to the graph, what significant change occurred in the year 2000? [1]

More girls were playing traditional games... fewer boys were playing traditional games... traditional games were played more by girls than boys... girls had overtaken boys in playing traditional games... 50 per cent of girls played traditional games, but only 40 per cent of boys did, and this was the opposite trend to that seen in the previous 20 years.

> **Our expert says:** A question based on a chart or graphic requires a basic understanding of statistical charts. However, the answer required will usually be language-based rather than just a number. The key here is to be precise, and use as few words as possible to convey the information highlighted in the chart. It is not normally acceptable just to convey the statistic: e.g. "50 per cent girls, 40 per cent boys" would not be credited because it does not answer the "significant change" element of the question.

k) Give four examples of games being used for socialization, quoting some evidence in each case. [4]

- *campana – drawing of lots of children playing it*
- *figurine – no point playing on your own*
- *table football – involved teams playing each other*
- *scubidù – friends collaborate on the designs*

> **Our expert says:** This question is testing synthesis skills. Students will need to revisit the text and locate four details that correlate to the given theme. As only content is assessed, it is advisable to use a list and bullet points here (not a paragraph). As there will usually be an explanatory element, single-word responses are not enough: e.g. an answer just listing the four games correctly will receive no marks because the second part of the question has not been attempted.

Study tips: listening

Listening to recognize ideas, opinions, and attitudes (see page 45 of the student book)

This short introductory exercise aims to help students recognize the underlying attitudes that speakers sometimes have. The key skill here is being able to work out inference – what a speaker means by what they say and/or imply. Inference can exist at a sophisticated or straightforward level. It is the latter context that features in several parts of the examination papers.

As students work through the Alex Zanardi interview, they will pick up several moments where speakers display their views and opinions. It should be stressed that different listeners will identify slightly different attitudes, and this is fine as long as they recognize the underlying attitude of each speaker. They could think of this skill as the ability to identify which speaker is most likely to have said or thought something, or reacted in a particular way – i.e. to identify the basic attitude of a person in a given context and then work out (infer) the rest.

Question 1 answers

Answer	Evidence
1a Male fan	"I had a bad accident once in a racing car and it took me nearly a year to get my confidence back. I wish I had acted more quickly now."
1b Female fan	"What I liked about you most was your approach to racing – even on the racing track, when you were pushing to win as much as the next man."
1c Alex Zanardi	"Maybe add another wheel and an engine? How about that? And then I shall come back to Brands Hatch and race again in a Formula 1 car. Adapted, of course. My great friend Jimmy Vasser, the US motor-racing impresario, telephoned me before the race. He said: 'If you win gold, I'm going to put you in a special car for the Indy 500.' So I'm going to call him back tonight and say: 'Jimmy, here I am. I've got the gold medal. How about that car?'"
1d Interviewer	"I'm very envious of you, actually, as I hardly ever try anything new or risky."

(Further in-depth work on listening to recognize attitudes and opinions appears on pages 64–5 of this teacher resource pack.)

☑ My progress

The four study skills are key skills for success in each of the examinations. In the "My Progress" section we invite students to select one skill that they can focus on and develop. However, you may like to ask students to prepare action plans to develop all four skills featured.

The table indicates where the skills feature in the examination papers and how they are applied. Where there is a difference between the Core and Extended levels, this is indicated. Otherwise, the skills and tasks are common to both levels.

Skill	Task	Positioning in examination papers
Broadening the theme into more general areas	Consider pros and cons, or consider the wider implications of the theme	Speaking ● Part D, Prompt 3
Writing a summary	Creating a coherent summary	Reading and Writing ● Exercise 5
Responding with concise and short answers	Complete comprehension exercise which uses short questions	Reading and Writing ● Exercise 2
Listening to recognise people's attitudes and opinions	Listening to several people talking about the same theme	Listening ● Exercise 6

Action plan

Skill I want to improve developing conversations by including related ideas.

- *planning* – how I will try to improve this skill
  have some informal conversations which last about 5 or 6 minutes and are based on one topic only.

- *implementing* – what I will need and what my exact strategy is
  find 3 or 4 adults from different backgrounds and have the conversations – all on the same topic.

- *monitoring* – how I will know I am improving and what evidence I might keep compare and contrast the way each conversation developed. What were the related ideas each adult brought in? Record the conversations as evidence for future reference.

Workbook practice

There were also other language learning skills that were covered in this chapter, and your Workbook provides further practice at these.

3 Communities

Student book content coverage

Segment 1	Pages 52–6 What makes a community?
Syllabus objectives	**R1** Identify and retrieve facts and details **L1** Identify and retrieve facts and details
Broader skills development	• Watch a video about ants and extract information from it. • Read about ants and extract information. • Collaborate to produce an ICT presentation.
Introducing the session	"Thinking out loud" (page 52): Ask students to spend five minutes in pairs talking about these questions, leading into "What ingredients make a community?"
Ensuring a skills balance	Suggested writing activity: Ask students to follow up "What ingredients make a community?" by writing a paragraph describing their "recipe" for a community.
Differentiated activities	Stronger students can be asked to write a short article, "What we can learn from the ants".
Teaching and learning methodologies	**1** Extract information from a variety of sources. **2** Prepare and give a PowerPoint presentation.
Building your vocabulary	Page 54: Ask students to work in pairs and to go on to use the words in sentences of their own.
Check your understanding	Page 55: Ask students to complete this in pairs.
Learner outcomes	By the end of this segment, students should be able to: • extract relevant information from audio/video and written sources • collaborate on a PowerPoint presentation.
Workbook	Page 23: Building your vocabulary Pages 23–4: Reading about bees Page 24: Check your understanding Pages 24–5: Writing about bees Page 26: Language focus – active and passive verbs
Worksheet	3.1: Writing a recipe for a community

Segment 2	Pages 57–61 Life in a commune
Syllabus objectives	**R3** Recognize and understand ideas, opinions, and attitudes and the connections between related ideas **W2** Convey information and express opinions effectively
Broader skills development	• Read accounts of community life. • Transfer details accurately. • Write about thoughts and feelings.
Introducing the session	"Thinking out loud" (page 57): Ask students to discuss the questions in pairs for up to five minutes.
Ensuring a skills balance	Suggested speaking activity: A volunteer phones/Skypes home – ask students in pairs to hold that conversation (perhaps based on the diary entry "Monday 10th May" on page 59).
Differentiated activities	Stronger students can research other examples of international community life and report on one of them.
Teaching and learning methodologies	1 Read personal accounts for information. 2 Transfer information accurately. 3 Fill in a form accurately.
Building your vocabulary	Page 57: Ask students to complete the sentences and then use the words in sentences of their own.
Check your understanding	Page 58: Ask students to complete this in pairs.
Learner outcomes	By the end of this segment, students should be able to: • identify and adapt personal reflections in reading and listening tasks • complete form-filling tasks with confidence • write personal reflections, e.g. in diaries.
Workbook	
Worksheet	3.2: Building your vocabulary

Segment 3	Pages 62–63 School as community
Syllabus objectives	**W6** Employ appropriate register/style **L3** Recognize and understand ideas, opinions, and attitudes and the connections between related ideas
Broader skills development	• Listen to an extract from an interview. • Write an informal letter/email.
Introducing the session	Ask students to talk for five minutes in small groups about ways in which their school is a community.
Ensuring a skills balance	Suggested speaking activity: Ask students to interview Dr Reese, the head teacher (page 62), about his school's scheme to have older pupils "parenting" new arrivals.
Differentiated activities	Stronger students can prepare and give a short talk, "Schools as communities".
Teaching and learning methodologies	1 Identify and use ideas and opinions in spoken material. 2 Write an informal letter.

Building your vocabulary	Ask students to list five adjectives to describe a school as a community, then share lists in small groups and note down striking examples.
Check your understanding	Page 62: Multiple-choice questions – these are best done in pairs.
Learner outcomes	By the end of this segment, students should be able to: • identify accurately inferred attitudes and opinions in listening tasks • write an informal letter making use of appropriate vocabulary.
Workbook	
Worksheet	3.3: A parents' evening role play

Segment 4	Pages 64–66 Life in an African village
Syllabus objectives	**R4** Understand what is implied but not actually written **S2** Convey information and express opinions effectively
Broader skills development	• Read about an African village. • Discuss issues presented in a passage. • Work together to plan an improvement programme.
Introducing the session	Ask students to think about the basic community needs of a village or small town (e.g. schools, doctors) – and, in pairs, discuss their importance for five minutes.
Ensuring a skills balance	Suggested writing activity: Ask students to imagine they visited Kitaisa for a day, and to write a diary entry/blog about the time they spent there.
Differentiated activities	Stronger students can choose one of the areas of need highlighted in "What would you do?" (page 66) and write up an improvement scheme for the village.
Teaching and learning methodologies	1 Read what is implied in a personal account. 2 Respond to what is implied.
Building your vocabulary	Page 64: Ask students, in pairs, to check the passage for any additional unfamiliar words.
Check your understanding	Page 66: Ask students, in small groups, to discuss the implications of these questions.
Learner outcomes	By the end of this segment, students should be able to: • read for inference • collaborate to respond to given and implied information.
Workbook	Page 27: Building your vocabulary Pages 27–8: Reading about Maasai village life Page 28: Check your understanding Pages 28–9 and 30: Note-taking, parts 1 and 2 Page 29: Listening – a day in a Maasai mother's life Page 30: Writing a summary
Worksheet	3.4: How would you spend it?

Segment 5	Pages 66–69 Village life in Peru
Syllabus objectives	**R2** Understand and select relevant information **W4** Demonstrate knowledge and understanding of a range of appropriate vocabulary
Broader skills development	• Compare contrasting descriptions. • Identify and make use of comparatives and superlatives.
Introducing the session	Ask students, in pairs, to discuss for up to five minutes what part of the world they would like to visit, choosing somewhere very different from where they live, and what they would look forward to.
Ensuring a skills balance	Suggested speaking activity: Ask students, in small groups, to discuss "The best place in the world", taking it in turns to say where they think that might be, and why.
Differentiated activities	Stronger students can imagine that a party from Colquemarca visits their country and, in small groups, discuss what differences they might notice.
Teaching and learning methodologies	1 Make comparisons between contrasting descriptions. 2 Write an informal letter.
Building your vocabulary	Page 66: Crossword – ask students to check the passage for other vocabulary on page 67 that might be unfamiliar to them.
Check your understanding	Page 68: Ask students to complete this in pairs.
Learner outcomes	By the end of this segment, students should be able to: • employ comparatives and superlatives in their descriptive writing • select appropriate vocabulary to write an informal letter.
Workbook	Pages 27–30: Any material not used in the previous segment could be useful in this one.
Worksheet	3.5: Comparing and contrasting

Segment 6	Pages 70–71 Literary connections
Syllabus objectives	**R4** Understand what is implied but not actually written **W1** Communicate clearly, accurately, and appropriately **S5** Engage in and influence the direction of conversation
Broader skills development	• Read a literary extract. • Talk about what might have happened. • Write a short story.
Introducing the session	Ask students, in pairs, to talk for up to five minutes about books they have read recently. What was the setting?
Ensuring a skills balance	Suggested listening activity: Read the extract from *Lord of the Flies* to your students, asking them to listen for clues to what is happening.
Differentiated activities	Stronger students can, in pairs, have a go at acting out the scene from the extract, making use of the dialogue.
Teaching and learning methodologies	1 Read a literary text for meaning. 2 Discuss what is implied in a text. 3 Write a short story.

Building your vocabulary	Ask students to note down any unfamiliar vocabulary.
Check your understanding	Page 71: Students may need careful guidance through the text to ensure that they understand what is said and implied. See worksheet 3.6.
Learner outcomes	By the end of this segment, students should be able to: • identify and understand atmosphere and setting • build discussion on textual clues • write an imaginative story.
Workbook	
Worksheet	3.6: Building your vocabulary – *Lord of the Flies*

Segment 7	Pages 72–75 The Big Issue – do jobs people do create a sense of community?
Syllabus objectives	**S1** Communicate clearly, accurately, and appropriately **S2** Convey information and express opinions effectively
Broader skills development	• Prepare and participate in a debate. • Reflect on, design, and present "your perfect community". • Understand the role of the warm-up in the speaking test.
Introducing the session	"Thinking out loud" (page 72): Ask students, in pairs, to discuss this for up to five minutes.
Ensuring a skills balance	Suggested writing activity: Students should write an advertisement for one of the community-based jobs they discussed in pairs (page 72).
Differentiated activities	Stronger students can discuss the question: "Why do some communities fail?"
Teaching and learning methodologies	**1** Debate the relative merits of jobs in the community. **2** Reflect on the variety of communities in the chapter. **3** Collaborate on a poster or computer-generated design.
Building your vocabulary	Ask students to check through the segment for any vocabulary that they are unsure of.
Check your understanding	
Learner outcomes	By the end of this segment, students should be able to: • contribute to a debate with confidence • collaborate in and participate in a visual presentation.
Workbook	Page 31: Building your vocabulary Page 32: Reading about an alternative community Page 33: Check your understanding Page 34: Writing an email Page 34: Discussion topic
Worksheet	3.7: Planning and having a debate
Further practice	**On completion of the chapter, ask students to complete questions 1–20 of the communities interactive activities.**

Links

Here are some links to use with your students:

- www.un.org – looking at peace and humanitarian affairs.
- www.animal.discovery.com/insects – one of many sites about insect colonies.
- www.MECP – the model European Communities Programme.
- www.chickenshed.org.uk – an inclusive community theatre group for children and young adults, started in the UK but now spreading to other countries.
- www.sportingequals.org.uk – using sport to bring diverse communities together.

Study tips: listening

Covering a range of question types (see page 52 of the student book)

This section is intended to familiarize students with or perhaps – as revision – remind them of the various question types used in the Listening examination at core and extended level. It also serves as practice for the interview scenario usually used for Question 7, and also sometimes for Question 5.

The audio recording provided – of Stanley, who lives in Hong Kong – offers your students opportunities to experiment with question setting (track 3.1). Students generally enjoy creating their own questions and posing these to their peers. You could add matching questions and true/false for more range – but be aware that true/false is no longer used in the examination papers.

We recommend that you look at the specimen papers produced by Cambridge for the 2015 examination session so that you can familiarize yourself with the full range of question types used across both listening papers. In short, all students will be:

- answering questions using no more than three words
- gap filling by using only one or two words
- matching six speakers to opinions stated (Speaker 1 – Opinion D, etc.)
- answering multiple-choice questions.

Extended-level students will also complete short notes with one or two words only.

This section does not contain sample student responses because it does not cover a specific examination question.

Study tips: reading

Transferring details accurately to a form (see pages 60–1 of the student book)

This section in the student book is an extensive and detailed analysis of the skills required to transfer information from one place to another – i.e. from an account written in the third person to a form written in the first person. In both papers, core and extended, candidates are tested to see how efficient they are at this skill, using different third-person accounts. There are common elements to Exercise 3 in both papers, but the exercise differs in these ways:

- Core paper – the third-person account is shorter, and the exercise carries 14 marks. The final section requires two sentences.
- Extended paper – the third-person account is longer, and the exercise carries 8 marks. The final section requires one sentence of between 12 and 20 words.

The advice in the student book makes it clear that the first person must be used when filling out the form – i.e. your students must pretend to be the person they are reading about when they fill out the form. Accuracy of language is expected, as is conciseness and the ability to carry out instructions as directed.

In the sentence pairs:

- B is correct because A is written in the third person and spells walking as waking
- A is correct because B has misspellings of save and enough
- B is correct because in A indoors is given as two words and I is not capitalized
- A is correct and B has one error of spelling (friends) and one of punctuation (a comma which is not needed).

Evaluating the sample student responses

- **Student A** has the most correct answers. In fact, Student A has been 100% accurate.

- **Student B** has made the following errors:

  1 Capital letters have not been used for the name.

  2 John has been identified as female.

  3 Months is spelled as moths.

  4 "No money" is not accurate; a small amount of money was provided.

  5 There are 21 words in this response, so no marks can be gained.

Exam focus: reading and writing

While there is a lot of commonality between the core and extended papers, we will focus on the form-filling exercise for Exercise 3 of the extended paper. (Chapter 5 focuses on the core-level paper.)

As can be seen from the assessment objectives below, Exercise 3 tests the integrated skills of reading and writing. The focus skill, however, is reading, but obviously writing skills are involved as the information is transferred to a form. Marks available are:

- 6 marks for reading skills
- 2 marks for writing skills.

Assessment objectives

R1 Identify and retrieve facts and details

R2 Understand and select relevant information

R4 Understand what is implied but not actually written, e.g. gist, relationships, writer's purpose/intention, writer's feelings, situation or place

W1 Communicate clearly, accurately and appropriately

W5 Observe conventions of paragraphing, punctuation and spelling

---

Ask your students to read the account below based on a teenager who is interested in spending some time living with another person in a different type of community.

A typical Exercise 3 at extended level

Yasmin Harare lives in an apartment with her parents in Belgium. Her address is 131a NeuStrasse, Pont Blanc. This is in the city of Brussels and the area code is 20120. The best way to contact Yasmin is by email at yasmin.h@yahoo.co.bg. Her parents are often working away, so they rely on email also. Yasmin attends a college – but she does have a free day each week, on a Tuesday. She is a full-time student studying the International Baccalaureate, or IB as it often called. She is studying at the Diploma level. She can be contacted at college by telephone in an emergency on 88-0104-2996.

Yasmin has always wanted to go on an exchange visit. In a few months time she will be 18, and she feels she is now ready to spend some time living with a host family. The place she really wants to go is Thailand. She has been researching for the last four months and has also considered Venezuela and Indonesia, but she settled on Thailand as her ideal destination for the exchange. If Thailand is not possible, Yasmin would like to go to Indonesia as she has a friend who has been there.

Yasmin's main objective is to find a family very different from her own, and Thai culture offers her a different cultural experience.

She has used a website to track down several people who are interested in an exchange, which means that they will come to Europe for a month and she will then stay in their house for the same length of time. The person she most likes is called Anchali Thomasin. Anchali lives with her older brother and sister in an area of Chiang Mai in a city called Sansiri. The area code is 50200. Full address details are not provided on the website for security reasons. From her profile on the website, Yasmin can see that Anchali goes to an International School and has been there since she was 10 years old. Anchali is 19 years old.

The next step for Yasmin is to register her interest by filling out a form on the website and the information she provides is then sent to Anchali. Yasmin cannot make direct contact at this point – but if Anchali is interested the company that operates the website begins liaising with both people and will, at the right time, put them in touch with each other.

There is a section on the form where Yasmin can ask questions about Anchali and about where she lives, etc. Yasmin will also need to explain why she is interested in Chiang Mai. What Yasmin found appealing about the city was its ancient history and its warm climate but she is a little concerned about the local food. Northern Thai food is famous around the word for being spicy and tasty and Yasmin is not used to this type of diet. She is particularly interested in the elephant sanctuary in the hills to the north of the city and would like to do some voluntary work there.

Imagine that you are Yasmin Harare and fill out the following registration form, to indicate your interest in a particular exchange visit.

Exchange visit registration form

SECTION A   **Personal details of applicant**

Full name ....

Contact address ....

Main contact details ....

Other contact ....

SECTION B   **Background information and reasons for application**

Your age (circle)

Under 16   16–17   18–21   Over 21

Research period (underline)

1 month   1–3 months   2–5 months   6–12 months

Chosen destination country

....

Other destinations in order of preference

1st ....   2nd ....

SECTION C   **Details of proposed trip and chosen host family**

Period of visit ....

Surname of exchange family ....

City ....   Area code ....

Status of person to exchange with (delete as appropriate)

Student Employed   Living with parents   Under 21

SECTION D

Write one sentence below of between 12 and 20 words describing two reasons why you have chosen the particular location.

....

....

[8 marks in total – 2 marks for Section D + 6 marks for the other sections.
Where there are 12 items, the total should be divided
by two to give a mark out of 6]

Answers

Exchange visit registration form (page 42)

Sections A–C

Full name	*Yasmin Harare*
Contact address	*131a NeuStrasse, Pont Blanc, Brussels 20120*
Main contact details	*(by email at) yasmin.h@yahoo.co.bg*
Other contact	*88-0104-2996*
Your age	*16–17*, to be circled
Research period	*2–5 months*, to be underlined
Chosen destination	*Thailand*
Other destinations	*1ˢᵗ, Indonesia; 2ⁿᵈ, Venezuela*
Period of visit	*1 month*
Surname of hosts	*Thomasin*
City and area code	*Chiang Mai 50200*
Status of exchange	*Student + Under 21*; the other two to be deleted/ struck through

Section D

The sentence should focus on the positive aspects of Chiang Mai. It must include therefore a reference to *two* of: ancient history, its warm climate, and its elephant sanctuary to qualify for the 2 marks. Then apply the following mark scheme:

- 2 marks: no fewer than 12 and no more than 20 words; proper sentence construction; correct spelling, punctuation and grammar; relevant to context.

- 1 mark: no fewer than 12 and no more than 20 words; proper sentence construction; 1–3 errors of punctuation / spelling / grammar that do not obscure meaning; relevant to context.

- 0 marks: more than 3 errors of punctuation / spelling / grammar; and/or irrelevant to context, and/or not a proper sentence; and/or fewer than 12 or more than 20 words.

Model answers and how to improve performance

In an exercise where absolute accuracy is required, a model answer will usually be the only acceptable response. However, there are occasions where alternatives might be accepted as long as they convey identical information. It is often more useful to look at responses that appear to be accurate but which, on closer inspection, are not and would not gain the mark(s).

The key skill that students need to develop therefore is the skill of accurate transcription. To do this, it is important that they select the appropriate pieces of information from the source and transcribe *only* that information and nothing more.

Much of what is tested from a reading perspective will be objectives R1 and R2. However, it is certainly possible to test R4 in form filling, where candidates will need to understand what is implied by what is written in the third-person source/account.

Acceptable responses

SECTION A

Full name:

- *Yasmin Harare*

- *Harare, Yasmin*

> **Our expert says:** In writing full names, both names must be given in full, so *Y. Harare* would not be allowed. Not using capital letters for the proper noun would also exclude the mark – e.g. *yasmin harare*. Examiners will recognize internationally accepted alternative conventions, however, so *Harare, Yasmin* would be credited, but only if it includes the comma.

Contact address:

- *131a NeuStrasse, Pont Blanc, Brussels 20120... 131a NeuStrasse, Pont Blanc, 20120 Brussels*

- *131a NeuStrasse, Pont Blanc, Brussels 20120, Belgium*

> **Our expert says:** The standard convention for transcribing an address is house number, street name, district, city, city code, in that order. However, the acceptable responses show that adding the country will be accepted as long as it is spelled correctly (even if the country is not mentioned in the source). Any error in spelling, not using proper nouns, or inappropriate punctuation will lead to the mark being disallowed. In the example above, if a candidate wrote the initial part of the address as 131A NeuStrasse or 131a Neustrasse, the examiner would not award the mark.

Main contact details:

- *(by email at) yasmin.h@yahoo.co.bg*

- *yasmin.h@yahoo.co.bg*

- *email: yasmin.h@yahoo.co.bg*

- *by using her email account which is yasmin.h@yahoo.co.bg*

> **Our expert says:** As with any mark scheme, details in brackets can be ignored. However, any additional detail included must be spelled correctly. Errors in unwanted information will result in the mark being lost in a transcription exercise. This re-affirms the need for students to provide *only* the information requested. It would be insufficient if a candidate simply wrote "by email" or "using her email". The email address will always be required. Forms are designed to mirror authenticity, so the principle here is that answers must be realistic. Simply writing "email" would not allow any contact to take place.

Other contact:

- *88-0104-2996*

> **Our expert says:** This would be the only response permissible for a telephone number – it is the specific detail needed to be able to contact Yasmin. It would not be acceptable to write things like:
> - by telephone...
> - by calling her at college...
> - contacting her parents...
> - phoning her other number...
> - emailing her parents.

SECTION B

Your age:

- *16–17* (circled as per the instruction)

> **Our expert says:** There are two relevant elements here:
> - the candidate has to work out the age from the information given: "she will be 18 in a few months"
> - any other way of identifying the 16–17 range – such as underlining, using a square and not a circle, or using an arrow – will not be allowed. The instruction is to circle and this is the only acceptable indication of understanding. However, an oval would be allowed!

Research period:

- *2–5 months* (which *must* be underlined)

> **Our expert says:** It follows also that anything other than underlining will not be rewarded. It is normal for the form to be designed so that the details from the source fit into it – hence using 2–5 months here and not just 4 months. Students will need to be trained to spot how specific information in the source may be presented in a different way on the form.

Chosen destination:

- *Thailand*
- *the country of Thailand*
- *I choose Thailand*
- *I prefer Thailand*
- *Thailand and not Indonesia*

> **Our expert says:** A pitfall here is that a candidate might slip into the third person and lose the mark, for example by writing "She chose Thailand". Other potential pitfalls would be misspelling of words not required, for example "I prefere Thailand" and responses lacking specificity, such as "The country where Thai people live" (as this could be any country).

Other destinations in order of preference:

- *Indonesia + Venezuela*
- *Indonesia initially + Venezuela after that*

> **Our expert says:** This is essentially a test of locating the information and spelling the countries correctly. In the second response above, the examiner would give the benefit of the doubt as the additional detail provided is indeed correct.

SECTION C

Period of visit:

- *1 month*
- *one month*
- *a month*
- *only a month*
- *the length of stay is 1 month*
- *1/12th of a year*

> **Our expert says:** As you can see above, only responses that are entirely synonymous are allowed. An examiner would not allow "4 weeks" for one month. Also, abbreviations are not likely to be acceptable here as only standard abbreviations are permitted. "One mnth" would therefore not receive the mark.

Surname of exchange family:

- *Thomasin*

> **Our expert says:** It is difficult to see what alternative might be allowed. Only the surname is requested so *Anchali Thomasin* would not be accepted. Additional information here loses the mark because any more information would contradict the question.

City and area code:

- *Chiang Mai + 50200*

> **Our expert says:** As separate spaces for each detail are provided on the form, candidates are expected to transcribe this accurately.

Status of person to exchange with (delete as appropriate):

Student + Under 21 should remain; "Employed" and "Living with parents" are not correct and should be deleted with a strikethrough

> **Our expert says:** When the instruction to delete is used, a strikethrough is required. No other means of identifying the correct details would be accepted. This item illustrates that sometimes more than one detail will be highlighted – in this case, two of the four details are correct. Students should not assume that only one detail is required in Exercise 3.

SECTION D

Write one sentence below of between 12 and 20 words describing two reasons why you have chosen the particular location:

- *I chose Chiang Mai because of its history and I love the idea of being warm for a month...*
- *I want to work with elephants and spend a month in a warm climate...*
- *The elephant sanctuary interests me but so does the ancient history of the city...*

> **Our expert says:** The first aim here is to stay between 12 and 20 words, and then of course to use accurate English. Simple, straightforward statements are therefore recommended, and students should avoid using too many short words or linking words. The degree of error will dictate the mark gained. "Relevant to context" here means that *two* reasons must be given – "I am looking forward to Chiang Mai because of its warm climate" would not gain a mark. Students should also avoid general responses such as "Thailand is a great place to visit and I want to go to see the culture", even if they are word perfect.

Study tips: writing

Writing an informal letter (see page 63 of the student book)

Exercise 6 of the core and extended papers asks students to write an informal letter, probably to a friend. Students are guided through a suitable style or register and are shown that informality is the key to successful "personal" writing. Examiners are looking for a coherent, fluent, and natural piece of extended writing. Students will of course need to minimize their errors and that comes about through general language development and practice. Here, we will try just to set the scene so that what follows has a greater chance of being productive.

The task set includes three prompts, and the only difference in the task at the two levels is the number of words suggested/required: 100–150 at core level and 150–200 at extended level. The mark scheme used is identical and the way in which the writing is marked is also the same.

Evaluating the sample student responses

- **Student A** has used the best style (or register): all the phrases are good examples of an informal, yet structured, piece of writing. This is clearly a letter written to a close friend.

- **Student B** is the weakest: the style is too formal for a letter to a friend. This style may have been the norm in 1850, but it is much too formal to be effective these days. It reads as if it is a letter to a colleague or even to someone the writer has not met. There is nothing wrong with each phrase; it is actually rather good language, but it is not of the appropriate register and thus is not fit for purpose.

- **Student C** is a reasonable attempt at an appropriate register. Apart from the last phrase, it is generally informal, though it tends towards keeping a little distance between the writer and the intended reader. It would be more suitable as a letter to an acquaintance than as one to a close friend.

Exam focus: reading and writing

Exercises 6 and 7 assess writing skills only. Exercise 6 focuses on testing a candidate's skill in informal writing, and Exercise 7 focuses on more formal writing. The purpose, format, and audience are therefore very different for each exercise.

The full range of writing skills is assessed in both exercises and at both levels.

Assessment objectives

W1 Communicate clearly, accurately, and appropriately

W2 Convey information and express opinions effectively

W3 Employ and control a variety of grammatical structures

W4 Demonstrate knowledge and understanding of a range of appropriate vocabulary

W5 Observe conventions of paragraphing, punctuation, and spelling

W6 Employ appropriate register/style

The required "essays" are in essence directed writing.

Exercise 6 follows a set pattern. There will be a picture or two which helps set the scene and then a lead-in sentence followed by details of the task and the mark scheme, as in this example.

Exercise 6

You have recently spent some time in a community very different from your own.

Write a letter to a friend telling her/him about the experience.

In your letter you should:

- tell your friend what the community was, and why it was so different

- say whether you enjoyed the experience and what you gained from it

- suggest whether you feel your friend would enjoy spending time there also.

The pictures above may give you some ideas, and you should try to use some ideas of your own.

Core: The letter should be between 100 and 150 words long. Do not write an address. There are 7 marks available for content and 6 marks for style and language accuracy.   [13 marks total]

Extended: The letter should be between 150 and 200 words long. Do not write an address. There are 10 marks available for content and 9 marks for style and language accuracy.   [19 marks total]

Model answers and how to improve performance

Here's a model response to the Exercise 6 task above:

Hi Jane

I've just got back from two weeks in a really interesting place. I wanted to write earlier but one of the rules there was "no writing"! Sounds really strict, doesn't it, and it was. Let me explain. My parents arranged what they said would be an "experience of a lifetime" for me as a surprise. They know how much I hated summer camp last year so this time they said it would be different. It certainly was. I was living among a community of people who are living the way that people lived 400 years ago.

I was a bit concerned at first that I just wouldn't fit in and that I'd find it really difficult to survive without modern conveniences. I was a bit suspicious when I was told that I couldn't bring my mobile phone or any music-playing devices. Two weeks without my phone. Two weeks without any music. Now that sounds like fun, I told myself. The first few days were tough, actually, because so much work needed to be done to support the community that I got really tired. There are people there who have been living in the settlement for months. I'm not sure I could stay that long, but one person I spoke to said he joined for a week and that was five months ago! I wanted to stay longer though; by the end of the second week I was really enjoying it.

I'm not sure you would enjoy it, though. I mean, you really need your social networking sites, don't you? I think you would miss the freedom of logging on when you want to and seeing who has posted what and who has messaged back, etc. You're a different kind of socializer from me.

Can't wait to see you to tell you more,

Jake

Rules for marking extended writing

The full assessment criteria grid can be found in the syllabus, but remember the following when marking a piece of extended writing:

1 The content must be relevant (the piece should fulfill the task and show awareness of purpose/audience/register) and show development of ideas (i.e. the detail/explanation provided and how enjoyable it is to read).

2 The language used covers style (i.e. complexity of vocabulary and sentence structure) and accuracy (of grammar, spelling, punctuation, and use of paragraphs).

3 The use of paragraphs should not be the primary basis of deciding which mark band the work is in. Look first at the language used and, once you have decided on the appropriate mark band, you can use the paragraphing as a factor in helping you decide whether the work warrants the upper or lower mark in the mark band.

4   If the essay is considerably shorter than the stated word length, put it in mark band 2–3 for content, or lower, for not fulfilling the task

5   If the essay is irrelevant and has nothing to do with the question asked, it should be given 0 marks for content and language, even if it is fluent and enjoyable to read.

6   If the essay is partly relevant and therefore in mark band 2–3, the full range of marks for language is available.

Students can improve their performance by practising this style of writing and by evaluating their weaknesses each time they make a mistake and noting where they need to improve. The student book provides ample opportunities for this style of writing and it is up to you to decide when to deploy these as summative tests and when to use them as formative assessment activities. The student book prefers a formative methodology within the framework that the IGCSE English as a Second Language examination requires, but we also realize that plenty of work in general language competency is the foundation for success in written English.

Study tips: speaking

The role of the warm-up (see page 73 of the student book)

The warm-up, Part B of the Speaking test, is not assessed. Only Part D of the test is assessed – the 6–9 minute discussion. However, teachers and students should do some work on the warming-up phase so that everyone can be as prepared as possible for the assessed phase.

The warm-up serves two purposes:

1 To place the student/candidate at ease and to settle him or her into the atmosphere of what will be a formal, summative test of speaking skills.

2 To explore, via a discussion of general interests, hobbies, and life outside school, an area in which the candidate has a strong interest, and if possible match this to a suitable and productive topic card from the ten available.

Warm-ups should last 2–3 minutes, after which the examiner chooses a topic card and the assessed phase begins, using the five prompts on the topic card.

The student-centred activity of the warm-up aims to increase the students' confidence so that they can give of their best during the assessed phase of the test – Part D. The warm-up should be fun, and create equality in the classroom. Remember that the Speaking test is not an interview; nor is it an occasion where the teacher/examiner is in the position of authority. It should offer a supportive atmosphere in which ideas are shared and developed. Very formal speaking tests offer no advantage to candidates and they will also generate negative feedback from the external moderators. While Part D should of course have a more formal feel than Part B, the warming-up of Part B should serve to generate productive Part Ds.

It is not always possible to match a candidate to a specific topic based on the warm-up. In these cases you can use a general and accessible topic card. There is a requirement that a school uses a range of topics, so this must occur also. It's a challenge to manage Part B as an effective and fair tool for all candidates taking part in the Speaking test. It is important therefore to allocate time and resources to this element of preparing for oral assessment.

Evaluating the sample student responses

- **Student A** should be given topic 3, The outdoor life.
- **Student B** should be given topic 2, Journalism.
- **Student C** should be given topic 1, Human nature.

☑ My progress

The four study skills – reading, writing, speaking, and listening – are key skills for success in each of the examinations. In the "My progress" section at the end of the chapter in the student book, we invite students to select one skill that they can focus on and develop. However, you may like to ask students to prepare action plans to develop all four of the skills.

The table indicates where the skills feature in the examination papers and how they are applied. Unless otherwise indicated, the skills and tasks are common to both levels.

Skill	Task	Positioning in examination papers
Covering a range of question types in the listening examination	Direct answers, gap filling, matching, MCQs (core and extended) Completing notes (extended)	Listening ● Core: questions 1–7 ● Extended: questions 1-8
Transcribing information to a first-person form	Completing a form with three sections (core) Completing a form with four sections (extended)	Reading and writing ● Exercise 3
Completing the warm-up phase of the speaking test	Conducting a 2–3-minute directed warm-up for specific purposes	Speaking test ● Part B
Using informal language and register in longer pieces of writing	Directed writing: 100–150 words (core) Directed writing: 150– 200 words (extended)	Reading and writing ● Exercise 6

4 Animals and us

Student book content coverage

Segment 1	Pages 78–81 Pets
Syllabus objectives	**R2** Understand and select relevant information **W2** Convey information and express opinions effectively
Broader skills development	• Design a questionnaire. • Fill out a questionnaire. • Analyse and evaluate information. • Write up results objectively.
Introducing the session	"Thinking out loud" (page 78): Allow students five minutes to compose their thoughts as a silent activity. Then ask them, in pairs, to share their thoughts informally.
Ensuring a skills balance	Suggested additional listening activity: Ask one group (who produced a strong piece of work) to present their findings orally. Ask the other groups to listen carefully and take notes. Compare the notes each group produced for consistency.
Differentiated activities	Stronger students can spend a few minutes discussing why people keep pets and why some don't.
Teaching and learning methodologies	**1** Manage group work. **2** Use writing frames. **3** Encourage collaboration with peers.
Building your vocabulary	Ask students, in pairs, to make a list of as many animals as they can in two minutes and then, in small groups, to pool vocabulary that they think will be useful in this segment.
Check your understanding	See segment 2.
Learner outcomes	By the end of this segment, students should be able to: • understand the basic requirements of a questionnaire • select, collate and present information in a written report format.
Workbook	Page 35: Building your vocabulary Pages 35–6: Reading advice for owning pets Page 37: Writing – guidelines for pet owners
Worksheet	4.1: Conducting a survey

Segment 2	Pages 78–80 Unusual pets – stick insects
Syllabus objectives	**R1** Identify and retrieve facts and details **W1** Communicate clearly, accurately and appropriately **W6** Employ appropriate register/style
Broader skills development	• Scan a short article. • Match vocabulary to definitions. • Role play. • Construct an advertisement.
Introducing the session	Ask students if they can think of any unusual pets. Does anyone have an unusual pet?
Ensuring a skills balance	Suggested additional speaking activity: Extend the role-play activity to include a speech from a parent about why stick insects or any other unusual pets would not be welcome in the house. This should be an authoritative speech with only one view/attitude presented.
Differentiated activities	Stronger students can use information in "Unusual pets – stick insects" to prepare and give a one-minute presentation on what children learn from having stick insects in the classroom.
Teaching and learning methodologies	**1** Manage a role play. **2** Construct an advertisement.
Building your vocabulary	Page 79: Stick insects – ask students, in pairs, to read the passage to each other, substituting similar words or phrases for the words in bold.
Check your understanding	Page 79: Ask students to discuss the questions with a partner as they go through them.
Learner outcomes	By the end of this segment, learners should be able to: • understand different viewpoints via role playing • engage with a range of approaches to advertisements.
Workbook	Pages 35–7: Any material on these pages not already used in segment 1 is also useful in support of this segment.
Worksheet	4.2: A practice exam question – listening; a model advertisement

Segment 3	Pages 82–3 Talented animals
Syllabus objectives	**L1** Identify and retrieve facts and details **S2** Convey information and express opinions effectively
Broader skills development	• Recognize and use similes and metaphors. • Match vocabulary to definitions. • Talk about how animals can help people.
Introducing the session	Ask students to think about how animals are used to symbolize or illustrate characteristics.
Ensuring a skills balance	Suggested writing activity: Ask students to write up a blog in which they talk about the talents of Eli. Recommend the YouTube video.

Differentiated activities	Stronger students can work in pairs to develop an interview with Lorna Marsh about her talented dog. They can then act out the interview, taking turns to be interviewer and interviewee.
Teaching and learning methodologies	**1** Enrich descriptive writing through the use of figurative expressions. **2** Develop a conversation.
Building your vocabulary	Page 82: Eli, a most talented dog
Check your understanding	
Learner outcomes	By the end of this segment, students should be able to: • make use of similes and metaphors to enrich their writing • convey information effectively • hold a meaningful conversation.
Workbook	Page 37: Language focus – similes and metaphors Page 37: Talk about training animals Page 38: Building your vocabulary Pages 38–9: Reading about training a puppy Page 39: Check your understanding Page 40: Listening to a guide dog owner Page 40: Multiple-choice response Page 40: Writing different viewpoints
Worksheet	4.3: Building your vocabulary

Segment 4	Pages 84–7 Animals under threat
Syllabus objectives	**R3** Recognize and understand ideas, opinions, and attitudes and the connections between related ideas **W2** Convey information and express opinions effectively
Broader skills development	• Think about conservation issues. • Plan extended writing. • Develop note-taking skills.
Introducing the session	"Thinking out loud" (page 84): Give students two minutes to collect their thoughts on endangered animals. Then give them five minutes to share, in small groups, what they know about tigers.
Ensuring a skills balance	Suggested listening activity: Ask students to listen to one another's short talks based on the "Save the tiger!" article and to note down constructive comments.
Differentiated activities	Stronger students can describe their thoughts and feelings about a visit they made to see an animal in captivity.
Teaching and learning methodologies	**1** Read about the threat to the tiger in the wild. **2** Write a magazine article.
Building your vocabulary	Page 84: When students have finished matching the words with their meaning, ask them to devise sentences of their own, using the words they have just learned.
Check your understanding	Page 85: Ask students to do this in small groups, discussing the information as they complete the exercise.

Learner outcomes	By the end of this segment, students should be able to:
	• reflect and comment persuasively on an issue
	• plan and write an extended piece
	• locate and produce relevant notes from a long passage.
Workbook	Page 41: Building your vocabulary
	Page 42: Reading about the giant panda
	Page 43: Check your understanding
	Page 43: Writing an email about the WWF
Worksheet	4.4: Planning an extended piece of writing

Segment 5	Pages 88–90 Animals being exploited
Syllabus objectives	**R4** Understand what is implied but not actually written
	L4 Understand what is implied but not actually stated
Broader skills development	• Build appropriate vocabulary to express attitudes and opinions.
	• Summarize concisely a response to a piece of writing.
	• Navigate multiple-choice options appropriately.
Introducing the session	"Thinking out loud" (page 88): Give students five minutes to consider issues relating to the ill treatment and exploitation of animals.
Ensuring a skills balance	Suggested speaking activity:
	Ask students, in small groups, to discuss the case of the mistreatment of dancing bears and other instances of cruelty to animals that they may have heard about.
Differentiated activities	Stronger students can put together a short speech either drawing attention to animal cruelty or in defence of the bear trainers and/or other such practices.
Teaching and learning methodologies	1 Read and respond to emotive material.
	2 Listen to and distinguish between strongly held opinions.
Building your vocabulary	Ask students, in pairs, to make a list of words and phrases to express attitudes and opinions.
Check your understanding	Page 88: Dancing bears
	Page 90: Multiple-choice questions – listening
Learner outcomes	By the end of this segment, students should be able to:
	• identify attitude and opinion in both written and spoken material
	• use appropriate vocabulary to express attitude and opinion
	• write a short summary of their response to a piece of writing.
Workbook	"Now it is your turn" (page 44): Students who feel strongly about the mistreatment of animals could use this writing exercise to tell a story in which an ill-treated animal gets its own back on its master.
Worksheet	4.5: A group discussion

Segment 6	Pages 91–2 The Big Issue – preservation or progress?
Syllabus objectives	**S5** Engage in and influence the direction of conversation **W6** Employ appropriate register/style
Broader skills development	• Present your view orally. • Assess the strengths and weaknesses of examples of formal letter writing. • Present your view in a piece of extended writing.
Introducing the session	"Preparing for a debate" (page 91): Give students five minutes to read and discuss in pairs the problem and the choice presented.
Ensuring a skills balance	Suggested writing activity: Ask students to email a friend about the debate they had.
Differentiated activities	Stronger students can write a critical report of the debate that takes place, summarizing the points made for and against and assessing the quality of argument.
Teaching and learning methodologies	**1** Take part in a debate. **2** Write a piece that takes into account the views of several people on a particular issue.
Building your vocabulary	Ask students to make a list of five unfamiliar words on pages 91–92 and, in pairs, compare lists, check the meanings, and add them to their personal vocabulary.
Check your understanding	
Learner outcomes	By the end of this segment, students should be able to: • prepare and present a point of view • appreciate both sides of an argument.
Workbook	
Worksheet	4.6: A studio debate – preservation or progress?

Segment 7	Pages 93–4 Animals in literature
Syllabus objectives	**R3** Recognize and understand ideas, opinions, and attitudes and the connection between related ideas **L3** Recognize and understand ideas, opinions, and attitudes and the connections between related ideas
Broader skills development	• Listen to fables being read to "get the gist" of what they mean. • Read an extract from a work of contemporary literature. • Write and tell an anecdote.
Introducing the session	Ask students what animal stories they have come across. Get them to share briefly what the story was about. For no more than five minutes, get them to think of animals that appear in stories (such as the wolf in *Red Riding Hood*). Introduce them to fables.
Ensuring a skills balance	Suggested writing activity: "What happens next?" Ask students to read the extract from *War Horse* (page 94) and then write the next episode in the story as they imagine it might continue.
Differentiated activities	Stronger students might have a go at rewriting the extract from *War Horse* as told by Albert.

Teaching and learning methodologies	**1** Listen to "get the gist" of what is being read.
	2 Read and respond to an extract from a novel.
Building your vocabulary	Ask students to check any vocabulary they are unsure of in the *War Horse* extract and add the new words to their personal vocabulary list.
Check your understanding	Ask students, in pairs, to discuss how many things they can find in the extract from *War Horse* that show that the horse is telling the story.
Learner outcomes	By the end of this segment, students should be able to:
	• listen critically to a reading
	• understand opinion and viewpoint when reading a piece of literature
	• convey a particular viewpoint when telling an anecdote.
Workbook	Page 44: Reading – *Belling the cat*
	Page 44: Listening – "Reading aloud"
	Page 44: Writing – "Now it's your turn"
Worksheet	4.7: Find out more about fables

Segment 8	Pages 95–7 Animals in the service of humans
Syllabus objectives	**R2** Understand and select relevant information
	W1 Communicate clearly, accurately, and appropriately
Broader skills development	• Read a surprising example of animals in the service of humans.
	• Contribute to a focused conversation.
	• Take part in a group writing activity.
Introducing the session	"Thinking out loud" (page 95): Give students five minutes to collect their thoughts and, in pairs, to complete the table listing animals that help humans.
Ensuring a skills balance	Suggested listening exercise:
	Ask students to listen again to the sample speaking test conversations and, in pairs, to pick up the discussions that they have sampled.
Differentiated activities	Stronger students can follow up the discussion about respecting all animals by writing a brief summary of their findings.
Teaching and learning methodologies	**1** Read and evaluate information that gives an unusual perspective on a subject.
	2 Take part in a group writing activity.
Building your vocabulary	Page 95: A very unusual little helper
Check your understanding	Page 96: A very unusual little helper
Learner outcomes	By the end of this segment, students should be able to:
	• reflect on what they have learned about listening and responding to different viewpoints
	• complete the "My progress" form at the end of the chapter and select one skill for their action plan.
Workbook	Page 44: Discussion topic
Worksheet	4.8: Building your vocabulary
Further practice	**On completion of the chapter, ask students to complete questions 1–20 of the animals and us interactive activities.**

Links

If you choose only one link to use with your students, try this:

- www.wwf.org
  This website provides a wealth of information about animals in their interaction with human beings worldwide, especially about endangered species. It offers an excellent opportunity for students to practise and extend their vocabulary.

You might also try:

- www.animalsnationalgeographic.com – this home page gives free access to news, pictures, articles, and film clips about animals of all kinds everywhere.

- www.animal.discovery.com – read and watch videos of animal activity throughout the world.

- www.rspca.org.uk/allaboutanimals – information about pets, wildlife, and farm animals.

If your students enjoyed Michael Morpurgo's novel *War Horse*, tell them to look out for the play and the film.

Study tips: reading

Note-taking (see page 87 of the student book)

Evaluating the sample student responses

- **Student 1** provides minimal responses and pure notes, and has followed the advice on useful techniques most closely.

- **Student 2** provides full responses and close to full sentences. All the required information is present but so is a lot of unnecessary additional detail. However, the notes provided are acceptable.

- **Student 3** has, by using their own words, slightly changed the meaning. The phrases "like to kill them", "stealing bits of the body", and "chopping down trees doesn't help them" have led to what examiners refer to as blurred meaning. This is the weakest response and these notes are not acceptable.

Note-taking skills are assessed differently at the core and extended levels of the Reading and Writing paper. The key skills are the same and common to both, but the formats of the questions vary. Further in-depth work on note-taking, illustrating these different formats, appears on page 180 (page 290 of the student book).

Study tips: writing

Presenting your view in a piece of extended writing (see pages 91–2 of the student book)

This activity offers students advice on how to to generate/write their own essays and asks them to analyse the strengths and weakness of three examples of other students' writing. You will need to do some preparatory work with your students to help them construct a marking scheme for assessing this type of essay writing.

This section is intended to mirror the work undertaken in Exercise 7 at both levels of the Reading and Writing paper. However, it will be interesting to allow students to be creative here in designing their own marking criteria, while ensuring with careful management that their schemes are reasonable and that they relate to how Exercise 7 is assessed by examiners.

Evaluating the sample student responses

- **Student 1** provides a strong, secure and confident response, considering both sides of the argument and recognizing that each has a rationale. It concludes by presenting a personal view and stating it clearly. The language is secure, accurate, and varied.

- **Student 2** conveys a clear preference and does consider both sides of the argument, but not fully. A major omission is not dealing with the relative cost of building the airport at the other site. There are some slips in language usage and it is not an accurate piece. However, it has its merits, which a marking scheme would recognize. It is a pleasant piece of work, adequate in parts and appealing in others.

- **Student 3** has written a piece with more weaknesses than strengths. The degree of error affects the fluency of reading and a key concern is repetition. The piece also shows only a superficial understanding of some of the main issues and problems.

Study tips: listening

Listening to a discussion (see page 93 of the student book)

This exercise provides practice for Part B by using Aesop's fables and allows students up to three words to complete each sentence. This is an informal and formative exercise to improve their skills, with students working through it in pairs or in small groups.

Evaluating the sample student responses

- **Q1:** Student A is the closest here. The man and the woman agreed. There is no evidence that they argued and, if listened was used, we would have "listened with each other", which is not accurate grammatically and would not therefore be credited.

- **Q2:** Student B provides the best answer here. Student A's response may well be true but there is no evidence for it in the recording. Student C is attempting to provide a response that fits and makes sense, but it bears no relevance to the context.

- **Q3:** Student C is correct. However, this is a difficult gap to fill because inference has to be used. Usain Bolt's name is mentioned and, since he wouldn't agree to or benefit from going carefully or taking his time, the only viable response is therefore "run very fast".

- **Q4:** Students A and B both provide responses that are not grammatically correct, so they cannot be correct. Student C has the accurate response here – the man relates closely to the mouse.

- **Q5:** Student A and Student B provide responses which work and which fit. However, Student B has selected the most accurate detail from the recording. Student A's response would not be allowed as it is too general and examiners are looking for precision.

- **Q6:** All three students suggest acceptable responses given the context, and all three provide responses that are grammatically acceptable. However, Student B has recognized that is the balance in life that the woman mentions, while there is no evidence for what the other two students say.

Exam focus: listening

For students taking the Listening paper at extended level, there is an additional exercise: Question 8. This question has two parts:

- Part A: an initial formal talk (5 marks)
- Part B: a discussion with two people discussing the contents of the talk (5 marks).

Both parts are assessed using sentences or statements that require one or two words for completion.

How Question 8 works: Part A

Here is a formal version of how a full Question 8 works, based on the interview with Bart Weetjens featured in the article on page 96 of the student book about using African pouched rats to help humans. Play students the recording for Part A of Question 8.

Students should now attempt to complete these notes, writing only one or two words in each gap. Each note is a statement or a short sentence that is missing a piece of information. Note that two or three full and complete statements are included.

Reasons why rats are used

1   Rats are .... to train than other animals.

Characteristics of rats

2   Rats are perceived as vermin and destroyers, but this is not necessarily the case. Rats exist in social groups and show clear signs of ....

Details of rats used

3   Sniffers and hero rats make up the crew. The .... shows images of some of the rats.

Schemes and ventures

4   An adoption scheme has attracted interest from .... people.

5   Some rats are being trained to find people who are trapped under ....

[5 marks – 1 mark for each correctly filled-in gap]

Answers

1   easier

2   intelligence

3   website

4   280

5   (collapsed) buildings

Model answers and how to improve performance

In Part A of Question 8, students listen to a talk and then complete statements by entering one of two words only in a gap. It is not a simple exercise in locating specific detail because it is testing all four assessment objectives. This means that some degree of inference skill will be required. For example, the words in the statements may not feature in the original talk/text, so students will need to listen carefully in order to be able to locate the parts of the speech being referred to.

This question tests higher-level skills and features only on the extended paper.

Level of achievement	Level descriptor
A grade	Select material from texts and develop it in relationship to the questions, sufficient to show some independence of thought
C grade	Select material from texts in answer to questions and provide straightforward explanations and developments to show relevance
E grade	Select material from texts in answer to questions and provide basic explanations

Here are some model answers to the Part A questions above. The first response is the ideal response, but the other responses are acceptable and would be credited by an examiner.

1 Rats are .... to train than other animals.

easier... less difficult... simpler... more straightforward

> **Our expert says:** The main idea is that rats are easier to train, so anything that equates to this will be accepted, as long as it provides a secure grammatical fit and uses only one or two words. For example, *not as hard* would not be credited and neither would *the easiest* as the superlative here is not grammatically sound.

2 Rats exist in social groups and show clear signs of ....

intelligence... being intelligent... intelligent behaviour...obvious intelligence

> **Our expert says:** Students need to convey the idea of intelligence and not a characteristic close to it – so *being clever* would not be credited, as it is not quite the same thing. *Intelligent* on its own would also not be credited because it is not grammatically secure.

3 The .... shows images of some of the rats.

website... web pages... company website...

> **Our expert says:** Since precision is important at this level, students suggesting *the Internet* or *the web* would not be given the mark as these responses are too broad. The reference must be to a specific website. *Website of rats* would also be not be allowed as it is three words.

4 An adoption scheme has attracted interest from .... people.

280...

5   Some rats are being trained to find people who are trapped
     under ....

buildings... collapsed buildings... demolished buildings...

How Question 8 works: Part B

In Part B of Question 8, students listen to a semi-formal discussion by two people who have just been listening to the talk. Or perhaps one of the two heard the talk and is discussing it later with the other. Part B involves different skills: synthesizing information, listening to two points of view, and recognizing attitudes in dialogue.

More about mine-detecting rats and other working animals

1   The things people say about rats can sometimes
     be ....

2   Animals are proving useful in helping to solve ....

3   Rats appear to .... when they repeat tasks.

4   Currently, there are ....of rats helping to detect
     landmines.

5   Another animal project, of a medical nature, makes
     use of ....

[5 marks – 1 mark for each correctly filled-in gap]

Answers

1   false

2   crime

3   get better

4   hundreds

5   cats

Model answers and how to improve performance

In these model answers to the Part B questions above, the first response is the best one, but the others are acceptable and would be credited by an examiner.

1   The things people say about rats can sometimes
     be ....

false ... not true... untrue... inaccurate... not reliable... wrong

> **Our expert says:** Any synonym for false would be accepted here. However, students need to be careful of the "one or two words" rule, so *not the truth* would not gain the mark, for example. If students have not heard the word "false" they may offer a word that fits but which doesn't have the same meaning, such as *misleading, critical, bad, unfair,* or *biased*. These all present a different shade of meaning.

2   Animals are proving useful in helping to solve ....

crime... criminal cases...drugs cases

> **Our expert says:** The recording stated that animals are proving useful in the prosecution of *criminals*, so students might suggest criminals in the gap and this would not be allowed as it is grammatically questionable, and the meaning is blurred. The word *drugs* on its own would also not be credited.

3   Rats appear to .... when they repeat tasks.

get better... improve...

> **Our expert says:** If a student used the full phrase from the recording – *get better and better* – it would not be credited because it is more than two words. Phrases broader in scope, e.g. *become experts, gain skills,* would not be accepted as they are imprecise. More general responses, such as *enjoy it* or *be happy,* would also not be credited as they are drawn from elsewhere in the recording and do not relate specifically to the task repetition action.

4   Currently, there are .... of rats helping to detect landmines.

hundreds... 100s

> **Our expert says:** It is always better to use figures rather than words when writing down numbers here – e.g. *1,001* rather than *one thousand and one*. When transcribing numbers it is important to be accurate, so *a hundred, 100,* or *about 100* would all fail to gain the mark. There is probably only one acceptable response here – *hundreds*. Adding *several* is poor grammar.

5   Another animal project, of a medical nature, makes use of ....

cats... felines... a cat...the cat...

> **Our expert says:** Inserting *diabetes* would not gain a mark as it makes the meaning unclear and is superseded by a much more appropriate response (cats). This question raises the issues of plurals, and here the singular would be accepted because it has the same meaning. (In a case where this would change the meaning, an examiner might insist on one or the other.)

Study tips: speaking

Speaking test – Prompt 4 (see page 97 of the student book)

This activity asks students to listen to and evaluate three examples of responses from a typical Speaking test.

Evaluating the sample student responses

- **Student 1** provides the best response to this section of the Speaking test, and is very skilled at understanding the concept, considering both sides of the suggestion, but having a firm and confident view in response to Prompt 4. It is particularly impressive where alternative ways are suggested to watch wild animals, and regarding the specific purpose of zoos. This student is clearly working at band 1 level in all areas.

- **Student 2** provides a safe and steady response. There is clear understanding of the concept that zoos might not be ethically sound, but the student stays in safe and more straightforward territory and does not possess the sophistication that Student 1 demonstrates. This response suggests competent band 3 achievement.

- **Student 3** is rather inflexible – stating a view and then sticking to it. The response certainly shows understanding of the concept raised in Prompt 4, but it is limited, thin, and contains some repetition. As a result, the vocabulary lacks breadth and the repeated short statements affect the range of structures. It is an acceptable, but a weak and limited, response that equates to band 4 performance.

Exam focus: the Speaking test and the topic card

As the grid in the syllabus shows, speaking skills are assessed against three criteria, each of which has a maximum of 10 marks available. The total available is therefore 30 marks for the full test. There are five achievement bands and the examiner commentary below places each response in a performance band. A mark out of 30 can only really be given for a full 6–9 minute discussion.

The following is an example of an oral test card, showing Prompt 4 in bold for you to practise with your students.

Oral test topic card
Animals and us

Across the world, people have different opinions and attitudes towards animals.

Discuss this theme with the examiner.

The following ideas *must* be used in sequence to develop the conversation:

1 Animals that you like or dislike

2 Whether you have a pet and, if not, which pet you would have

3 How different animals live in different parts of the world

4 **The suggestion that all animals could be pets if we treated them correctly**

5 The idea that animals are on the planet for our benefit – to use in any way we like.

You are free to consider any other *related* ideas of your own.

Remember, you are not allowed to make any written notes.

Model answers and how to improve performance

In addition to demonstrating a safe and good range of structures, a wide range of vocabulary, and the ability to speak fluently using appropriate pronunciation and intonation, a highly competent performance will need to engage fully with the concepts raised in Prompts 4 and 5 of the Speaking test.

Prompt 4 here asks whether *all* animals could be pets. We heard a woman earlier talking about the unusual animals she kept as "pets" and this serves as an example of the concept – that a pet means different things to different people.

The following comments from students are examples of model responses, achieving the top band of achievement.

Student A

"Yes, I agree with that. Or at least I agree with the principle – that more animals could be treated as pets. It depends really on a person's attitude towards animals. One person's pet is probably another person's pet hate. Take snakes, for example. I know that some people who own snakes will pick them up, caress them, be playful with them – all the kinds of things that you do with a pet. Other people are frightened of them, though, and some people have even worse reactions, panicking."

Student B

"Some animals – say, farm animals – can be both. I've heard that sheep, for example, can be wild and can run a mile from humans. But there's a situation in sheep farming where a lamb, a young sheep, can be very friendly to humans and it feels to the human like the lamb is a pet dog. It's when a lamb is an orphan, and doesn't have a mother. These lambs, when reared by humans, make a bond with the human. You can stroke the lambs, play with them – just like a pet."

Student C

"I'm not sure though that the suggestion works all the time. All animals, it says. What about insects? I'm not sure we can treat a spider correctly, or a fly. So I think the suggestion really means that more animals could be closer to humans, but not all. The best example maybe is a shark. I don't know of any of those that have been trained to be pets like dolphins. I know I wouldn't trust a shark. Even if it had a nice name."

Student D

"And when we do treat animals correctly, that's not to say that they become pets – for example, crocodiles. If you kept one of those in a large tank and fed it properly and kept it healthy, how would you know if it created a close bond to you? I think you'd always be looking over your shoulder to see what it was up to. And that's not what a pet is, surely?"

Each case demonstrates a deeper understanding of the issue, an ability to see both sides of it, an ability to draw upon relevant examples, and enough confidence to be able to present these to the examiner on equal terms.

☑ My progress

The four study skills – reading, writing, speaking, and listening – are key skills for success in each of the examinations. In the "My progress" section at the end of the chapter in the student book we invite students to select one skill that they can focus on and develop. However, you may like to ask students to prepare action plans to develop all four of the skills.

The table indicates where the skills feature in the examination papers and how they are applied. Unless otherwise indicated, the skills and tasks are common to both levels.

Skill	Task	Positioning in examination papers
Taking notes based on an article	Locate seven notes (core) Locate nine notes (extended)	Reading and writing ● Exercise 5 (core and extended)
Presenting a view based on the opinions of others	Write an essay of 100–150 words (core) Write an essay of 150–200 words (extended)	Reading and writing ● Exercise 7 (core and extended)
Listening to a talk and a follow-up conversation about the talk	Identifying details from the talk and then identifying information based on the subsequent dialogue	Listening ● Question 8, Parts A and B
Responding to a strong point of view	Speak with conviction when asked about a view or an idea	Speaking test ● Prompt 4 ● Prompt 5

5 Working life

Student book content coverage

Segment 1	Pages 100–2 The best job in the world?
Syllabus objectives	**R2** Understand and select relevant information **W2** Convey information and express opinions carefully
Broader skills development	• Distinguish between fact and opinion. • Write a letter of resignation. • Collaborate in group writing.
Introducing the session	"Thinking out loud" (page 100): Ask students to spend five minutes discussing these introductory questions informally in pairs.
Ensuring a skills balance	Suggested listening and speaking activity: Ask students, in small groups, to take turns to choose one of the dream jobs and give a short talk advertising its benefits. As the members of the group listen to these talks, they can note down their responses.
Differentiated activities	Stronger students can write an imaginative account of six months as a chocolate consultant or in one of the "dream jobs".
Teaching and learning methodologies	**1** Develop a discussion. **2** Look for the "twist in the tale".
Building your vocabulary	Ask students to reinforce their understanding of the words on page 100 by using them in sentences of their own.
Check your understanding	Ask students to check one another's understanding of the dream job accounts by taking it in turns to ask each other questions about them.
Learner outcomes	By the end of this segment, students should be able to: • sift through a passage to establish what is actually being said • convey their thoughts and feelings in a letter • collaborate in a group writing activity.
Workbook	Page 45: Building your vocabulary – further useful job advertisement and application words Page 45–6: Reading about summer jobs for teenagers Page 46: Check your understanding Page 47: Writing a dairy entry
Worksheet	5.1: Building your vocabulary

Segment 2	Pages 103–6 The Big Issue – what job will you choose?
Syllabus objectives	**R4** Understand what is implied but not actually written **L4** Understand what is implied but not actually stated
Broader skills development	• Practise form filling. • Develop a conversation.
Introducing the session	"Thinking out loud" (page 103): Ask students to discuss what jobs they would like to sample to find out more about them.
Ensuring a skills balance	Suggested writing activity: Ask students to write "Case study 4" about their own work experience, real or imagined.
Differentiated activities	Stronger students can, in pairs, discuss what the main requirements are for a successful work experience placement, before going on to note down a short list of recommendations.
Teaching and learning methodologies	**1** Read through case study reports. **2** Continue a conversation.
Building your vocabulary	Page 103: Ask students to reinforce their acquisition of new words by using them in sentences of their own. Page 106: Ask students to make a list of idioms used in the workplace, with their meanings.
Check your understanding	Page 106: Multiple-choice questions – ask students to complete this in pairs, discussing their choices as they work through the exercise.
Learner outcomes	By the end of this segment, students should be able to: • understand and evaluate feedback • continue a conversation using the appropriate register.
Workbook	Pages 45–7: Any material on these pages not already used will also be helpful in support of this segment.
Worksheet	5.2: Role playing – Pete's work experience

Segment 3	Pages 107–8 A day in the life of …
Syllabus objectives	**L3** Recognize and understand ideas, opinions, and attitudes and the connections between related ideas **S1** Communicate clearly, accurately, and appropriately
Broader skills development	• Read about a day in the life of a social worker. • Listen to a flying doctor speaking about his work and respond appropriately. • Set up writing and speaking activities to welcome and interview a special guest.
Introducing the session	"Thinking out loud" (page 107): Allow five minutes for students, in pairs, to discuss the routine of work.
Ensuring a skills balance	Suggested writing activity: Ask students to follow up "A special guest" by writing a blog about Ceinwen's visit.
Differentiated activities	Stronger students can go on to give a talk welcoming Ceinwen as the special guest.

Teaching and learning methodologies	1 Read an account of a Ugandan social worker's day and from it reconstruct a counselling session.
	2 Listen to a flying doctor's account of his life and work.
	3 Work as a group to organize the visit of a special guest.
Building your vocabulary	Page 107: Ask students to practise using these words in sentences of their own.
Check your understanding	Page 107: As students listen to track 5.2, "A flying doctor", ask them, in pairs, to note down any expressions they are unsure of and check with one another the meaning of each before going on to the other work based on this.
Learner outcomes	By the end of this segment, students should be able to:
	• recreate a scene or setting from given information
	• contribute to a group activity developing ideas from information in a talk.
Workbook	Page 48: Check your understanding – multiple-choice questions
Worksheet	5.3: Building your vocabulary

Segment 4	**Page 109–11 Jobs involving travel**
Syllabus objectives	**R1** Identify and retrieve facts and details
	R3 Recognize and understand ideas, opinions, and attitudes and the connection between related ideas
	W6 Employ appropriate register/style
Broader skills development	• Read job descriptions and extract particular information from them.
	• Read job applications and assess the information given or implied.
Introducing the session	"Thinking out loud" (page 109): Ask students to spend five minutes discussing the questions.
Ensuring a skills balance	Suggested speaking activity:
	In small groups, ask students to discuss the "Careers for travellers" and decide together which one most appeals to them.
Differentiated activities	Stronger students can write to apply for one of the jobs involving travel.
Teaching and learning methodologies	1 Read a description of three top travel jobs.
	2 Transfer information to complete an assessment form.
	3 Assess information to match applicants to jobs.
Building your vocabulary	Page 109: Crossword – ask students in pairs to check the meaning of any other vocabulary new to them in the segment.
Check your understanding	Page 111: Answer the questions in small groups as preparation for the suggested speaking activity above.
Learner outcomes	By the end of this segment, students should be able to:
	• analyse written presentations and extract appropriate notes from them
	• assess suitability from written applications and match these to jobs.

Workbook	Page 49: Discussion focusing on an international aid worker
	Page 49: Building your vocabulary – multiple choice
	Page 50: Reading a blog by an international aid worker
	Page 51: Check your understanding
	Page 51: Language focus – reported speech
	Page 52: Extended writing
Worksheet	5.4: Looking at skills, experience, and personal qualities

Segment 5	Pages 112–15 A career in sport or leisure
Syllabus objectives	**W4** Demonstrate knowledge and understanding of a range of appropriate vocabulary
	L2 Understand and select relevant information
	S5 Engage in and influence the direction of conversation
Broader skills development	• Create a puppet show.
	• Write a descriptive letter.
	• Sustain a conversation.
Introducing the session	"Thinking out loud" (page 112): Ask students to discuss the questions in small groups for five minutes.
Ensuring a skills balance	Suggested speaking activity:
	Develop the "Famous people" topic card as an informal small-group discussion.
Differentiated activities	Stronger students can go on to present the puppet play prepared in "Creating a puppet show" (see template in worksheet 5.5).
Teaching and learning methodologies	**1** Prepare and script a puppet play.
	2 Improve the flow of a conversation.
	3 Look critically at content in descriptive writing.
Building your vocabulary	Ask students to note down any unfamiliar words as they listen to the interview with Kim and watch and read about Corina and her puppets. For each, they should check the meanings in pairs.
Check your understanding	Page 112: Ask students to answer individually and then in pairs compare and discuss their answers.
	Page 113: Answer informally in pairs.
Learner outcomes	By the end of this segment, students should be able to:
	• sustain a relevant conversation on a prepared topic
	• assess the style and content of their descriptive writing
	• engage in a group activity to mount a puppet show.
Workbook	Page 53: Building your vocabulary
	Page 54: Reading – further information about Corina and her puppets
	Page 55: Check your understanding – students to discuss the answers informally in pairs
Worksheet	5.5: Creating the script for a puppet show

Segment 6	Pages 116–17 Literary connections – *To Kill a Mockingbird*
Syllabus objectives	**R3** Recognize and understand ideas, opinions, and attitudes and the connections between related ideas
	S2 Convey information and express opinions effectively
Broader skills development	• Read and assess a short literary extract.
	• Create a play scene.
Introducing the session	"Thinking out loud" (page 116): Ask students to spend five minutes discussing the questions, then ask if anyone has read *To Kill a Mockingbird* or seen the film.
Ensuring a skills balance	Suggested writing activity:
	Take the discussion topic on page 56 of the workbook and post a blog, giving your personal thoughts on "What do I want to do?"
Differentiated activities	Stronger students can write an introduction to the careers stand featured in "Reflection" that could be used as a handout to give visitors to the stand.
Teaching and learning methodologies	**1** Read a literary extract.
	2 Collaborate to develop a play scene.
	3 Work as a group to create a publicity display.
Building your vocabulary	Go through the extract from *To Kill a Mockingbird* (page 116) as a teacher-led activity to achieve understanding of the complex vocabulary – especially the idioms used. This is supported by worksheet 5.6.
Check your understanding	Page 116: Students could answer in pairs.
Learner outcomes	By the end of this segment, students should be able to:
	• act out a short scene exploring a difficult work situation
	• work with others on a group presentation.
Workbook	Page 56: Discussion topic
Worksheet	5.6: Looking at the extract from *To Kill a Mockingbird*
Further practice	**On completion of the chapter, ask students to complete questions 1–20 of the working life interactive activities.**

Links

The most helpful links are likely to be specific to a country or region, such as:

- www.network4africa.org

Others to try are:

- www.totaljobs.com – information about unusual jobs.
- www.work-experience.org – ideas to follow up.
- www.workexperienceabroad.co.uk – individuals' accounts of their work experience.
- www.theguardian.com/series/a-day-in-the-life-of – an occasional series.

If your students have read *To Kill a Mockingbird* and enjoyed it, they might also like Mildred Taylor's *Roll of Thunder, Hear my Cry,* a story set in the Mississippi Delta during the Great Depression of the 1930s.

Study tips: reading

Form filling (see page 105 of the student book)

This activity introduces the format of application and feedback forms to the students. When students complete their form-filling task on the examination paper, they will incorporate elements of applying for something and providing some sort of evaluative comment. The informal pair work here encourages students to discuss and design some feedback questions, and this is then followed by some feedback linked to the three case studies.

Evaluating the sample student responses

- **Student C** provides the most useful information from a data-gathering perspective. Everything that is given is given exactly as it was requested and the respondent has clearly understood what the questions were getting at. She listed two concerns as requested.

- **Student A** does not convey any issues, concerns, or problems. This is unlikely for a person taking on a work placement. Also, she hasn't really understood what benefits are/mean. In the last question, she has not explained *why* she would recommend the experience. In terms of data collection, this feedback form is the least useful.

- **Student B** provides three issues where two were requested. This is a more useful response than Student A's, but it skews the data because we are not sure which two were the biggest concerns. Also, the issues were entirely personal. This person has understood what benefits mean but has given only one and could have said more. A similar pattern is seen in the response to the last question: partial understanding and data that is partly useful.

This section therefore raises the issue of the aptness and usefulness of data provided on a form. You may like to emphasize and explore this with your students and to get them used to responding in Exercise 3 with details that give the form designers the information they actually want.

Exam focus: the Reading and Writing paper

For in-depth coverage of the skills involved in filling out the forms used in Exercise 3 of the Reading and Writing paper, see chapter 3, pages 40–45. Many of the skills are common to both tiers, but here we will focus on the core paper. In chapter 3, the focus is on the extended-level paper.

As can be seen from the assessment objectives below, Exercise 3 tests the integrated skills of reading and writing. The focus skill, however, is reading, but obviously writing skills are involved as the information is transferred to a form. Marks are awarded as follows:

- Reading skills: 10 marks
- Writing skills: 4 marks

R4 is not tested at core level – students do not need to understand what is implied but not actually written. The form is simpler and asks for the location of more straightforward details than the form used at extended level.

There are usually only three sections of the form – sections A and B for obtaining details, and section C asking for two sentences (but with no word limits) relating to specific reasons or preferences shown in the original account.

A typical Exercise 3 at core level

Ask your students to read the account below about someone interested in applying for a new job.

Miriam Kelly graduated approximately two years ago from university. She currently lives at 1a Cedar Apartments, 12th Avenue, Manhattan, New York City. She is 23 years of age, is not married and she lives alone. It is best to contact her using her mobile number, which is 07770 212312. She spent four years studying for her degree course, and graduated in Economics, which included a placement year working in Chicago for a bank. She graduated in 2012 from Chicago State University.

She has been working as a personal assistant in a fashion company, but it is not a job she likes and she is looking for a job in finance. Her current boss is the Director of Creative Fashion. At the moment, Miriam earns $28 000 a year, and receives four weeks holiday. She has been with the company for exactly 20 months. Miriam has just seen an advertisement for a job that she thinks is ideal for her and she is going to make an application. It is based in New York and the position is as finance controller for a commercial bank. The form she needs to fill in asks about her qualifications, experience, and previous jobs, but it also asks her for other information. Miriam has two references, one from her university professor and one from her current employer.

In a new job, Miriam is looking for more freedom to express herself, and she is keen to use some of the experience she gained from studying economics. She feels that she is under-performing in her current job, and as a result she is quite often not being challenged at work.

Imagine you are Miriam and fill out the following application form applying for the new job.

Application for the post of finance controller

SECTION A   **Personal details of applicant**

Full name ....

Contact address ....

Age (circle)

18–25   26–40   41–60   over 60

Status (delete as appropriate)

Single   Married   Own accommodation   Living with parents

Telephone ....

Qualifications ....

SECTION B   **Current position**

Position held ....

Responsible to ....

Salary per year (tick box)

less than $10 000 ☐ $10 000–$19 999 ☐ $20 000–$30 000 ☐   more than $30 000 ☐

Time in employment (underline)

less than 2 years   2–5 years   6–10 years   more than 10 years

SECTION C

Write one sentence below stating what you are looking for in a new job, and write one sentence about why you would like to leave your current job.

1 ....

2 ....

[14 marks in total: 4 marks for Section C + 10 marks for the other two sections.]

Answers

Section A

Name: | Miriam Kelly |

Address: | 1a Cedar Apartments, 12th Avenue, Manhattan, New York City |

Age: | circle 18–25 |

Status: | delete married + living with parents |

Telephone: | 07770 212312 |

Qualifications: | Degree in Economics |

Section B

Position held: | personal assistant (in a fashion company) |

Responsible to: | Director of Creative Fashion |

Salary: | tick $20 000 – $30 000 |

Time in job: | underline "less than 2 years" |

NB: For sections A and B, a single mark is awarded for each item on the form. Unlike the extended paper, core does not use half marks or divide the total by 2, so 10 items = 10 marks.

Section C

Sentence 1 should convey either her need for more freedom to express herself (at work) *or* her need to use her degree/studying of economics. If both are given that is fine.

Sentence 2 should convey her view that she is under-performing *or* that she is not being challenged by her current work. If both are given that is fine.

For each sentence:

- proper sentence construction; correct spelling and punctuation; gives the information asked for: 2 marks

- proper sentence construction; one to three errors of punctuation and/or spelling (without obscuring the meaning); gives the information asked for: 1 mark

- more than three errors of punctuation and/or spelling; and/or does not give the information asked for; and/or not a proper sentence; and/or meaning obscure: 0 marks

NB: Section C carries 4 marks, 2 marks for each sentence.

Model answers and how to improve performance

In an exercise where absolute accuracy is required, a model answer will usually be the only acceptable response. However, alternatives might sometimes be accepted as long as they convey identical information. It is perhaps more interesting in this section to look at some responses which appear to be accurate but which, on closer inspection, are not and would not gain the mark(s).

The key competence that students therefore need to develop is the skill of accurate transcription. To do this, they must be able to select the appropriate pieces of information from the source and to transcribe only that information and nothing more.

Sections A and B

For a detailed analysis of the approaches to marking form-filling work, refer to chapter 3, pages 40–45. Here, we will focus on a few interesting responses that might occur in the exercise above.

Contact address: *1a Cedar Apartments, 12th Avenue, Manhattan, New York City*

> **Our expert says:** This must be as above and it must contain all the correct capital letters and commas. A response such as *1a Cedar apartments, 12th Avenue, Manhattan, New York City,* where a lower case "a" is used for Apartments, would not be credited. Neither would *1a Cedar Apartments, 12th Avenue, Manhattan New York City,* as the comma is omitted before New York City. Should a candidate write just New York, this would also not be allowed because New York might be New York State.

Status (delete as appropriate): *delete BOTH married AND living with parents*

> **Our expert says:** Remind students that "delete as appropriate" can mean the deletion of more than one item in the list. Also, the examiner will not accept underlining as deletion. Delete must be shown as a striking through or a crossing out completely.

Qualifications: *Degree in Economics... Economics degree... Economics at degree level...*

> **Our expert says:** Examiners are likely to accept lower case for "degree" if it is used as a common noun and not capitalized in the source. However, Economics does use the capital so that must be accurate. If the candidate puts a gap in their writing, *degree in Eco nomics* for example, an examiner might give the student the benefit of the doubt in this case, as the gap does not change the meaning. However, if the answer changes the meaning (e.g. if *Wildlife* is required and *wild life* is given), the mark would not be allowed.

Position held: *personal assistant... Personal Assistant... personal assistant in a fashion company...*

> **Our expert says:** These answers show that, where lower case is used, using upper case does not affect the mark. As for the extended level, the rule is that, should a candidate add unnecessary detail, it must be accurately transcribed, so *personal assistant in a fashon company* would lose the mark. It is always best in Exercise 3 to give *only* the information required.

Responsible to: *Director of Creative Fashion*

> **Our expert says:** By contrast to the last item, this must be capitalized as it is a proper noun and capitals are used in the source. For successful form filling, the language skills of correct grammar are clearly essential, as is a sound understanding of language conventions.

Salary per year (tick box):

If a cross (x) or forward slash is used here, the mark will not be given – it must be a tick.

Section C

The two sentences are not restricted to minimum and maximum word limits but must relate clearly to the content stated. Otherwise, the marking approach is the same as for the extended paper Exercise 3.

Study tips: listening

Listening to a talk based on a job (see page 108 of the student book)

This exercise tests listening skill, which is a feature of several parts of the Listening examination. The students first listen to a talk by someone describing their career, current job, and working life. In the Listening test, students will probably experience talks both about a particular subject (e.g. the state of the world's oceans) and about someone's life and work (e.g. how a captain of a ship copes with his job on the oceans).

Here, Ceinwen's talk about his work with the Royal Australian Flying Doctor Service (Track 5.2) is used as the basis for giving students further practice at completing sentences with one or two words. Ask your students to work informally in pairs or small groups to complete the five statements by filling in the gaps. They must use good grammar and their word choices must make sense.

It is important that your students practise this skill – of completing statements or sentences using only one or two words – because it will improve their chances of success in the examination considerably. You could give them short segments of speech to use for further practice, but try to use clips of someone talking enthusiastically about an interesting subject.

Evaluating the sample student responses

Question 1

- **Student C** gives the best response. We would prefer "taught English" at the end of the sentence, but "taught" on its own is fine.

- **Student A** provides an incorrect response. Three words are one too many in the first gap (and it is grammatically incorrect with "an" added after "a") and "Australian" in the second gap is poor grammar.

- **Student B** also provides an incorrect response, using – like Student A – the wrong article and too many words. "Worked in the building industry" is accurate but at five words would not be allowed.

Question 4

All three answers have complied with the one or two words requirement, but only one is correct.

- **Student A** suggests that the long distances and the flying are problematic for Ceinwen, but although he mentions these aspects, there is no evidence that he either likes or dislikes them. If we were testing assessment objective L4, an incorrect gist would have been reached. No marks.

- **Student B** suggests that Ceinwen dislikes the long hours and the heat and flies. Counting the conjunction, this is strictly a three-word answer, and even if it were not we can't award a mark because Ceinwen clearly states the opposite – he doesn't mind working long hours as the job is so rewarding.

- **Student C** provides the only accurate response, with "high temperatures" and "insects", using two words or fewer for each gap.

The final activity in this section invites the students, in pairs, to mark each other's answers to the other three questions. This will train them to look for what examiners require in *close attempts*.

Study tips: speaking

Improving the flow of a conversation (see pages 112–13 of the student book)

The Speaking test is assessed using three criteria:

- Structure: 10 marks

- Vocabulary: 10 marks

- Fluency and development: 10 marks

It is a challenging task for an examiner – who is usually but not always the students' regular classroom teacher – to mark candidates for Part D of the Speaking test: the conversation/discussion. Some examiners prefer to assess candidates "on the spot"; others prefer to make rough notes and then listen again before deciding on a final mark. Larger departments in schools or colleges might hold a departmental meeting at which borderline cases are revisited before the team decides on the final mark to submit to Cambridge. Cambridge insists on this internal moderation in all centres using more than one examiner. Whatever approach is taken in deciding on the final marks for students, Cambridge expects some sort of professional discussion relating to those marks to have taken place in centres.

We strongly recommend that you familiarize yourself with Cambridge's advice on conducting and assessing the tests in its *Handbook for Centres Conducting Speaking Tests* for English as a Second Language. Use the practice (audio) material it contains, so that you can check your marks against marks awarded by Cambridge moderators.

Fluency and development

A student who is able to monitor the flow of the discussion, logically developing the topic from Prompt 1 through to Prompt 5, is likely to perform well. While it is natural for a 16-year-old to perhaps be the more passive participant in a topic-led discussion with an adult, we do encourage you to build your students' confidence so that they can, on occasion, reach equal terms. Very strong students will show signs of being able to respond with success to changes in the direction of the conversation.

Assessing fluency is not about judging the student's ability to speak at length, as in a formal speech or an oratory. It is fluency in the context of a two-way conversation.

Pronunciation and intonation are not likely to hinder a discussion that is developing each prompt with confidence. Our advice is to make a judgment first about development and fluency, and then consider the extent to which pronunciation and intonation affect this.

Evaluating the sample student responses

The teacher's comments on three students' responses show how an examiner might evaluate a candidate's contribution and overall performance.

- **Student C** impressed the examiner the most – particularly the balanced account of responding to Prompt 3, which often asks about pros and cons, advantages and disadvantages. What was most impressive to the examiner was the way in which Prompts 4 and 5 led on from the discussion of general matters. This was clearly a focused conversation from the beginning and, as a result, likely to be considered a band 1 performance and certainly no lower than band 2.

- **Student A** did not really understand the aim of the conversation – to develop a discussion. It is tempting for students to stay in the "safe zone" with a topic like this – i.e. to talk for 2–3 minutes about a famous person or two. But in a 6–9-minute discussion all five prompts need to be used, so it is unwise to allow one of the earlier prompts to dominate and prevent the development of the discussion. These comments suggest that the candidate in question is within band 3.

- **Student B** has also not grasped the main objective of the Speaking test and has failed to cover all five prompts, choosing instead to develop just one area of the subject about which he/she has a strong view. It is permissible to bring in related ideas not covered by the prompts, but only when the prompts have been exhausted. Student B may well have band 2 ability, but would be awarded a band 3 mark because of the lack of any logical development of the topic.

Exam focus: speaking

The Speaking test is a formal examination, conducted under strict examination conditions. You can see from our commentary above that it has two key requirements:

1   The examination paper (the topic card) must be utilized properly, fully, and competently.

2   Students must adhere to the structure of the five prompts, showing development and fluency; if they don't, they are unlikely to perform as well as they might have done.

The following six assessment objectives can all be met in a two-way focused conversation. A candidate who can achieve these objectives will almost certainly perform well in any speaking test.

Here is a typical topic card on the theme of working life.

Oral test topic card

University and work

Some people attend university after school with a view to getting a better job, while other people go straight to work after school.

Discuss this topic with the examiner. You *must* use the five prompts below in the sequence provided.

1　Your own current plans for continuing your education after school

2　Some people you know who are graduates, and others you know who did not attend university

3　The pros and cons of going to university

4　The suggestion that achieving success is due to good luck and other factors, not hard work at all

5　The idea that a little knowledge is a dangerous thing

Model answers and how to improve performance

Part C of the test is when the candidate can look at the topic card and plan for the upcoming discussion. In the 2–3 minutes allowed for this, it is probably best to think of two ways in which to *develop* each prompt. Here's how a strong candidate might approach the topic card above:

Prompt 1

1　I will talk about my plans to take a year off – a gap year – before going on to study journalism at university.

2　But I will also mention that I will not stop learning during my year off. I will read books about journalism, read a lot of newspapers and Internet-based news sites, and I will practise doing some mock interviews with people during my travels and work experience.

Prompt 2

1 I will quote the example of my uncle who is a graduate in Design & Technology and who now runs his own successful creative design business, employing people and leading a full life.

2 I'll also mention my brother who chose not to attend university but who is the most well-read and clever person I know. Everyone asks him where he went for his degree, and he always responds with "What degree?"

Prompt 3

1 Best here to think of one pro: it provides a secure and safe period when someone is 19–23 years old as he/she is gaining a qualification, whether they choose to use it later or not.

2 And a con: what if there are too many graduates in, say, Chemistry and no jobs in that field? In the real world of work, the number of jobs = the actual need for jobs. Too many university graduates end up doing basic jobs such as working in shops.

Prompt 4

1 The world is not a fair place. I understand that now at my age, so yes, I can see how some people get success through being lucky. Or far worse, through being dishonest – e.g. crime.

2 Hard work is rewarded, though. Maybe people should always be made to work hard, even when they are unemployed? A strong work ethic is a good thing, surely? I might ask the examiner what he thinks about that.

Prompt 5

1 I think this means that someone who is well educated and trained properly will get results if given responsibility. Seems a good idea to me.

2 An example of where it seems to apply, though, is where people are arrogant about their ability and don't research or prepare enough. Like a builder trying to construct a five-storey building without an architect's plans.

This example shows a model candidate working at band 1 level, but students of lower ability can use the same approach – of thinking ahead – to help them ensure some degree of development.

Study tips: writing

Descriptive writing (see page 114–15 of the student book)

This detailed and comprehensive section engages with the type of writing that will be assessed in Exercise 6 of both the core- and extended-level examinations. The key skill, and perhaps the biggest challenge, is to make descriptive writing vibrant and lively – so as to engage the reader fully. The activity is therefore intended to get your students thinking about audience.

The purpose of a letter or any other piece of writing will be strongly influenced by its audience – indeed, the audience for a piece of writing should be signposted by its purpose.

Working in pairs or small groups, the students should discuss the three letters written in response to the task. This is intended as a relatively informal and collaborative activity, with students sharing their views on the strengths and weaknesses of the three letters. The students are not in productive mode here, but in analytical and evaluative mode.

Evaluating the sample student responses

Descriptive writing is assessed using two criteria: content and accuracy of language. The marking scheme your students should use here to evaluate each of the three sample responses should be based on content alone.

1 How well has each piece of writing responded to the three prompts?

2 What content – e.g. points and examples – has been provided and developed?

The examples contain some errors – spelling errors, weaknesses in grammar, etc. – to reflect the reality of writing seen at this level.

- **Student A** responds well in terms of suitable content. All three prompts are covered in a balanced way and the piece reads as a safe and competent letter.

- **Student B** also responds well and covers each prompt appropriately. However, there is a strong sense that this is higher-level content than Student A produced. The lexis is more sophisticated and the sense of audience is better developed.

- **Student C** has the weakest English. However, there is still a pleasing level of engagement with the prompts. It is a weaker piece than those by the other two students but it certainly has its merits.

If we were marking these three examples out of 10 and we used a holistic approach based on sense of purpose and the development of content, we would award:

- Student A: 7 marks

- Student B: 10 marks

- Student C: 4 marks (we thought 3.5, really, but we always round up!)

☑ My progress

The four study skills – reading, writing, speaking, and listening – are key skills for success in each of the examinations. In the "My progress" section at the end of the chapter in the student book we invite students to select one skill that they can focus on and develop. However, you may like to ask students to prepare action plans to develop all four of the skills.

The table indicates where the skills feature in the examination papers and how they are applied. Unless otherwise indicated, the skills and tasks are common to both levels.

Skill	Task	Positioning in examination papers
Form filling, including application information and feedback	Completing a form with three sections (core)	Reading and writing ● Exercise 3 (core)
Listening to people talking about specialized jobs and careers	Filling in gaps in statements with specific details (using only one or two words)	Listening ● Question 5
Improving the flow of a two-way conversation	Planning for a 6–9-minute discussion which develops a topic at key stages (using five prompts)	Speaking test ● Part C (planning) ● Part D (enacting)
Matching content to purpose and audience in descriptive writing	Directed writing – 100–150 words (core) Directed writing – 150–200 words (extended)	Reading and writing ● Exercise 6

6 Travel and transport

Student book content coverage

Segment 1	Pages 120–2 Travelling around
Syllabus objectives	**R1** Identify and retrieve facts and details **W1** Communicate clearly, accurately and appropriately
Broader skills development	• Think about an exciting journey you have been on in the past. • Look at both advantages and disadvantages of travel. • Read about forms of transport in Montevideo.
Introducing the session	"Thinking out loud" (page 120): Allow students five minutes to think about the most exciting journey they have been on.
Ensuring a skills balance	Suggested listening activity: Ask students to listen to each other talking about an exciting journey. They can then ask the speaker a question about what has just been said.
Differentiated activities	Stronger students can write a response to the email on page 121. They need to respond to the information given by their friend and include their reactions to it.
Teaching and learning methodologies	**1** Think about different forms of transport and the advantages and disadvantages of the different forms. **2** Read about the transport system of Montevideo.
Building your vocabulary	Page 120: Modes of transport. Ask students, in pairs, to copy and complete the chart.
Check your understanding	Page 121: Transport in Montevideo. Ask students to work on their own to complete the five statements.
Learner outcomes	By the end of this segment, learners should be able to: • use the language of transport • talk about the advantages and disadvantages of different forms of transport.
Workbook	Page 57: Building your vocabulary – cycling Page 57–8: Check your understanding – cycling Page 58: Writing – spreading the word
Worksheet	6.1: Talking about your favourite place in the world

Segment 2	Pages 122–3 Travel guides
Syllabus objectives	**R2** Understand and select relevant information **W2** Convey information and express opinions effectively
Broader skills development	• Locate specific detail in an information task. • Read a travel guide and make notes on the details it contains. • Use insider knowledge while writing your own travel guide.
Introducing the session	Ask students what they might look for when locating specific detail in an information text. They should take no longer than five minutes doing this.
Ensuring a skills balance	Suggested speaking activity: Ask students to tell their classmates one piece of insider knowledge about a city they live in or have been to.
Differentiated activities	Stronger students can give a one-minute presentation on the insider knowledge they have learned about, to try to persuade their classmates to go to the place they are describing.
Teaching and learning methodologies	**1** Read a travel guide and think about what facts are in it. **2** Locate specific detail in an information text.
Building your vocabulary	Ask students to make a list of five tourist destinations in a town that they might not know the word for, to add to their vocabulary.
Check your understanding	Ask students to pick out the most interesting piece of insider knowledge they have learned during the session.
Learner outcomes	By the end of this segment, learners should be able to: • convey information clearly • express opinions effectively.
Workbook	Page 59: Reading – polar explorer Pages 60–61: Check your understanding: Polar explorer; Arctic explorer Page 61: Language focus – relative pronouns
Worksheet	6.2: Travel writing

Segment 3	Pages 124–8 Working in the travel industry; Holidays
Syllabus objectives	**S1** Communicate clearly, accurately, and appropriately **L2** Understand and select relevant information
Broader skills development	• Listen to a pilot who has overcome the odds to succeed. • Create your own drama based on changes in transport. • Use your personal experiences to get the conversation going in the speaking test.
Introducing the session	Ask students to choose a job in the travel industry and why they would wish to do it.
Ensuring a skills balance	Suggested writing activity: Ask students to imagine they have been to Ski Dubai and are now updating their blog. They should give facts about it, as well as their opinion on their time there.

Differentiated activities	Stronger students can read the postcard from Mauritius on page 127 and then write their own postcard from a destination of their choice. Ask them to include task-specific vocabulary, as the postcard they have read has done.
Teaching and learning methodologies	**1** Listen and react to a pilot. **2** Use Prompt 2 of the speaking test. **3** Listen to a talk and select relevant information from it.
Building your vocabulary	Ask students to make a list of five words from the pilot interview that they do not regularly use. Ask them to find a synonym for each word.
Check your understanding	Ask students to pick out three interesting facts about Jessica Cox.
Learner outcomes	At the end of this segment, learners should be able to: • communicate clearly • understand how to use Prompt 2 of the speaking test effectively.
Workbook	Page 62: Building your vocabulary – holidays Pages 62–3: Check your understanding – holidays Page 63: Writing – Diving to shipwrecks
Worksheet	6.3: Increasing your travel vocabulary

Segment 4	Pages 129–131 Operation Raleigh
Syllabus objectives	**L3** Recognize and understand ideas, opinions, and attitudes **R2** Understand and select relevant information
Broader skills development	• Think about which charity you would help if you could work for one for a month. • Analyse questions to predict the types of responses needed. • Fill out a form based on the information you have been given.
Introducing the session	Ask students to think about which charity they would support for a month if they could.
Ensuring a skills balance	Suggested reading activity: Ask students to check the answers their partner has completed for the "Check your understanding" exercise – do they agree that their partner has the correct answers? Ask them to specify any errors.
Differentiated activities	Stronger students can be placed in pairs. Ask them to imagine they have spent some time on an Operation Raleigh trip and are back, telling each other about it.
Teaching and learning methodologies	**1** Analyse questions. **2** Complete a form.
Building your vocabulary	Ask students to make a list of five factors they consider when choosing a charity to support.
Check your understanding	Page 130: Operation Raleigh. Ask students to complete this individually and then check their answers in small groups.
Learner outcomes	By the end of this segment, learners should be able to: • hear a listening passage and select relevant information • select relevant information from a written passage.

Workbook	Page 64: Building your vocabulary – flying crossword
	Page 65: Reading – flying
	Page 65: Check your understanding – flying
Worksheet	6.4: Reading about the London Transport Museum

Segment 5	**Pages 132–7 Eco-friendly holidays; Holidays with health benefits**
Syllabus objectives	**R3** Recognize and understand ideas, opinions, and attitudes
	S4 Demonstrate knowledge of a range of appropriate vocabulary
Broader skills development	• Give a presentation about a great holiday destination.
	• Talk about eco-friendly holidays.
	• Talk about the advantages and disadvantages of spending a day in a cave.
Introducing the session	Ask students if they have been on an eco-friendly holiday. If they have, ask them to tell the class about it; if they have not, ask them to tell the class what kind of eco-holiday they would like to go on, if they had the chance.
Ensuring a skills balance	Suggested writing activity:
	Ask students to imagine that they have been either on the Florida ecotour or to the salt-mine cave. They then email a friend to say why they enjoyed the trip and its ethical side, and to ask them to join them next time.
Differentiated activities	Stronger students can respond to the suggested writing activity by phoning their friend and discussing the eco-holiday with them.
Teaching and learning methodologies	**1** Give a presentation.
	2 Develop a conversation.
Building your vocabulary	Page 132: Eco-friendly holidays. Ask students to add the words to the sentences within a five-minute time limit.
	Page 134: Holidays with health benefits students can complete this activity in pairs.
Check your understanding	Page 135: Salt mine. Students could complete this individually.
	Page 136: Juan the caver. Students could complete this in pairs.
Learner outcomes	By the end of this segment, learners should be able to:
	• complete a form based on the information given
	• talk about eco-friendly holidays.
Workbook	Page 66: Writing – update your blog
Worksheet	6.5: Speaking about transport

Segment 6	**Pages 138–41 Space travel**
Syllabus objectives	**S2** Convey information and express opinions effectively
	W4 Demonstrate knowledge and understanding of a range of appropriate vocabulary
Broader skills development	• Tell each other what your main goal in life is and how you will achieve it.
	• Write a letter home while you are on the International Space Station.
	• In groups, prepare a bid to win the chance of travelling to a planet of your choice.

Introducing the session	Ask students to consider the idea that some people are braver than others. They can then spend up to five minutes discussing their ideas.
Ensuring a skills balance	Suggested writing activity: Ask students to read about Felix Baumgartner and then write down six questions they would like to ask him.
Differentiated activities	Stronger students can put up a tweet of their reaction to Felix Baumgartner's jump. Make several copies next to the tweet, so classmates can take one if they like the comment and add it to their own, retweeting the comment.
Teaching and learning methodologies	1 Ask and respond to a series of quick questions. 2 Use relative pronouns.
Building your vocabulary	Page 138: Space jump. Give students five minutes to complete the crossword – who will finish first?
Check your understanding	Pages 138–9: Space jump. Students can answer these questions in pairs.
Learner outcomes	By the end of this segment, learners should be able to: • recognize and use relative pronouns • complete the "My progress" chart and pick one skill for their action plan.
Workbook	Page 67: Discussion topic – building a new holiday complex
Worksheet	6.6: Using vocabulary in a dialogue
Further practice	**On completion of the chapter, ask students to complete questions 1–20 of the travel and transport interactive activities.**

Links

If you choose only one link to use with your students, try this:

- www.kids.nationalgeographic.com – exciting stories, news, and quizzes about our planet

You might also try:

- www.telegraph.co.uk/travel – news and reviews about the best holiday destinations.
- www.timeout.com – find out what is happening in the most exciting cities on the planet.
- www.beaulieu.co.uk – everything you wanted to know about the history of transport – cars and motorbikes; old cars and new cars; and film cars, from James Bond to Chitty Chitty Bang Bang – all under one roof.
- www.svr.co.uk – the Severn Valley Railway has steam trains and diesel trains, as well as Classic Car Days.
- www.nasa.gov – for those not just interested in travel on Earth, but also space, space travel, and space exploration.

If your students enjoyed reading about Felix Baumgartner, they can find out more about him and his future projects at www.felixbaumgartner.com

Study tips: reading

Locating specific detail in an information text (see page 122 of the student book)

This section invites students to think about approaches to skimming and scanning texts to find particular information based on a question. The first two questions in the examination of reading skills (Exercises 1 and 2) test these skills. Since they account for approximately 25 per cent of a candidate's mark for the whole Reading and Writing paper, it is certainly worth practising and refining skimming and scanning skills.

The first task is to answer three questions about the article on transport in and around Montevideo on page 121. Students should read the three questions without reading the article again. The aim here is to practise predicting probable answers based on the types of question set. The pedagogy here is of course when to apply deduction and when to apply induction. The task introduces students to both approaches, allowing them to locate and convey specific detail from both perspectives.

The second task asks students to fill the gaps in some bullet points offering sound advice on how to complete this type of information transfer.

We recommend completing these tasks informally and in pairs or small groups, as this will generate further discussion about how best to answer these types of "locating details" questions.

Evaluating the sample student responses

Task 1

Question 1 From the question we can see that two details are required, and that we are looking for a service or facility for travellers. We then skim the text quickly to find what we need and we find that the terminal (the key word we are looking for when skimming) offers five benefits for travellers. We only need two. We now scan for those specific details.

- **Student A** has provided a succinct response and it is the best answer of the three.

- **Student B** chooses to list four of the five benefits. All four are correct, so this would be accepted, but it is not a sensible approach because it takes longer to write unnecessary details, and it increases the risk of making errors in the additional information. For responses like this, all the information given has to be correct.

- **Student C** has given only one detail and it is inaccurate. The student has complicated things by inferring a discount where there is no evidence of one.

Question 2 It's clear from the question that a means of transport is needed, but the key word is "cheapest". There will always be a key word that points the candidates towards the correct detail(s). We also know, however, that the location is Buenos Aires, so this question can be factored down to: cheapest cost + Buenos Aires.

- **Student A** has again provided exactly the right answer – the Trans Uruguay combined service gives the detail we need succinctly.

- **Student B** presents us with a slight dilemma, but "the $599 one" is correct, it is this service which is the cheapest route. An examiner would have to accept this as it answers the question.

- **Student C** gives us a response that is too general. Where Student B's response was specific, Student C's is not. Examiners will not reward responses that reword the question and then lack specificity – even if it is a logical answer. The cheapest one is likely to be the less expensive one – but which one is that, exactly?

Question 3 A "where" question usually requires an answer that is a specific location. We can work out from this question that it is a destination reached by air, so our key phrase here is "fly direct". A candidate will need to understand what is mean by direct, of course, to be able to respond successfully. They will also need to know the collocations "via" and "non-stop". Induction and deduction skills are being tested here. We induce that a destination is required; we then deduce which ones are reached without stopping.

- **Student A** is clearly the most competent of the three students in skimming and scanning skills. The response is again accurate and succinct.

- **Student B** provides an incorrect response, and has failed to deduce that there are two destinations.

- **Student C** is the weakest of the three and appears not to have understood the question by suggesting that there are no direct flights.

Note: examination questions will never ask for detail or information that is not evident in an article. Student C's response to question 3 is therefore never going to be an "educated guess".

Task 2

The answers are:

- Read the questions FIRST…
- Scan the text for some CLUES…
- SKIM read the text quickly…
- …from the text without CHANGING…
- …they do not have to be full SENTENCES.

Exam focus: reading and writing

Exercise 1 of the Reading and Writing papers uses the same source text for both core and extended levels. There are 7 marks available for core and 9 marks for extended level. The two extra marks available at extended level are achieved by answering additional questions.

Only two objectives are tested but if we arrange their key words differently, we have:

- understand
- identify
- select
- retrieve.

Share these with your learners as you work through the activities. This should help them with the cognitive processing involved.

> ## Assessment objectives
>
> **R1** Identify and retrieve facts and details
>
> **R2** Understand and select relevant information

Exercise 1 will probably feature one of the following:

- an advertisement
- a brochure or leaflet
- a guide
- a report
- a manual or series of instructions.

This source material will be approximately 350 words long.

The following example of source material is an information leaflet about a trip across the United States by motorcycle on Route 66. It is advertising a company that organizes 15-day cross-country excursions.

Route 66 by motorbike

The original Route 66, known as the "Main street of America" runs from Chicago to Los Angeles, and crosses three time zones and eight states: Illinois, Missouri, Kansas, Oklahoma, Texas, New Mexico, Arizona, and California. Route 66 has been the pathway of migrants, dreamers, and holidaymakers ever since it opened. The 1950s were the Route 66 glory days and much of Route 66's classic roads, restaurants, petrol stations, and nostalgic landmarks are preserved just as they were in the 1950s.

Day 1 Begin in Chicago at 9 a.m., where you can enjoy the famous skyline. We hope you will be relaxed after listening to the 66-ers jazz band on the rooftop restaurant of your hotel the night before.

Itinerary details

- 15 days/14 nights
- Distance: 4,406 kilometers
- Seasons available: spring, summer, autumn
- Temperature: 13° to 41°C

Highlight of Day 11: the Grand Canyon

For those looking to get the best view of the Grand Canyon, we will arrange a thrilling early morning helicopter ride over the heart of the South Rim. In the afternoon, we will have plenty of time to ride along the rim and stop for amazing vistas and photos as the sun goes down. We will leave the Grand Canyon at sunrise and pick Route 66 back up in Williams, Arizona, stopping for the night at a hotel in Kingman, the next town.

Testimonial from Peter

"We were on the tour beginning on 25 August and rode the full length of Route 66. Congratulations on the excellent planning of the tour, and for keeping the riding group small – too many motorbikes would have made it less enjoyable for us. We are promoting your tours to all our friends now. It was really good value for money because everything was taken care of. And we love our Route 66 riding jackets – an unexpected bonus."

What's included

- All hotel accommodations
- Motorcycle rental (but insurance must be provided by second rider)
- Free fuel and oil
- Helmet for driver (passenger to provide own helmet)
- Daily breakfast
- Support vehicle equipped with spare bike and room for additional luggage
- National Park entrance fees
- Custom riding jacket

Day 15: Los Angeles

Complete your journey in the city of Angels, where a farewell dinner on the beach is planned for all!

Adapted from http://www.eaglerider.com/ motorcycle-tours/guided-motorcycle-tour/ route-66-motorcycle-tour.aspx

Exercise 1

Read the advertisement for a motorcycle trip across the United States and then answer the following questions.

a) Where will the journey start from and what entertainment is planned?

....

b) What distance will the motorcyclists travel over the 15 days?

....

c) Which is the only time of the year when the trip is not offered?

....

d) What is the most exciting way to see the Grand Canyon?

....

e) Which two towns will be visited after leaving the Grand Canyon?

....

f) What was Peter's view of riding in large groups of motorbikes?

....

g) What types of people have always used Route 66? Give two details.

....

[7 marks total]

For candidates taking the extended paper:

h) For people riding as a pair, what two additional items must be obtained?

....

[9 marks total]

Model answers and how to improve performance

Answers should be as brief as possible. Students do not need to write in whole sentences, as this simply wastes time. The best way to ensure accuracy is to use the words as they appear in the source material. "Lifting" is therefore not only permissible: it is encouraged. Exercise 1 does not test gist understanding; it tests precision.

The key skill that students need to develop is the ability to locate the details relating specifically to the question. However, candidates may not always follow this advice. Many of the answers mentioned below could, with some improvement, have obtained the mark. The first responses listed, however, are all model responses.

a) Where will the journey start from and what entertainment is planned?

Chicago, a jazz band... The state of Chicago, jazz music... Chicago, an evening of jazz...chicago, some jazz... Chicago Illynoy, jaz music

> **Our expert says:** As only reading skills are assessed, weak spelling and grammatical slips will be tolerated, so *jaz* and *chicago* would be allowed. However, the mark will not be awarded where the meaning is changed, becomes blurred, or is too general, as in *in Chicago which is in Nevada... start from Chicago in a jazz place... Chicago and music.*

b) What distance will motorcyclists travel over the 15 days?

4,406 kilomters... 4,406 km... km = 4,406

> **Our expert says:** When asking questions about measurements, examiners will expect accuracy. A very close attempt would not be allowed – e.g. *4,405 km* – and neither would a broad response, even if it is generally accurate, such as *a very long distance... almost 5,000 km.*

c) Which is the only time of the year when the trip is not offered?

winter... winter time... in the winter

> **Our expert says:** An interesting response would be the *time of the year except spring, summer, and autumn*. This is a long-winded way of trying to say winter. Examiners would allow this clumsy response as it has to mean winter – there is no other season. However, *offered in spring, summer, autumn* would not gain a mark because it does not answer the question.

d) What is the most exciting way to see the Grand Canyon?

helicopter ride... by helicopter... going in a helicopter

> **Our expert says:** This requires precision, so these three responses would all gain the mark. Responses that seem to understand the gist but lack specificity, such as *by taking a thrilling ride... by getting up very early*, show only partial understanding and would not be allowed.

e) Which two towns will be visited after leaving the Grand Canyon?

Williams and Kingman... Kingman and Williams... Williams, Arizona Kingman

> **Our expert says:** Staying with required specificity, a response such as *the next two towns* would be disallowed even though it is not incorrect. Neither would a *town in Arizona, and Kingman* be credited. If one town only is given, a mark cannot be awarded. Half marks are never deployed, so two details means two details.

f) What was Peter's view about riding in large groups of motorbikes?

too many motorbikes would have made it less enjoyable... it would be less enjoyable... not as enjoyable... not enjoyable

> **Our expert says:** Although a student could use his or her own words in such a question, it is not recommended. Synonymous responses are accepted but they must have the same meaning. For example, *Peter was unhappy... he didn't like it... he hated the idea... he has a negative view... etc.* would all be disallowed as they convey different views from "less enjoyable". Since gist understanding is not tested in Exercise 1, convey to your students that these types of questions are still testing the location of stated details/information and do not therefore require interpretation.

g) What types of people have always used Route 66? Give two details.

migrants and dreamers... migrants and holidaymakers... dreamers and holiday makers

> **Our expert says:** If more than two details are given, as long as the additional detail is correct, a mark will be awarded. If a candidate uses more words than necessary a mark will still be given – e.g. *people who dream and people who migrate.*

h) For people riding as a pair, what two additional items must be obtained?

insurance and a helmet... helmets and insurance

> **Our expert says:** A slightly harder question is set for extended-level candidates. Here they have to scan through the list and analyse the information in the brackets. They also need to equate "second rider" and "passenger" to riding in a pair. There are only two possible answers here, and the key word in the question is of course "additional". An examiner would tolerate the use of a plural as the candidate has understood, identified, selected, and retrieved the appropriate details.

Study tips: speaking

Prompt two of the Speaking test (see page 125 of the student book)

This section focuses on the second prompt of the five provided on the topic card. The first prompt will have asked the student about his or her direct experience of the topic or theme – and this is therefore very straightforward. The aim is to settle the student with an easy opening minute or so where he or she can relay real experiences. Prompt 2 will often take the form of asking the student either to talk about people close to them (friends and family) and experiences they have had, or to present their own views about an aspect of the topic. Prompts 1 and 2 both remain in the area of personal discussion, or discussion of personal experience and views. Prompt 3 then moves the discussion into more general matters.

Evaluating the sample student responses

- **Student A** is likely to provide a satisfactory response to the prompt. She covers both aspects of the prompt – the past and the future – and is able to prepare a few examples.

- **Student B** is likely to lose focus and lead the conversation into the discussion of living in space in the future, which is not quite the same thing as space travel. He is not preparing to discuss how people travelled in the past and appears not to have any examples of forms of travel in the past in mind. There is a danger that living on space stations will be the subject dominating this phase of the discussion.

- **Student C** is likely to have plenty to say in response to the prompts and has prepared a number of pertinent examples. She mentions one of Da Vinci's inventions, and the impact of the motor car, and how computer technology has changed transport beyond recognition.

Model answers and how to improve performance

Here is another example of a Prompt 2 related to the theme of travel and transport:

Oral test topic card

Technology and transport

Transport has changed almost beyond recognition since the days of horses and carts, and technology has played a big part in this.

Discuss this topic with the examiner.

1 Transport you use and how often you use each type

2 Other people you know who depend on transport and how they are affected by this

Prompt 2 on this topic card asks candidates to focus on how people they know use and rely on transport. It is not asking them about their own use of transport, which has been covered in Prompt 1, or about their personal views; rather it involves talking about people they know – i.e. friends and family.

A model candidate is likely to have made a few mental notes along the following lines:

- It says "depend" on transport, so I must stay on task. I shouldn't talk about lots of people and just list the transport they use. It's better to talk about a few people and say how much they need their transport.

- I'll talk about my dad. He travels with his job a lot. He's often in other countries and uses airplanes. He likes flying! He prefers trains, though, to cars, so I could explain why that is.

- And I will mention how much my older sister was affected by the strike by air traffic control last year. She was due to take a flight to France for work and couldn't get there. I think it cost her company thousands of dollars in the end.

- A really good, and different example, will be my uncle who uses his boat for taking tourists around the rivers. They recently passed a new law that requires people who take members of the public on journeys of more than one hour to have a special licence. He had to stop his business for three months to apply for it and was not happy at all. He's OK now, though, and despite his earlier complaints he thinks a licence is a great idea for several reasons. I know these reasons and I could discuss those.

- My friend at school is always complaining about his taxi. He has to get one to school every day because his parents don't want him to take the bus. He wants to use the bus. So he is affected by the transport he has to use and would prefer an alternative.

- I think this prompt is all about examples – examples that bring out the "depend on" and "affected by" bits.

Students can certainly improve their performance in the Speaking test if they start out strongly and with confidence. Bringing in interesting and pertinent examples for Prompt 2 will go a long way towards ensuring this.

In the early stages of the 6–9 minute discussion, it is likely that Prompts 1 and 2 will take up about 3 minutes or so. S2 is the key assessment objective at this stage (see below) but the other speaking objectives also all play a role. After about 3 minutes the examiner will begin to move the discussion into general matters and on to Prompt 3, thus broadening out the conversation. It is likely that Prompt 3 would introduce the theme of technology and transport.

Assessment objectives

S1 Communicate clearly, accurately, and appropriately

S2 Convey information and express opinions effectively

Study tips: listening

Listening to a talk and selecting relevant information (see page 128 of the student book)

This activity provides practice in answering Question 5 of the Listening examination. The question is the same for core and extended levels, with a possible 8 marks for each. Students will listen to a talk, or an interview where the interviewer is passive, and then complete a gap-filling exercise like the example given here: "Ski Dubai – indoor ski centre".

Students are invited to practise pre-listening skills, which for this exercise means trying to predict content. You might like to ask your students to form pairs and try to guess what answers are likely to occur in the gaps: what works and what doesn't. Suggestions will need to make sense in the context and will need to be sound grammatical fits. For example, sentence 4 makes sense thus: "There are quality ski runs and we even have a professional run." This is not the correct answer but there is nothing wrong with the sentence as it stands.

Only one or two words are allowed in a gap for this question, so it is best, while practising, to remember to stay within these parameters. You could ask students to make up their own sentences with gaps and pass these along to another pair of students for them to try to complete. A lot of detail in the speech given by Franz is unused, so you could use this recording for further practice.

Evaluating the sample student responses

- **Student A** is correct to state that the centre opened in 2006, but then makes an inference that Franz is a ski instructor. There is no direct evidence of this in his speech; in fact, he says that he is the manager of the ski slope. For sentence 4, Student A is right to say that there are "5 ski runs", but in suggesting "extremely difficult" we have "and we have even have a extremely difficult run". There are two reasons why this is not correct:

  - It is the incorrect article – it needed "an".

  - A more precise answer is "black" run.

This student therefore scores 0 marks.

- **Student B** suggests "for ages" so we have "since for ages", which is not a grammatical fit and lacks precision. However, this student has recognized that Franz is a manager. Unfortunately, there are 5 runs and not 6, so we cannot accept "5 or 6" for the first gap of sentence 4. The answer in the second gap is correct, however. Like Student A, Student B provides some accurate responses but makes some slips and also scores 0 marks.

- **Student C** also makes an article error with "a area manager there" for sentence 1. In sentence 4, we see "blacker" run but adding the -er creates a comparative that is not present in the source material. This is therefore incorrect grammar and would not be allowed. Student C also scores 0 marks.

This is therefore an interesting piece of peer assessment for students, as they can see that absolute precision is needed to gain marks in Question 5. All three students provide acceptable responses in some of the gaps but, overall, fall down because of a lack of consistency.

Study tips: writing

Completing a form (see pages 130–1 of the student book)

Completing forms usually requires two main skills: reading for relevant information and writing this down accurately. The balance in the examination is tilted towards testing reading more than writing, but if information is written down inaccurately, no marks will be given.

This section provides students with a full Exercise 3 which is not specific to either level but which incorporates features of both levels. It can therefore be used for all students.

The focus is not on asking your students to fill out the form – though you could ask them to do this if you prefer – but to analyse the forms filled out by other students and to ascertain whether responses provided are accurate (PA), close (CA), or not acceptable (NA). It is intended therefore as a formative exercise, encouraging collaboration and teamwork. We recommend making this a low-key, fun activity, with plenty of discussion and evaluation of the three responses.

The surprise in store for students is that there are hardly any correct responses – only 3 are PA out of a possible 36! We hope that it is much more interesting to explore the large number of CA responses.

Evaluating the sample student responses

1   a) and c) are CA. It is Elizabeth with a z; and Jones must be capitalized. Liz Jones is not an accurate transcription so that is NA.

2   c) is a CA. The postcode is B32 not B34, but a) is NA: 4 Bushy Avenue is an incomplete address. b) is certainly NA and is a very weak response to an address.

3   Elizabeth is 17 years and 8 months old, so a) and b) are NA as they are not close enough. However, c) is a CA as it is only 2 months out, but it is still wrong and would not gain a mark.

4   It is clear that Elizabeth is a female, so we need MALE to be deleted. None of the three responses gets close to this so they are all NA. c) has used deletion but has deleted the wrong word.

5   b) appears to be a CA when read out, but this is an exercise of accurate transcription so emails must be exactly as they are written in the source material. a) is clearly NA. c) is CA, though, as only "mail" is misspelled.

6   As she has applied for work in Costa Rica, it is a safe inference to make that this is her preferred destination. a) is therefore a PA (our first one). b) is not close, so it's NA – central USA is not the same as Central America. c) is clearly NA; even though she loves Spain it is not one of her preferences.

7   a) is NA: there is no evidence for this. b) would have been correct if it had been circled and not underlined – it is therefore CA with no mark. c) is also CA, but as with b is not circled but written down.

8   a) is NA. b) is NA also at six weeks. c) is CA because the answer needed is six months, so it lacks precision but is not technically incorrect. No mark is awarded for a lack of specificity.

9   The correct date to enter on the form is the one she is able to start on, not the date she would actually like to – hence 15/03/2016. Answer a) is therefore clearly NA. b) is also wrong and NA as October is a date she cannot attend. c) is almost there, so CA, but it lacks the day, the 15th. A starting date needs to be a specific date.

10   She wants to learn Spanish, and we can infer this from her keenness to join a language class. However, we cannot accept a) as "Spain" is not a language but a country. It is a CA, though. b) is NA – there is no evidence that Costa Rican is Spanish. c) is also NA – there is no such language as South American.

11   Answers a) and c) here are PA. We can allow "resources room" as it is synonymous with library. b) is wrong, however, but it is a CA, as a reasonable inference. At this stage, there is no evidence that Elizabeth has heard anything from Operation Raleigh.

12   a) is NA as the convention of writing in the first person has not been followed. b) is a CA but it lacks precision – "projects" is too broad. c) is NA because there is no evidence that this is a motivating factor; indeed, there is evidence that it is just a consequence of wanting to visit the region and work on conservation projects.

☑ My progress

The four study skills – reading, writing, speaking, and listening – are key skills for success in each of the examinations. In the "My progress" section at the end of the chapter in the student book we invite students to select one skill that they can focus on and develop. However, you may like to ask students to prepare action plans to develop all four of the skills.

The table indicates where the skills feature in the examination papers and how they are applied. Unless otherwise indicated, the skills and tasks are common to both levels.

Skill	Task	Positioning in examination papers
Locating details by skimming and scanning	Read a brochure and answer a series of open questions: ● seven at core level ● eight or nine at extended level	Reading and writing ● Exercise 1
Listening to a talk given by a specialist and selecting relevant details	Fill in gaps in short statements with specific details and using only one or two words.	Listening ● Question 5
Talking about own views and/ or about other people's relevant experiences	Develop the early stages of a discussion	Speaking test ● Part D, Prompt 2
Transcribing information from source material written in the third person and converting to first person	Complete a form	Reading and writing ● Exercise 3

7 Leisure and entertainment

Student book content coverage

Segment 1	Pages 144–5 Music
Syllabus objectives	**R1** Identify and retrieve facts **S1** Communicate clearly, accurately, and appropriately
Broader skills development	• Imagine being in a band. • Read about someone who created a band. • Use prefixes to indicate numbers.
Introducing the session	Ask students which girl bands they know and like. Do the girls play any instruments and, if so, which ones? Allow up to five minutes for this activity.
Ensuring a skills balance	Suggested listening activity: Ask students to listen to their favourite girl band song and, in small groups, to explain what they like about it for about one minute each.
Differentiated activities	Ask stronger students to find out about a boy or girl band from the past – the recent past or longer ago. Who was in it and what hits did they have? Having listened to some of their songs, ask them to explain why they like the music. Ask them to report back to the whole class.
Teaching and learning methodologies	**1** Learn to think in different ways. **2** Use vocabulary for precision.
Building your vocabulary	Page 144: Ask students to complete this in pairs.
Check your understanding	Page 145: Tine Thing Helseth – ask students to complete this alone.
Learner outcomes	By the end of this segment, students should be able to: • use specific vocabulary connected to music • use prefixes to indicate number.
Workbook	Page 69: Building your vocabulary Pages 69–70: Reading Page 70: Check your understanding Page 70: Speaking
Worksheet	7.1: Writing a song lyric

Segment 2	Pages 146–51 Crime fiction and drama
Syllabus objectives	**R2** Understand and select relevant information **L1** Identify facts and details
Broader skills development	• Sequence conversation. • Think about characteristics. • Use a range of conjunctions.
Introducing the session	Ask students which detective shows they enjoy watching. Do they know the names of any of the actors who play the detectives?
Ensuring a skills balance	Suggested speaking activity: After reading the extract from *Black Ice*, ask students to discuss in pairs who they think is the most interesting character in the extract, and why.
Differentiated activities	Ask stronger students to imagine a Sherlock plot. A blue diamond has been stolen; the gardener has been injured and the chauffeur is missing. Ask them, in pairs, to write a dialogue, with Holmes, Watson, and up to two other characters of their choice, to suggest what happens next.
Teaching and learning methodologies	**1** Conduct an interview. **2** Write a job description.
Building your vocabulary	Page 150: "Who could that be at this hour?" Ask students to do this individually.
Check your understanding	Page 149: Sherlock Holmes Page 149: Daniel Handler
Learner outcomes	By the end of this segment, students should be able to: • use the first two prompts in the speaking test • develop characters by thinking about their characteristics.
Workbook	Page 71: A. R. Rahman – listening Page 71: Check your understanding
Worksheet	7.2: Using persuasive vocabulary

Segment 3	Pages 152–6 Going out; Bollywood Oscars
Syllabus objectives	**W2** Convey information effectively **L2** Understand and select relevant information
Broader skills development	• Talk about a favourite film or stage show. • Learn a little more about Bollywood. • Write a storyboard.
Introducing the session	Ask students about the last time they went to the theatre. What did they go and see? Did they enjoy it and, if so, why?
Ensuring a skills balance	Suggested writing activity: Your favourite stage show has not yet been made into a film. Write to a famous director explaining why you think it should be.
Differentiated activities	Ask stronger students, in small groups, to give a short talk about their favourite type of cinema and the reasons for their choice. They should include examples of films they have seen in this genre.

Teaching and learning methodologies	1 Learn about adaptations.
	2 Use linking words.
Building your vocabulary	Page 152: The Lion King
Check your understanding	Page 152: The Lion King
	Page 154: Milkha Singh
	Page 156: Bollywood
Learner outcomes	By the end of the segment, learners should be able to:
	• compare film and stage shows
	• use linking words in a summary.
Workbook	Page 71: Floella Benjamin
	Pages 71–2: Reading
	Page 72: Check your understanding
Worksheet	7.3: Reading and answering short-answer questions

Segment 4	**Pages 157–62 Organizing large-scale events**
Syllabus objectives	**L2** Understand and select relevant information
	S2 Convey information and express opinions effectively
Broader skills development	• Learn about organizing a large-scale event.
	• Think about ways to raise money.
	• Use numbers and figures correctly.
Introducing the session	Ask students if they have ever been to a large-scale event like the Olympics or to a big concert. What was it like? If they have not been to one, ask them which one they would like to go to, and why.
Ensuring a skills balance	Suggested reading activity:
	Once students have watched the Rio 2016 and Tokyo 2020 Olympic bids, ask them to think back to London 2012 and research five interesting facts about it.
Differentiated activities	Ask stronger students to imagine they are watching a large-scale event. What is it like and what can they see? Ask them to describe it in their blog update.
Teaching and learning methodologies	1 Think about how to raise money for a good cause.
	2 Learn how best to tell others about your fundraising event so they can take part and/or support it.
Building your vocabulary	Page 158: Comic Relief – ask students to complete this on their own.
Check your understanding	Page 159: Comic Relief
	Page 161: Eddie Izzard
Learner outcomes	By the end of the segment, students should be able to:
	• work with numbers and figures
	• include adverbs more readily in their language.
Workbook	Pages 72–73: Adverbs
	Page 73: Speaking
	Pages 73–4: Richard Whitehead
Worksheet	7.4: More practice with adverbs

Segment 5	Pages 163–5 Apps
Syllabus objectives	**R3** Recognize and understand ideas
	L3 Recognize and understand ideas
Broader skills development	• Think about new aspects of modern life.
	• Use task-specific vocabulary.
	• Make comparisons.
Introducing the session	"Thinking out loud" (page 163): Allow students to complete this in small groups, in no more than five minutes.
Ensuring a skills balance	Suggested writing activity:
	Ask students to compare the apps described on page 164. Which do they like best and why? Tell them to use the language of comparison when writing their response.
Differentiated activities	Ask stronger students to make a table to compare three apps. Compared features could include price, resolution, special features, and animation, although students can, of course, use their own ideas.
Teaching and learning methodologies	1 Think about what we need in real life.
	2 Make comparisons between apps.
Building your vocabulary	Page 163: Ask students to complete this in pairs.
Check your understanding	After reading page 164, students should summarize each app in one sentence.
Learner outcomes	By the end of this segment, students should be able to:
	• understand a little more about apps
	• follow up a discussion.
Workbook	Page 74: Theatre
	Page 75: Check your understanding
	Page 75: Speaking and writing
Worksheet	7.5: Reading and answering short-answer questions

Segment 6	Pages 166–7 Gaming
Syllabus objectives	**R3** Recognize and understand ideas
	S4 Demonstrate knowledge of a range of appropriate vocabulary
Broader skills development	• Learn about gaming history.
	• Use task-specific vocabulary.
	• Work as a group to decide on an adaptation.
Introducing the session	Ask students whether they game on their smartphone. Which games do they enjoy playing the most?
Ensuring a skills balance	Suggested writing activity:
	Tell students that a close relative wants to borrow their favourite game while they are away. Ask them to write down the instructions so that the relative can play the game.
Differentiated activities	Ask stronger students to talk for one minute about their favourite game. They then need to compare their games in pairs, writing up to four comparative sentences.

| Teaching and learning methodologies | **1** Give instructions to play a game. |
	2 Make comparisons between games.
Building your vocabulary	Ask students to research up to five games. What vocabulary keeps appearing? Ask students to write a list of up to ten words or phrases.
Check your understanding	Page 166: Ask students to complete this individually.
Learner outcomes	By the end of this segment, learners should be able to:
	• explain their favourite game
	• compare games and their content.
Workbook	Page 75: Listening
	Page 76: Check your understanding
	Page 76: Discussion topic
Worksheet	7.6: Writing a summary
Further practice	**On completion of the chapter, ask students to complete questions 1–20 of the leisure and entertainment interactive activities.**

Links

If you choose only one link to use with your students, try this:

- www.bbc.co.uk/programmes/p00999wm

  Watch more interviews about Sherlock Holmes.

You might also try:

- www.bbc.co.uk/childreninneed – a big charity organizing annual events to raise funds.

- www.jeansforgenesday.org – on one day a year, wear your jeans and raise money for research into genetic disorders.

- www.olympic.org – find out more about the International Olympic Committee and the Olympic Games.

- www.madametussauds.com – help bring all your entertainment favourites to life.

- www.demelza.org.uk – have a look at how a smaller charity raises money to look after children.

If your students enjoyed reading the extract from *Black Ice* by Andrew Lane, why not suggest they try reading the whole book?

Study tips: speaking

Sequencing the early part of the conversation (see page 146 of the student book)

This section on the Speaking test focuses on the links between the first three prompts on the topic card – from the personal through to the general. The activity invites students to engineer some prompts to exemplify this development. Prompts 4 and 5 take the discussion into more sophisticated territory, but it is Prompts 1, 2, and 3 that set the scene for this.

Examiners will be prepared to use all five prompts in sequence, but will also have practised paraphrasing the more challenging prompts to suit the level of the candidate. All five prompts must be used, and in order, but it is permissible to paraphrase to suit the candidate in front of you.

Prompt 3 links the early part of Part D (the discussion) to the final part and is, more often than not, a broad-based, general discussion of the topic. In many cases this will be presented to the candidate as pros and cons, or advantages and disadvantages. It is useful therefore for teachers to do plenty of oral work with students, discussing a wide range of contemporary issues of which students have had direct experience and that can be explored in much more depth. The topics used for the Speaking examination will vary greatly and it is useful to refer to previous examination material to see the range covered. A topic could be regarded as a theme that the conversation covers with increasing depth as the discussion develops from the prompts.

A useful exercise with students is to talk about something they have done, or seen, and to extend this out to other people they know who have done or seen similar things, and then link this to what this says about society. An ideal 6–9-minute Speaking test should then include a strong view about the issue, followed by a final abstract idea to round everything up.

It is a good idea therefore to get students talking for 2–3 minutes about their experiences and views, and to include such a discussion in as many of your lessons as you can. This will increase their confidence and prepare them informally for the test of spoken language to come.

Sequencing exercise

Copy the following charts and give them to students to complete with some brief examples of their ideas for discussion against the first two prompts. What content would be appropriate for Prompts 1 and 2 to lead into Prompt 3? They could work in pairs to do this.

Topic: An evening out	
Prompt	**Spoken content**
1 My personal experience and thoughts	
2 What other people I know do or think	
3 General matters	The pros and cons of staying in vs. going out for entertainment

Topic: A great trip to the cinema	
Prompt	Spoken content
1 My personal experience and thoughts	
2 What other people I know do or think	
3 General matters	The pros and cons of being a film fan

Then ask them to think of a third topic within the theme of leisure and entertainment and repeat the exercise.

Study tips: writing

Using linking words in a summary (see page 156 of the student book)

This section focuses on the key skill of summary writing – Exercise 5 in the examination paper. Students at both levels will be asked to write a summary, but the approaches are very different:

- At core level, students will use notes they have made previously, based on an article they have read, to produce a 70–80 word summary. This is worth 5 marks and is marked for language skills only.

- At extended level, students will read an article that is new to them, and which is longer and more detailed, and they will then write a summary of 100–120 words. This is worth 11 marks and is marked for content (6 marks) and language (5 marks).

Summary writing therefore requires a blend of reading and writing skills in both examinations.

The student book offers plenty of informal practice at constructing summaries of longer texts and advice on the type of language – grammar and vocabulary – they need to use to create effective and concise summaries. In the examination, a summary will always be a guided summary – i.e. candidates will be shown/told the headings and subheadings required.

Evaluating the sample student responses

It will be interesting to see how your students assess the two sample responses, as the students are both strong writers.

- **Student B** would have scored the most marks for using more effective linking words and discourse markers.

- **Student A** is strong in terms of appropriate content but fails to bind this together in secure language.

Model answers and how to improve performance

To produce a successful summary, a candidate will have:

- covered most of the important (salient) points in the content
- not left out anything significant
- not included anything irrelevant or unproductive
- linked the content together in a logical sequence
- used strong linking language to ensure a smooth flow.

These integrated reading and writing skills are shown in the assessment objectives here.

Assessment objectives

At *both* levels:

W1 Communicate clearly, accurately, and appropriately

W2 Convey information and express opinions effectively

W3 Employ and control a variety of grammatical structures

W4 Demonstrate knowledge and understanding of a range of appropriate vocabulary

W5 Observe conventions of paragraphing, punctuation, and spelling

In addition, at *extended* level:

R1 Identify and retrieve facts and details

R2 Understand and select relevant information

R3 Recognize and understand ideas, opinions, and attitudes and the connections between related ideas

Here is a typical article that candidates might be invited to summarize at extended level in relation to leisure and entertainment.

Read the following article about directing a film. Write a summary of the different approaches to film directing, and what all good film directors share.

Your summary should be about 100 words long (and no more than 120 words long).

You should use your own words as far as possible.

You will receive up to 6 marks for the content of your summary, and up to 5 marks for the style and accuracy of your language.

The film director

A modern film director makes sure that all parts of a film are creatively produced and brought together to achieve a single perfect product lasting about two hours or so. A modern director interprets the script, coaches the actors, and tries to create a work of art. According to expert Eric Sherman, the director begins with a general idea of the entire film and uses this to help him determine what is to be done. He gains most when others taking part are given freedom to show what they can do. A film director brings out the best therefore in everyone involved.

The position of the director in the traditional filmmaking process, however, is different. The traditional film director is seen as a leader of others, providing a strong guiding force. According to this view, the final outcome is more or less predetermined by the requirements of the script, camerawork, acting, and editing; the director provides an organizational context to the picture.

Judging from the comments of most professional directors, there is very little agreement as to what exactly their main function should be. Some directors say that they must concentrate primarily on the script. If their films are to be successful, it will be because of the inherent beauty in the writing and dialogue in the script. Other directors are occupied primarily with the performance of actors. To them, the success of the film will be connected to the quality of acting.

Some directors attend primarily to the camerawork, their chief concern being for pictorial beauty. Still other directors say that the art of film is in the editing process. For them, all steps prior to editing yield crude and distorted material, which will be shaped and lent artistic worth by a skilled director.

When we watch a film for the first time, we see glimpses of the actor concentrating on every gesture, the writer concerned with logical narrative and captivating dialogue, the cameraman dealing with isolated images, and the editor concerned with the rhythmic flow. But it is the director who grasps the film as a whole. And all good directors are able to achieve certain aims and objectives.

Only the director stands apart from any one particular contributory element. Only the director has a sense of the films' entirety. Many of the strongest directors have refrained from virtually any function besides that of overseer of the film.

The successful director approaches a film with a more-or-less well-defined sense of its meaning, selecting and guiding all the work and shaping it along the necessary route to achieve (as closely as possible) what he or she has in mind.

Could a director be compared to an architect, a bricklayer laying brick upon brick, or a conductor of a great orchestra? No. These descriptions all fall short of the mark because what is being built is more volatile than stable, more fluid than secure. Director Roland Joffe (*The Killing Fields*) stated, "Being a director is like playing on a multilayered, multidimensional chessboard, except that the chess pieces decide to move themselves." The best directors are able to weave all these volatile pieces together and find harmony.

Adapted from www.filmmakers.com/stories/Director.htm

The article is 528 words long. Only 100 words or so are needed for the summary, but which ones? It is probably best to get your students to deconstruct the article first, by extracting some notes, ideas, and segments that align to the subheadings.

A strong candidate might produce a plan along the following lines:

How directors differ

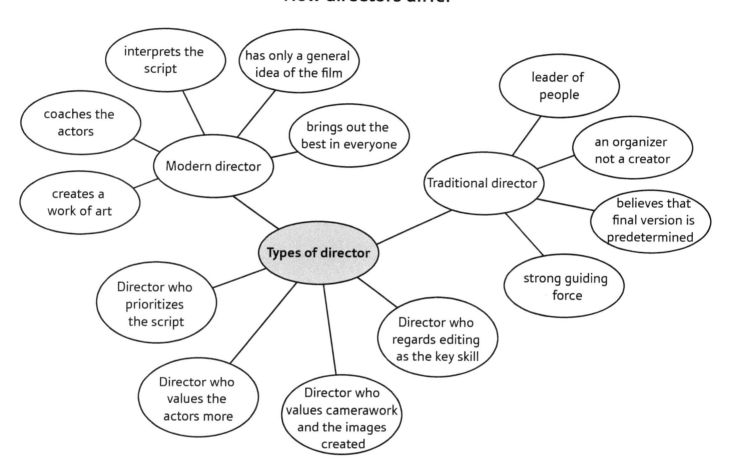

The common elements of being a good director

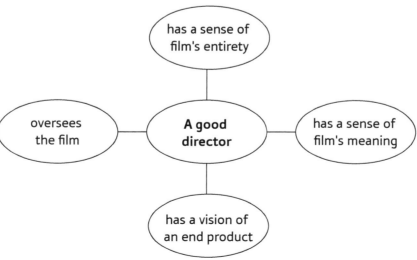

The challenge now is to bring all these separate notes together into a coherent piece of writing with fewer words than the original piece.

Here's a model answer for discussion with your students.

> "There are two basic types of director, one who has a modern outlook and another who prefers a more traditional style. The modern director is aiming to create a work of art by coaching the actors, interpreting the script as he or she goes along, aiming to create a work of art. This is in contrast to the traditionalist, who believes that the film's structure is preset, and that the job of the director is to act as a strong guide, leading the various people involved to produce an organized product.
>
> "However, even though there are differences in approach, most directors believe that good directing incorporates common skills, such as having a sense or a vision of the film's final form. A very good director is able to generate harmony from all the various disjointed pieces."

You might like to set this as an exam-based task first and then distribute the model answer.

- What makes this a model response?
- What are its strong points?
- Refer back to the bullet points at the beginning of this section – does this summary satisfy those objectives?

It is a challenging text and would not be suitable for core-level candidates.

Study tips: reading

Working with numbers and figures (see page 160 of the student book)

Both the Reading and Writing examination paper and the Listening paper will have questions that use numbers, so it's sensible to prepare your students thoroughly for these. It's a good idea to do plenty of classroom work testing their understanding of measurements, distance, weights, currency, times, dates, etc., to build up their knowledge of a wide range of numerical measurements.

It can be a fun activity to create imaginary questions with numerical answers and do this regularly. This exercise asks students to think of as many occasions as possible where numbers are used on a daily basis.

We strongly recommend classroom work on listening to numbers. Candidates often mishear 13 for 30, for example, and 15 for 50. We believe that practice makes perfect here, so repeatedly listening to various people pronouncing numbers will help students recognize the differences. It is also worth working on the differences between certain measurements – kilograms and kilometres, for example – as students often find these confusing.

It is likely, of course, that questions testing comprehension will feature numbers – e.g. Exercises 1 and 2 and Questions 1–4 on the Reading and Writing paper. Numbers may be used in all the questions in the Listening examination, and especially in Question 5. Numbers are not assessed in the Speaking test, however.

NB: all measurements featuring in the examination will be based on metric and not imperial scales. For example, kilometres will be used and not miles; kilograms and not pounds; centimetres and not inches, etc.

The sample student responses

Questions 1, 3, 4, 5, and 8 are all correct.

Study tips: listening

Listening to a follow-up discussion (see page 165 of the student book)

This exercise revisits Question 8b on the Listening paper at extended level. In Chapter 4 of this resource pack, "Animals and us", you'll find a detailed analysis of how this question works, with a sample of a typical Question 8 along with a mark scheme and a commentary. Question 8b appears only at extended level and it therefore assesses higher-level listening skills. The aim is to create a dialogue between two people who themselves have just listened to a talk (which is assessed in Question 8a). We listen in on that semi-formal conversation and answer five questions to assess how well we have understood the dialogue.

Question 8 can test all four assessment objectives, L1 to L4, but we will focus our attention here on L3 and L4.

Evaluating the sample student responses

- **Student A** infers too much from the dialogue. It's not stated that that phones and apps are having a negative effect on most users, or that a lot of people become addicted. We only have evidence of one person becoming addicted. The reference to governmental action is entirely inferred. So while this student has certainly understood the underlying issue, there is far too much inference to count as an accurate test of listening.

- **Student B** has understood the dialogue with the most accuracy and reports back exactly how each of the people feel.

- **Student C** appears to take the side of one of the people and even states that the person with the negative view is wrong. If we ignore that last statement, the rest of the response is an accurate portrayal of the views of one person. However, it does not convey fully the views of both people and is therefore only partially accurate.

This exercise demonstrates how difficult it is to identify a speaker's attitude and views. Conclusions about attitudes need concrete evidence from the text. Students need to infer less and seek out concrete evidence from the recording, and simply relay what has been stated. Work in the classroom on this key skill is recommended: differentiating between what is said, what is meant, and what can safely be inferred.

Model answers and how to improve performance

If we focus on assessment objective L4 we can see that it is gist understanding that is being assessed. Inferring something from what has been heard is a different skill, however, from inferring from what has been read. In everyday oral/aural communication, we probably see the person we are listening to, which allows us to look at their "body language" – their movements, gestures, and facial expressions, etc. This also lets us gauge emphasized language more easily, e.g. tone, intonation, stress, and other devices that can be used to convey irony, double meaning, sarcasm, etc.

In the Listening examination, candidates do not see the speakers but only hear them. It cannot be safe, therefore, to draw an inference from any of the devices or indicators mentioned above. To "understand what is implied but not actually stated" will need to be based on what is actually said. Let's practise this below.

Assessment objective

L4 Understand what is implied but not actually stated, e.g. gist, relationships between speakers, speaker's purpose/intention, speaker's feelings, situation, or place

You can use the following table with students. You could either recreate the table but leave the second and third columns empty and ask students to fill them in, or leave just one column empty – any of the first three – for lower-ability students. Feel free to add more statements on the theme of leisure and entertainment.

The model answers are given for you and you can see in each case that an accurate inference has been made. It might be interesting and fun if you invited your students to provide inaccurate inferences – i.e. add a fourth column with the heading "What cannot be safely inferred". For example, we cannot infer that the driver is "nervous" or "scared".

What was said (stated)	What was meant (implied) – model answers	What can be safely inferred – model answers		What cannot be safely inferred
"I'm never going to that cinema again. Did you see how dirty it was everywhere? It ruined my evening."	The cinema should be clean and pleasant, for an enjoyable experience.	1	The person did not enjoy the film. 2 The person was unhappy with the cinema owners.	
"That was the best evening out I've had for ages. The food was excellent and, actually, I didn't mind at all paying those prices on the menu."	The restaurant was of very good quality and gave value for money.	1	The person had a great night out. 2 The person had not expected the cost of the meal to be so high.	
"This is my first time driving a sports car. I'm probably going to go faster than I ever have. And that is maybe beyond me at the moment."	The driver wants to drive very fast but has doubts about achieving his/her personal best.	1	The driver is not completely confident. 2 The driver knows something that he/she is not telling us.	The driver was nervous or scared.
"Do we have to go there? I'd like to go somewhere new on holiday. And somewhere which is more exciting and with lots of things to do."	The suggested holiday destination is not appealing and lacks variety.	1	The traveller has been to the suggested location before and did not particularly like it. 2 A more adventurous destination is preferred. 3 An active holiday is preferred.	

☑ My progress

The four study skills – reading, writing, speaking, and listening – are key skills for success in each of the examinations. In the "My progress" section at the end of the chapter in the student book we invite students to select one skill that they can focus on and develop. However, you may like to ask students to prepare action plans to develop all four of the skills.

The table indicates where the skills feature in the examination papers and how they are applied. Unless otherwise indicated, the skills and tasks are common to both levels.

Skill	Task	Positioning in examination papers
Speaking about my own experiences and views and about the views of people close to me	Develop the early and less formal stages of a discussion	Speaking • Part D Prompts 1 and 2
Writing coherent summaries using linking words and discourse markers	Write a 100-word guided summary based on reading an article of 600 words (extended level only)	Reading and writing • Exercise 5 (extended)
Dealing with numbers, figures and measurements	Respond with precise detail in numerical form	Reading and writing • Exercises 1, 2 and 3
Listening to two people having a follow-up discussion on a stated theme	Provide five pieces of information that complete statements made by or about the two people (extended level only)	Listening • Question 8b (extended only)

8 Hobbies and interests

Student book content coverage

Segment 1	Pages 170–71 Hobbies
Syllabus objectives	**L4** Understand what is implied but not actually stated **S1** Communicate clearly, accurately, and appropriately
Broader skills development	• Think about hobbies/leisure activities. • Discuss new/unusual hobbies and what it might be like to try them. • Explore topic cards.
Introducing the session	"Thinking out loud" (page 170): Ask students to spend five minutes in small groups informally discussing the introductory questions. This can lead naturally on to the "What's my hobby?" miming game and speaking exercises.
Ensuring a skills balance	Suggested writing exercise: Ask students to write a blog saying how they spend their leisure and what new activity they might consider.
Differentiated activities	Stronger students can be asked to research unusual hobbies and report back to their group on one of their choice.
Teaching and learning methodologies	1 Explore possibilities in leisure pursuits. 2 Investigate the use of topic cards.
Building your vocabulary	Ask students to build their vocabulary by compiling a list of words associated with hobbies and leisure pursuits – with supporting worksheet 8.1.
Check your understanding	
Learner outcomes	By the end of this segment, students should be able to: • use topic cards correctly • identify and respond to inference and implication in a discussion.
Workbook	
Worksheet	8.1: Building your vocabulary – hobbies and pastimes

Segment 2	Pages 172–7 Collecting
Syllabus objectives	**R1** Identify and retrieve facts and details **W2** Convey information and express opinions effectively **L1** Identify and retrieve facts and details **S2** Convey information and express opinions effectively
Broader skills development	• Read about a royal collector. • Learn to write persuasively. • Listen to an autograph hunter. • Prepare and give an informative talk
Introducing the session	Ask students to talk about the things people collect. Are any of them collectors?
Ensuring a skills balance	Suggested writing activity: "Role playing – guess who I met today?" – Ask students to write an email to a friend about the conversation they have just had.
Differentiated activities	Stronger students can follow up the key skills persuasive writing tips on page 174. Ask them to use the same techniques to compose an advert for eBay, or similar online salesroom, to sell a small collection of stamps or autographs.
Teaching and learning methodologies	**1** Read about collections. **2** Prepare and write a persuasive letter.
Building your vocabulary	Page 172: Crossword – ask students to complete this individually and then compare results in pairs. Page 177: Prefixes
Check your understanding	Page 173: Ask students to work on these individually and then compare their answers. Page 175: Multiple-choice questions Page 176: Use this as preparation for the speaking exercise on page 177.
Learner outcomes	By the end of this segment, students should be able to: • write a persuasive letter • give an informative talk
Workbook	Page 77: Building your vocabulary Page 78: Read about postcard collecting Pages 78–9: Check your understanding Page 79: Descriptive writing Page 80: Language focus – prepositions Page 80: Check your understanding – multiple-choice questions
Worksheet	8.2: Preparing a talk on autograph collecting

Segment 3	Pages 178–81 Listening to music
Syllabus objectives	**R2** Understand and select relevant information **L2** Understand and select relevant information
Broader skills development	• Locate and select particular information from a written report. • Transfer information and fill out a form. • Prepare and present the radio programme *Desert Island Discs*.
Introducing the session	Ask students, in small groups, to discuss the importance of music to them. What kind of music do they like?
Ensuring a skills balance	Suggested writing activity: Ask students to write a blog about a piece of music they have heard recently.
Differentiated activities	Stronger students can choose their own famous person to invite on to *Desert Island Discs*. They can say what questions they would like to ask and have a go at suggesting the music their guest might choose.
Teaching and learning methodologies	**1** Listen to a speaker's ideas and opinions about music. **2** Read about a *Desert Island Discs* guest.
Building your vocabulary	Page 178: Appreciating music
Check your understanding	Page 178: Ask students to work informally in pairs, discussing their answers. Page 180: Ask students to answer individually, comparing their answers in pairs.
Learner outcomes	By the end of this segment, students should be able to: • listen critically to and evaluate opinions • collaborate in preparing and presenting a small-group activity.
Workbook	Page 81: Building your vocabulary – crossword Page 82: Reading an online discussion Page 83: Check your understanding Page 83: Joining in the conversation
Worksheet	8.3: Your *Desert Island Discs*

Segment 4	Pages 182–5 Learn to play an instrument
Syllabus objectives	**W4** Demonstrate knowledge and understanding of a range of appropriate vocabulary **L3** Recognize and understand ideas, opinions, and attitudes and the connections between related ideas
Broader skills development	• Listen to a conversation where different views are expressed. • Distinguish and evaluate views. • Identify and use appropriate vocabulary.
Introducing the session	"Thinking out loud" (page 182): Ask students to reflect individually on the questions before sharing thoughts in pairs for up to five minutes.
Ensuring a skills balance	Suggested speaking activity: In small groups, students prepare a short presentation to the class/school publicizing a forthcoming "sing along" evening – see page 184.

Differentiated activities	Stronger students can write a follow-up blog, "My first lesson".
Teaching and learning methodologies	**1** Match information from written and spoken sources. **2** Develop a critical understanding and response.
Building your vocabulary	Page 185: Language focus – musical imagery
Check your understanding	Page 183: Ask students to work through this informally in pairs.
Learner outcomes	By the end of this segment, students should be able to: • recognize and critique different opinions • draw together information from a range of sources.
Workbook	Page 84: Building your vocabulary Pages 84–5: Reading – learning the drums Page 85: Check your understanding Page 86: Writing
Worksheet	8.4: Building your vocabulary – "Ukepleyle"

Segment 5	Pages 186–8 Literary connections
Syllabus objectives	**R4** Understand what is implied but not actually written **W5** Observe conventions of paragraphing, punctuation, and spelling
Broader skills development	• Construct a questionnaire. • Conduct a survey of reading habits. • Read a poem and write a response to it.
Introducing the session	Ask students, in small groups, to talk about their reading interests, taking it in turns to say what they have recently read and what it was about.
Ensuring a skills balance	Suggested speaking activity: Ask students in small groups to read W. H. Davies's poem "Leisure" and discuss together what they would make time for.
Differentiated activities	Stronger students can have a go at writing their own poem about leisure in a technological age.
Teaching and learning methodologies	**1** Collaborate to produce a survey. **2** Write up the findings of a survey. **3** Read and appreciate poetry.
Building your vocabulary	Ask students to find five useful words from pages 186–8 or from their current reading and to share these in pairs.
Check your understanding	
Learner outcomes	By the end of this segment, students should be able to: • analyse and report on the findings of a survey • respond to a different genre (in this instance, poetry) • write an article making effective use of paragraphs.
Workbook	
Worksheet	8.5: Questionnaire for a reading survey

Segment 6	Pages 189–93 Getting away from it all
Syllabus objectives	**R3** Recognize and understand ideas, opinions, and attitudes and the connection between related ideas **S5** Engage in and influence the direction of conversation
Broader skills development	• Take part in a debate. • Sift through and evaluate opposing opinions. • Plan a series of lessons.
Introducing the session	"Thinking out loud" (page 189): Ask students to consider the questions together in pairs. How many outdoor pursuits can they come up with in two minutes? Are they outdoor types? Take up to five minutes altogether.
Ensuring a skills balance	Suggested writing activity: Follow up the study tips exercise on pages 192–3 by writing a paragraph summarizing one of the arguments.
Differentiated activities	Stronger students can, in pairs, act out a scene in which someone fishing quietly by a river is confronted by someone from an anti-fishing group.
Teaching and learning methodologies	**1** Contribute to a debate. **2** Use topic sentences and paragraphing. **3** Put together a lesson plan.
Building your vocabulary	Page 189: Ask students, in pairs, to match the words to their definitions and then to use them in sentences of their own.
Check your understanding	Page 190: Fishing as a hobby Page 191: Don't go fishing!
Learner outcomes	By the end of this segment, students should be able to: • recognize and respond to opinions they disagree with • locate and make use of appropriate content for a summary.
Workbook	Page 86: Discussion topic
Worksheet	8.6: The Big Issue debate: to fish or not to fish
Further practice	**On completion of the chapter, ask students to complete questions 1–20 of the hobbies and interests interactive activities.**

Links

If you choose only one link to use with your students, try this:

- www.about.com/hobbies

This website provides plenty of information about a whole range of hobbies. It also lists useful links to other sites.

You might also try these more specialized sites:

- www.collectibles.about.com – it's amazing what's considered collectible.
- www.hobbycraft.co.uk – a commercial site but offering useful information.

Particular hobbies and interests can be followed up on a variety of websites, such as:

- www.learntouke.co.uk
- www.fishing4fun.co.uk
- www.stanleygibbons.com/Stamp-Collecting

Study tips: speaking

Using paraphrasing and examples to work with prompts (see page 170 of the student book)

This activity looks at the structure of a topic card for the Speaking test. It invites students to act as question setters so that they can familiarize themselves with the pattern and the purpose of each of the five prompts. The way each prompt works and how each prompt develops into further discussion are covered elsewhere in this teacher resource pack. The activity here shows how students – and the examiner conducting the test – can paraphrase and use examples to clarify each of the prompts.

The focus is on paraphrasing the more challenging prompts (3, 4, and 5) and providing examples for each of them. A strong candidate should be able to give three or four examples for Prompts 3, 4, and 5 and be able to react to any changes in the direction of the discussion and, to some extent, be able to initiate changes. Working with the prompts in this fashion will therefore give a better chance of a higher mark for development and fluency, the third assessment criteria.

Here's a chart that you can use with students to allow them to demonstrate these skills. The prompts are based on topic cards that could be used for a hobbies and interests theme (but they are not drawn from the same card). The first row is completed; your students could fill in the gaps in the other rows.

Prompt as it is set	Paraphrased version	Possible examples
• The pros and cons of a dangerous hobby	Why some people like to take risks and the possible consequences of this	1 Caving – exploring underground caves and how this could go wrong 2 Motor racing – what some people get from the thrill of driving cars very fast
• The suggestion that a hobby can very easily become an obsession		1 Even collecting coins could lead to negative characteristics in someone – e.g. hoarding rather than sharing 2
• The suggestion that all hobbies are just a waste of time	A person's time could be used much more productively	1 2
• The advantages and disadvantages of having a hobby	The good things and bad things about a hobby and how it can enhance or ruin someone's life	1 2

• The idea that without a hobby a person is not achieving a full life		1 Someone who works all the time may work too much and a hobby would break this pattern 2
You can of course add further prompts to this chart, but focus on Prompts 3, 4, and 5.	Any paraphrasing is useful. If sometimes the paraphrase appears more difficult, this doesn't matter if clearer meaning is achieved.	It's a good idea to provide examples that support both sides of an argument and cover a wide range of possibilities.

Study tips: listening

Recognizing the opinions and attitudes of several people (see pages 183–4 of the student book)

In Question 6 of the Listening test at both core and extended levels, there will be a scenario during which six people are expressing their views and opinions on the same topic. Candidates are asked to match the six speakers to six different views out of seven views given; one is redundant.

This activity provides informal practice in applying this skill with an example of this question. It is based on a recording of the views of six people on music (the theme in this segment of the student book). Since this should be a formative and fun activity, we recommend playing the recording several times and pausing it on occasion if it helps students.

Evaluating the sample student responses

1 Which musician would be best to learn a new instrument with?

• **Student A** suggests the pianist but he has stated that he hated having lessons and there is no evidence that he has ever taught piano or has even wanted to.

• **Student B** suggests the violinist. However, she has said that she doesn't particularly enjoy teaching music. She prefers to perform.

• **Student C** suggests the drummer but, again, there is no evidence that he would make a good tutor.

It could be argued therefore that none of these six musicians would make ideal teachers/tutors... but that those with some experience of music lessons should be preferred.

2 Which musician is most accurately described or portrayed?

• **Student A** suggests the conductor, but since he has stated that there is "no room for error in what we do", he is hardly sensitive or very sympathetic to his orchestra.

• **Student B** provides a selective response with regard to the guitarist, omitting that the guitarist has been playing since he was 12, loves his guitar, and does indeed own an expensive guitar.

• **Student C** provides the most accurate portrayal, of the violinist.

Model answers and how to improve performance

Question 6 on the Listening paper is largely focused on testing candidates' ability to reach assessment objectives L3 and L4 (see below). Much of the teaching work that needs to be done to prepare students to perform at their best in this question is, however, at L3 – to recognize ideas, attitudes, and opinions.

> ## Assessment objectives
>
> **L3** Recognize and understand ideas, opinions, and attitudes and the connections between related ideas
>
> **L4** Understand what is implied but not actually stated, e.g. gist, relationships between speakers, speaker's purpose/intention, speaker's feelings, situation, or place

You can use the following Question 6 scenario as a summative test. The recording should be played only twice, as it will be in the Listening examination. This particular question is identical for both tiers, core and extended, and carries 6 marks on both papers.

The key skill here is to match the opinion, which is stated on the examination paper in the first person, to the likely speaker. It may well be that more than one speaker could hold the opinion, but candidates need to balance this and decide which opinion best fits the particular speaker. It is a challenging exercise and should therefore be practised as much as possible. Useful source material is panel-based discussions, with several people present, and each person presenting a different, or slightly different, point of view.

Play students the recording on the CD (Track 8.1), where they will hear six people offering their views on hobbies, and then ask your students to complete the question below:

Question 6

For each of the speakers 1 to 6, choose from the list, A to G, which opinion each speaker expresses. Write the letter in the box. Use each letter only once. There is one extra letter, which you do not need to use.

Speaker 1 ☐   **A** I'm happy that my hobby fills a gap in my life.

Speaker 2 ☐   **B** I think that hobbies are useful ways to build confidence in people.

Speaker 3 ☐   **C** I'm not addicted, I'm just very keen on what I do.

Speaker 4 ☐   **D** I thought I knew all about hobbies until I tried something different

Speaker 5 ☐   **E** Hobbies get in the way of work, so I avoid them.

Speaker 6 ☐   **F** I avoid hobbies now as I can't trust myself to keep them simple.

                     G I've never had a hobby that I didn't enjoy.

Answers

Speaker 1: C   Speaker 2: A   Speaker 3: E

Speaker 4: B   Speaker 5: D   Speaker 6: F

Study tips: writing

Using paragraphs and appropriate verbs (see pages 187–8 of the student book)

This section brings together two aspects of successful essay writing: using topic sentences and using a wide range of verbs. Topic sentences provide the framework for structured paragraphs, and irregular verbs in particular supply range and precision. If both these elements are strong in a piece of writing, it is likely to be fluent and convincing.

Both Exercises 6 and 7 on the Reading and Writing paper require the candidate to supply around 150–200 words of extended writing. This is not many words at all, so the key skill is to ensure that the whole piece has direction, focus, and is as accurate as possible. Many other elements make up a successful piece of writing, of course – accurate grammar, a wide range of vocabulary, the appropriate register, a strong sense of audience, etc. But perhaps the best place to start is with the structure of the piece. This is best initiated with secure topic sentences.

Here are some topic sentences for your students to enhance, using the suggested supporting points or examples. Ask them to work these into a paragraph. They don't have to use all the points provided: they should get the idea with the examples given.

Topic sentence	Ways it could be developed
There are many factors that make for a successful film.	(i) Good reviews (ii) An impressive cast of actors (iii) Strong directing (iv) Dramatic, exciting, lots of action (v) Clever advertising and promotion
Since I started that particular hobby, it has changed my life.	(i) In a positive way (ii) And also in a negative way (iii) It led me to change my job (iv) I met some very unusual people (v) I used to have a simple life

Evaluating the sample student responses

Students A and B have both made basic verb tense errors. Invite students to identify these and then to change the verbs to alternative ones – irregular verbs if possible. They could also look back at the paragraphs created in the topic sentence exercise above and explore the verbs they used and, again, seek out alternatives that are more apt.

Study tips: reading

Locating appropriate content for a summary (see pages 192–3 of the student book)

The two articles on fishing are ideal for creating summaries. Both can be summarized in around 70–100 words. This activity describes the key skills for writing a good summary: a combination of selecting appropriate content and using fluent and precise language. Indeed, when people create summaries, they are nearly always blending content and language.

The activity aims to demonstrate that selecting the content points is only half the task. Of equal importance is deciding on the order in which the content points are used. There is some flexibility in ordering content, but there is also probably a preferred order and it is this that students can learn. They need to know that there must be a logical pattern to a successful summary. This is where the use of secure language comes in, of course – i.e. linking words and phrases to bind the content points together and give the effect of a logical development. This is not an easy skill to learn.

You could explore this with your students by creating eight content points (eight will work well as practice for the exam) and asking them, in pairs, to string these together in both a logical and an illogical order. For example, here are eight content points for a summary of "How to go about collecting letters and manuscripts". Invite your students to play with the order of these until they arrive at the most logical.

---

1. There are specialist shops in many countries that sell very old letters.

2. It's useful to register with the British Library Antique Documents department, and it's free.

3. Some are inexpensive; others are very expensive.

4. Check the validity of older letters; many on the market prove to be fakes.

5. One of the best resources is the Internet.

6. Join your local collectors' group.

7. Speak to an expert.

8. Don't put old letters in frames as it can damage them; they should be kept in cabinets.

Evaluating the sample student responses

- **Student A** provides the weakest response, and it is the response with the highest degree of error.

- **Student B** provides a competent summary but prefers the listing approach.

- **Student C** provides the best summary and attempts to synthesize, integrating pros and cons.

Model answers and how to improve performance

In Chapter 7, Leisure and entertainment, we focused on writing a summary for the extended-level paper. Here, we will look at the same task but for the core-level paper. In both papers, the summary task appears in Exercise 5.

At core level, the summary is worth 5 marks and is assessed on language competence only. Candidates will have read an article for Exercise 4 and will have produced a series of notes based on the article; this provides the content element for the summary. It is likely that these notes will then be used again for another purpose – e.g. to prepare a talk – and a good way to finish this off is to write a brief summary based on the notes.

Here's an example of how it might work in an examination paper.

> In Exercise 4 you made some notes on the article "The science of sleep" [included in Chapter 1 of this teacher resource pack]. Use these notes to write a summary of the new research and its findings. Your summary should be about 70–80 words long and you should use your own words as much as possible.

A model student would have recorded the following notes. It would be more authentic, of course, for your students to use their own notes based on their response to Exercise 4.

Roles of sleep

1. Wash away waste toxins
2. Fix memories
3. Enhance learning
4. Do "housework"

Waste removal

5. Brain cells shrink to open up gaps to allow cleansing fluid in
6. A series of pipes/plumbing /glymphatic system carry waste material out
7. Becomes ten times more/much more active when the brain is in sleep mode

Implications of the research

8. Need to learn more about the physical element of sleep/effect on brain of physical and chemical changes
9. Sleep may contribute to the restoration of brain-cell function
10. Failing to clear away some toxins may result in disorders (allow specific disorders)
11. We may understand better how some diseases of the brain may come about

The new research into sleep and its findings – a model answer

"It has been found that while we are asleep waste toxins are washed away by using a series of pipes called the glymphatic system. By doing this, sleep may well improve the function of the brain. Some scientists think that failing to wash away these toxins could be the cause of brain problems, and further research is needed to explore this physical element of sleep. It was also found that this plumbing system is much more effective while we sleep." [80 words]

> **Our expert says:** Notice how the candidate selects the relevant content only and then uses a logical sequence to link this together. A strong summary is one that selects appropriate content and also therefore ignores less important content. Summarizing is not trying to include all the original material or points but prioritizing some material over other material.

A weaker response is likely to have one or more of these deficiencies:

- It will be too long and well over the word count.
- It will choose a linear approach, offering a list.
- It will try to use *all* the content points.
- It will be structured with short and simple sentences.
- It will not use linking words or conjunct phrases.

☑ My progress

The four study skills – reading, writing, speaking, and listening – are key skills for success in each of the examinations. In the "My progress" section at the end of the chapter in the student book, we invite students to select one skill that they can focus on and develop. However, you may like to ask your students to prepare action plans to develop all four of the skills.

The table shows where the skills feature in the examination papers and how they are applied. Unless otherwise indicated, the skills and tasks are common to both levels.

Skill	Task	Positioning in examination papers
Paraphrasing and using examples when speaking in a conversation	Ensure that the second half of the conversation is clearly understood and appropriately developed	Speaking • Part D, Prompts 3, 4 and 5
Recognizing opinions when listening to a group of people discussing the same topic	Match six opinions to six speakers	Listening • Question 6
Using topic sentences and verbs to structure extended writing	Write 150–200 words of extended but focused and structured writing on a given theme	Reading and writing • Exercises 6 and 7
Locating and selecting suitable content and writing a summary	Write a guided summary of about 70–80 words (core level)	Reading and writing • Exercise 5 (core only)

9 Customs and cultures

Student book content coverage

Segment 1	Pages 196–200 Greetings, all!
Syllabus objectives	**R2** Understand and select relevant information
	W3 Employ and control a variety of grammatical structures
	L1 Identify and retrieve facts and details
	S2 Convey information and express opinions effectively
Broader skills development	• Read about greetings customs around the world.
	• Discuss and write about different greetings customs.
	• Learn about accurate sentence structure.
Introducing the session	"Thinking out loud" (page 196): Ask students to spend five minutes discussing the questions.
Ensuring a skills balance	Suggested writing activity:
	Ask students to write about meeting someone from another country for the first time.
Differentiated activities	Stronger students, in small groups, can discuss the way that greetings customs differ worldwide and how these are changing with the times.
Teaching and learning methodologies	**1** Read about greetings customs worldwide.
	2 Compare different greetings customs.
	3 Learn about accurate sentence structure.
Building your vocabulary	Pages 196–7: Multiple choice – ask students to discuss the options informally in pairs.
Check your understanding	Page 199: Greetings around the world – ask students to work at these individually and then compare answers in pairs, leading into the discussion activity that follows.
	Page 199: Māori greetings – discuss in small groups.
Learner outcomes	By the end of this segment, students should be able to:
	• develop a discussion based on varied input
	• write accurate sentences.
Workbook	
Worksheet	9.1: Building your vocabulary – crossword

Segment 2	Pages 201–2 Birth customs
Syllabus objectives	**R1** Identify and retrieve facts and details **S1** Communicate clearly, accurately, and appropriately
Broader skills development	• Read about different customs worldwide celebrating birth. • Give a short talk about celebrating a birth in different cultures.
Introducing the session	"Thinking out loud" (page 201): Ask students to spend five minutes talking about the questions.
Ensuring a skills balance	Suggested writing activity: Ask students to write an entry for their country, to add to the web page.
Differentiated activities	Stronger students can write a blog about their visit to a friend from another country and culture who has invited them to the celebration of the birth of a baby in the family.
Teaching and learning methodologies	**1** Understand variations in customs celebrating birth. **2** Adapt written information for a short talk.
Building your vocabulary	Page 201: Ask students to match the words and meanings and to check their answers in pairs.
Check your understanding	Page 202: Baby customs – ask students to work at these singly in preparation for giving a short talk on the subject.
Learner outcomes	By the end of this segment, students should be able to: • distinguish detail in varied descriptions • prepare and present a short talk based on given material.
Workbook	Page 87: Building your vocabulary Page 87: Bringing up baby – listening Page 88: Check your understanding – multiple choice Page 88: Read about putting baby to bed Page 89: Check your understanding – setting the questions Page 90: Interview time – speaking
Worksheet	9.2: Giving a presentation

Segment 3	Pages 203–5 Coming of age
Syllabus objectives	**L3** Recognize and understand ideas, opinions, and attitudes and the connections between related ideas **S5** Engage in and influence the direction of conversation
Broader skills development	• Watch and listen to an account of the bullet ant test. • Participate in an interview. • Identify and make use of emotive language in writing.
Introducing the session	Ask students, in small groups, to discuss for up to five minutes the ways in which the transition to adulthood is marked in their culture.
Ensuring a skills balance	Suggested writing activity: When they have watched the bullet ant test video, ask the students to write an email to a friend, beginning: "I've just seen a most amazing video clip. You won't believe what they do …"

Differentiated activities	Stronger students can discuss and then write their response to the question: "Would you take part in a bullet ant test or its equivalent?"
Teaching and learning methodologies	**1** Prepare and take part in an interview. **2** Handle emotive language.
Building your vocabulary	Ask students to find five new sets of contrasting words to express feelings.
Check your understanding	Page 203: Multiple choice – ask students to work in pairs and discuss the various possibilities.
Learner outcomes	By the end of this segment, students should be able to: • participate in conversation with confidence • identify feelings and attitudes in speech and writing.
Workbook	Page 90: Emotive writing
Worksheet	9.3: Language focus – trick or treat?

Segment 4	Pages 206–7 Marriage customs in Europe; literary connections
Syllabus objectives	**R3** Recognize and understand ideas, opinions, and attitudes and the connection between related ideas **W4** Demonstrate knowledge and understanding of a range of appropriate vocabulary
Broader skills development	• Read about customs associated with weddings. • Understand and appreciate traditional verse.
Introducing the session	Ask students to spend five minutes, in small groups, talking about any weddings they may have attended. What wedding customs and traditions do they know about?
Ensuring a skills balance	Suggested speaking activity: Ask students to follow up the "Poetry please!" activity by holding a verse-speaking session. In small groups, they first need to prepare, making use of the examples on page 207, their own poems and others they research, and then present a reading.
Differentiated activities	Stronger students can research marriage customs and present a short talk summarizing their findings.
Teaching and learning methodologies	**1** Write for a specialist magazine. **2** Read traditional verse.
Building your vocabulary	Page 206: Ask students to work on these individually and then compare their results with others.
Check your understanding	Page 206: Work on these in pairs; the answers will be useful notes for subsequent discussions.
Learner outcomes	By the end of this segment, students should be able to: • research and gather information from a variety of sources • use appropriate vocabulary and structure to write for a specialist audience.

Workbook	Page 91: Building your vocabulary – crossword
	Page 92: Read about Greek marriage customs
	Pages 92–93: Check your understanding
	Page 93: Watch a video of a Greek wedding
	Page 93–94: Write a descriptive email
Worksheet	9.4: Composing a speech

Segment 5	**Pages 208–11 Chinese wedding traditions**
Syllabus objectives	**R1** Identify and retrieve facts and details
	W2 Convey information and express opinions effectively
	W5 Observe conventions of paragraphing, punctuation, and spelling
Broader skills development	• Read about traditional Chinese marriage customs.
	• Recognize different points of view in a piece of writing.
Introducing the session	Ask students to talk about the traditional wedding customs they came across during the previous segment. What might a traditional wedding in their culture be like?
Ensuring a skills balance	Suggested speaking activity:
	Ask students to use the notes they made for "Comparisons" (page 210) to form the basis of a small group discussion.
Differentiated activities	Stronger students can, in pairs, role play an interview with a Chinese woman matchmaker about her job. They need to agree questions and then take it in turns to be interviewer and matchmaker.
Teaching and learning methodologies	**1** Extract information from extended writing.
	2 Identify a balanced argument.
	3 Present a balanced argument.
Building your vocabulary	Scan the article on Chinese marriage customs and note down any unfamiliar words. Compare lists in pairs and establish their meaning. Use them in sentences of your own.
Check your understanding	Check that students understand all that is taking place in the article on Chinese marriage customs. Worksheet 9.5 helps with vocabulary of this piece.
Learner outcomes	By the end of this segment, students should be able to:
	• recognize a balanced argument
	• sift and scan longer pieces of writing.
Workbook	Pages 91–4: Any activities not covered in the previous segment will be useful for this one.
	Page 94: Further punctuation practice
Worksheet	9.5: Building your vocabulary

Segment 6	Pages 212–5 Death customs
Syllabus objectives	**R2** Understand and select relevant information **L2** Understand and select relevant information **L4** Understand what is implied but not actually stated
Broader skills development	• Investigate the customs of a selected ancient civilization. • Collaborate in a multimedia presentation.
Introducing the session	"Thinking out loud" (page 212): Ask students to talk about these questions for up to five minutes.
Ensuring a skills balance	Suggested writing activity: Ask students to write letters as part of the Reflection activity (page 215), either to the media about the campaign or to invite the special visitor to take part.
Differentiated activities	Stronger students can choose one of the practices featured in "Caring for the dead" and, imagining that they were present at the time, write a short eyewitness account.
Teaching and learning methodologies	**1** Prepare and present a multimedia project. **2** Select a tradition in danger of dying out and collaborate in a campaign to preserve it.
Building your vocabulary	Page 212: Listening exercise
Check your understanding	Page 213: This is best done in pairs.
Learner outcomes	By the end of this segment, students should be able to: • understand what is implied in listening activities • contribute with confidence to collaborative activities.
Workbook	Page 95: Building your vocabulary Pages 95-6: Reading about death ceremonies Page 96: Check your understanding Page 96: Discussion topic – contemporary culture
Worksheet	9.6: Listening – understanding what is implied

Links

A wealth of websites offers information about cultures worldwide. Good places to start are:

- www.britishmuseum.org/explore/cultures.aspx – specializing in the history of cultures.
- www.atozworldculture.com – an A to Z of world culture; a comprehensive resource.
- www.cultures.com – a site devoted to cultures, living and ancient.
- www.culturecrossing.net – a guide to cross-cultural etiquette and understanding.

For birth and childhood customs, try:

- www.disneybaby.com/blog/baby-customs-traditions-rituals-around-world

For marriage customs, try:

- www.livescience.com/16810-10-world-wedding-traditions.html

For customs related to caring for the dead, try:

- www.about.com/genealogy

Study tips: writing

Writing accurate sentences
(see pages 199–200 of the student book)

This is a straightforward reference to Exercise 3 of the extended Reading and Writing paper (form filling), part of which asks candidates to write a sentence of between 12 and 20 words. The activity provides practice at this skill, while also bringing in a broader understanding of what a proper sentence is. You may like to precede this activity therefore with a segment on "what constitutes a proper sentence".

Building up students' confidence in writing medium-length competent sentences will of course help them to become better writers in general, and will help them when they are completing Exercises 5, 6, and 7.

You could use the following activity to enhance the section. Split your class into groups of three and ask them to fill out a chart like the one below. They should then compare and contrast their findings with another group. Five points should be sufficient to provide a challenge.

What a sentence should have	When a sentence would not be a proper sentence
1	1
2	2
3	3
4	4
5	5

Evaluating the sample student responses

- **Student A** is the more competent writer of sentences and the author of sentences b, d, and e.

- **Student B** is the less competent sentence writer and is the author of sentences a, c, and f.

Study tips: speaking

Expressing your opinions and taking control of a conversation (see page 204 of the student book)

The two objectives stated at the beginning of this section send a key message to students: if a candidate can meet both of these objectives, he or she is likely to perform very well in the Speaking test.

During the Speaking test, candidates can offer opinions and influence the direction of the conversation from the outset. They don't have to wait until Prompts 4 and 5 have been introduced in order to demonstrate these skills. They are not higher-level skills, but the weaker performances in the speaking test are generally those in which the candidate is passive, and responds "in turn".

This section aims to show that it's important to take control of the conversation where possible. This doesn't necessarily mean challenging the examiner, but just steering the discussion into new, productive areas. Several sections of the student book emphasize this message, and it's important if you are an examiner of the Speaking test to structure your approach so that you support candidates in developing the points they make.

Evaluating the sample student responses

All three students provide good responses, as all three engage with the concept and have understood what the examiner is getting at. However, there are differences:

- **Student A** provides one secure example, but could have developed this further. The examiner would have responded with "Why is it such a serious matter, then?" so Student A may well have been able to provide more depth and more examples.

- **Student B** is almost there but there is slight blurring of understanding and the personal example is not quite what is meant by a ritual.

- **Student C** provides the response that shows the most profound understanding.

Model answers and how to improve performance

The key skill for success being practised in this section is closest to these assessment objectives for the component.

> ## Assessment objectives
>
> **S2** Convey information and express opinions effectively
>
> **S5** Engage in and influence the direction of conversation

The following topic card is based on the theme of customs and cultures. To demonstrate how these two assessment objectives can be met effectively, the card is followed by what a strong candidate might say in response to each prompt. It shows that there are several points during the discussion where a candidate could take the reins and influence the direction of the conversation.

Oral test topic card

Traditions

Most cultures have some traditional values.

Discuss this topic with the examiner.

You should use all five prompts in the order given, to develop the conversation.

1   Something you or your family do which you regard as a tradition

2   Other traditions you know about

3   The pros and cons of maintaining traditional values

4   The suggestion that tradition is just a way for people who control society to maintain order

5   The idea that at the end of each century all traditions should be scrapped and a society is allowed to start again

You can include additional, related ideas of your own to help develop the discussion.

Prompt 1: "We have a strong tradition in my family of going to see our grandparents every week. We like to maintain that connection and although at times it's a little bit boring for me and my sister, we really appreciate how important it is for our grandparents. If everyone did this, wouldn't society be a better place?" [teasing the examiner to engage... which he/she should do].

Prompt 2: "I know that a penfriend I've got goes to camel races every month with his family. They also show falcons at these events and this is a tradition that has been going on for centuries. I'm not aware of too many other traditions but this example shows that different cultures have different traditions. I can imagine that people who live close to the sea have their particular traditions. For example ..." [showing that logical progression of the discussion is better than being passive].

Prompt 3: "Although people like to make progress, sometimes this can happen too fast and we lose sense of our identities. This is where traditions help. They can fix us to our past and make us feel a sense of belonging – a sort of comfort zone. Mind you, a comfort zone can sometimes become a danger zone..." [showing a clear depth of understanding and, again, teasing a response from the examiner].

Prompt 4: "You mean like in schools – the way that we have assemblies, and rules, and an established way of doing something? Yes, I'd agree with that prompt. But not just in schools; I'm sure that keeping order is really important in a court of law, so I'm guessing that the legal system has lots of established traditions. Is that right? [a very good way to bring the examiner in and influence the discussion... though students should not use this device more than two or three times in Part D of the test].

Prompt 5: "It's a radical idea. At first I liked it, but now I'm not so sure. I can see how it would work, but I can also see how we might end up with just the same in time ... different traditions but with the same effect. So the prompt should really say, 'It's impossible to get rid of tradition'." [rewording the later prompts to show conceptual understanding is very impressive and the examiner has to respond to this sophisticated change of direction].

All these responses show that what is required more than anything in the speaking test is a healthy debate, where both parties are attempting to reach equal terms. Candidates must be given the chance to achieve this, so the worst possible examining technique is an interview scenario where the examiner represents authority, as the "question asker".

Study tips: reading

Recognizing a balanced argument (see page 211 of the student book)

We have already focused on the key skill of writing an essay that considers several views of a topic and concludes with a balanced personal view. This skill is especially required in Exercise 7 of the Reading and Writing examination at both core and extended levels. This section takes a different approach and offers students some work from the reading perspective.

The first task asks students, in pairs, to come up with a first draft (so no need to check for errors) for a piece of writing of about 200 words and then another pair evaluates it for balance. This informal peer assessment is a useful and effective teaching tool on the course.

The second task – to locate on the Internet a balanced piece of writing of about 500 words – is also good exam practice because texts featuring in the examination are likely to be around 450–600 words. A key skill for success – not just in the Reading and Writing exam but also in the Listening and Speaking tests – is being able to recognize different points of view in relation to a theme or a topic.

Sample student responses

- **Student A** has a plan that is likely to suffer from a lack of structure. It lacks the means to develop a pros and cons of marriage argument.

- **Student B** has a better response, but it would be even better if it had an introduction and a conclusion that settled on a preference, or overall point of view. Essays that just list both sides without having a sense of ownership are not likely to achieve top band marks.

- **Student C** has the best response: a plan with a logical flow that also considers both sides, and then also offers a conclusion and a rationale.

Study tips: listening

Understanding what is implied (see page 214 of the student book)

This section looks at the generic skill of inference in listening. It is important to convey to students that we are trying to infer meaning only from something actually said – and not from any use of intonation, expression, or even body movements. The implication therefore will be in the words used by the speaker; the inference is a way that the listener processes and understands those words.

The skill runs through much of the listening examination and is a key skill in trying to work out what someone means from what they have said. Synonymous phrases are useful here in ascertaining meaning, and these could form the basis of an activity. Question 6 on the examination paper, which uses MCQs, is where this skill is most pertinent, and we have already covered this question on several occasions.

The focus of this activity is on the different views that people hold about the same topic or issue. Here, we are exploring the skill in a collaborative, informal, and fun way that makes it a general lesson rather than fixing it to an examination question.

Another useful activity is to use large groups of five or six students and give each group a point of discussion, for example how a culture should deal with death. Then ask each participant to present a different point of view from the other participants. At no point should a similar point of view emerge. It's quite a challenge, but it helps students get used to the scenario used in Question 6.

Model answers and how to improve performance

In Question 6, candidate performance is formally assessed by means of MCQs. It is therefore difficult to provide model answers. However, we can demonstrate strong performance by analysing a student's response to the following scenario. We will be using synonym phrases.

Three people are talking about the future of marriage, and each person presents his or her view early on in the conversation:

Person 1: "I have been married now for 20 years and it was the best decision I made in my life. Yes, we've had a few differences over the years, but that always led to healthy debate, and I'd say my wife and I are both better people for it. We have become good listeners and it's nice to have someone close to share ideas with."

Person 2: "I will never marry. I think that it would compromise the way I like to do things. I like my independence, and I like being able to just get up and go where I want to go. I've also got used to my personal space, and I can't imagine another person living in my house and changing things."

Person 3: "If I do marry, it must be on equal terms. And that will always involve a compromise in my book. So when I'm ready for a compromise I'll think about getting married. At the moment, my boyfriend and I enjoy being so different from each other, so we're very happy with the way things are."

Here's how a strong candidate summarized each person, using different words and inference:

- "Person 1 believes that a wife has to be a good listener for a marriage to be successful."

- "Person 2 believes that he would need to consult his wife whenever he wanted to go out."

- "Person 3 believes that marriage could upset the way things are in a negative way."

We are of course exploring L4.

Assessment objective

L4 Understand what is implied but not actually stated, e.g. gist, relationships between speakers, speaker's purpose/intention, speaker's feelings, situation, or place

Your students can improve their performance in the Listening test by practising this key skill of using different words to mirror what a speaker has said, as long as those words convey the same meaning, whether stated or implied.

Person 3 also believes that marriage is a union where two people become one ... or is this an inference too far?

☑ My progress

The four study skills – reading, writing, speaking, and listening – are key skills for success in each of the examinations. In the "My progress" section at the end of the chapter in the student book, we invite students to select one skill that they can focus on and develop. However, you may like to ask your students to prepare action plans to develop all four of the skills.

The table shows where the skills feature in the examination papers and how they are applied. Unless otherwise indicated, the skills and tasks are common to both levels.

Skill	Task	Positioning in examination papers
Writing short, accurate, controlled sentences	Write sentences of between 12 and 20 words (extended)	Reading and writing • Exercise 3 (extended)
Influencing the direction of a conversation	Bring in relevant discussion points during the speaking test	Speaking • Part D
Listening to infer with precision what someone has said	Provide synonymous phrases to mirror implied meaning	Listening • Question 6 • Question 8 (extended)
Recognizing a balanced set of views in a reading text	Separate out two or more sides of an argument and conclude with own view	Reading and writing • Exercise 7

10 The past and the future

Student book content coverage

Segment 1	Pages 218–21 Progress
Syllabus objectives	**R1** Identify and retrieve facts and details **S2** Convey information and express opinion effectively
Broader skills development	• Read about ten things that have changed our lives. • Prepare and deliver a talk.
Introducing the session	"Thinking out loud" (page 218): Ask students to spend five minutes individually and then in pairs thinking and talking about the questions. What changes have they seen – locally – in the way we do things?
Ensuring a skills balance	Suggested writing activity: Ask students to choose one item not mentioned in the top ten (pages 219–20) and write a paragraph/post a blog saying why it should be included in the list.
Differentiated activities	Stronger students can, in small groups, discuss five advances that might be made in the next ten years of progress and produce a short piece: "Five things that could change our lives".
Teaching and learning methodologies	**1** Read and evaluate a list of things that have changed our lives. **2** Discuss what has been the greatest influence on progress.
Building your vocabulary	Page 219: Ask students, in pairs, if they can add to this important list of mainly technical words.
Check your understanding	Page 221: Ask students to complete this individually.
Learner outcomes	By the end of this segment, students should be able to: • scan technical information critically • engage in discussion at a sophisticated level.
Workbook	
Worksheet	10.1: Your top ten things that have changed our lives

Segment 2	Pages 222–6 Life in England 100 years ago
Syllabus objectives	**R2** Understand and select relevant information **W1** Communicate clearly, accurately, and appropriately **L2** Understand and select relevant information **S5** Engage in and influence the direction of conversation
Broader skills development	• Sift and scan for note taking. • Write a diary entry. • Take part in a chat show.

Introducing the session	Ask students to think what life might have been like for them 100 years ago and talk about it in pairs.
Ensuring a skills balance	Suggested speaking activity: "A remarkable old lady" (page 226): before students proceed to write the magazine article, ask them in pairs to draw up the questions they would like to ask the lady. They can then take it in turns to act out the interview.
Differentiated activities	Stronger students can extend their diary entry (page 225) to include reflections on other things that have happened during the week.
Teaching and learning methodologies	**1** Read an account of life 100 years ago. **2** Identify redundant material. **3** Listen to and respond to an interview.
Building your vocabulary	Page 222: Fill in the blanks and then, in pairs, use the words in sentences.
Check your understanding	Page 222: Ask students to check their answers with their neighbours. Page 226: Multiple-choice questions
Learner outcomes	By the end of this segment, students should be able to: • identify redundant detail in a passage • use relevant information from a passage in written and spoken activities.
Workbook	Page 97: Building your vocabulary Page 98: Reading a letter Pages 98–9: Check your understanding Page 99: Speaking – asking questions Page 99: Writing an email
Worksheet	10.2: Note-making – life in England 100 years ago

Segment 3	**Pages 227–9 Family life in Ancient Egypt**
Syllabus objectives	**R3** Recognize and understand ideas, opinions, and attitudes and the connections between related ideas **W5** Observe conventions of paragraphing, punctuation, and spelling **W6** Employ appropriate register/style
Broader skills development	• Read an extended piece about life in Ancient Egypt. • Summarize accurately and concisely. • Distinguish accurately between homophones.
Introducing the session	"Thinking out loud" (page 227): Ask students, in pairs, to talk about the questions for five minutes.
Ensuring a skills balance	Suggested spoken activity: Ask students to discuss what life would have been like for them in Ancient Egypt.
Differentiated activities	Stronger students can write a paragraph of 80 words summarizing growing up in Ancient Egypt.
Teaching and learning methodologies	**1** Extract relevant information from a passage. **2** Write accurate summaries using your own words.
Building your vocabulary	Page 226: Crossword

Check your understanding	Page 227: Ask students to complete this individually.
Learner outcomes	By the end of this segment, students should be able to: • use synonyms in summary writing • be more confident in accurately distinguishing between homophones • adapt information gleaned from a given passage to their own writing.
Workbook	Page 101: Building your vocabulary Pages 101–2: Reading more about life in Ancient Egypt Page 102: Check your understanding
Worksheet	10.3: Using synonyms

Segment 4	Pages 230–32 The Terracotta Army
Syllabus objectives	R4 Understand what is implied but not actually written L1 Identify and retrieve facts and details
Broader skills development	• Read about the Terracotta Army. • Give a presentation about Emperor Qin, making use of information given or implied.
Introducing the session	Ask students to talk together in small groups for up to five minutes about what other ancient civilizations were like.
Ensuring a skills balance	Suggested writing activity: Ask students to write a paragraph describing two of the statues.
Differentiated activities	Stronger students can write the message that the first archaeologist on the scene in 1974 might have sent about the discovery.
Teaching and learning methodologies	1 Extract and adapt information, stated or implied. 2 Collaborate to produce a presentation about the first emperor of China. 3 Ensure appropriate and grammatically accurate responses to listening.
Building your vocabulary	Ask students to note down and check the meaning of any words they are unfamiliar with, comparing notes with their neighbour.
Check your understanding	Page 231: Ask students to complete this individually.
Learner outcomes	By the end of this segment, students should be able to: • research material from a variety of sources • contribute to a collaborative presentation.
Workbook	
Worksheet	10.4: Building your vocabulary – a crossword

Segment 5	Pages 233–4 The future
Syllabus objectives	R2 Understand and select relevant information W3 Employ and control a variety of grammatical structures
Broader skills development	• Read an imaginative account of what life might be like in the future. • Accurately identify and use correct tenses.
Introducing the session	"Thinking out loud" (page 233): Ask students, in pairs, to think about and then discuss life 10 years from now, then 40, then 1,000.

Ensuring a skills balance	Suggested speaking activity: Ask students, in pairs, to interview Katy about her weekend.
Differentiated activities	Stronger students, in pairs or small groups, can discuss what education might be like for students like them in 2050.
Teaching and learning methodologies	**1** Understand ideas about the future and imaginatively build on them. **2** Write as if you were someone else.
Building your vocabulary	Ask students to scan the passage for any words they are unsure of.
Check your understanding	Page 234: Forty years from now …
Learner outcomes	By the end of this segment, students should be able to: ● identify and transfer complex ideas into their own writing ● accurately handle past and present tenses.
Workbook	Page 103: Building your vocabulary – crossword Page 104: Listening to a talk about the world in 100 years Page 104: Check your understanding – multiple choice; talk through this in pairs Pages 104–5: Writing down your thoughts Page 105: Listening to a "Bygones" talk Pages 105–6: Check your understanding Page 106: Listening – discussion topic
Worksheet	10.5: Writing about life in 2050

Segment 6	Page 235 The Big Issue – a Golden Age?
Syllabus objectives	**L4** Understand what is implied but not actually stated **S1** Communicate clearly, accurately, and appropriately
Broader skills development	● Prepare and present a debate. ● Listen to an interview with someone from 1,000 years in the future. ● Develop the theme.
Introducing the session	"Thinking out loud" (page 235): Ask students, in pairs, to talk for up to five minutes about escaping to their ideal world. Where and when would this be?
Ensuring a skills balance	Suggested writing activity: Ask students to imagine they met Minqq and to write one paragraph describing him.
Differentiated activities	Stronger students can do some research about the Golden Age and report back to the class or group.
Teaching and learning methodologies	**1** Collaborate to present a debate. **2** Write an imaginative interview.
Building your vocabulary	"The Golden Age" extract is complex and would benefit from a teacher-led reading/explanation. This is supported by a worksheet. Ask students to note down unfamiliar words.
Check your understanding	

Learner outcomes	By the end of this segment, students should be able to:
	• contribute successfully to a debate
	• understand and respond to inferred attitudes and feelings.
Workbook	
Worksheet	10.6: Building your vocabulary

Segment 7	Pages 236–7 Literary connections
Syllabus objectives	**R3** Recognize and understand ideas, opinions, and attitudes and the connections between related ideas
	S2 Convey information and express opinions effectively
Broader skills development	• Read an extract from a work of literature.
	• Collaborate to prepare and present a short scene.
Introducing the session	Ask students what historical fiction and stories from the past they have read. Get them to talk about them in small groups.
Ensuring a skills balance	Suggested writing activity:
	Ask students to write a description of a famous historical event as though they were there.
Differentiated activities	Stronger students can imagine that they time travel to the same place twice, once to 100 years in the past and once to 100 years in the future, and then write two contrasting descriptions of that place.
Teaching and learning methodologies	**1** Read a work of literature.
	2 Collaborate to recreate a scene from the past.
Building your vocabulary	Guide students carefully through this literary extract and ask them to note down any words unfamiliar to them.
Check your understanding	
Learner outcomes	By the end of this segment, students should be able to:
	• contribute to a joint project
	• reflect on famous people/events from the past.
Workbook	
Worksheet	10.7: Reflection – speaking activity

Links

A useful link on all things related to the past is:

- www.britishmuseum.org

  This website covers every continent, not just Britain.

You might also try:

- www.horrible-histories.co.uk – based on the books, but also now the stage productions.
- www.bbc.co.uk/history/forkids – history, quizzes, and information
- www.royaldeaf.org.uk/newsid_122/Parliament's_debate_on_deaf_children – the future for deaf children being debated in parliament but with some general ideas as well.

Study tips: speaking

How to approach Prompt five in the Speaking test (see page 221 of the student book)

Prompt 5 is the final prompt on the topic card used in the Speaking test. The pattern of the five prompts and advice on tackling the other four are covered elsewhere in the student book and in this teacher resource pack. The purpose of the later prompts is to raise the level of difficulty and to challenge stronger candidates. Prompt 5 is designed to raise the topic to a sophisticated level.

This activity invites students to share ideas with each other about the nature of abstract vs. concrete discussion. It is probably accessible only to more able students. As mentioned before, managing the Speaking test from an accessibility perspective is a key part of a teacher's/examiner's role. Candidates achieving lower band 3 or band 4 performance (see the full oral assessment criteria grid in the syllabus) are not likely to be able to engage effectively with sophisticated and abstract ideas. Lower-ability learners should therefore focus on making a good job with Prompts 3 and 4.

Evaluating the sample student responses

All three students have some good points to make and none of them is a weak candidate.

- **Student A** shows some understanding but lacks the confidence to be more convincing by giving more examples.

- **Student B** has the strongest response and really gets to grips with the abstract nature of the prompt.

- **Student C** takes a more simplistic view and focuses on the concrete rather than the abstract.

Model answers and how to improve performance

The Speaking test takes the form of a 6–9-minute discussion to test a range of spoken language skills. The assessment criteria used by the examiner, to award a mark out of 30, are:

- accuracy and range of structures

- use of vocabulary

- whether the discussion is developed fluently.

The assessment objectives, all six of which are in play during Part D of the test, reflect these criteria.

Assessment objectives

S1 Communicate clearly, accurately, and appropriately

S2 Convey information and express opinions effectively

S3 Employ and control a variety of grammatical structures

S4 Demonstrate knowledge of a range of appropriate vocabulary

S5 Engage in and influence the direction of conversation

S6 Employ suitable pronunciation and stress patterns

When Prompt 5 is being considered and discussed, all six of these objectives are being tested at the highest level.

Here's another Prompt 5 that could feature in a topic card on the past and the future:

> **5** The idea that the future is simply the past reappearing in a different form

As you can see, this is a challenging concept, even for adults to engage with. Examiners are looking at how well the candidate can use English at this conceptual level, however. A test that stays at the same level of language and content through all 6–9 minutes is not likely to achieve more than a mid-band 3 performance.

 Track 10.1 Here's how student B from the previous activity might have dealt with this prompt. Play students the extension to Track 10.1.

You might like to ask your students to play out the prompt informally in pairs, taking it in turns to be the examiner, before playing the model answer.

> **Our expert says:** When suggesting ways for your students to improve their performance in response to Prompt 5, remind them that it's OK to:
> - keep an open mind and to try to relate to several sides of an issue
> - relay an abstract idea by using concrete examples
> - provide analogies to explain the concept
> - draw the examiner into the discussion at this stage
> - change your mind if, when exploring the concept, it raises new ideas
> - present your views, even if they are unpopular.

Study tips: reading

Identifying redundant material in a written text (see page 224 of the student book)

Identifying redundant material is just as useful a skill as being able to identity and retrieve required details and information. Indeed, a strong candidate will have shown both skills working together.

This activity involves doing some interesting collaborative work to create a new piece of writing and then to decide on headings that effectively exclude some of the original text. The aim is to look at the balance of useful vs. redundant material in a given text. What it shows is that all the contents of a text could be useful, depending on the headings or the reasons we want to reduce the text to focus points. The exercise also shows that, by contrast, should we want to focus on only one or two key aspects of it, much of a text can be redundant.

Exercises 3, 4, and 5 of the Reading and Writing examination paper all test this skill of having the confidence to regard some material as not fit for purpose – in other words, as redundant.

Evaluating the sample student responses
- **Student A** has not made notes relevant to the article heading.
- **Student B** has identified the correct information but in less detail than Student C.
- **Student C** has been able to identify the appropriate details from the passage.

Study tips: writing

Summarizing in your own words (see pages 228–9 of the student book)

This activity focuses on using own words when summarizing, and provides a collaborative "synonym activity". It is also a reminder of the other key aspects of a successful summary for the Reading and Writing examination: correct number of words, selection of relevant material, and the maintenance of the original meaning.

At both core and extended levels, five marks are available for the language element of writing a summary, and it is clear in the descriptors used to assess a summary that using their own words can help students gain a higher mark. They do not need to change the original text radically; rather, they should use just a few new words and phrases to demonstrate confidence. Too many summaries copy from the original source and lift large chunks of it. Reorganizing the content a little helps the candidate to convey their level of understanding.

From an "own words" perspective, this is what examiners are checking for:

Level	Descriptor
Excellent	Accurate use of own words, which helps to organize and sequence content points cohesively
Good	Good attempt to use own words and to organize and sequence points cohesively but with slips and a few stretching errors
Satisfactory	Some reliance on language from the text, but with a reasonable attempt to organize and sequence using some alternative words
Weak	Heavy reliance on language from the text, with very little attempt to organize and sequence points using own words
Very weak	Copying without discrimination from the text

The "Building your vocabulary" sections in the student book will help to provide a wide range of vocabulary that will be useful for students looking for alternative words and phrases to use in a summary.

Evaluating the sample student responses

- **Student A** has the weakest response.
- **Student B** does a better job than Student A.
- **Student C** is the strongest and is able to use own words concisely.

Study tips: listening

Accuracy in gap-filling exercises (see page 232 of the student book)

As a general principle, what candidates at both levels write in their examination paper must be grammatically sound. Phonetic attempts are accepted but incorrect grammar and structures are not. The best way to improve performance in Question 5 of the listening text is by practising grammatical and contextual fit through gap-filling exercises, using many different examples.

The example used here is the Terracotta Warriors video (see page 229 of the student book) and a series of statements related to it. The students are then asked to create two more sentences with two gaps in each. We will look at this aspect further by analysing responses to a Question 5, set out below. You can use it as a summative test for your students (along with some formative feedback!).

Evaluating the sample student responses

As stated in the student book, these are all wrong.

Here's a typical Question 5 based on the theme of the past and the future.

Question 5

You will hear a talk given by a woman who is showing a group of people the home of the future.

Listen to the talk and complete the details below. Write one or two words only in each gap.

You will hear the talk twice.

a) By ...., services in most people's homes will be ....

b) The device which controls the new system is called the .... for short.

c) At the moment there is approximately .... of cabling, but later on this will reduce to ....

d) The control unit, called The Maestro, was named after a ...., and it communicates ....

e) CPU 125 performs .... even if nobody is in the house.

f) Currently there are .... such houses and .... are interested in them.

g) The main drawback is the high ....

h) If a human is in one of the rooms, the temperate will reach .... centigrade, and then .... to 12 degrees centigrade when the human leaves the room.

Model answers and how to improve performance

Question 5 is the same for both core and extended levels and it is always based on a formal talk. The candidates listen to the talk twice and then demonstrate understanding by filling in gaps in eight statements. There are 8 marks available, one for each statement. Correctly filling in one or two gaps in each statement – with only one or two words in each gap – gains a mark.

A key skill for success is to listen for the word in the talk that closely matches the key word or words needed for the gap. The objective of this question is to focus on details and information and not on recognizing opinions or attitudes.

> ## Assessment objectives
>
> **L1** Identify and retrieve facts and details
>
> **L2** Understand and select relevant information

Answers

a) 2050, integrated

b) CPU

c) 55 metres, zero/none/0 metres

d) conductor, wirelessly/without wires

e) daily tasks/duties/jobs

f) 25, 100 people/100 applicants

g) cost

h) 20 deg/20 degrees, return/go back

> **Our expert says:** Here are some interesting responses to these questions. They are close attempts but would not be allowed under the grammatical and contextual fit rule:
>
> **a)** services will be *integrate* – not allowed due to incorrect use of the verb
>
> **b)** *See Pee You* – not allowed as, even though it is phonetically accurate, it uses three words
>
> **c)** *No messy cables* – again, three words are used, but only two are allowed in a gap
>
> **d)** *Wireless* – the adverb is needed for accuracy
>
> **e)** *Task* – the singular would not be accepted here, as it is not grammatically acceptable (However, a task would be allowed, as it is an accurate contextual fit.)
>
> **f)** *100 persons* – not allowed, as it is not grammatically sound
>
> **g)** *money* – while the idea is clearly there, this is not the right word. "Price" would be allowed, but money does not convey full understanding in the context.
>
> **h)** *returning* – the present continuous is not appropriate here, so this would be disallowed.

☑ My progress

The four study skills – reading, writing, speaking, and listening – are key skills for success in each of the examinations. In the "My progress" section at the end of the chapter in the student book, we invite students to select one skill that they can focus on and develop. However, you may like to ask your students to prepare action plans to develop all four of the skills.

The table shows where the skills feature in the examination papers and how they are applied. Unless otherwise indicated, the skills and tasks are common to both levels.

Skill	Task	Positioning in examination papers
Speaking about abstract and sophisticated matters	Spend 2–3 minutes discussing a prompt that poses an abstract concept	Speaking • Prompt 5
Identifying redundant material when reading	Read an article of about 600 words and ignore redundant content	Reading and writing • Exercise 4, Exercise 5
Using own words when compiling summaries	Write a summary of 70 words (core level) or 100 words (extended level)	Reading and writing • Exercise 5
Providing accurate grammatical and contextual fit when relaying what has been heard	Gap filling, sentence completion	Listening • Questions 1–4 • Question 5 • Question 8 (extended)

11 Communication

Student book content coverage

Segment 1	Page 240 Why do we need to communicate?
Syllabus objectives	**R1** Identify and retrieve facts and details **S1** Communicate clearly, accurately, and appropriately
Broader skills development	• Collaborate with peers. • Think about communication. • Tell an anecdote.
Introducing the session	"Thinking out loud" (page 240): Ask the students, in small groups, to spend five minutes telling each other what they think.
Ensuring a skills balance	Suggested writing activity: Ask students to practise what they have learned about anecdotes by writing another one, this time about their partner rather than themselves. Then swap with their partner.
Differentiated activities	Stronger students can ask their partner for more detail about the anecdote, and ask a couple of questions about it.
Teaching and learning methodologies	1 Improve communication skills. 2 Relate detail in an interesting way.
Building your vocabulary	Ask students to make a list of the most common ways we communicate. How has this list changed over the past 50 years?
Check your understanding	
Learner outcomes	By the end of this segment, learners should be able to: • use communication to collaborate • tell an anecdote in an interesting way.
Workbook	Page 107: Every picture tells a story Page 107: Writing Page 108: Speaking
Worksheet	11.1: Building your vocabulary – synonyms

Segment 2	Pages 241–7 How do we communicate?
Syllabus objectives	**R2** Understand and select relevant information **W1** Communicate clearly, accurately, and appropriately
Broader skills development	• Design an application form. • Write a poster. • Discuss the way we communicate.

Introducing the session	"Thinking out loud" (page 241): Ask students to discuss the questions. What do they use to write – a keyboard or a pen? Which is better, and why?
Ensuring a skills balance	Suggested speaking activity: In pairs, ask students to discuss what they found interesting about Laszlo Bíró. What information did they not know before? Ask them to pick out one detail.
Differentiated activities	Stronger students can research another inventor connected to writing and communication. They can then give a one-minute speech to the class about their chosen inventor.
Teaching and learning methodologies	1 Learn about purpose and register. 2 Design an application form.
Building your vocabulary	Ask students to design a poster to encourage their classmates to participate in No Pens Wednesday. Ask them to use some task-specific vocabulary.
Check your understanding	Page 242: Laszlo Bíró – ask students to complete this individually. Page 243: Tommy Harrison – ask students to complete this in pairs. Page 245: Satellite talk – ask students to complete this individually.
Learner outcomes	By the end of this segment, learners should be able to: • use relevant and appropriate language • use a formal register.
Workbook	Page 108: Listening Page 108: Check your understanding
Worksheet	11.2: A guessing game

Segment 3	Pages 247–9 Communication in the past
Syllabus objectives	**R2** Understand and select relevant information **L2** Understand and select relevant information
Broader skills development	• Use the correct register. • Persuade someone. • Understand how communication has changed.
Introducing the session	The year is 1850. Tell the students to imagine they live in the far south of the country. How would they get an urgent message to the far north of the country as soon as possible? Ask them to work in small groups to work out what they would do.
Ensuring a skills balance	Suggested speaking activity: Ask the students to imagine they work for Wells Fargo and discuss, in small groups, whether to keep the Pony Express or not, and give reasons for their choice. Once each person has spoken, they vote.
Differentiated activities	Ask stronger students to imagine they are time travellers and have gone back in time to be riders on the Pony Express. Ask them to write a blog about their experiences.
Teaching and learning methodologies	1 Write a letter using the correct register. 2 Use language to persuade.

Building your vocabulary	In pairs, students prepare language for a formal letter, focusing on the correct register. What phrases and language would they expect to use?
Check your understanding	Page 247: The Pony Express Page 248: Homing pigeons Page 249: Morse Code
Learner outcomes	By the end of the segment, learners should be able to: • talk about old ways of communicating quickly • use an appropriate register.
Workbook	Page 109: Formal and informal language Page 109: Building your vocabulary Page 109: Check your understanding
Worksheet	11.3: Using persuasive language

Segment 4	Pages 250–52 Communication in children
Syllabus objectives	**R3** Recognize and understand ideas, opinions, and attitudes **L2** Understand and select relevant information
Broader skills development	• Think about how people communicate. • Choose the correct tense. • Decide which words are important.
Introducing the session	Ask students how they would feel if they could not use speech to communicate. How would it change their lives?
Ensuring a skills balance	Tell students to imagine they can understand what babies are saying. They are to write a short dialogue between two babies in a nursery.
Differentiated activities	Ask stronger students to think about the way teenagers communicate. What teen-only words can they think of?
Teaching and learning methodologies	**1** Understand how to communicate without words. **2** Choose the correct tense.
Building your vocabulary	Page 251: Babies communicating – ask students to complete this activity in small groups.
Check your understanding	Page 250: Oxana Malaya Page 252: Is your baby talking to you?
Learner outcomes	By the end of the segment, students should be able to: • talk about the different ways to communicate • use different tenses correctly.
Workbook	Page 110: Speaking Page 110: Building your vocabulary – crossword
Worksheet	11.4: Writing a communication passport

Segment 5	Pages 253–9 Communicating without speaking
Syllabus objectives	**L3** Recognize and understand ideas, opinions, and attitudes **S2** Convey information and express ideas effectively
Broader skills development	• Talk about graffiti. • Improve structure when speaking. • Listen to responses with follow-on information.
Introducing the session	"Thinking out loud" (page 253): Do this as a whole-class activity.
Ensuring a skills balance	Suggested writing activity: Ask students to pick one of the people they have read about in this segment. They need to write them a letter explaining what they have found so interesting about them.
Differentiated activities	Ask stronger students to think of three words they would like to introduce to the language. What would they be and what would they mean?
Teaching and learning methodologies	**1** Understand how to speak in the speaking test. **2** Understand detail and follow-on information.
Building your vocabulary	Page 257: Dolphins – ask students to complete this activity in pairs.
Check your understanding	Page 255: Evelyn Glennie Page 256: Sonia Hollis Page 258: Dolphins Page 259: Chimpanzees
Learner outcomes	By the end of the segment, learners should be able to: • understand better what ways are open to us to communicate • understand better the requirements of the speaking test.
Workbook	Page 111: Reading – Esperanto Page 111: Check your understanding – Esperanto
Worksheet	11.5: Writing a letter

Segment 6	Pages 260–62 The Big Issue – alternative ways to communicate
Syllabus objectives	**R4** Understand what is implied but not actually written **S5** Engage in and influence the direction of conversation
Broader skills development	• Learn what may cause a stoppage in communication. • Use language to compare and contrast. • Ask interesting open questions.
Introducing the session	Ask students what they would do if they could not move their bodies. How would they communicate? How would they feel? Ask them to write a few notes individually.
Ensuring a skills balance	Suggested listening activity: Ask students to listen to each other's questions about Bauby or Hawking (see page 262) and then write down how they think either Bauby or Hawking would respond to at least two questions.
Differentiated activities	Stronger students can research a little on either locked-in syndrome or motor neurone disease. They need to find out how it affects communication before reporting back in small groups.

Teaching and learning methodologies	1 Use language to compare and contrast.
	2 Ask interesting questions.
Building your vocabulary	Ask students to think of five adjectives to describe how they would feel if they could not move their body.
Check your understanding	In pairs, ask students to discuss their reaction to Bauby and Hawking, giving reasons why they think people admire them.
Learner outcomes	By the end of the segment, learners should be able to:
	• compare and contrast ideas well
	• use language to develop questions and answers.
Workbook	Page 112: Saying what we mean
Worksheet	11.6: Emailing about the Deaflympics

Segment 7	Pages 263–4 Literary connections
Syllabus objectives	**R4** Understand what is implied but not actually written
	W6 Employ appropriate vocabulary
Broader skills development	• Think about first-person narrative.
	• Develop the way discussions progress.
	• Discuss being a code breaker.
Introducing the session	"Thinking out loud" (page 263): Ask students to discuss the questions in small groups.
Ensuring a skills balance	Suggested listening activity:
	Ask students to tell each other what they would say to someone who looked different from our idea of normal, and explain why their suggestion is a good idea.
Differentiated activities	Stronger students can write a letter to Anna. They need to tell her that they have read about her and would like to know more – asking her at least two appropriate questions.
Teaching and learning methodologies	1 Develop a discussion.
	2 Understand implication.
Building your vocabulary	Page 263: *World Enough and Time* – ask students to complete this in pairs.
Check your understanding	Page 264: *World Enough and Time* – ask students to complete this individually.
Learner outcomes	By the end of the segment, learners should be able to:
	• talk at length in an interesting way
	• use discussion to reach a conclusion.
Workbook	Page 112: Discussion topic
Worksheet	11.7: Communicating with your idol

Links

If you choose only one link to use with your students, try this:

- www.janegoodall.org

  Find information on gorillas and how they communicate with each other and with humans.

You might also try:

- www.bslzone.co.uk/sofia-2013-deaflympics

- www.makaton.org – sign language.

- www.encyclopedia.kids.net.au/page/mo/morse_code – learn more about Morse Code, among other things.

- www.alzheimers.org.uk – talking about the difficulties people with dementia have with communication.

If your students enjoyed reading *World Enough and Time*, they might also like *Wonder* by R. J. Palacio, on the same subject. If they do decide to read *Wonder*, they can answer questions about it afterwards, at: www.rjpalacio.com/for-teachers.html

Study tips: writing

Using a formal register (see pages 245–6 of the student book)

In Exercise 7 on both the core and extended level Reading and Writing papers, candidates will be asked to write an essay based on an issue that can clearly have different viewpoints. Indeed, the examination paper gives several views for candidates to read and consider. However, the aim of the essay is for candidates to present their own views *in the light of* those offered by others.

This activity emphasizes that this style of writing needs to be formal and that the register must match both the purpose of the text and its audience. Students are invited to explore this relationship here. It is useful to point out to your students that Exercise 7 demands a very different piece of writing from Exercise 6. We could say that the bar is raised in Exercise 7 and students with stronger writing skills are likely to perform better, as they can demonstrate their skills of writing formally, with concision, and with a clear purpose.

With this type of directed and controlled writing, students will be assessed on their ability to:

- bring in and develop appropriate content

- write fluently, accurately, and concisely.

Evaluating the sample student responses

- **Student A** provides only one example of the negative aspects of modern communication. The writing also contains several basic errors, which show a lack of competence. However, it is a reasonable attempt.

- **Student B** introduces more complexity than Student A, but the writing suffers from "stretching" errors and is not accurate enough to gain a higher mark. However, it is stronger than Student A's work because it does attempt to consider a wider range of views.

- **Student C** provides the strongest response. This essay is largely error-free and considers contrasting views before making a conclusion; it is a balanced piece of extended writing.

Model answers and how to improve performance

Exercise 7 in both examination papers (core and extended) uses the same topic or issue, but the requirements and marks are different:

- Core level requires 100–150 words and 13 marks are available (7 for content and 6 for accuracy).

- Extended level requires 150–200 words and 19 marks are available (10 for content and 9 for accuracy).

The marking schemes for extended writing are published by Cambridge after each examination session, and are also available on the Teacher's Support site for all registered centres. We cannot reproduce them in full here, but the commentary on the model answer below extracts the salient points.

Exercise 7 texts all six assessment objectives, but W6 is particularly important.

Here's how a typical Exercise 7 might work for the theme of communication:

A billionaire has announced on a radio programme that he is seeking volunteers to go on a one-way trip to Mars, to try to communicate with any life forms that might be there.

Here are some responses to this announcement by people who have phoned in:

"I'm in. There's nothing much to keep me on this planet any more. I have a boring and low-paid job and this trip could open up so many interesting opportunities."

"No way. A one-way trip? I think that means I'd probably die in space, or on Mars. Anyway, I'd miss my friends and family far too much."

"As a scientist, I feel that I have to put myself up for this. I'm not married and I don't have any children so it's not a huge sacrifice. I would be useful on the science side of things."

"It's a silly idea. It must be costing millions of pounds, and for what? I think the money should be spent on people on Earth who really need it."

The comments above might give you some ideas but you should try to use ideas of your own.

NB: Two or four views are usually given, and there will always be contrasting views so that the candidate is aware of the balance needed. It is also worth noting that a candidate is not obliged to use or refer to any of the views and can produce an essay based on his/her own ideas in the light of various other viewpoints.

Model essay from a strong candidate

"On the one hand, it could be argued that the destiny of mankind is in exploring the planets. Earth is clearly starting to struggle to maintain the human population, which reached 7 billion people in 2012. The prospect of being on a space trip, with lots of other people, with the aim of setting up a space station is a very strong motivating force. It's also fascinating that we might find life on Mars.

However, it won't be an easy journey. It will take 18 months to reach Mars and once we are there, we expect to find a dry planet with no signs of life as we know it. But the scientists are not 100% sure of this, so imagine being one of the first few human beings to communicate with aliens.

There has been criticism from people who feel that the money should be spent on solving problems on Earth, and whoever goes on this trip will live the rest of their lives in a small space station. It's clearly a very difficult decision for anyone to make. It's not surprising, though, that in the first week of the radio programme, over 240 000 people around the word have applied."

[201 words]

Our expert says: As we have pointed out, the candidate does not have to refer to the views given, or may choose to pick out just one or two views to bring into the essay. The candidate above has done this and has chosen to present arguments from both sides. The strong points of the essay are that it is focused on the topic (it stays on task), it includes additional and relevant content, and it presents a clear view using accurate language. The register is nicely formal, and there is a good sense of audience. The content that has been chosen has been used well, and the style of the writing fits the purpose.

Successful performance for Exercise 7 therefore requires:

- relevant content which is then developed with argument and/or examples
- interesting facts and details
- good background knowledge of the theme
- the inclusion of contrasting views, considered objectively
- the confidence to present own view
- to be written ideally in the third person
- the use of controlled and pertinent language.

Study tips: speaking

The structure criterion (see page 254 of the student book)

In this section, we try to highlight the first assessment criterion: structure. It is probably the most difficult of the three criteria to work with and to apply when assessing a student's speaking skills. We can think of structure as the accuracy of a person's speaking if we were to write down what they have said and check for errors. But this is not all that is encompassed by structures. To achieve a high mark, we would expect a speaker to use a wide and appropriate range of structures in a natural manner.

This activity provides some examples of weak and incorrect structures, and invites students to identify these. The main aim in ensuring appropriate structures is to improve the cogency and fluency of speaking in the context of a conversation. It is much better for a student to use accurate if simple structures than to use more complex structures and make a lot of mistakes, as the latter will affect the development of the conversation and make it hard for the listener to follow the meaning.

A good way to ascertain whether a student has strong, average, or weak structures is to record the student speaking about a topic – any topic. This works well with two students having a conversation with each other, and then listening to their conversation afterwards. It's also interesting to listen to the conversation that another pair of students have just had. Students are generally surprised when they hear themselves talking, but, rather like a golf swing, it's hard to see what's going on until you look at things from a distance.

The following topic card is on a subject that will be particularly accessible to candidates and could therefore be given to a student with slightly weaker structures.

Oral test topic card
Mobile phones

It could be argued that the greatest technological advance of the last 20 years is the mobile phone, or cellphone.

Discuss this topic with the examiner.

You must use the following five prompts in the order given, to develop the conversation.

1 Your mobile phone and what you use it for

2 Other phones you know about – maybe owned by friends or family – and your views on them

3 The pros and cons of having a mobile phone

4 The suggestion that someone without a mobile phone is someone to admire

5 The idea that mobile phones are just another form of addiction

Remember, you are not allowed to write down any notes.

Our expert says: The ten topic cards are designed with a range of ability levels in mind, so some topics will be more accessible than others. The above card, for example, would be widely accessible. However, while weaker speakers will feel more comfortable with a straightforward topic like this one, strong speakers are likely to fare better with a more challenging topic.

In other words, it is acceptable in the Speaking test to differentiate by topic. There are ten topic cards and if the warm-up (Part B) does not indicate a productive topic, the examiner should then consider how accessible a topic is likely to be. Selecting an appropriate topic is not an easy task, but the structures displayed by the candidate in the warm-up may give an idea of which topic card to deploy.

Evaluating the sample student responses

- **Student A** uses a wide range of accurate structures.
- **Student B** has limited structures and this can be seen clearly to limit fluency and development.

Study tips: listening

Responses to follow-on information (see pages 255–6 of the student book)

At both tiers the Listening examination starts with four scenarios, covered by Questions 1 to 4. Each question has two parts, and these are connected – i.e. the second part follows on from the first part.

This activity demonstrates how this works by giving an example, and by asking students to work again with the talk given by Sonia Hollis, the sign language expert. So although there are eight pieces of information (and 8 marks available), these are essentially 4 × 2 pieces of information. It is important therefore that your students are aware of this, so that they can practise this skill.

Questions 1 to 4 on the examination paper will each be based on a different scenario – i.e. there is no continuous theme running through the eight items. There are four scenarios or themes and it is likely that these will be very different from each other.

Evaluating the sample student responses

- **Student A** gains no marks as we need the book included along with the DVD, and in the second part there has been a misunderstanding of "What are you likely to working on…?"

- **Student B** provides an accurate response to both parts and therefore gains 2 marks.

- **Student C** is accurate in the second part (the follow-on) but incorrectly suggests that being qualified equates to making knowledge available.

Model answers and how to improve performance

Since Questions 1 to 4 each have two parts – a) and b) – there are therefore 8 marks available. Candidates' understanding is tested by asking questions, and candidates are allowed to use up to three words in an open response. The questions are the same for both core and extended levels.

At this early stage of the Listening test, candidates are conveying straightforward understanding and are locating specific information. The assessment objective is therefore as follows.

Assessment objective
L1 Identify and retrieve facts and details

Exam focus: listening

 Track 11.1

Here is how a typical Listening examination might begin.

Questions 1–4

You will hear four short recordings. Answer each question on the line provided. Write no more than three words for each detail.

You will hear each recording twice.

1 **a)** Who sent the two boys to the shop?

....

  b) What does David's friend need to buy?

....

2 **a)** How much time will the passengers be allowed for lunch?

....

  b) Where is the nearest stop if a passenger needs to get some money?

....

3 **a)** What was it about the storm that surprised the weather centre?

....

  b) What was one of the effects of the bad weather?

....

4 **a)** How long has the family been in the chocolate business?

....

  b) Why has the demand for dark chocolate probably increased?

....

Model answers

1 a) David's mother	**1** b) Gift for sister/gift
2 a) one hour	**2** b) Stop H
3 a) it made land/it changed direction	**3** b) boats sank/fishermen lost fish/ fish escaped
4 a) 55 years	**4** b) it's healthier/uses less sugar

> **Our expert says:** The recordings are likely to include situations where two people are having a dialogue but scenarios may also feature speeches or monologues. These can take the form of announcements or narratives. In all cases, the scenarios aim to mirror authentic real-life contexts.

Let's look more closely at some responses to the above questions that were not awarded the mark, and the reasons why.

The examples demonstrate that it is important to remind candidates that:

- they need to be careful to stay within the rubric of "no more than three words", even if what they say is 100 per cent correct

- only the ability to identify and retrieve facts and details is being tested in Questions 1 to 4; the ability to infer is *not* being tested.

Question	Incorrect answer	Reason
1 a)	His mother	Not clear whether it is David or his friend who is being referred to
1 b)	A gift for his sister	Too many words – only three are allowed
2 a)	1 h	"h" too ambiguous to be allowed for hour, though "hr" would be allowed
2 b)	The bank	While that is where the money is, it is not an actual stop on the route
3 a)	It caused damage	No evidence that the damage surprised the weather centre staff
3 b)	Fishermen lost their fish	Too many words – only three are allowed
4 a)	15 years	This is only the grandson's time as manager
4 b)	They don't know	The use of "probably" in the question allows the responses on the mark scheme above; this is an incorrect inference

Study tips: reading

Scanning a text for themed detail (see page 258 of the student book)

This section serves as a reminder to students that getting the gist of a reading text is as important as understanding the details within it. Although the examination paper does not have a specific question asking about general understanding, scanning for detail is an important skill for success in various areas, including making notes and writing a summary, which are tasks that *assume* gist understanding. The last question in Exercise 2 on the extended paper also requires scanning skills to identify a running theme.

Practising this skill will increase the students' confidence in reading more complex articles. It is always a good idea to ask students "What is the gist of this piece?" when they have just read an article for the first time. Topic sentences are usually a big clue to what is to come in the paragraphs, so writing down the topic sentences in a list will often summarize the gist of the piece of writing.

Many of the articles in the student book have a single theme, which is the nature of the source material that should be used in teaching and assessing English as a second language. Successful performance in the Reading and Writing examination will depend to some extent on how well and how quickly your students are at "getting the gist". Skimming and scanning are so much easier and more effective if you know why you are scanning.

Evaluating the sample student responses

Student B has the best approach and possesses better study skills than Student A.

☑ My progress

The four study skills – reading, writing, speaking, and listening – are key skills for success in each of the examinations. In the "My progress" section at the end of the chapter in the student book, we invite students to select one skill that they can focus on and develop. However, you may like to ask your students to prepare action plans to develop all four of the skills.

The table shows where the skills feature in the examination papers and how they are applied. Unless otherwise indicated, the skills and tasks are common to both levels.

Skill	Task	Positioning in examination papers
Using a formal register when writing essays	Express your views on an issue which several people hold contrasting ideas about (100–150 words at core level; 150–200 words at extended level)	Reading and writing • Exercise 7
Speaking with accurate and wide-ranging structures	Talk clearly, with precision, using more complex structures in the context of a developed discussion	Speaking • Parts A, B, C, and D – i.e. the whole test
Listening to follow-on details and connected information	Respond to four short questions, each of which has two parts, and each of which relates to a different short scenario	Listening • Questions 1 to 4
Identifying a running theme in a written article	Write a summary Make notes	Reading and writing • Exercise 2, final question • Exercise 4 • Exercise 5

12 Global issues

Student book content coverage

Segment 1	Pages 268–71 Global trade and advertising
Syllabus objectives	**S5** Engage in and influence the direction of conversation **W4** Demonstrate knowledge and understanding of a range of appropriate vocabulary
Broader skills development	• Develop a discussion. • Use open questions. • Write a review.
Introducing the session	"Thinking out loud" (page 268): Allow students up to five minutes to discuss the global brands they know and use; they could do this in pairs.
Ensuring a skills balance	Suggested speaking activity: Ask students to pick out three logos they can see in the classroom, explain what they like or dislike about each one and how they would improve it.
Differentiated activities	Stronger students can research specific colours and fonts for specific products and companies.
Teaching and learning methodologies	**1** Learn to understand and use open questions. **2** Write a review.
Building your vocabulary	Page 270: Words advertisers use – ask students to watch the clip and tick the boxes.
Check your understanding	Page 270: Students read one another's reviews. Pick two or three and highlight where each bullet point has been answered.
Learner outcomes	By the end of this segment, learners will be able to: • use open questions • write a review.
Workbook	Page 113: Using global brands to learn
Worksheet	12.1: Writing an email

Segment 2	Pages 271–5 Early traders
Syllabus objectives	**R2** Understand and select relevant information **L3** Recognize and understand opinions, ideas, and attitudes
Broader skills development	• Create your own label. • Write an account of a journey. • Discuss global transport.

Introducing the session	Ask students to think about how people traded before the Internet. How did they get the items they needed for everyday living and how did they pay for them? Spend no more than five minutes on this activity.
Ensuring a skills balance	Suggested writing activity: Ask students to update their social media page by telling friends how they enjoyed reading about the Silk Road, picking out one fact they found particularly interesting.
Differentiated activities	Stronger students can find out which trade routes there were in their country in the past. Where were the routes and what was traded?
Teaching and learning methodologies	1 Respond concisely and with appropriate detail. 2 Learn to use conjuncts and conjunct phrases.
Building your vocabulary	Page 271: The Silk Road – ask students to add the word to the correct sentence, working individually.
Check your understanding	Page 273: The Silk Road – ask students to complete the short-answer responses in small groups.
Learner outcomes	By the end of this segment, learners should be able to: • talk about old trade routes • write a travelogue.
Workbook	Pages 114–15: Better brands
Worksheet	12.2: Language focus on conjuncts

Segment 3	Pages 276–7 Global population
Syllabus objectives	W2 Convey information and express opinions effectively S2 Convey information and express opinions effectively
Broader skills development	• Talk about global populations. • Prepare a question for a public meeting. • Write a letter to a newspaper editor.
Introducing the session	"Thinking out loud" (page 276): What do students think about the global rise in population? What are the advantages and disadvantages they can think of? Spend about five minutes on this activity, with students in small groups.
Ensuring a skills balance	Suggested reading activity: Ask students to find information about hotels in their favourite city and pick out five useful task-specific lexical items to add to their vocabulary – for example panoramic, skyline.
Differentiated activities	Stronger students can think about how their local area would change if its population doubled and report on the changes that would have to take place.
Teaching and learning methodologies	1 Discuss global population and related issues. 2 Respond to the views of other people.
Building your vocabulary	Page 277: The sky's the limit – ask students to spend five minutes choosing the correct word for each sentence. They could do this alone.
Check your understanding	Page 276: Ask students to make a list of key phrases about global population that might be used in a formal letter to a newspaper editor.

Learner outcomes	By the end of this segment, learners should be able to:
	• write a formal letter, giving their opinions on global population
	• use an increased lexical range on global population in cities.
Workbook	Pages 116–19: Recycling
Worksheet	12.3: Speaking about global population

Segment 4	Pages 278–81 Carbon-neutral
Syllabus objectives	**R3** Recognize and understand ideas and the connections between related ideas
	S1 Communicate clearly, accurately, and appropriately
Broader skills development	• Think about leading a carbon-neutral life.
	• Compare ideas with classmates.
	• Talk about diagrams and charts.
Introducing the session	"Thinking out loud" (page 278): Ask students what technology they would miss if they had to live without it for a week. Spend five minutes on this activity.
Ensuring a skills balance	Suggested speaking activity:
	In pairs, students discuss who they preferred reading about – Don or Vimod – and give the reasons for their choice.
Differentiated activities	Stronger students can discuss what will happen if we use too much carbon dioxide. Ask them to write down five task-specific words as they are talking together in pairs.
Teaching and learning methodologies	**1** Use language to compare and contrast.
	2 Understand diagrams and charts.
Building your vocabulary	Page 278: A carbon-neutral life – ask students, in pairs, to find a synonyms for each word or phrase.
Check your understanding	Page 279: A carbon-neutral life – give students five minutes to complete the questions on their own.
Learner outcomes	By the end of this segment, learners should be able to:
	• talk about a carbon-neutral lifestyle
	• compare and contrast ideas.
Workbook	Page 118: Language focus
Worksheet	12.4: Writing a newspaper report

Segment 5	Pages 282–4 Meat-free diets; Global hunger
Syllabus objectives	**R2** Understand and select relevant information
	L2 Understand and select relevant information
Broader skills development	• Learn more about a meat-free lifestyle.
	• Read about global hunger.
	• Use reported speech.
Introducing the session	Page 282: Ask students where their food comes from and how what they eat has an impact on the global environment. This could be a whole-class activity.

Ensuring a skills balance	Suggested listening activity: Ask students to listen to the protest songs their classmates have written (page 282). What qualities do the best ones have?
Differentiated activities	Ask stronger students to list what they ate during their last meal. What distance did each item travel to reach their plate? Could they have chosen a closer alternative?
Teaching and learning methodologies	**1** Write a song, or the lyrics to a song. **2** Use reported speech.
Building your vocabulary	Ask students to think of five dishes they enjoy that contain no meat. What ingredients do they contain? How do you make it? Ask them to tell their partner about one of the dishes and then tell their partner to ask one question about it – then swap roles. Allow up to ten minutes for this activity.
Check your understanding	Page 282: Meat-free Monday – ask students to complete this exercise in pairs. Page 283: Global hunger – give students no more than five minutes to complete this exercise.
Learner outcomes	By the end of this segment, learners should be able to: ● talk about global hunger ● use reported speech with precision.
Workbook	Pages 118–119: Recycled clothes
Worksheet	12.5: Using vocabulary in a meat-free recipe

Segment 6	**Pages 285–8 The global energy problem; Recycling**
Syllabus objectives	**R1** Identify and retrieve facts and details **L3** Recognize and understand opinions, ideas, and attitudes
Broader skills development	● Talk to classmates about global energy. ● Listen to a nuclear power plant worker. ● Use role play to talk about modern jobs.
Introducing the session	"Thinking out loud" (page 285): Take five minutes to discuss the questions about global energy supplies.
Ensuring a skills balance	Suggested writing activity: Ask students to imagine their school is going to start its own "Landfillharmonic" and to write a poster explaining how it is different from an ordinary orchestra and encouraging people to join, telling them where and when they can sign up.
Differentiated activities	Stronger students could find out more about the nuclear power plant closest to where they live – which could be close by or quite far away – by discovering three facts about it and reporting back in small groups.
Teaching and learning methodologies	**1** Share views on renewable energy. **2** Present a talk.
Building your vocabulary	Ask students to list five discarded items that could be used to make an instrument, then say which instrument they will be making and how they will adapt the item(s) so it can be played.

Check your understanding	Page 285: Nuclear power plant – ask students to complete answers individually before comparing responses in a small group.
	Page 286: Pollution – ask students to give responses individually.
	Page 287: Bottled water or tap water? – give students no more than five minutes to complete the sentences individually.
Learner outcomes	By the end of this segment, learners should be able to: • understand better about bottled water and the environment • think about what we could do with rubbish.
Workbook	Page 120: Earth Hour
Worksheet	12.6: Delivering a news report

Segment 7	Pages 289–90 The Big Issue: cyber bullying
Syllabus objectives	**R3** Recognize and understand ideas, opinions, and attitudes and the connections between related ideas **S4** Demonstrate knowledge of a range of appropriate vocabulary
Broader skills development	• Find out what to do when you face a difficult problem. • Learn how to talk to people about their problems.
Introducing the session	"Thinking out loud" (page 289): Spend up to five minutes asking students about global problems they may be facing.
Ensuring a skills balance	Suggested writing activity: Ask students to tweet what they think about cyber bullying and why it should be stopped.
Differentiated activities	Stronger students can read a real cyber-bullying story (from a selection you have chosen) and then write a response to it.
Teaching and learning methodologies	**1** Complete a note-taking exercise. **2** Talk about acting kindly to others.
Building your vocabulary	Ask students to make a list of modern problems which they and/or their peers may be facing. In small groups, ask them to pick three and suggest how to stop these problems. Allow up to ten minutes for this activity.
Check your understanding	Ask students to pick one of the modern problems they have discussed in small groups and then write an open letter to anyone who may be facing this problem. The open letter should be supportive and give kind and helpful advice.
Learner outcomes	By the end of this segment, learners should be able to: • talk about Internet bullying • talk about how cyber bullying can be stopped.
Workbook	Page 120: Discussion topic
Worksheet	12.7: Using global issues vocabulary
Further practice	**On completion of the chapter, ask students to complete questions 1–20 of the global issues interactive activities.**

Links

If you choose only one link to use with your students, try this:

- www.kidsgoglobal.net

  Explore more of the issues that are affecting us all.

You might also try:

- www.walkingforwater.eu – learn more about World Water Day and how you can get involved.

- www.dosomething.org – how to make a difference with campaigns such as Teens for Jeans.

- www.globalfootprints.org – find out how big your global footprint is and how to make it smaller.

- www.globaleducation.edu.au – more about the issues that affect us all.

- www.worldhunger.org – all you need to know about where and why people are going hungry.

If your students enjoyed reading about brands, suggest that they try checking the packaging next time they buy something to see whether the product is ethical – and remind them to think about how big their carbon footprint might be.

Study tips: speaking

Using open questions (see pages 268–9 of the student book)

In the Speaking test, students need to be able to ask open questions and this activity shows them how to improve this skill. The student should not only expect to answer open questions but also be able to ask them in order to help move the conversation along. However, the examiner usually leads the way, and it is crucial to the success of the test that he or she deploys open questions and productive prompts throughout the 6–9 minutes.

Cambridge will of course have set five prompts, which must be used, but it is expected that examiners will add to these where appropriate. Closed questions can stifle a discussion and should be avoided. It is up to you, the teacher/examiner, to ask the kinds of questions that will sustain a discussion. Since the third assessment criterion is *Development and fluency*, students will need to improve these skills, but it will be difficult for candidates to score highly if there are no open questions, i.e. little development. Examiners should therefore be trained and/or experienced in using open questions and productive prompts.

The following table exemplifies this point, illustrating how key aspects of discussions around global issues might be developed.

Closed question	Open question	Productive prompt
Is the world we live in a global community or not?	Tell me what you do to engage with the global community.	Some people argue that we will never be a truly global community. What do you think about that?
I think we need to develop nuclear power now, as it's the only form of energy which will serve everyone's needs, isn't it?	You hinted earlier that you weren't keen on nuclear energy. Can you tell me why that is?	There is an idea that nuclear energy is never worth the risk. What's your view?
Do you care about fish and other sea life?	How would you feel if we were to lose all our stocks of fish in the oceans?	It's much more important that we build even bigger ships to carry containers, despite the damage to the oceans. That's what global trade is. Surely nobody can argue against that.

If you are an examiner of the Speaking test, or are about to become one, please practise developing open questions and productive prompts. They will give your candidates the best chance of performing well, and they will also help generate a smooth, flowing discussion. Open questions make your job easier.

Evaluating the sample student responses

Here are the correct answers to the questions relating to Track 12.1:

- **Discussion A** is the least productive and has far too many closed questions.

- **Discussion B** is the most effective because it utilizes straightforward open questions and prompts. The candidate is given every chance to respond.

- **Discussion C** is partly successful, but the examiner speaks a little too much at times and the flow of the conversation suffers as a result. The candidate is given chances to develop his/her own thoughts, but is sometimes not sure how to respond.

Study tips: listening

Recognizing and understanding opinions and attitudes (see page 274 of the student book)

This section provides more practice for Question 6: matching people to their opinions. Students need to listen to the soundtrack on the CD (Track 12.4) and match the speakers to the opinions listed on the page.

The skill has been covered elsewhere in the student book – and in this teacher resource pack – so it is up to you how you teach this activity. You might like to cover pre-listening skills here and spend 20 minutes or so inviting students to predict what the six different people might think about the proposed train line development. You could also discuss post-listening skills – perhaps evaluating why some students (or groups) did not match certain people to their views accurately. What was it they each said that led the students to make the incorrect match? This could lead to a short session on inappropriate or unrealistic inference.

Study tips: reading

Questions using diagrams or charts (see page 281 of the student book)

In the Reading and Writing examination paper, only Exercise 2 presents information in diagrammatical form. At both levels this exercise requires students to skim and scan to locate specific information, so these skills should be taught to everyone.

A simple bar chart or pie chart is often used and it will contain all the detail needed to answer the question correctly. Mathematical skills are not tested (e.g. addition, subtraction, etc.) but recognition of numbers, distances, measurements, etc. is tested. The student book shows an example of a typical chart used in the examination, and a further activity asks students to find other, similar charts.

Students need not practise this skill too much, however, as it accounts for only a small proportion of possible marks in the examination paper. It is a useful life skill, though, and as such should be incorporated into schemes of work which comprise an article in which data or figures feature. It should be introduced as a natural rather than a mathematical skill. Useful source material is newspaper articles, magazines, and science journals – anywhere where a diagram has been used to emphasize a statement in the text.

Evaluating the sample student responses

- **Student A** provides the correct answer to Q1.
- **Student A** also comes up with the best answer to Q2.

Study tips: writing

Note making (see page 290 of the student book)

Making notes requires the integration of both reading skills – to capture the content – and writing skills – to convey that content in a concise format. This activity focuses on the writing aspect of note making. The activity provides the subheadings to be used, and advises students to write notes that are as short as possible and which convey each specific point on a separate line.

Both core and extended papers include a specific examination exercise that tests candidates' skill in making notes. The stimulus, or source, for the notes varies slightly, and we have explored this variance elsewhere in the student book and in this teacher resource pack. However, the ability to write the notes effectively is equally relevant to both tiers.

Here are some more examples of note making. Notice how "The essential notes" are phrases and not complete sentences. This is the ideal way in which to present the notes for the examination exercise.

Text containing the note we need	The essential notes
If we carry on as we are, the global population will be over 10 billion people by the year 2018, and this will make life very difficult for the poorest people in some of the third-world countries whose daily lives will suffer.	• More than 10 billion people by 2018 • Poorest people will suffer daily • Third-world countries most at risk
There is surely a responsibility held by the wealthier nations to help out here and for governments to plan ahead by initiating aid schemes to develop infrastructure in countries that need it...	• Richer countries need to help • Aid schemes need to be developed • Need to develop infrastructure
If nothing is done, we anticipate that people will die as a result of disease, malnutrition, unsafe water supplies, and poor sanitation. It is in the third-world countries where population growth can so easily get out of control. A side effect of this is mass emigration, with millions of people seeking better lives in other countries, and this brings its own set of new problems.	• Deaths due to disease, poor diet, unclean water • Population growth a concern in third world • Mass emigration results • Mass emigration causes more problems

You could practise reducing sentences to phrases in this way by using virtually any article of around 600 words with a lot of information in it. Useful articles are those with a strong theme or topic and which stay closely connected to that theme. Discursive pieces are not therefore recommended, as students at this level will probably struggle to complete the jigsaw of non-linear connectives.

Evaluating the sample student responses

- **Students B and C** provide the better notes.
- **Student C** provides the most concise notes.
- **Student A** provides the least effective notes.

☑ My progress

The four study skills – reading, writing, speaking, and listening – are key skills for success in each of the examinations. In the "My progress" section at the end of the chapter in the student book, we invite students to select one skill that they can focus on and develop. However, you may like to ask your students to prepare action plans to develop all four of the skills.

The table shows where the skills feature in the examination papers and how they are applied. Unless otherwise indicated, the skills and tasks are common to both levels.

Skill	Task	Positioning in examination papers
Using open questions and productive prompts	Sustain a conversation and develop key prompts/themes	Speaking • Part D
Recognizing people's attitudes and opinions when listening to them in a group setting	Decide which person's views equate to a brief statement about them	Listening • Question 6
Interpreting charts or diagrams to extract specific information	Analyse a simple chart/diagram and answer one question based on data within it	Reading and writing • Exercise 2 (one item only)
Using subheadings and writing concise notes	Read an article of around 600 words and make a series of related notes	Reading and writing • Exercise 4

Student book answers

All answers are for the "Check your understanding" questions unless otherwise stated.

1 Science and technology

Page 3
1 13 years
2 It has an extraordinary capacity to adapt to the world around it
3 How to make friends; how to interact with people
4 Teenagers are more globally minded than in the past
5 30 years old
6* extraordinary (capacity); flexible; capable

Page 4
1 20 years old
2 Decide when there will be an exhibition; choose the theme of the exhibition; decide how the items will be shown; help with the music; help with the lighting
3 History of art
4 Monitor the atmosphere; monitor the temperature
5 It is a stepping stone of phone technology
6* Model answer: I would like to know more about Jose's favourite item and why he likes it so much.

Page 5
1 Science; technology
2 They date from the Stone Age
3 One quarter: 25 per cent
4 The first motorized aircraft built by the Wright brothers
5 On its website
6* Model answer: I would be surprised to see the aeroplane in the museum

Page 6
1 False
2 False
3 True
4 False
5 True
6 False
7 False
8 False
9 False
10 False

Page 7 (Building your vocabulary)
1 demonstrate
2 engineering
3 develop
4 prototype
5 manufacturers
6 patent
7 perseverance
8 architecture

Page 8
1 Architect
2 He enjoyed creating new things
3 In 1993
4 The Dyson vacuum cleaner
5 The ballbarrow; fan; washing machine; hand drier; taps
6* Model answer: I would like to patent the vacuum cleaner as it is not only a good product, but it looks good too.

1 The Woman of the Future Award
2 Prestigious; nice
3 Stair Steady
4 Lets people walk up and down their stairs
5 She has done so much at such a young age
6* Model answer: I would recommend this invention to my neighbour as she is elderly and would be able to stay in her house longer if she had it

Page 10
1 15 000
2 He has to plan what he is going to write
3 23
4 As places of chance and mystery
5 Comedy
6* Model answer: creative, independent, exciting

Page 12
1 Venice
2 Cornelius; the Doctor; Urquart; Hari; Amy
3 How to dance
4 Less than a week
5 Once every 250 years
6* Golden, rich, lively

Pages 12 and 13 (Language focus)
1 The car is the best and the cheapest as well.
2 My phone is the newest and the lightest - I like it the most.
3 I have seen Avatar and I thought the special effects were the best.
4 The objects in the museum were the most unusual I have ever seen.
5 I liked the Martian Chronicles the most.

Page 14
1 They looked at the city
2 Pink; silver; blue; purple
3 Three
4 An atomic radio
5 A map of the world
6* Model answer: to forget their old life; so no-one would find out about their old life; so no-one would find them

Pages 14 and 15 (Language focus)
1 He buys all the things he needs from the hypermarket.
2 They go to work by train but don't like it.
3 She thinks he is nice but her friends don't like him.
4 We walk to town every Wednesday.
5 He listens to the radio every day but does not download music any more.

Page 18
1 2 years old
2 He clicks
3 He thinks it is amazing
4 He sometimes wishes he could see
5 He is positive about it
6* Model answer: He has remained positive despite what has happened, and has not let him miss out on things other children his age can do.

Page 19
1 She did some work experience at a local optician's and really enjoyed it
2 3 to 4 per cent
3 Teach them to use special magnifying glasses; teach them about eye health; put them in touch with rehabilitation workers
4 Regular eye tests; a healthy diet; protect your eyes from UV; don't smoke
5 Rewarding; challenging; varied
6* Model answer: you can help people see clearly; you can help people with low vision; you can help prevent diseases the patient may have

Page 20
1 More than ten years
2 The thrill of taking off and landing; seeing places all over the world
3 The Maldives; Madeira; Cyprus
4 Science; engineering
5 New navigation displays
6* Model answer: I would enjoy being able to use the latest technology in my job.

2 Food and fitness

Page 25
1 January and February
2 15 days
3 It is a lucky colour; it is supposed to frighten off (the monster) Nian
4 Wealth
5 It is thought to be lucky
6* Model answer: I like the dancing the most, as it makes everyone really happy.

1 1963
2 Up to 15 000
3 Mythical creatures; historic monuments
4 Up to 10 million cubic feet
5 With multicoloured lasers/lanterns
6* Model answer: I would create a castle, as the straight sides would make it easier to do; I would create a swan, as it would look so elegant in the ice.

Page 30
1 Money and truffles
2 Nearly one third
3 Up to US$180 000
4 The US and Japan
5 Deep black with a lacing of white veins through them
6 Agriculture, development, weather, deforestation

Page 31
1 His mother
2 Onion and garlic
3 They took the meatballs too early, before they were cooked
4 At catering college (in Lagos)
5 About a month
6* Model answer: flexible hours, creative, working with a range of people

Pages 41 and 42 (Language focus)
1 When I saw him again, I ran towards him and wept for joy.
2 I had a smartphone 1 but last week I bought a smartphone 6.
3 My mother liked her but I did not like her as much.
4 She enjoyed putting up the party decorations but did not enjoy taking them down again.
5 I started the book last year and last week I finished it.

Page 46 (Key skills: Answering multiple-choice questions)
1 A
2 B
3 C
4 A

3 Communities

Page 55
1 Queens, males, workers
2 A real family life
3 Dirt that piles up at the entrance to the nest
4 Hundreds, thousands, millions
5 To lay eggs
6* any appropriate answer

Page 57 (Building your vocabulary)
1 volunteer
2 graffiti
3 wardrobe
4 privacy
5 camaraderie
6 aloof
7 commodity; hose down
8 motto
9 allocated; dreaded
10 organic

Page 58
1 Unimpressed; disappointed
2 Because of the bare room, graffiti, and cracked windows
3 With water play
4 (Swimming); football
5 Machu Picchu
6 Teamwork; friendship; camaraderie; doing everything together; making (unpleasant) things fun; organic eco-farming; lasting friendship; contact

Page 62
1 B
2 C

3 A
4 C
5 C

Page 66
1 They know someone living there
2 Porridge
3 For the eggs
4 In Busunju, 15 kilometres away
5 It has to be carried from a distance
6* Any appropriate answer

Page 68
1 Gathering in the market; soccer
2 Money place
3 Adobe
4 The poorest
5 Because they were special guests
6* Any appropriate answer

Page 71
1 Are there any adults/grown-ups?
2 Having fun and games; playing
3 Because of the smoke; the island is on fire
4 Anything appropriate: playing at soldiers
5 Anything appropriate: when Ralph says that two have been killed
6* grown ups; a semicircle of little boys; fun and games; little scarecrow; kid; nose wipe

4 Animals and us

Page 79
1 In classrooms
2 Their unique appearance; their simple care needs
3 Anything; bramble; ivy; lettuce
4 Because they like to hang; they grow up to 10 centimetres long; they need room to climb out of their skin
5 They shed/climb out of their skin
6* Any reasonable suggestions

Page 85
1 India to north-eastern China; from the Russian Far East to Sumatra
2 For their skins; for their body parts (for medicine)
3 Clearing forests for agriculture/the timber trade/ development/roads
4 Decline in the number of animals that tigers prey on; tigers coming too close to humans; tigers and people being killed
5 Security; legislation; conservation; planning
6* Any reasonable answer

Page 85 (Language focus)
1 My father will come to see us. He will be our first visitor this week.
2 He will train guide dogs for a living. They will help blind people to find their way about.
3 We shall give him our support. I shall follow in his footsteps one day.

Page 88
1 The wild
2 They are red-hot/glowing hot

3 It's an automatic response – associating the music with pain
4 By inflicting pain; by rings fitted through their nose/ bear's nose very sensitive/no anesthetic
5 Their teeth are broken or removed and their claws are trimmed several times a year
6* Any reasonable answer, including: descriptions; choice of vocabulary (examples); contrast between entertainment and cruelty.

Page 90
1 B
2 A
3 B
4 A
5 C
6 A
7 B
8 B

Page 94
1 15
2 A soldier
3 A war horse
4 The (outbreak of) war
5 Any appropriate answer: Albert excited, Mother sad, Father worried
6* Thinks he will be a good one; look good in uniform; wants to march to a band; wants to ride Joey to war; full of youthful enthusiasm; has idealised view of war as adventure

Page 96
1 Smell out land mines
2 Nine months
3 In two hours
4 People don't like them/are afraid of them
5 Putting nice pictures on the website; calling them "hero rats"; launching an "Adopt-a-Rat" scheme
6* any appropriate answer

5 Working life

Page 106
1 B
2 A
3 A
4 C
5 A

Page 107
1 Patongo Counselling Community Outreach
2 About three hours
3 (She counsels them about) money problems/ savings advice
4 She is dedicated
5 She can bring about change/improvements
6* Something like:
5.30 a.m. get up, fetch water, make breakfast, get daughters ready for school
6.30 a.m. housework, cooking
7.30 a.m. leave for work
8.30 a.m. group planning session
9.00 a.m. visiting outreach groups
5.00 p.m. office closes, extra evening session(s), return home

Page 108 (Study tips)

1 teacher; built houses
2 health education; medical chest checks
3 family-run cattle stations; mine sites
4 flies; heat
5 promotion; niche

Page 111

1 Any appropriate answer – more than just "travel" involved
2 Variety, moving around, different every day
3 For emergencies; when medical help is not nearby
4 A desire to help others
5 The gratification of helping people; good salaries/ earnings
6* any reasonable answer, including: caring for people; demanding physically/mentally; rewarding; adventure; challenge

Page 112

1 Spartaco
2 Being leading scorer with the youth side; two years with Spartaco
3 Train; clean gear; study
4 A (road/bike) accident; crushed ankle
5 sports commentator/reporter
6* Anything appropriate: check carefully, prepare

Page 113

1 Argentinian/Venezuelan
2 In a charity shop
3 Teaching autistic/handicapped children (puppetry)
4 Her father's job involved travelling
5 Anything appropriate: around 29
6* Anything appropriate

Page 116

1 A lawyer
2 "Other folks"
3 Tom Robinson
4 Guilty
5 His conscience won't let him
6* Anything appropriate

6 Travel and transport

Page 121

1 3 km; $83
2 two; four
3 $599; eight hours
4 604-0272; 8 a.m.
5 three; five

Page 124 (Listening)

Put the given words into each gap in this order:
without arms; pilot; 120; schools; future

Page 126 (Language focus)

1 As I was sitting on the sofa, I suddenly heard a crash from outside.
2 When James was walking along the road, he noticed a shiny coin on the pathway.
3 They were watching their favourite television show when the telephone rang.

4 The meal was cooking on the stove but then he forgot all about it and it boiled over.
5 He was thinking about the solution to the problem when his friend rushed in and said "I have solved it!"

Page 130

1 He saw a poster at university
2 Ten weeks
3 The same one as Jake/to help a local community project build a better hospital
4 She fell into a river
5 You can achieve more by keeping on going and not giving up.

Page 132 (Building your vocabulary)

1 pristine
2 marine
3 curious
4 swampy
5 wetland
6 appeal
7 impact
8 aware

Page 134 (Building your vocabulary)

1 unique
2 responds
3 mine
4 impressions
5 chamber
6 stable
7 hike
8 manner

Page 135

1 Bathe in it, drink it
2 For mental and physical rest
3 Warm, comfortable clothes; hiking shoes; light sports shoes; sleeping bag
4 10°C
5 The Tourist Route; The Mining Route
6* Model answer: exciting, healthy, cold, eerie

Page 136

1 They were small and beautiful
2 His father and a friend of his father
3 He had been a champion caver
4 A thrill; inspiring
5 Not being able to go caving for a few days; the cold under ground
6* Model answer: map, light, helmet, warm clothes, sturdy shoes

Page 138 (Building your vocabulary)

Across: 3 helium; 6 ambition; 7 skydive; 8 harness

Down:1 hero; 2 humble; 4 capsule; 5 inspire

Page 139

1 Military parachutist
2 Smashed
3 Dropped to his knees; punched the air (in celebration)
4 Firefighting; perform mountain rescues; move to the country; fly helicopters
5 He would not have broken the speed record

6* Model answer: it shows we can conquer space; he has explored the limits of the human body

7 Leisure and entertainment

Page 144 (Building your vocabulary)

Put one of the given words into each gap in this order: soloist; generation; awards; outstanding; highlights; fusion; quintet; ensemble

Page 144 (Language focus: Using prefixes to indicate numbers)

pentagon: the number 5; a five-sided shape

triplets: the number 3; three siblings born at the same time

unicorn: the number 1; a mythical horse-like animal with one horn

Page 145

1 18 years
2 Australia; Monte Carlo; Germany; Hong Kong
3 To celebrate the 150th anniversary of his birth
4 10
5 10
6* Model answer: She has been able to perform with different instruments and so play a wider range of music.

Page 146

1 Baker Street
2 He is Sherlock Holmes restored
3 The police
4 Cardiff
5 His superiority; he is usually right
6* Model answer: we see how it is solved through their conversations; we see their relationship

Page 149

1 14
2 How to fish
3 From the surroundings; the position of the sun; the way moss grows
4 Mycroft
5 The next day
6* Model answer: They will travel upto London and perhaps meet Mycroft; if they do, Mycroft will explain everything to them; if he is not there, they may have to work things out for themselves.

1 A brown suit with blue stripes; an orange tie his mother gave him
2 Children; teenagers
3 An accordion
4 He gets to meet young people
5 He loves the paper dust covers which you get on books.
6* Model answer: patience, a good memory, logic

Page 150 (Building your vocabulary)

theft	the taking of an item which is not yours to take
investigate	try to solve a mystery by finding facts
hiding place	a secret place where it is hard to be found

curious	unusual or strange
alley	a narrow pathway between two buildings
hired	employed
nosy	wanting to know too much information

Page 151

1 In a cafe
2 Like a tiny horse's galloping
3 An envelope
4 A note
5 Five minutes
6* Model answer: He noticed she had a small coin in her hand.

Page 152 (Building your vocabulary)

stage show	a performance in a theatre
represent	take the place of something
act of a show	a section of a stage show
Hollywood	an area famous for film-making in California, USA
stampede	the fast movement of many animals of the same type, often through a desert
Broadway	an area famous for theatre in New York
inspiration	the cause of the idea for something
essence	the central part of something

Page 152

1 More than 74 minutes
2 Getting the audience to accept that the actors are representing animals
3 None
4 Four (shadow puppet, rod puppet, hand puppet, and human actor)
5 The music
6* Model answer: I would enjoy going to see The Lion King because the story sounds interesting and I would like to see how they show the animals on stage.

Page 154

1 400 metres
2 38 years
3 Milkha's record-breaking achievements
4 He had to
5 He likes it

Page 156

1 More than 800 million
2 Super Bowl; Republican National Convention
3 Hot; 85°C
4 More than 23 500
5 Kollywood; Tollywood
6* Model answer: The films are being released in more and more cinemas over the world; as people are moving between countries, so the demand for their native films is increasing in their new countries.

Page 158 (Building your vocabulary)

Put one of the given words into each gap in this order: relief; raising money; fun run/sponsored walk; fundraisers; sponsored skydive; aid/help/cure/treat

Page 159

1 Christmas Day/25 December 1985
2 A famine in Ethiopia
3 £15 million
4 Sport Relief
5 Make Poverty History; Live8; America Gives Back; United Against Malaria coalition
6* Model answer: I would ask them to support WaterAid, as this charity helps ensure people all over the world have fresh, clean water.

Page 162

1 He wanted a big, physical running challenge
2 Olympic experts
3 43
4 Over 6,000 a day
5 Sports Personality of the Year Special Award
6* Model answer: I would like to know what motivates him to do such an amazing run.

Page 163 (Building your vocabulary)

Put one of the given words into each gap in this order: high-tech; high resolution; interface; GPS; terrain; interactivity; database; reinforce

Page 166

1 At a New York bus station
2 People played it too much
3 1981
4 2006
5 Facebook; iPhone
6* Model answer: The game which appeals to me the most is Angry Birds because all my friends play it and we really enjoy talking about it and comparing our scores.

8 Hobbies and interests

Page 173

1 His son/the Duke of York
2 King; George V
3 The (unused) Two Pence 'Post Office' Mauritius stamp
4 Its completeness
5 Three afternoons a week (when in London)
6* Any reasonable answer

Page 175

1 B
2 C
3 B
4 A
5 B

Page 176

1 Enjoyment, their financial value
2 A self-addressed envelope
3 That you are an autograph hunter/collector
4 That they don't mind (you asking)
5 By exchanging/swapping (autographs)
6* Any appropriate answer

Page 178

1 Every day

2 Rhythm & blues
3 Anything appropriate: passion/addicted/love listening to/name almost every song/takes the stress away/ listen to many genres: rhythm & blues/pop/songs …
4 He can't
5 Any appropriate answer

Page 180

1 Her secretary liked it
2 Kirsty Young
3 Largo (movement) from Dvorak's New World Symphony
4 Bob Marley and the Grateful Dead
5 To get the skin crispy for Peking Duck
6* Any appropriate answer

Page 183

1 The ukulele
2 It was free
3 She was lent a better one
4 Online
5 Sang/chose songs to sing
6* Any appropriate answer

Page 190

1. People fish for different reasons. Recreational fishers fish for pleasure or sport. Commercial fishers fish for profit.
2. The use of nets and the catching of fish with hooks not in the mouth.
3. You forget about the hustle and bustle of city life.
4. James works indoors so he loves to get fresh air. / Fishing is relaxing and satisfying. / It promotes a healthier lifestyle. / It offers the chance to improve your self-esteem through respect for the environment.
5. Patience.
6* Any appropriate answer

Page 191

1 Fish die unnecessarily just for the pleasure of humans.
2 A fish gets stressed and out-of-breath. Just like a person, if a fish can't breathe, it will die.
3 The fish can experience serious exhaustion or injury during the process.
4 Hundreds of thousands of birds die each year in gillnets around the world. The birds get tangled in the nets and drown because they can't get out.
5 Any appropriate answer

9 Cultures

Page 199

1 Men kissing men
2 With one kiss (on the cheek)
3 Being tactile/touching/making (physical) contact
4 Touching their feet
5 Her boyfriend's parents
6* Anything appropriate

1 For a greeting; sharing common breath
2 A greeting; connecting thoughts
3 Any appropriate answer
4 Trinidad (& Tobago); West Indies
5 Any appropriate answer

Page 202

1 Puerto Rico and the Bahamas
2 To bring prosperity and blessings to the newborn
3 Brazil
4 It's shaved off/removed and weighed
5 Gifts are brought for/showered on the baby
6* Provision of meals (USA); general help in the home for 40 days (Mexico); shower part gifts (Canada)

Page 203

1 C
2 A
3 A
4 C
5 A

Page 206

1 Being seen (in her wedding dress) by the groom
2 Friends or relatives (of the prospective groom)
3 Seeing (nanny) goats, pigeons, or wolves
4 By replacing the hawthorn branch he left at her door with a cauliflower
5 Practise writing her new name
6* Appropriate answer

Page 213

1 How a culture lives
2 Because the burial sites have been built over by later generations
3 All they might need in an afterlife: ship; weapons; horses; food
4 To prevent the soul escaping from the body
5 The idea that evil spirits hovered/lingered round/tried to steal the soul of/dead bodies
6* Appropriate answer

10 The past and the future

Page 221

1 Advertising, entertainment, news
2 Orville and Wilbur
3 By steam turbines
4 With their speed
5 So much of what we depend on uses it
6* Appropriate answer

Page 222

1 There were fewer industries/opportunities; qualifications didn't count
2 The (social) class you belonged to
3 Don't compete with boys in exams
4 Once a week (at most)
5 It meant remaining dependent on parents (for rest of your life)
6* Appropriate answer

Page 226

1 B
2 A
3 A
4 B
5 C

Page 227

1 Pray (to gods/goddesses)/write to/ask dead relatives to plead for them/resort to magic/adopt
2 (Queen) Hatshepsut
3 At 7 years old
4 Their children
5 Farmer, business owner, acrobat, dancer, singer, musician, priestess, professional mourner, perfume maker
6* Any appropriate answer

Page 231

1 To protect him/help him retain power in the afterlife
2 They were painted/lacquered/holding real weapons
3 They represented men from different parts of China/different personalities
4 Farmers were digging for a well
5 A (type of) hard baked clay
6* Any reasonable answer

Page 234

1 A robot (vac)
2 A computerized/barcoded fridge/delivery system links directly with supermarkets
3 By driverless electric postal truck
4 By automatic electric car (delivered from car pool); (Victoria line) tube
5 It changes her diet and books (extra) gym sessions
6* Any reasonable answer

11 Communication

Page 242

1 At the Budapest International Fair
2 Desk; pocket; handbag; bag; car
3 As a form of advertising
4 Marcel Bich in 1950
5 It is the birthday of Laszlo Bíró
6* Model answer: they are cheap; they are convenient

Page 243

1 To save energy; they help us think
2 No time at all
3 Email; social media websites
4 What he is doing
5 Focus on your activities
6* Model answer: Write a note to someone, rather than emailing them

Page 245

1 Satellites were used by armies to find their way and to spy.
2 Today, satellites are used in weather reports and telephone calls.
3 Newspapers use satellites to speed up local distribution.
4 Some reliable taxi drivers use GPS to find their way.
5 Search-and-rescue teams use satellites to find ships and planes.

Page 247

1 1,966 miles
2 20 days
3 April 1861

4 October 1861

5 19 months

Page 248

1 For centuries

2 Finding out how pigeons find their way home

3 They follow the magnetic curves of the Earth's surface; they use the sun; they use landmarks; they use their sense of smell.

4 A road; a river

5 Blood samples

6* Less than 70 years

Page 249

1 By foot; by pony; by ship

2 Painter

3 So that he could study art

4 Electricity

5 Three dots

6* Students report back individual names to the class.

Page 250

1 Runs on all fours; barks; pants; paws at the ground; drinks noisily; shakes her head free of the water

2 8 years old

3 It has no cadence/rhythm/music/inflection/tone

4 She can count

5 By 5 years of age

6* Model answer: she can talk again; she can walk upright; she can eat with her hands; she can communicate like a human being

Page 251

1 1993

2 A computer

3 Nothing rhymed with 'tiger'

4 Funny; brilliant

5 101

6* Model answer: they provide images of the characters in the story; they provide ideas about the location of the story

Page 251 (Language focus)

1 walks

2 leaves

3 learning

4 kicking

5 telling

Page 252

1 Newborn

2 She picked out patterns when the babies cried

3 0–3 months

4 Owh; heh; eh; neh

5 They praise it

6* Model answer: She helps parents understand their babies.

Page 255

1 To feel the sound of the music

2 More than 100

3 Over 1,800

4 12

5 Sound-making

6* Model answer: young people who are deaf and are interested in music; anyone with an impairment who is interested in music

Page 255

1 Sonja is a fully qualified British Sign Language interpreter.

2 Sonja started to learn sign language to communicate with a small nursery child.

3 When learning the signs, at first Sonja felt a bit shy.

4 Sonja feels sign language is incredibly important.

5 Sonja has just produced a set of DVDs.

Page 257 (Building your vocabulary)

echolocation	a way of locating an object using sound which can be reflected off the object
vocalization	giving words to thoughts
clicks	short sounds like taps
evolved	developed over a period of time
gestures	hand signals used to communicate or reinforce words
convey	transmit a feeling or thought
emotional state	the way a person is feeling
communication system	the way someone passes a message to others

Page 258

1 A gentle nuzzle; a playful bite; an aggressive bite; a smack

2 A bobbing of the head; a wide open gaping mouth; an S-shaped swimming position

3 Chimpanzee; bird

4 Their emotional state; their gender; their age

5 What communication signals dolphins use; what these signals might mean

6* ants; bees; chimpanzees

Page 259

1 95 to 98 per cent

2 By kissing; by embracing; by patting on the back; by touching hands; by tickling

3 More than 240

4 About 21

5 The rainforests are being cut down; commercial hunting for meat

Page 260

1 His left eyelid

2 By blinking

3 Every quarter of an hour/every 15 minutes

4 It feels heavy and stops him from moving

5 Castles in Spain; discovering imaginary worlds

6* Model answer: He has been able to write a book with virtually no body movement.

Page 261

1 It was exactly 300 years after the death of Galileo

2 Maths was not available at his university

3 He uses a computer

4 He opened the Games

5 His daughter

6* I like the way he has written a children's book with his daughter, it shows another side to him.

Page 263 (Building your vocabulary)
Put one of the given words into each gap in this order: mission; dressing table; flattering; convince; illusion; articulate; indicate; hazy; reactions; toddler

Page 264
1 Sits in front of the television
2 A stranger staring; a toddler asking its mummy what's wrong with the big girl
3 Most school subjects apart from PE; playing the piano; writing; acting; public speaking; being confident; being articulate
4 Beautiful
5 Transplant some rib into where her jawbone should be; transplant some flesh
6* Model answer: Hope you are OK. Don't worry. I shall come and visit you as soon as you are out of hospital.

12 Global issues

Page 269
1 She is interested in ethical products
2 Fair trade for all; the products are sustainable; caring for the environment
3 Anyone
4 To the farmers; to environmental care
5 From the website; from Facebook; from Twitter
6* Model answer: Body Shop; Neil's Yard, Lush

Page 270 (Building your vocabulary)
Words to tick: traceability; hand-gathered; highest quality; organically certified; best-selling; fair price

Page 271 (Building your vocabulary)
1 stock
2 import
3 valuable
4 caravan
5 region

Page 273
1 202 BC
2 Within China
3 Iran; Iraq; Syria; China; India
4 Jade; silver; gold
5 It exposed people to different cultures and religions
6* Model answer: it was successful; people beyond China were willing to trade for silk

Page 277 (Building your vocabulary)
1 accommodation
2 panoramic
3 skyline
4 complex
5 crowning

Page 278 (Building your vocabulary)

symbolizes	represents
energy efficiency	using less energy
sacrifices	gives up
responsible	in charge

climate change	global warming or cooling
motivation	incentive
sustainable	maintainable
participated	took part

Page 279
1 Nearly 1,400 people
2 Changes in their transport, food, energy, and water use
3 Turn off the lights
4 The No Impact Week program
5 Go paperless; be more energy efficient; go vegetarian
6* Model answer: it symbolizes progress and highlights climate change

Page 282
1 livestock
2 80
3 choose mainly plant foods; limit red meat; avoid processed meat
4 £1.2 billion each year
5 10
6* Example model answer: money

Page 283
1 870 million
2 almost 15%
3 563
4 about 100 million
5 US$ 3.2 billion
6* hunger

Page 285
1 Nearly seven years
2 A bit surprised; worried
3 Safe; clean; a long-term option
4 Chemistry teacher
5 Amazing; the best job in the world
6* Model answers: Will it last forever? Is there a safer way to get our energy?

Page 286
1 Carbon dioxide
2 Gasoline; natural gas
3 Volcanoes
4 Drive less; fly less; recycle; promote conservation
5 Cut carbon dioxide emissions; tax carbon emissions; put higher taxes on gasoline
6* Higher taxes on carbon emissions and gasoline.

Page 287
1 29 billion
2 crude oil
3 one-sixth
4 in rivers; in lakes; in the ocean
5 six hours
6* it is convenient

Workbook answers

All answers are for the "Check your understanding" questions unless otherwise stated.

1 Science and technology

Pages 1 and 2
1 Hydrogen
2 diamond, graphite or coal (any two)
3 the Egyptian language; it means 'earth'
4 around 9% more space
5 Quartz
6* Example answer: I was surprised that only 1 per cent of the sun's mass is oxygen, so this is my favourite fact.

Page 2 (Language focus)
1 friendliest
2 cleanest
3 most intelligent
4 calmest
5 most inspirational

Page 3 (Building your vocabulary)
1 telescope
2 privileged
3 spectrum
4 distinction
5 self-made
6 molecule
7 emits
8 galaxy

Page 4
1 Edwin Hubble
2 He changed the way we think about the cosmos twice
3 That there was more than one
4 Away from the Earth
5 The Big Bang Theory
6* Example answer: They are interested in finding life on other planets.

Page 6
1 Aston Martin; Lotus Esprit
2 Sean Connery; George Lazenby; Roger Moore; Timothy Dalton; Pierce Brosnan; Daniel Craig
3 It can travel under water
4 In briefcases, belts, glasses, pens or watches
5 As state of the art; totally believable
6* Example answer: I would most enjoy using the underwater car as it would be really exciting to be able to drive underwater.

Page 7
1 New inventions
2 Sue them
3 It must be new; it must have an inventive step; it must be capable of being made or used in some kind of industry
4 A scientific or mathematical discovery, theory or method; a literary, dramatic, musical or artistic work; a way of performing a mental act; playing a game or doing business; the presentation of information; some computer programs; an animal or plant variety; a method of medical treatment or diagnosis; or something against public policy or morality.
5 Up to 20 years

6* Example answer: I wish I had been able to patent the tablet, as it has become a world-wide success.

Page 8
1 The phonograph
2 Mary had a little lamb
3 Recording and reproducing sound; letter writing and dictation; phonographic books for blind people; a family record; music boxes and toys; clocks that announce the time; and a connection with the telephone
4 One and a half years
5 Money
6* I think his most significant achievement was the phonograph, as it was one of the first times sound was recorded and replayed for others to hear.

Page 8 (Language focus)
1 I dream every night but my friends never do.
2 My mum cooks a great lunch when all the family gets together.
3 Dad always asks me to call when I get home safely.
4 She drinks tea but she doesn't drink coffee.
5 He drives a very expensive car now he is famous.

2 Food and fitness

Page 11 (Building your vocabulary)
Put one of the given words into each gap in this order: virtually; influences; prime, celeb; achievement; stable; renovated; intrusive

Page 12
1 London
2 Over 30 years
3 A year
4 Theatre-goers, celebs/celebrities
5 A stable
6 Cookery courses, wine courses
7 European
8 Perfectly/expertly cooked food; plenty of vegetables; knowledgeable staff

Page 14
1 Checks that kitchens are clean; checks that food is kept in appropriate conditions
2 The built-in thermometer can be inaccurate
3 3–5°C
4 −18°C
5 Wash your hands
6* Example answer: It is important so that a minimum standard of food preparation is kept by all companies.

Page 15
1 Checks their health history
2 Three to four times a week
3 Make sure Ash or one of his colleagues is with him
4 By holding on to the handles
5 A cycling class
6* Example answer: I would take up running, as you are warm and safe in a gym to go running.

Page 15 (Language focus)
1   He set up the charity because he wanted to make a difference.
2   After the performance, there was a long round of applause.
3   He went into the restaurant but then decided to go and eat some fast food.

Page 16 (Building your vocabulary)
Put one of the given words into each gap in this order: prize-winning; martial arts; blended; outbreak; recreational; self-defence; devotee; posture

Page 17
1   He was a gymnast
2   He wanted to restore his health
3   Bodybuilding; gymnastics; boxing; recreational sports
4   A Greek statue act
5   Martha Graham
6   Breathing; proper posture; correction of various physical ailments
7   1945
8   In studios; gyms; universities; grade schools

Page 18 (Building your vocabulary)

record	best achievement
champion	the top person in a competition
debut	first time at an event or competition
adolescents	young teenagers
contribution	what you give to something
convinced	persuaded
promotes	highlights and encourages
beneficiaries	people who gain from something else
collaborating	partnering
implement	make happen

Page 19
1   Bjorn Borg
2   In 2005
3   One
4   November 2007
5   To help socially disadvantaged children and adolescents
6   In Manacour; it is his home town
7   Sport
8   Other foundations; organizations

Page 20
1   To fill the time he had after he had finished the marathon
2   2,500 metres
3   21 miles
4   Pilates; light weights
5   Cold, painful, fantastic
6* Example answer: incredible; amazing; fantastic

Page 21 (Building your vocabulary)

global	worldwide
exhilarating	exciting
blend	mix
quarterly	four times per year
impact	influence
initiatives	plans
motor neurone disease	disease mainly affecting the muscles
vision	idea for the future

Page 22
1   2001
2   Fitness; entertainment; culture
3   Quarterly
4   151
5   Breast cancer; motor neurone disease; heart health
6* Example answer: It is fun and energetic, so keeps them fit.

Page 22 (Language focus)
1   We cooked a wonderful meal for our parents last night.
2   I liked strawberries when I was younger.
3   He never brushed his teeth when he was a small boy and now they are falling out.
4   They touched the stone and were surprised to feel it was warm.
5   Every spring, my mother cleaned the house from top to bottom.

1   I went to town and saw my Mum.
2   I drank coffee when I was younger but I don't any more.
3   She took some fantastic photos of the mountains.
4   He was a chef and so cooked some very tasty meals.
5   They had a dog and then they bought a cat.

3 Communities

Page 23 (Building your vocabulary)

caste system	different classes in society
assume	to take on
drone	male bee
sterile	infertile
duel	fight between two
anatomical	of the body
chore	unpleasant task
comb	wax structure containing honey
evaporate	convert to liquid
swarm	a massed colony

Page 24
1   (Female) worker bees
2   Fights to the death with/kills any other queen
3   She destroys them before they hatch
4   Honey; eggs
5   Workers
6* Any appropriate answer

Page 26 (Language focus)
1   Active
2   Active; passive
3   Active; passive; active
4   Passive; active
5   Active; active

Can you change these sentences so that the active voice is passive, and vice versa?
1   Bees were kept by my father in the small vegetable patch behind our house.
2   His bees produced all the honey eaten by us.
3   We gave a jar of honey that had been extracted by him from his honeycombs to everyone by whom we were visited.
4   One of his bees sometimes stung him but they were never complained about by him.
5   It was said by him that the queen then would be looked after by one less worker.

Page 27 (Building your vocabulary)

1 kraal
2 ochre
3 whisk
4 igloos
5 draped

Page 28

1 Nkaradu; his mother; his sister; the whole family
2 Tree branches, grass and leaves, dung and mud/clay
3 Beans and corn
4 Lions and water buffalo
5 Beaded jewellery/beads, decorations for special ceremonies
6* Any answer including reference to beads, jewellery, ochre, blue - sky, green - peace/vegetation, ceremonies

Page 29

1 B
2 C
3 A
4 B
5 A

Page 31 (Building your vocabulary)

1 humus
2 strategically
3 tolerance
4 marginalized
5 operational
6 elevated
7 consciousness
8 interns
9 located
10 agronomist

Page 33

1 63 kilometres
2 Chile; Ecuador; Colombia; Bolivia
3 Sandy, unworkable land
4 By providing an example/model of sustainable, alternative solutions; by showing how good/ eco-friendly techniques can improve conditions; modelling good, cheap forms of agriculture
5 Any appropriate ones, including: friendly, relaxing, educational, stress-free, peace-loving, community-based

4 Animals and us

Page 35 (Building your vocabulary)

bonds	close friendships
forged	made
nurtured	nourished
behavioural	what you do
preventive	avoiding
abandoned	left behind
suitability	appropriateness
consistent	regular
environment	living conditions
factors	things to consider

Page 36

1 Respect, friendship
2 Time, money, commitment

3 It depends on the species or breed
4 A healthy/consistent diet/food, clean/fresh water
5 The wrong choice of pet
6* Any appropriate answer

Page 38 (Building your vocabulary)

Put one of the given words into each gap in this order: sponsor; crucial; immunisation; harness; treated; misconception; gradually; navigate; obstacle; negotiated; kerb; napping

Page 39

1 Patience, time, money
2 20 months
3 Check traffic lights
4 When a car is coming
5 17–22 months
6* Any appropriate answer

Page 40 (Listening in)

1 C
2 B
3 A
4 A
5 C

Page 41 (Building your vocabulary)

1 encroachment
2 subsist
3 bulk
4 logging
5 integral
6 founding
7 monitoring
8 furry (down)
8 function (across)

Pages 42 and 43 (Language focus)

Tomorrow will be my birthday and I shall celebrate it at the zoo. I shall watch the pandas playing. It will be their first day on view to the public. My sister will be there, too. She will stay with me for the week and will be keen to see the pandas. She will love their cuddly appearance and will want to take one home with her. My brother won't be with us as he will be working in London this week and will not be able to get time off to join us. I shall miss him but shall enjoy the day with my sister.

Page 43

1 1961
2 Bamboo
3 By creating green corridors
4 (Panda) reserves are now spread across a wide area/3.8 million acres of forest
5 A worldwide conservation movement
6* cuddly; peaceful; distinctive black and white coat; features; furry; appealing (black-patched) eyes

5 Working life

Page 45 (Building your vocabulary)

Put one of the given words into each gap in this order:

caddie; shift; interact; prime; typically; anonymous; survey; eligible; elementary; retail

Page 46

1 No schoolwork
2 Those who like dealing with people
3 (Knowing basic) first aid; (knowing how to) handle various emergencies; (the ability to) stay calm in a crisis
4 Monitor the children closely
5 Survey-filling
6* Any appropriate answer

Page 48

1 B
2 A
3 A
4 C
5 B
6 Sad, miserable, helpless, desperate
7 Model answer: Grateful, enthusiastic, fulfilled, happy

Page 49 (Building your vocabulary)

implemented	carried out
affected	altered
launched	started
monitor	keep an eye on
set my sights on	aim for
assignments	jobs to do
stability	steadiness
stay focused	keep mind on job
complex	involving several different things
passion	something you are really keen about

Page 51

1 Canada
2 Its excellent reputation in disaster response
3 It's neutral; it's independent
4 In Canada; in his own community
5 Positive: a chance to develop new friendships; negative: difficult to maintain stability with friends and family; difficulty in maintaining friendships
6* Any appropriate answer

(Language focus)

1 He (said that he) came from Canada and worked for the Red Cross in Senegal.
2 (He said that) his family was very understanding and wished him well.
3 (He told me that/us that) if I/we wanted to be an international aid worker/international aid workers, he recommended the Red Cross.
4 I am standing at the spot where the temple was.
5 I consider working as an aid worker a privilege.
6 We don't know the answer, but fortunately John does.

Page 53 (Building your vocabulary)

1 latex
2 torso
3 wardrobe mistress
4 atmosphere
5 enhanced
6 prestigious
7 projection
8 sculpted
9 mainstream
10 veil
11 resurgence

Page 55

1 (Live) music/poetry
2 Create and take part in the stories
3 The puppet body is held in front of the puppeteer's
4 The function of the puppets, the ability of the puppeteers, the budget
5 Sewing
6* Any appropriate answer

6 Travel and transport

Page 57 (Building your vocabulary)

mayor	the person in charge of a town or city
potholes	holes in the road caused by erosion, cold weather, or age
pollution	noise, fumes, and rubbish which make a place dirtier
chime	ring (e.g. a bell)
ferry	type of boat on a river or water channel

Pages 57–8

1 The mayor
2 About a month
3 More pollution
4 The chimes on the clock tower; the ferries
5 Use the cycle paths
6* Example answer: Yes, because I want to be healthier and cause less harm to the environment

Page 59 (Building your vocabulary)

Place one word in each gap in this order:
steep; sledge; drifts; altitude; summit

Page 60

1 –19°C
2 9 miles
3 Scott; Wilson; Evans
4 About 80 miles
5 Very wet bags, they need more sleep
6* Example answer: Low temperatures; southerly wind; people pulling possessions on sledges; bags getting wet

Pages 60–61

1 Physics
2 Cambridge
3 Six months
4 His friends and family
5 Patience
6* Example answer: I think the hardest part of his job is living in such cold conditions for such a long time.

Page 61 (Language focus)

1 whose
2 whom
3 which/that
4 which/that

Page 62 (Building your vocabulary)

1 Shoal
2 Clam
3 Exhilarating
4 Shipwreck
5 Reminder

Pages 62–3

1 Since the age of 18
2 19 years old

3   Australia; the Great Barrier Reef
4   The feeling of flying
5   (In) his office
6* Example answer: I would feel scared but excited at the same time; maybe more scared at the time and more excited afterwards.

Page 64 (Building your vocabulary)
1   stunt-flying
2   ticker tape
3   convictions
4   biplane
5   prank
6   altitude
7   aviation
8   conventional
9   canary
10 relented

Page 65
1   She was not impressed
2   Financial/money; finances; prejudicial; prejudice
3   Second-hand; two-seater; yellow
4   17 June 1928
5   A ticker-tape parade; a reception at the White House
6* A challenge to others

Page 68 (Language focus)
1   When she was cooking the dinner, she heard the good news on the radio.
2   It was when he was using his knife that night that he realised he wanted to be a surgeon.
3   They saw the Milky Way for the first time as they were standing in the garden of their new house.
4   He was looking for the remote control when he saw a ring on the floor.
5   They sang the beautiful music they were practising each week this term.

7 Leisure and entertainment

Page 69 (Building your vocabulary)
Place one word in each gap in this order:
consultant; relic; era; noughties; soared; stacked; cast

Page 70
1   Play well
2   1958
3   More than 300 million
4   Teacher who had become a consultant
5   Will Ferrell; Liam Neeson; Morgan Freeman
6* He was a carpenter

Page 71
1   Impossible things
2   Trigger his senses; feel alive; ease things
3   Tolerance
4   Trunk; leg; tail; tusk
5   The whole image of things
6* Any appropriate answer

Page 72
1   Bed; side-table; duvet; alarm clock; old sheet
2   The room is bare
3   7 a.m.

4   Jasmine
5   Barbados
6* Example answer: No, I don't think she is looking forward to it because she is reluctant to leave her bedroom.

Page 73 (Language focus)
Possible answers:
1   deafeningly
2   flawlessly
3   entirely
4   utterly
5   exceedingly

Page 75
1   *Hamlet; A Midsummer Night's Dream*
2   Chekhov
3   How to react
4   *Noises Off*
5   While filming a period drama
6* Example answer: I would like to go and see Noises Off as it sounds funny and Michael Frayn is a good writer.

Page 76
1   Good; original
2   The music
3   Des says it is not realistic
4   During the 1980s
5   17 years old
6* Any appropriate answer

8 Hobbies and interests

Page 77 (Building your vocabulary)
1   pedigree
2   cartoons
3   stashed
4   canyons; focus
5   depict; dimension
6   bolster
7   unique; indulge

Pages 78–79
1   Collect postcards
2   A specific animal; wildlife; structures such as tall buildings/bridges; natural wonders such as waterfalls/canyons; household items such as teapots; artwork from museum collections; transport such as trains/trams/planes; beach scenes; Valentine's Day; Christmas; Star Trek
3   Collect postcards on that theme
4   It means you have at least one good photo of the place
5   Postcards showing the place at different times of year or in different weather
6* Rewarding; flexible; can be done anywhere; opens up (new) opportunities; means of learning; developing interests you already have; provides record of places you visit

Page 80 (Language focus)
check a reference	look up
consider (someone as)	look upon
check (for mistakes)	look over; look through
investigate	look into
be a spectator (but not take part)	look on

feel superior to	look down upon/on
expect	look for
beware	look out
take care of	look after
admire	look up to

Page 80
1 C
2 A
3 C
4 A
5 B

Page 81 (Building your vocabulary)
1 utilitarian
2 fleeting
3 avenues
4 interspersed
5 fragment
6 bizarre
7 craniotomy
8 rural
9 shiver
10 neurological
11 familiarity

Page 83
1 Sound, silence
2 (You can be reduced to) tears
3 It can make you shiver
4 It manages to communicate (when other means fail); it gets through to residents who have lost their memory
5 Music played to her helped her recover from serious head/brain injury and surgery
6* Any appropriate answer

Page 84 (Building your vocabulary)
decent	reasonable
religiously	very conscientiously
rudiments	basics
in retrospect	thinking about it later
potential	possible
accomplish	successfully do
gear (verb)	adjust to fit
complex	involved and difficult

Page 85
1 Practise
2 In a friend's (parents') basement
3 Learn the rudiments (of music); join the school band
4 A rock band
5 Simple songs
6* Frequent use of first person; use of personal example; friendly tone as if speaking directly to you; some unusual advice

9 Customs and cultures

Page 87 (Building your vocabulary)
norm	what is usual
prevalent	widespread
routinely	as part of regular practice
outsource (verb)	pay someone else to do something
phenomenon	occurrence

schedule (verb)	set a time for
variability	difference
decade	period of ten years
health-promoting	encouraging good health
peers (noun)	equals

Page 88
1 A
2 C
3 A
4 B
5 A

Page 90 (Language focus)
1 I like nut and peppermint ice cream.
2 My boyfriend's family greeted my parents.
3 Grandparents looked after the children.
4 The boys underwent coming-of-age rites at 16.
5 I failed my exams.

Page 91 (Building your vocabulary)
1 prosperity
2 fertility
3 bouquets
4 substitute
5 felicity
6 colleagues
7 pinning
8 determined

Pages 92 and 93
1 Money and young children
2 Prosperity and fertility
3 (Flower) bouquets; (a bunch of) flowers
4 Rice and flowers
5 Sugar-coated almonds
6* Any appropriate answer

Page 94 (Key skills)
1 "Our friend Spyroulla married George at a Greek wedding," said Suki.
2 "Where was it held?" I asked.
3 "In Birmingham," she replied. "I was one of the guests."
4 "Lucky you!" I said. "I never get invited to anything."
5 "Poor you!" said Suki. "When I get married I'll let you come."
6 "You're too kind!" I said. "I shall look forward to that day."
7 "Me too!" she replied. "They made a lovely pair."
8 "Who did? I don't know who you're talking about."
9 "George and Spyroulla, of course. Their wedding was special."
10 "You can see it on the video," she added.

Page 95 (Building your vocabulary)
entourage	group of attendants
lamas	Mongolian or Tibetan priests
flanked	to have alongside
yurt	a central Asian tent
predators	flesh-eating animals
karma	distinctive atmosphere
ensue	follow
dismembered	cut into pieces
sustenance	nourishment
interment	burial

Page 96

1 Lamas/monks/priests
2 To keep out evil spirits
3 Through a window or hole cut in the wall
4 Bad karma
5 A stone outline
6* Any appropriate answer

10 The past and the future

Page 97 (Building your vocabulary)

prescriptions	instructions for (medical) treatment
acquaintances	casual friends
dignified	respectful
concealment	hiding
melancholy	sadness
sentimental	overly emotional
benevolence	kindness
endeavour	try
fatigue	tiredness
underrate	underestimate the value/ importance of
rational	reasonable

Pages 98 and 99

1 Because he also suffers from "low spirits"/depression
2 Just cold; cool; cool enough to give a slight sensation of cold
3 She should be open about them/tell as much as she likes/talk of them freely
4 Tea and coffee
5 Comedies
6* Reading (amusing books); keeping busy; meeting plenty of good friends/people who like/respect you/ amuse you; doing good; pleasing everyone; plenty of fresh air; pleasant surroundings; a good fire; religion

Page 100 (Language focus)

Past tense:
I lived in London and travelled by underground every day to the British Museum where I worked. I was based in the Ancient Egyptian rooms and was always amazed at the details of daily life in that ancient civilization that had been preserved in the relics on display. My favourite exhibit was the Rosetta Stone. It was such an important discovery because it opened up the way for scholars to read and translate what is written in hieroglyphics. I was responsible for the security and safety of exhibits, some of which had been around for thousands of years. I was learning to decipher inscriptions and was beginning to understand how to go about dating them. I thought it was a wonderful job.

Future tense:
I shall be living in London and shall travel by underground every day to the British Museum where I shall be working. I shall be based in the Ancient Egyptian rooms – I am always amazed at the details of daily life in that ancient civilization that have been preserved in the relics on display. I think that my favourite exhibit is going to be the Rosetta Stone. It was such an important discovery because it opened up the way for scholars to read and translate what is written in hieroglyphics. I shall be responsible for the security and safety of exhibits, some of which have been around for thousands of years. I shall be learning to decipher inscriptions and begin to understand how to go about dating them. It will be a wonderful job, I think.

Page 101 (Building your vocabulary)

1 nude
2 braided
3 sequins
4 kilt
5 pendants, amulets
6 Loin cloths

Page 102

1 For decoration and for protection from the heat
2 Pigtails, a braided lock, hair pieces
3 Ears, fingers, arms, wrists, ankles, neck
4 Linen
5 Bare feet
6* wigs; jewelled/braided collars (wesekh); necklaces; pendants; gold/silver jewellery; precious stones; pleated kilts; beaded dresses (women)/(additional) long robe/pleated dress and shawl (women); sandals; gloves (king)

Page 103 (Building your vocabulary)

1 biodegradable
2 composite
3 squabbling
4 wizard
5 fossil fuels
6 optimistic
7 instilling
8 crystal ball gazing
9 debris
10 utilizing

Page 104

1 B
2 A
3 B
4 B
5 C

Pages 105 and 106

1 Thermo-bottled water, instaheater tap
2 In junk shops
3 Thought scanners, i-pins
4 A ballpoint pen/biro
5 Advertising, writing
6* Any appropriate answer

11 Communication

Page 108

1 Watching the film 'Quest for Fire'
2 How to make a fire using sticks
3 Fire is important in our evolution
4 He has a warm bed every night
5 Cooking food
6* Example answer: I would like to teach Kanzi how to paint a beautiful picture.

Page 109 (Language focus)

Formal language: article in a newspaper, letter to your boss, essay in an examination
Informal language: speech, blog, text message, tweet

Page 109 (Building your vocabulary)

pride	pleasure
professionalism	proper, formal way of behaving at work
key	most important
hesitated	paused
trend	direction
turnover	amount of money spent on products

Page 109

1 BCD Enterprises
2 Their professionalism; the ability to communicate to customers
3 A strong leadership team; junior members have learned from senior members; good communication throughout the company
4 The last 12 months
5 A bonus
6* Example answer: There is good communication in the company; you get a bonus for good work

Page 110 (Building your vocabulary)

1 incurable
2 strict
3 version
4 poverty
5 determined
6 specialize
7 adopted
8 register

Page 111

1 It is Zamenhof's birthday
2 14 years old
3 It would be fair; people would be able to talk to each other
4 Felix (his brother); his school friends
5 So that the Esperanto users could be introduced to each other
6* Example answer: I would like to learn Dutch as it is an interesting language and a pretty country to travel in.

Page 112 (Saying what we mean)

1 Can we stop?
2 I'd like a drink
3 It's horrible!

Possible answers:
1 I'd prefer to go to the market.
2 I don't want to see the new Sherlock movie.
3 I don't really like him.
4 My uncle designed it.
5 I don't intend to watch it.

12 Global issues

Page 114 (Building your vocabulary)

prioritized	made the most important
cited	quoted
mutually exclusive	not having anything in common
cynical	taking a sceptical or negative view
intentions	planned way
associated	related
assurances	guarantees
substantial	considerable

substitute	something used in place of something else; unavailable
reputation	how something or someone is seen

Page 115

1 Prioritizing corporate social responsibility
2 Over 800
3 Best, safest, most suitable
4 Over $60 million
5 It was too noisy
6* Example answer: It is more important to me that a brand is ethical as I would not want to buy something where a person or animal has suffered during its manufacture

Page 116

1 Children asking for things
2 freecycle.org
3 Request things you need; give away things you want to dispose of
4 Your postcode
5 Furniture; dishes; toys; backpacks; computers; phones; sports equipment
6* Example answer: I am most interested to hear they have mobile phones, as the one I had broke last week.

Page 117

1 Develops technologies for a sustainable energy future; expands energy resources; reduces carbon dioxide emissions
2 Energy; science; technology
3 Floating offshore wind farms
4 More than 85 per cent
5 Because space usage per person is also high
6* Example answer: Solar energy interests me the most as you can just put a few solar panels on your roof and save energy.

Page 118 (Language focus)

1 17
2 Ethical
3 Appropriate; paying their employees well
4 Ten
5 Celebs

Page 119

1 To launch Recycle Now Week
2 42
3 Throwing food away
4 Recycling exhibitions; environmental magicians; composting displays; eco-fashion shows
5 Local authorities; community groups; supermarkets; businesses
6* Example answer: I shall try and recycle newspapers; plastic bags; cardboard boxes.

Page 120

1 planets
2 turning
3 5,000
4 share
5 inspiration

Worksheet answers

1.1
be globally minded; posting updates; multitasking;
keep up with; digital trend; capacity; impulse control;
cut-off point

1.3
1 Albert Einstein
2 Vienna
3 Clark Gable; Judy Garland
4 Bluetooth; Wi-Fi
5 It was Hedy Lamarr's birth date

1.4
1 The building was more impressive than the town hall.
2 Jan thought the view was lovelier than the view at
   the bottom of the mountain.
3 The dress the princess wore was more stunning than
   the one her sister had worn two years earlier.
4 The child was hungrier than the child who lived in
   the big house.
5 Paulo was thought to be a more fashionable designer
   than his older colleague Davide.

1.5
1 1888
2 A technology workshop
3 The OCT
4 Diabetes; glaucoma; high or low blood pressure
5 Every two years

2.2
Across: 1 truffle; 3 coconut milk; 4 coriander;
5 olive oil; 7 meatball

Down: 2 fortune cookie; 6 lime; 8 squash

2.4
1 The celebrity fitness DVD market
2 How they keep fit
3 Home; workplace
4 Clothing; gym membership; music; beauty
   products
5 Their fame may not last long

2.5
Add the words in this order:

training; inspiration; commitment; combination; charity;
participants; finish line; accomplishment

3.2
Across: 2 anticipation; 6 aloof; 9 privacy;
10 permanently

Down: 1 wardrobe; 3 commodities; 4 volunteer;
5 laundry; 7 toiletries; 8 graffiti

4.2
a 7 years/centipede(s) OR lizard(s)
b food/warm
c dark/black leg(ged)
d small/outside
e lizard(s)/house OR home
f monthly/positive
g rescued/injured
h network/help OR support

4.3
Across: 1 carer; 4 preventive; 5 autism; 6 abandoned;
9 quadriplegia; 10 factor

Down: 2 repertoire; 3 uttering; 7 consistent

5.1
Across: 1 ultimate; 4 survey; 7 client; 8 budget;
9 anonymous

Down: 2 typical; 3 simultaneously; 5 eligible; 6 exotic;
10 retail

6.3
holidaying; hike; guide; mapmaker; marine; pristine;
wetland; mine

6.4
1 In the heart of London; central London
2 1863
3 Large box; small television; large round sofas
4 Bobby Charlton, Franz Beckenbauer, Tony Adams,
   Rafael Benitez
5 Music; art; film

6.6
Put the words in the gaps in this order: plane; driver; tram;
mountain rescue; harness; parachutist; skydive; pilot

7.3
1 Jackie Chan; Michelle Yeoh; Jet Li
2 A rural village
3 2,000 years old
4 Catering facilities; a large hotel; a theme park
5 To see the film studios; to celebrate a seasonal
   festival; to see their favourite film star

7.5
1 Eliminate parts; reach a certain score
2 April 2012
3 One in seven
4 Tiffi; Mr Toffee
5 9 October 2013

8.1
Across: 2 antiques; 5 miniatures; 8 recreation; 9 spectator

Down: 1 field; 2 album; 3 browsing; 4 vintage; 6 amateur;
7 relaxation

9.1
Across: 1 collaborative; 7 conservative; 9 guaranteed

Down: 1 contributors; 2 beaming; 3 effusive; 4 blushed;
5 peck; 6 tactile; 8 routine

10.4
Across: 1 customized; 4 scouts; 6 lacquer; 9 massive

Down: 2 torso; 3 immortality; 5 condition; 7 despite;
8 elixir; 9 mace

11.3
Across: 4 explain; 5 publicity; 7 avoid; 8 profit

Down: 1 benefit; 2 upgrade; 3 improve; 6 competitors

12.5
tofu; paprika; cumin; soya; vegetable; soya